STABILITY AND THE LEBANESE STATE IN THE 20TH CENTURY

STABILITY AND THE LEBANESE STATE IN THE 20TH CENTURY

Building Political Legitimacy

Tarek Abou Jaoude

I.B. TAURIS
LONDON • NEW YORK • OXFORD • NEW DELHI • SYDNEY

I.B. TAURIS
Bloomsbury Publishing Plc
50 Bedford Square, London, WC1B 3DP, UK
1385 Broadway, New York, NY 10018, USA
29 Earlsfort Terrace, Dublin 2, Ireland

First published in Great Britain 2023
This paperback edition published 2024

Series design by Adriana Brioso
Cover image: General Maxime Weygand in Beirut,
Lebanon, 1923. (© Culture Club/Getty Images)

A catalogue record for this book is available from the British Library.

A catalog record for this book is available from the Library of Congress.

ISBN: HB: 978-0-7556-4414-8
PB: 978-0-7556-4418-6
ePDF: 978-0-7556-4415-5
eBook: 978-0-7556-4416-2

Typeset by Newgen KnowledgeWorks Pvt. Ltd., Chennai, India

To my mother, who handed me my first book. Now, I hand her mine.

CONTENTS

List of Maps viii
List of Figures ix
List of Tables x

INTRODUCTION 1

Chapter 1
THE ILLEGITIMATE CREATION OF THE LEBANESE STATE 17

Chapter 2
THE IMMEDIATE EFFECTS OF ILLEGITIMACY 45

Chapter 3
COMPROMISE AND ENSURING THE SURVIVAL OF THE STATE 81

Chapter 4
THE FIRST SIGNS OF DISINTEGRATION 115

Chapter 5
DELAYING THE INEVITABLE? 153

Chapter 6
DESCENT INTO CIVIL WAR 183

CONCLUSION 201

Bibliography 213
Index 231

MAPS

1.1	Map drawn by the topographical brigade of the French Expeditionary Force in 1860–1	27
1.2	Visualization of the expansion of the borders of Mount Lebanon, and the addition of Beirut, in the Maronite state-building project	29
2.1	Divisions of the first years of the mandate	51
2.2	Map of Lebanon	55

FIGURES

TABLES

1.1	Petitions Received by the King-Crane Commission from the O.E.T.A (West) Region according to Political Programme	34
2.1	Results of the Census Conducted during 1921–2	50
2.2	Population Figures in Lebanon as Indicated in a 1922 Report from the British Consul General in Beirut	50
5.1	Socio-economic Indicators	160
5.2	Political Indicators	163

INTRODUCTION

Over a hundred years after the creation of the Republic of Greater Lebanon, the functionality of the Lebanese state remains an enigma. At the time of writing, the country is going through what will potentially be its worst economic crisis, which is largely a result of the shortcomings of its political system. Overall, the post-war 'Second Republic' of Lebanon has been characterized by extensive clientelism, political sectarianism and systemic corruption, all of which engender ineffective public institutions and an inherently weak state. And, despite the Taif Agreement in 1990 declaring that the abolition of political sectarianism was a 'fundamental national objective', the post-war system has so far failed in decreasing confessional tensions and political polarizations. Instead, political relations have been established on an 'incentive structure operating at the structural, institutional, and individual levels [which] is distorted in a manner that serves the reproduction of the sectarian system and its concomitant dislocations'.[1] Still, the effects of the sectarian nature of Lebanese political culture have long been established, and it was long ago that its pitfalls were uncovered. In fact, almost sixty years ago, J. C. Hurewitz portrayed the issues with Lebanese sectarianism perfectly in this short anecdote:

> On the Lebanese front in the Palestine war of 1948 a Maronite Lieutenant found a Greek Catholic platoon in a state of complete inactivity despite the unabating and still vigorous exchange of fire. 'Sergeant,' bellowed the company commander, 'don't your men know that this is war? [W]hy aren't they fighting? If they do not take up their arms at once, I shall have you and them executed as deserters!' 'But one of our men was just killed, sir. We are therefore waiting for three Maronites, two Sunnis, two Shi'is, two Greek Orthodox, and one Druze also to be killed before we resume fighting.'[2]

Those acquainted with the Lebanese political scene – or with Middle Eastern politics more generally – will not find such satirical expressions surprising. What remains truly astonishing, however, is that long after the 1948 Arab–Israeli war, two subsequent civil wars, a redrafting of the constitution and concurrent occupations by both Syria and Israel, the application of such sectarian formulas to Lebanese politics in the 2020s remains as accurate as ever.

It is precisely the endurance and evolution of this political system in the face of such formidable aggression, a multitude of obstacles and demonstrably obvious deficits that form the central theme of this book. Like many of its counterparts in the region, the Lebanese state is still in the process of being built, and that state-building endeavour started more than a century ago. What is of interest here, however, is the central cog in any state-building project: political legitimacy. The aim of this book is to present a new lens through which one can look at a sequence of political events in and around Lebanon during the twentieth century, identifying a causal chain between them that can clarify many aspects of the Lebanese state's legitimacy (or lack thereof) over the years. It is the author's belief that much of the issues present in Lebanon today can be made clearer through a deeper understanding of the relationship between the state and political legitimacy. As such, the arguments developed throughout the book will need to rely on a specific understanding of the existing theories. Particularly, the analysis proposed will draw on the concepts of state-building, nation-building and stability to look at how these ideas manifested themselves in Lebanese twentieth-century politics.

The principal benefit of examining these concepts within one case study is the ability, and the space, to delve into as much detail as necessary. The freedom afforded by this approach will allow for a more rigorous examination of the nature between theory and practice, in a manner which appreciates the complexity and multifaceted nature of such concepts. In fact, this is the general advantage of single case studies, as Robert Yin showed: they are useful when dealing with 'how' questions 'because such questions deal with operational links needing to be traced over time, rather than mere frequencies or incidence'.[3]

In this regard, Lebanon serves as a perfect case study. The problematic interplay between state and society is naturally very apparent in an example like Lebanon: from its inception as a 'nation-state', questions of the identity of its 'nation' have been debated not only in the relevant literature but also by those domestic and foreign actors who have themselves been engaged in the state-building process.[4] As the book will later demonstrate, Lebanon's political history is drawn along the ambiguous line that links state-building with nation-building. To put it simply, those that were working towards building the Lebanese state were acutely aware of the imperative to work towards building the Lebanese nation. As such, the book will show the extent to which the relation between the two (nation and state) has shaped the legitimacy of the Lebanese state. Before emphasizing the importance of the book relative to the extensive work that has already been done on Lebanese political history, however, it is more immediately important to establish the conceptual framework within which this analysis will operate, thus elucidating the significance of the research which it includes.

State-building and nation-building

First of all, it must be stated that the general attention of this book will be directed towards Lebanese state-building. State-building itself represents a somewhat timeless endeavour that looks to explain the development of the way in which humans choose, or are perhaps made to choose, the means with which to govern themselves. Practically, the modern conception of state-building became prominent through the emergence of the nation-state, and the development of the modern notion of the state and its institutions. The academic field of state-building has also grown concurrently, and as the conceptual elements of nation-state and public administration were developed, the twenty-first century saw the subfields of institution-building and nation-building emerge in their own right. Despite this evolution of state-building over the years, however, it is still quite difficult to shake off the original ambiguity found in the concept of the nation-state, an imperfect notion from the start that seemed to provide a solid-enough framework for political development, particularly in Western Europe. And so, it cannot be overlooked that there is still some confusion in the state- and nation-building literature over the terms of 'state-building' and 'nation-building'. Equally, it is not illogical to assume that an element of this confusion comes down to the ambiguous definitions of, and distinction between, state and nation. It therefore behoves us to establish some clear, albeit somewhat convenient, definitions for these concepts, if only for the purpose of clarifying what this book will mean when it uses those terms but, more importantly, to establish how these concepts fit in the framework of our study.

Partha Chatterjee described 'nation' as 'the one most untheorized concept of the modern world', though that hasn't stopped others from trying to tackle the issue.[5] Sarah Paine, for example, argued that the word has two usages: one related to a place, a territory with a sovereign government, and the second to a 'community of people usually with a shared language, religion, culture, and society'.[6] Paul James tried to link the word 'nation' back to its original Latin roots and then study the development of its use throughout the years. He found that the Latin concept of 'natio' has been a very flexible term over the years, ranging from the designation of 'communities of foreigners at the newly formed universities, in refectories of the great monasteries, and at the reform councils of the Church', to that of 'uncivilized peoples', later to mean the ruling classes, up until the sixteenth century when it began taking a more political meaning to refer to the 'whole people of a country'.[7] Guido Zernatto and Alfonso G. Mistretta had already confirmed this flexible use of the word, comparing it to a coin the value of which changes according to its context.[8] James believes that the joining of 'nation' with the state became generalized in the eighteenth century, when the term 'nation' came to replace the notion of 'kingdom', yet even then there was tension over whether the concept referred to a community tied together through genealogy or through sharing a somewhat similar culture and living within certain boundaries.[9]

The evolution of the word 'nation' is important to our study through its inherent link to what has come to be understood by state-building. In fact, it is clear that at one point, a 'nation' became so intimately linked to the state that they became intertwined. For example, Anthony Giddens defined the nation as a 'collectivity existing within a clearly demarcated territory, which is subject to a unitary [and uniform] administration, reflexively monitored both by the internal state apparatus and those of other states'.[10] He then goes on to specify that in his definition, a nation 'only exists when a state has a unified administrative reach over the territory over which its sovereignty is claimed'.[11] Conversely, Timothy Mitchell highlighted how state theorists also struggle with finding the distinction between the state and the population it governs: 'a definition of the state always depends on distinguishing it from society'.[12] James acknowledged the advantages of Giddens's definition but does not agree with how Giddens conflates 'nation' with 'nation-state', his definition implying that there was no nation before nation-states, something which the history of the word 'nation' contradicts. In addition, James believes that Giddens's definition is too exclusive, focusing only on the institutional aspect of a nation, in the form of a nation-state. Similarly, Benjamin Akzin defined 'nation' as 'a certain type of ethnic group and the relations based thereon'.[13] Akzin accepted that nation has been and can be used 'to denote concepts intimately linked to the State', but also did not agree with this use.[14] John A. Armstrong attributed political consciousness to any group that wants to develop some form of 'ethnic identification', in his studies on pre-modern forms of nations. Additionally, symbolic boundaries play a crucial part in the self-identification of an ethnic community; specifically, the persistence of such symbols is what matters rather than the actual origins of them. According to Armstrong, individual mythic structures tend to become more legitimate as they fuse with other myths 'in a *mythmoteur* defining identity in relation to a specific polity'.[15] The problem that Armstrong runs into, according to Anthony D. Smith, is the lack of specificity and depth when it comes to distinguishing between 'ethnicities' and what differentiates one group (and their social boundary) from another, in terms of their development. Moreover, Smith believes that Armstrong was still not able to clearly establish what the relation is between pre-modern ethnic communities and modern nations. While one distinguishing factor according to Armstrong is the modern nation's conscious effort for establishing political structures based on group identities, he still credits the emergence of those nations to their pre-modern predecessors, indicating a more continuous relationship between the former and the latter. This, Smith believes, leaves the issue unresolved.[16]

It is clear through the examples touched on above that the relation between a nation's political consciousness and the establishment of its political structures proves to be the most challenging obstacle in defining the nation. Essentially, the use of 'nation' in modern times can be brought down to two main notions – one in which the nation is inherently linked to the state within which it exists, and another where nation refers to a community of people linked together, culturally, in one way or another. For the sake of this study, just as in Akzin's or James's, the former definition would not serve a purpose, and any such definition would lead to the very confusion that this research aims to avoid. So, whether it refers to an ethnic community, a linguistic one or simply a politically conscious community driven by 'constitutive myths', 'nation' in this sense cannot be synonymous with, or even dependent on, the state as a political institution. Ernest Gellner stressed this point: arguing that both state and nation are contingencies that cannot be said to be inevitable to mankind's social life. Crucially, he emphasized that they cannot be seen to be the *same* contingency: their respective histories show that state and nation developed separately and independently.[17]

Thus, using the above distinctions between 'nation' and 'state', one can proceed to separate state-building and nation-building in the following manner: state-building concerns the establishment, maintenance and preservation of political institutions which aim to govern over a certain people and territory, while nation-building refers to the attempts at establishing and/or preserving strong cultural and identity-related ties between different sections of particular people, usually with the purpose of removing internal cleavages as obstacles to harmonious transactions and peaceful cohabitation. As such, this study will consider nation-building to be a subfield of state-building, and which can therefore be subsumed within the latter.

Legitimacy: Institutional and societal

Having established such terms, we must now consider the role of political legitimacy within state-building, and consequently its role in this book's study. After all, any approach to state-building strives to understand and explain the circumstances under which a *legitimate* state is built, while assuming that legitimacy is concurrent with stability. In other words, what is considered a successful state-building project? If the answer to this question is characterized by the definition of the state itself, then the answer becomes 'once a state is established', and one is then tempted to use a definition like Max Weber's: a state is a 'human community that successfully claims the monopoly of the legitimate use of physical force within a given territory'.[18] It is fairly easy to surmise that for Weber and his successors, stability was key for the establishment of the state, and use of force was the most direct way to ensure such stability. However, notwithstanding the more obvious criticisms that have formed over the years of this definition, the central and key term in Weber's characterization remains the 'legitimate' nature of this monopoly of the use of force: what characterized the state's use of force, apart from its monopoly, was its rightfulness in doing so compared to other users of this force. Weber's definition will be discussed later on in detail, but it will be sufficient to establish the centrality of legitimacy – seen as rightfulness – in his definition, which itself provides the objective of stability as a key purpose of the state.

As Talcott Parsons contended, however, no 'society can maintain stability in the face of varying exigencies and strains unless interest constellations of its members are grounded in solidarity and internalized loyalties and obligations',[19] and the last two notions in particular highlight another facet of legitimacy that is just as central to Parsons's contrary approach, as it was in Weber's definition. Parsons's approach to stability emphasizes the acceptability of this 'society' as a prerequisite for its stability in the face of adversity, which every society can be expected to meet in the long term. Naturally, the state is also affected by this and one can presume that the stability of the state is also in question in Parsons's point. Though the example of Weber and Parsons offers two contrary views on the stability of the state, there is a unity in their schools of thought with regard to the *purpose* of the state, that is, its stability. And further still, they are also united by an emphasis on an additional element that is essential to this stable state: legitimacy as rightfulness and legitimacy as acceptability. In essence, all literature on political legitimacy will deal with those two concepts, and as a result, it becomes obvious that legitimacy can be broken down to those two values: rightfulness and acceptability. To return to the question asked: what makes a state-building project successful? The answer that can be provided is, 'when a legitimate – in other words, a rightful and an acceptable – state has been established'. It is through the legitimacy caveat that one can then make the argument that only in such a case can we expect the state to remain stable. It is with that information in mind that I propose a focus on this one element that is not only found at the heart of any approach to state-building but also found – in one way or another – in every governing apparatus: political legitimacy.

If, as deduced above, legitimacy represents the willingness of recipients (i.e. the people) to accept the governing body (i.e. the state) and its right to rule, and if the ultimate goal of any state-building endeavour is to establish a legitimate governing body, which is assumed to bring about stability, then new questions arise: is legitimacy a prerequisite for stability or can effective institutions bring legitimacy *through* their ability to maintain stability? In a sense, the question is also a temporal one: where does legitimacy come from *first*? Society or state? And can long-term stability come without legitimacy? As for what is generally meant by political stability, a summary of Leon Hurwitz's more extensive definition can provide a useful characterization: political stability can be understood as a dynamic phenomenon that involves one or more of the following: the absence of violence, governmental longevity or endurance, and societal harmony.[20]

Generally speaking, there are two approaches to state-building that are divided on this issue. The institutional approach operates under the assumption that political legitimacy originates *within* the state. Legitimacy, in that sense, is in the state's control, and serves as another tool which the state structure can make use of. From modernization, to liberalization, to war-making, the institutional approach identifies the tools which are at the disposal of the state to achieve a belief in its rightfulness to rule, and thus pave the road to internal stability. One can see in these institutionalist writings the influence of social contract theory: in institutional state-building, the state is founded on the specific will of a certain society and, in that sense, remains viable so long as that agreement is convenient.[21] Its convenience being defined by its ability to satisfy society's different demands, it then follows that the ultimate legitimacy of the state must lie in its institutional performance in relation to society's demands. The tools proposed by institutionalists serve to meet this purpose. Nonetheless, while political legitimacy is usually subsumed into the strong state apparatus by institutionalists, its implicit presence can shed enough light on the role that it plays in successfully building a stable state. In most institutionalist theories, legitimacy is 'claimed' by the state, and 'legitimation' – or the development of the belief in the rightfulness of the state – must come from the state itself.[22] De Jasay's criticism of Weber's definition of legitimacy illustrates the state's role in achieving legitimacy: 'The use of physical force by the state is legitimate for no more fundamental and logically prior reason than that it *has* successfully claimed a monopoly of it and has thus become a proper state.'[23] Such a tautological understanding of Weber's concepts certainly highlights some of the institutional approach's shortcomings.

Meanwhile, the societal approach generally assumes that political legitimacy cannot be derived from within the state, since the state is merely a reflection of a particular idea, and will thus originate from outside it. Not only do the formal institutions of the state need to be adequately set up in the organizational sense, but they also need to embody 'the idea of the state', a notion espoused by Barry Buzan which refers to a common identity that the population feels somewhat close to and a broad set of values of social and legal justice which they accept.[24] The manifestations of that idea can vary: pragmatic agreements, ideological or religious conviction, or the support of one particularly dominant group within society. In all cases, the state can only derive the legitimacy it needs to remain stable from outside the realm of its own institutions. Therefore, the state must always remain conscious of this, and adapt both functionally and institutionally, or risk collapsing when its authority 'fragments or evaporates in direct proportion to the loss of governmental legitimacy in society and its component groups'.[25] So long as the objective of state-building is to provide a stable relationship between the state and its citizens, then societal legitimacy needs to be present. As Parsons argued, no 'society can maintain stability in the face of varying exigencies and strains unless interest constellations of its members are grounded in solidarity and internalized loyalties and obligations'.[26] The societal approach, in turn, can certainly risk underappreciating the role that strong institutions can play in ensuring a stable, even if temporary, environment in spite of the absence of 'internalized loyalties'. This limitation will certainly be highlighted in the Lebanese case study within this book.

In either approach, however, legitimacy shows itself to be the crucial analytical variable in state-building. If one understands where legitimacy originates in a certain state, the analysis of state-building that the latter has undergone becomes much more straightforward, in accordance with one approach or the other. But is it possible to really rely one approach irrespective of the other? With this dilemma in mind, this book will attempt to take both approaches in consideration when studying the Lebanese state. In other words, both the institutional and societal legitimacy of the Lebanese state will be analysed as the book traces the relevant Lebanese events. The most obvious purpose for including both approaches to legitimacy is to be able to definitively and accurately establish the relationship between legitimacy and stability in Lebanese state-building during the twentieth century.

The last issue to be addressed with regard to legitimacy in this case study is its measurement. Historically, to measure the degree of institutional legitimacy, certain variables have been taken into consideration: functioning democratic institutions, efficiency of service delivery, degree of monopolization of force, levels of corruption. Societal legitimacy, however, is much harder to measure and, in this particular case, is best seen through a look at the history of political actors' actions and rhetoric, the vertical and horizontal divisions in Lebanese society, and the way in which state policy and messaging reflects the Lebanese identity (or lack thereof). These policies and this message are, especially in the case of Lebanon, related to particular actors whose actions need to be studied. In this book, these actors will include (but will not be limited to): community leaders, political parties and interest groups, external actors, public institutions and administration, and socio-cultural institutions. As for the required data to 'measure' both institutional and societal legitimacy, it will include (but will not be limited to): the manner of the creation of the power-sharing system, the level of group/individual representation, the performance of those institutions, the level of democracy and inclusive institutions, the degree of patron–client relationships, the discursive element of the media and the dependency of groups on external actors. For this purpose, a holistic and thorough approach is needed, because of the inherent need to take both hard data and the contextual political climate into account when analysing the state of legitimacy in a particular timeline. Additionally, the importance of contextualization pushes for the need to situate whatever political phenomenon is observed in its appropriate historical setting. By setting out a timeline a priori like this book has done, one can trace the relationship between the legitimacy and stability within the Lebanese state-building project for most of the twentieth century.

Lebanese history

It was mentioned above that the survival of the Lebanese system in the face of all manners of socio-political obstacles is at the heart of this book. That being the case, it is now appropriate to briefly assess the existing literature on Lebanese politics, in order to grasp the general ideas that have been developed around the political system. There has not been, for some time, any significant piece of research on Lebanon that deals with the concept of political legitimacy in pre-war Lebanon. As for the works that bring up such notions as state-building and nation-building, they simply do not go as far back as Lebanon's creation in the early twentieth century and focus instead on post-war Lebanon.[27] There are quite a few possible reasons for this that are not worth delving into, such as the trend in Middle Eastern countries of not 'opening up past wounds', which is seen as counterproductive.

On the whole, however, both historians and political analysts have completed extensive and detailed works on the development of Lebanese political life, and many have had the exceptional advantage of being personally connected with much of the political dealings that have affected, or have been affected by, the state's institutional and ideational development. These detailed accounts of the Lebanese state serve as an exceptionally helpful resource for those that want to understand where and why the state failed in grasping opportunities to better itself and avoid its own demise during the end of the twentieth century.[28] Through the many works in the field written in English, Arabic and French, notable authors like Kamal Salibi, Albert Hourani, Hamdi al-Tahiri, Ali Abed al-Ftuni, Stephane Malsagne, Franck Salameh and Hassan al-Hallaq have done a tremendous job covering the different perspectives on Lebanese events pre-1975. Many of these historical studies, naturally, do not provide as much theoretical or analytical insight into the structural and systemic surroundings that might have affected the state (both internally and externally). And although there are some exceptions, particularly from more writers like Fawwaz Trabulsi,[29] most only marginally approach the subject of state-building – and specifically political legitimacy – through a description of the facts. Still, the historian's work, which involves the picking and choosing of specific events and accounts, does enough to shed light on a perspective on the obstacles to Lebanese state-building, and how such issues were dealt with.

Lebanese nation-building, however, and in particular the struggle to create an overarching and binding Lebanese identity, is one issue that repetitively comes up. As established above, nation-building is itself a part of state-building and functions as a useful indicator of societal legitimacy through its ability to affect the state's acceptability in the eyes of the population. Related works on Lebanon usually delineate the different nationalist movements and show the dynamic that has existed between these convictions, as well as their manifestations in Lebanese socio-political life. A recent example of such work would be Carol Hakim's *Origins of the Lebanese Idea*,[30] which looks at the development of local forms of nationalism in Lebanon prior to 1920. Hakim explicitly tries to 'disengage the historiography of Lebanese nationalism from past and current controversies and from nationalist ideological moulds'.[31] While not directly touching upon the concept, there is no doubt that works like Hakim's play a crucial role in elucidating some societal elements behind the Lebanese state's current legitimacy, and such extensive research will be helpful for this book's tracing of the development of that legitimacy. Other extensive works on Lebanese identity include Kais Firro's *Inventing Lebanon: Nationalism and the State under the Mandate*, Raghid el-Solh's *Lebanon and Arabism: National Identity and State Formation*, Ghassān Fawzī Tah's *Hawiyat Lubnān* and Asher Kaufman's *Reviving Phoenicia: In Search for Identity in Lebanon*.[32] Contrarily, there are also Marxist analyses of the development of Lebanese identity as an exploitative tool, most notably the works of Mahdī Āmil.[33] This book plans to make use of all such resources, particularly in its quest to establish the status of societal legitimacy – which itself heavily relies on the strength of, and the belief in, national identity – though there will be no need to delve too deeply into the theoretical elements on how Lebanese identity has grown or receded; what is of more importance is the actual degree to which that identity was ubiquitous at different points in time.

Among the many authors who have studied the different facets of Lebanese history and identity, a clear division emerges between those that see a natural development of Lebanese exceptionalism into the supposedly overarching national identity of the country, and those that attribute the imposition of that national identity to powerful actors that acted in their interests to rip much of the native population from its existing cultural attachments. Eyal Zisser has outlined what he identified as these two schools of thought: one represented by scholars such as Kamal Salibi, Albert Hourani, Nadim Shehadi and Ghassan Salamé, who refuse to regard Lebanese history as having been decreed by fate. They interpret it in terms of continuity and coherence, consider the Lebanese state as legitimate and viable, and point to the many years of prosperity as evidence corroborating their view.[34] The second school was represented by writers like Meir Zamir and Elie Kedourie whose 'approach led to the conclusion that the Lebanese state … was an artificial creation lacking legitimacy and … was incapable of survival in the longer term'. Overall, a reasonable conclusion is that Lebanese historiography, just like so many others in the postcolonial world, cannot but touch on the viability of the country in which it emerges. While some writers, such as Eli Fawaz, have argued that the 'accumulation' of social, geographical and historical circumstances makes it so that the 'Lebanese experience must be reinforced and kept going',[35] others like Muḥammad Jamīl Bayhum have worked to 'uncover the veil on [Lebanon's] history which has been ignored by historians', due to the image 'intended by colonialism'.[36] Will this book be guilty of the same issue? Perhaps, since the research will make use of all the resources mentioned above, and this certainly seems to be the 'business' of historical studies, such a risk only highlights the importance of remaining aware of the existing literature, especially as one makes use of the extensive research that has already been conducted on Lebanese politics.

Another significant section of the literature is comprised of those who have explicitly undergone a study of Lebanese state-building, though most focus on specific institutions.[37] The majority of such work has centred around the dynamics of consociationalism as a political tool. Modernization theorists have usually found in consociationalism, and its effects, the main obstacle towards the progression of the state into a full-fledged, modern version of itself that can realistically deal with Lebanese society's evolving demands.[38] On the one hand, modernization and organizational theorists who advocate for a more systematic state unladen from the constant pressures of communal demands for representation run into the historical fact that the Lebanese communities had never accepted such a system, which would subsequently fall short of the democratic standards that they espouse. Pluralists, on the other hand, who attempt to show a way in which the state can adapt to its role as mediator, struggle to wrestle away the reality that state mediation has been historically extremely difficult in Lebanon, if not impossible. Overall, the theories provided in the literature fall short of accounting for many realities that have been witnessed throughout Lebanese history. Points of debate revolve around the nature of the confessional system that has remained in place in Lebanon, how inherent this power-sharing structure is to Lebanese political culture, if it has been imposed upon its population, whether or not it has actually been successful in the creation of social cohesion and/or a functioning democracy, and whether or not it *could* be successful in the future.

Eduardo Wassim Aboultaif's *Power Sharing in Lebanon* and Tamirace Fakhoury Mühlbacher's *Democracy and Power-Sharing in Stormy* are both recent works that dissect the system in place, tracing the history of Lebanese confessionalism. Aboultaif suggests some lessons to be drawn from the Lebanese case, not least of which is the emphasis on the system's ability to strengthen itself internally. Such an argument can function as a response to the traditional analysis of consociationalism, such as the one found in Michael Kerr's *Imposing Power-Sharing*, which emphasizes exogenous variables in the development of consociational systems in Lebanon and Northern Ireland,[39] and Arend Lijphart's consociationalism theory which highlighted,[40] especially in the developing world, the role of 'government by elite cartel [which is] designed to turn a democracy within a fragmented political culture into a stable democracy'.[41] Similarly, Mühlbacher argues that confession-based consociationalism had shown signs of success in the past,[42] though she also believes that the 'power-sharing system which provided a basis for its strength and stability was in a self-contradictory manner at the same time a tool of disintegration'.[43] Still, she states, 'it is of paramount importance to highlight that the main danger did not lie in the power-sharing arrangements themselves, but in the fact that they remained unchanged'.[44] Though it is important to establish this recent literature on Lebanese power-sharing (and there are other older works, such as Helena Cobban's *The Making of Modern Lebanon*[45]), it must again be stated that, though inherently central to this book's study, our focus on political legitimacy means that the emphasis throughout this work will be on the effects of power-sharing on the state's legitimacy, both in the social and in institutional sense. As for the question of the system's improvement as a form of consociationalism, or its ability to satisfy the democratic needs for a successful system, these factors will only matter when they directly affected the state's overall legitimacy. In other words, the system's success or lack thereof will serve only as an indicator of political legitimacy in Lebanon, irrelevant of what could have – or could be – done to improve its efficacy.

In fact, a common characteristic in all sections of the literature is an underdeveloped analysis of political legitimacy. Indeed, the word 'legitimacy' as defined above doesn't come up often in the recent literature on Lebanese politics. This wasn't as much the case in the early to mid-twentieth century, when questioning the very existence or 'viability' of a state was a bit more common. When recently used, however, the word replaces terms such as 'sustainable' or 'legal', usually during discussions about particular (private or public) organizations or rules. While there are – in the political literature – general theories on legitimacy, its parameters, its origins, its indicators, its consequences and its relation to nation- and state-building, this has been largely overlooked in the literature on Lebanese politics. That is not to say that the literature does not come into contact with legitimacy; in fact, it could be argued (and this author would) that all the works mentioned so far do, though very rare are the instances where a theoretical discussion on legitimacy has been conducted beforehand, or an application of such theories to the Lebanese case has been effected. For example, Zisser himself argued that the Lebanese state remained legitimate after its independence since it embodied the only system that could function, and 'for all the weakness of the central government, Lebanon was a vital and viable state with broadly accepted concepts of legitimacy', though again, he fails to delve into what those accepted concepts of legitimacy are and what they mean.[46] Michael Hudson's work is the closest to truly bring up legitimacy consistently. In his *Precarious Republic*, he mentions insufficient 'system legitimacy' in his introduction as a result of state deficiency in leadership and participation, though he does not define the terms of his wording. As he carries out his study, he continues to use 'legitimacy' many times.[47] Hudson also clearly believes in 'degrees' of legitimacy. Mentions of 'added legitimacy', 'sufficient legitimacy' and 'the little of what remained of the regime's legitimacy' point to such a conceptualization of legitimacy, though there is no discussion as to why this is the case. Most importantly, however, Hudson immediately equates legitimacy with stability: 'The legitimacy, and therefore the stability, of this "mosaic" system was being eroded by an insufficient broadening of political participation.'[48] Thus, in his search for stability, Hudson has to 'get past' legitimacy, since the two go hand in hand, and this particular connection with stability will appear throughout this book as more concrete conceptions of legitimacy are touched upon.

As mentioned above, this book's focus on political legitimacy means that it will touch upon many of the issues touched on in the literature on Lebanese politics, though its focus will remain on the effects of those issues when they are relevant to either institutional or societal legitimacy, in order to assess the Lebanese state's overall legitimacy. The aim of this undertaking is to look at the relation between legitimacy and stability in pre-war Lebanon, and to show how it varies from established understandings and expectations of how legitimacy and stability in and around the state interact. And while this study's logical and methodological presuppositions necessitate an in-depth, historical study into Lebanon's own struggle for legitimacy, there is another implicit aim to the book: to stress the need to reassess how we look at state legitimacy in developing countries in general, particularly ones with colonial pasts, especially if we are to start approaching the problems therein at their roots. This reassessment of conventional, Western-centric, concepts and their application in the developing world is certainly not a new one, and many, more established, authors have made immense strides in this effort. The internalization, and naturalization,[49] of political and legal structures has proven to be one of the bigger enforcers of the paralysed status quo in countries like Lebanon, so it is only natural to question those structures at their theoretical roots, and their practical transformations. As such, I hope that this study can add another piece to the wider puzzle.

The approach

This type of historical explanation can be quite complicated since it is almost impossible to account for all the causal relations that might be hypothesized in a relation between legitimacy and state-building. Without drawing on all the potential causal factors, I will attempt to uncover a link between the *illegitimacy* of the Lebanese state during its formation and the political instability that has followed since that application. It is also important to reiterate here that in the context of this book, I shall mean by instability that the very existence of the

Lebanese state has been questioned time and again by a group or groups of the population of Lebanon; that there has not been any real consensus over the Lebanese constitution, nor a resolution to the question of Lebanese identity; and that these fundamental disagreements resurface periodically in forms of conflict that often include armed violence.

With regard to the variables taken into consideration for this research, it is just as complicated to gauge the feelings and aspirations of the different Lebanese groups and communities. Surveys, polls and individual interviews were not as common an occurrence in Lebanese academic, or even journalistic, life as they might be nowadays (which is still relatively little). Instead, one must rely on the actions, decisions and internal policies of different groups and individuals that claimed, and have historically been proven, to speak in the name of their supporters and, in some cases, their communities. The validity of that claim is then assessed against the adjacent and relevant actions (and reactions) at the time. Still, there is some inevitable room for inaccuracy with regard to the exact line of thought which these actors possessed at the time. Thus, the reader must bear in mind that, though the evidence itself is accurate, it will also only be used when relevant, and does not necessarily dictate that the actors involved did not possess other, sometimes contradictory, convictions and plans. Indeed, the history of political Lebanon has been distinguished with unlikely alliances and paradoxical arrangements.

Hence, in order to conduct such a complex study, the structure of the book must reflect the above-mentioned aims while also allowing for as accurate as possible an investigation into the socio-political developments within Lebanon in the relevant timeframe. Chapter 1 analyses the political environment in which the state was built, so as to get a good understanding of the role that legitimacy played in the creation of the Lebanese state. Chapter 2 looks at the period from 1920 to 1943, in which the state of Greater Lebanon tried to stand on its own feet despite a struggle to overcome its own creation. Chapter 3 studies Lebanon's first independent presidential term, which provides the perfect timeframe to study the immediate effects of the infamous National Pact on Lebanese state-building. Chapter 4 follows the previous one by looking at the period immediately succeeding it: Kamīl Sham'ūn's presidential term between 1952 and 1958. Chapter 5 focuses on what many consider the only period in which the Lebanese state underwent a modernizing experience: the period that came to be characterized by a current known as Chehabism. Finally, Chapter 6 will study the sharp changes that characterized the transition from Chehabism to the civil war. The conclusion will then lay out the causal chain established throughout the book to show how the events covered are all interlinked through their relationship with the political legitimacy of the Lebanese state.

Notes

1 Bassel F. Salloukh et al., *The Politics of Sectarianism in Postwar Lebanon* (London: Pluto Press, 2015), 175.

2 J. C. Hurewitz, 'Lebanese Democracy in Its International Setting', in *Politics in Lebanon*, ed. Leonard Binder (New York: Wiley, 1966), 213.

3 Robert K. Yin, *Case Study Research: Design and Methods* (London: Sage, 2009), 9.

4 It is unsurprising that to this day, one is still likely to run into essays that include the title 'Parody of a Nation'. See *Lebanon: Parody of a Nation? A Closer Look at Lebanese Confessionalism*, by Turkmen-Dervisoglu, a 2012 essay for *The Yale Review of International Studies*: http://yris.yira.org/essays/316. Accessed on 27 March 2020. Similarly, as recently as December 2019, the essay *Is Lebanon Becoming a Real Nation?* was published by Amir Asmar for the Council on Foreign Relations: https://www.cfr.org/blog/lebanon-becoming-real-nation. Accessed on 27 March 2020.

5 Partha Chatterjee, *The Nation and Its Fragments: Colonial and Postcolonial Histories* (Princeton, NJ: Princeton University Press, 1993), xi.

6 S. C. M. Paine, *Nation Building, State Building, and Economic Development: Case Studies and Comparisons* (New York: M.E. Sharpe, 2010), 7.

7 Paul James, *Nation Formation: Towards a Theory of Abstract Community* (London: Sage, 1996), 10–11.

8 See G. Zernatto and Alfonso G. Mistretta, 'Nation: The History of a Word', *Review of Politics* 6, no. 3 (1944): 351–66.

9 James, *Nation Formation*, 12.

10 Anthony Giddens, *The Nation-State and Violence: Volume Two of a Contemporary Critique of Historical Materialism* (Berkeley: University of California Press, 1985), 116.

11 Giddens, 119.

12 Timothy Mitchell, 'The Limits of the State: Beyond Statist Approaches and Their Critics', *American Political Science Review* 85, no. 1 (1991): 77, https://doi.org/10.1017/s0003055400271451.

13 Benjamin Akzin, *State and Nation* (London: Hutchinson University Library, 1964), 10.

14 Akzin, 9.

15 John A. Armstrong, *Nations before Nationalism* (Chapel Hill: University of North Carolina Press, 1982), 9.

16 Anthony D. Smith, 'Nations before Nationalism? Myth and Symbolism in John Armstrong's Perspective', *Nations and Nationalism* 21, no. 1 (2015): 169.

17 Ernest Gellner, *Nations and Nationalism* (Oxford: Blackwell, 1983), 6.

18 Max Weber, David Owen, Tracy B. Strong, *The Vocation Lectures* (Indianapolis: Hackett Publishing, 2004), xlix.

19 Talcott Parsons, *Societies: Evolutionary and Comparative Perspectives* (Englewood Cliffs, NJ: Prentice Hall, 1966), 14.

20 See Leon Hurwitz, 'Contemporary Approaches to Political Stability', *Comparative Politics* 5, no. 3 (1973): 449–63.

21 See Robert M. MacIver, *The Modern State* (London: Oxford University Press, 1926), 447–8, for a brief criticism on the shortcomings of social contract theory.

22 Max Weber, *Economy and Society: An Outline of Interpretive Sociology* (Berkeley: University of California Press, 1978), 213.
Also see David Beetham, 'Max Weber et La Légitimité Politique [Max Weber and Political Legitimacy]', *Revue Européenne Des Sciences Sociales* 33, no. 101 (1995): 11–12.

23 Anthony de Jasay, *The State* (Indianapolis, IN: Liberty Fund, 1998), 74.

24 See Barry Buzan, *People, States and Fear: An Agenda for International Security Studies in the Post-Cold War Era* (Boulder, CO: Lynne Rienner, 1991).

25 K. J. Holsti, *Taming the Sovereigns: Institutional Change in International Politics* (Cambridge: Cambridge University Press, 2004), 56.
26 Parsons, *Societies*, 14.
27 In his 2012 book on Lebanese post-war state-building, for example, Reinoud Leenders argued that he 'found no detailed characterization of the contemporary Lebanese state or its institutions'. See Reinoud Leenders, *Spoils of Truce: Corruption and State-Building in Postwar Lebanon* (Ithaca, NY: Cornell University Press, 2012), 8.
28 For examples of such works, both in English and Arabic, see: Kamal Salibi, *The Modern History of Lebanon* (New York: Praeger, 1965); Carol Hakim, *The Origins of the Lebanese National Idea, 1840–1920* (Berkeley: University of California Press, 2013); William Harris, *Lebanon: A History, 600–2011* (New York: Oxford University Press, 2012); Ḥassān Al-Ḥallāq, *Tārīkh Lubnān Al-Mou'āṣir 1913–1952* [Modern History of Lebanon 1913–1952] (Beirut: Dār al-Nahḍa al-'Arabiyya, 2010); Nasser M. Kalawoun, *The Struggle for Lebanon: A Modern History of Lebanese-Egyptian Relations* (London: I.B. Tauris, 2000); Caroline Attié, *Struggle in the Levant: Lebanon in the 1950s* (London: I.B. Tauris, 2004); Max Weiss, 'The Historiography of Sectarianism in Lebanon' *History Compass* 7, no. 1 (2009): 141–54; Ḥamdi Al-Tāhiri, *Siyāsat Al-Ḥokm Fī Lubnān: Tārīkh Lubnān Min Al-Intidāb Ḥatta Al-Ḥarb Al-Ahliya, 1920–1976* [Regime Policy in Lebanon: Lebanes History from the Mandate to the Civil War, 1920–1975] (Paris: Manshūrāt Asmar, 2006).
29 An example of this sort of exception is Traboulsi's *A History of Modern Lebanon*, which attempts to focus on specific socio-economic aspects of Lebanese history.
30 Hakim, *The Origins of the Lebanese National Idea, 1840–1920*.
31 Hakim, 261.
32 Kais Firro, *Inventing Lebanon: Nationalism and the State under the Mandate* (London: I.B. Tauris, 2002); Raghid el-Solh, *Lebanon and Arabism: National Identity and State Formation* (London: I.B. Tauris, 2004); Ghassān Fawzī Tah, *Hawiyat Lubnān ('ind Al-Kiyāniyīn – Al-Qawmiyīn – Al-Islāmiyīn)* [Lebanese Identity (in Lebanism – in Nationalism – in Islamism)] (Beirut: al-Markaz al-Islāmī lil-Dirāsāt al-Fikrīyah, 2009); Asher Kaufman, *Reviving Phoenicia: In Search for Identity in Lebanon* (London: I.B. Tauris, 2004).

In addition, see Franck Salameh, *Language, Memory, and Identity in the Middle East: The Case for Lebanon* (New York: Lexington, 2010); Tamara Chalabi, *The Shi'is of Jabal 'Amil and the New Lebanon: Community and the Nation-State, 1918–1943* (New York: Palgrave Macmillan, 2006).
33 Two important examples are: Mahdī Āmil, *Madkhal Ila Naqḍ Al-Fikr Al-Tā'ifī: Al-Qadiya Al-Falastīniya Fī Īdiyōlojiyat Al-Būrjwāziya Al-Lubnāniya* [An Introduction to a Critique of Sectarianism: The Palestinian Cause in the Ideology of the Lebanese Bourgeoisie] (Beirut: Dār al-Fārābī, 1989); Mahdī Āmil, *Fī Qadāyā Al-Tarbiya Wal-Siyāsa Al-Ta3līmiya* [On the Issues of Education and Pedagogic Policies] (Beirut: Dār al-Fārābī, 1991).
34 Eyal Zisser, *Lebanon: The Challenge of Independence* (London: I.B. Tauris, 2000), x.
35 Eli Fawaz, 'What Makes Lebanon a Distinctive Country?', in *Lebanon: Liberation, Conflict and Crisis*, ed. Barry Rubin (New York: Palgrave Macmillan, 2009), 33.
36 Muḥammad J. Bayhum, *'Urubat Lubnān, Tatawuraha Fi Al-Qadīm Wal-Hadīth* [Lebanese Arabness, Its Past and Modern Development] (Beirut: Dār al-Riḥānī, 1969), 5.
37 For works on specific Lebanese institutions, see (among others): Leenders, *Spoils of Truce*; T. Gaspard, *A Political Economy of Lebanon, 1948–2002: The Limits of*

Laissez-Faire (Leiden: Brill, 2004); Roger Owen, 'The Political Economy of Grand Liban, 1920–1970', in *Essays on the Crisis in Lebanon* (London: Ithaca Press, 1976), 23–32; Pierre Rondot, 'Lebanese Institutions and Arab Nationalism', *Journal of Contemporary History* 3, no. 3 (1968): 37–51; Oren Barak, *The Lebanese Army: A National Institution in a Divided Society* (Albany: State University of New York Press, 2009).

38 The most famous of the application of modernization theory to Lebanon is Michael C. Hudson's *The Precarious Republic: Political Modernization in Lebanon* (Boulder, CO: Westview Press, 1985).

39 See Michael Kerr, *Imposing Power-Sharing: Conflict and Coexistence in Northern Ireland and Lebanon* (Dublin: Irish Academic Press, 2006).

40 See, for example, Arend Lijphart, 'Consociational Democracy', *World Politics* 21, no. 2 (1969): 207–25.
Also see Arend Lijphart, *Thinking about Democracy: Power Sharing and Majority Rule in Theory and Practice* (New York: Routledge, 2008).

41 Lijphart, 'Consociational Democracy', 216.

42 Mühlbacher argued that Lebanese traditional communal ties, conflict-resolution policies on the part of elites, political institutionalization and increased liberalization were indicators of the strengths of the pre-war consociational model.
See Tamirace Fakhoury Mühlbacher, *Democracy and Power-Sharing in Stormy Weather: The Case of Lebanon* (Wiesbaden: VS Verlag für Sozialwissenschaften, 2009).

43 Mühlbacher, 93.

44 Mühlbacher, 101.

45 Helena Cobban, *The Making of Modern Lebanon* (London: Hutchinson Education, 1985).

46 Zisser, *Lebanon*, 243.

47 For example, in one instance he argues that '[Lebanese] formal institutions ... do not engender the kind of positive legitimacy inherent in the Western notion of rule of law', implying a degree of responsibility on the part of the state to engender 'a kind of positive' legitimacy. See Hudson, *The Precarious Republic*, 9. This also begs the question of the nature of legitimacy when it is not 'positive'.
In another instance, he uses the following phrase: 'The November crisis stamped a seal of legitimacy on the National Pact.' This implies a different form of legitimacy which comes from outside the state. In this case, legitimacy can be substituted by 'support' since Hudson was discussing the demonstrations by the Lebanese communities in support of the 'resistance government' – the members of which were arrested during November of that year, Hudson, *The Precarious Republic*, 45.

48 Hudson, xiii.

49 To borrow a term from Joel Migdal. See Joel S. Migdal, *State in Society: Studying How States and Societies Transform and Constitute One Another* (Cambridge: Cambridge University Press, 2001).

Chapter 1

THE ILLEGITIMATE CREATION OF THE LEBANESE STATE

The introduction outlined the general theories of legitimacy. Those theories were shown to be, on the one hand, too focused on the institutional make-up of the state at the expense of the effects of national identity and, on the other hand, too ambiguous and too reliant on the societal make-up of a nation where political stability becomes untenable. Additionally, the relation between legitimacy and state-building was proven to be largely overlooked and underestimated. Our understanding of these concepts having been assessed, we can now begin to establish a link that will shed further light on the relationship between legitimacy, state-building and political stability during pre-war Lebanon, as per the purpose of this book. This demands the establishment and tracing of a causal link in which different chronological events are themselves results of specific causes, with the underlying mechanism linking them all and leading them towards the ultimate outcome of state collapse. This being the case, this chapter serves to shed light on the first link in that chain, that is, the first event: the formation of the Lebanese state. For the sake of clarity, and in accordance with the earlier chapter, it is important to show a lack of ambiguity with regard to political legitimacy. Thus, both institutional and societal legitimacy will show to be lacking in the formation of the Lebanese state. Using both aspects of legitimacy allows this chapter to show how the latter was not wholly present in the newly formed Lebanese state of the early twentieth century, and that it had not originated from any political institution or Lebanese society itself. Thus, the state of Greater Lebanon, founded in 1920 on the basis of power-sharing, was neither given legitimacy through representation nor was it set up to garner belief in representative legitimacy. This is evident when one looks at the prior state-building projects that were proposed and argued for before 1920,[1] including the one that would ultimately shape the Lebanese Republic. Seeing that the focus of this section is on the period just before the formation of the state, there will naturally be more emphasis on societal legitimacy since the nature of pre-existing institutions in most of the Lebanese territory disappeared during and after the collapse of the Ottoman Empire.

The chapter will follow the structure of the overall book, that is to say it will attempt to remain accurate to the chronological progression of events. Firstly, it is important to set out the predecessors for any state-building projects for the

Lebanese territory, and also show how and where those projects originated. This is done by briefly going over the contextual environment (up until the end of the First World War) of Lebanon's four major political actors: the Maronites, the Druzes, the Shīʿa Muslims and the Sunni Muslims. The focus on these ethno-religious communities is not dictated by a presupposition that such divisions in Lebanon are primordial or ever-lasting. Instead, this perspective is guided by the historical fact that, as part of the Ottoman political system, and through local sentiments of identity, political positions and actions were usually siphoned through local religious (or religiously affiliated) leaders. This, combined with the adjacent fact that gauges of more individual opinions were essentially non-existent (or at the very least inaccessible), forces us to frame the picture of nationalist sentiment through locally representative actors like those of each of community. As for the central focus on the variable of nationalist sentiments (or lack thereof), it quite simply serves to show the potential for support of different state-building projects, which forms the second part of this chapter, and where hindsight proves beneficial in a retrospective tracing of possible causal relations. Those state-building projects, which arose after the end of the First World War, evidently took different forms and, more importantly, included within them specific objectives regarding the integration of different communities. Those projects will be dissected, with the understanding of conceptions of state-building and legitimacy, in order to assess how reflective they were of local and communal sentiments as well as cultural and social ties. Those projects observably panned out in different manners and, as the formation of the Lebanese state took place, the Franco-Maronite alliance took control of building such a state, which resulted in a lack of legitimacy for the resulting state of Greater Lebanon. This illegitimacy is the focus of the third and final part of this chapter. By setting these chronological events in their context and exposing (through the use of the conclusions in the previous chapter) their causal role, this chapter will establish the first link in the overall causal chain of the book.

Forms of Lebanese nationalism

It is the particular objective of this chapter to show how the Lebanese state apparatus was created without the existence of an established nation, yet was burdened with all the other expectations of a nation-state. To show the absence of a somewhat coherent nation, integrated on socio-political levels and with common – to a certain extent – political aspirations, it is helpful to focus on the different aspirations that the Lebanese people envisaged for themselves,[2] since their socio-political divisions are somewhat clearer and more historically established. This is useful not only because the differing aspirations among the Lebanese are diverse[3] but, more importantly, because they meet at certain points in history, and have clashed whenever they do. Nationalist movements are a good indicator of political aspirations because they represent, especially in pre-nation-state terms, a form of social evolution for a group of people when it becomes politically self-conscious. In addition, the role of nationalism as a nation-building tool has been well established in the literature.[4] In this case, nationalist sentiments and movements in Lebanon, for a retrospective research, play that role even more strikingly, as one can trace the development of those same 'nationalisms' throughout Lebanese political history, can observe their links with Lebanese state-building projects and can look at their direct effects.

'Mt Lebanon' nationalism

'Lebanese' nationalism as it appears in the literature is usually associated with the nationalist movement that developed in the area geographically and historically known as Mount Lebanon; it is sometimes referred to as 'Lebanism'. This area refers to the mountain range known as the Lebanon that stretches from the north to the south of the current Lebanese borders, east of the Lebanese coast and west of the Biqāʿ plain that separates that range from the Anti-Lebanon mountain range on the borders of what is currently Syria.[5] The reasons for the historical monopoly of Lebanism over other forms of nationalism are multiple, but most importantly, they include: firstly, that the vision for a modern Lebanon that practically manifested itself in actual results arose from Lebanism, and secondly, that the political entity that existed in the Mountain – and some of its surroundings – strived to separate itself from the rest of the Levantine region, which added to its particularity.

The existence of a separate political entity in Mt Lebanon dates back to the Druze Emirate, which operated as its own 'sanjak' under Ottoman rule.[6] The relationship between the Emirate and the High Porte of the Ottoman Empire oscillated, with different consequences that varied from more autonomy afforded to the Mountain, to direct clashes and battles with its princes and nobles, to the fluctuation of the exact boundaries of the Emirate.[7] These direct confrontations with a foreign authority have arguably played the biggest part in the development of a distinct collective identity among the residents of the Mountain, despite their confessional differences.[8] In addition, the occurrence of violent battles (small manifestations of a war, as it were) that directly affected authority, territory and pride also played its part in uniting the residents of the Emirate and allowing them to develop a sense of national pride and a feeling of common destiny.[9]

The back and forth between the Emirate – and other variations of political forms of autonomy in the Mountain[10] – along with the continuous search for identity between the Mountain's two biggest factions[11] ultimately led to the form of nationalism that became overwhelmingly dominant in the Mountain. Having said that, however, there is an argument to be made that the resulting nationalism wasn't as overwhelming as it is historically painted, since that nationalist movement, and its accompanying literature, was undoubtedly dominated by Maronite figures.[12] And while it is true that, by the twentieth century,[13] the Maronites attained a demographic majority in the Mountain,[14] the differences in self-identification between the confessions were still significant enough to highlight this possible bias in the historiography and depiction of Mt Lebanon nationalism, both in the literature and in the archival documents.[15] This overwhelming representation of Maronite thought and identity in the history of the Mountain can itself be traced to the foreign backing and support that this community enjoyed, which led to a significant intellectual revolution for the community, due to the abundant access to health and education (mostly through missionary establishments), jobs (largely as a result of their superior education), emigration to and back from Europe, involvement in trade relations and so on.[16]

The contextual information regarding the development of 'Mt Lebanon' nationalism, and the beginning of the idea of a nation in the Mountain, allows for a further understanding of the origins of such thought and, more importantly, of its aspirations. There are also observed differences in behaviour between the Maronites and the Druzes of the Mountain, with regard to the surrounding peoples and rulers that have existed throughout their respective histories. The Maronites, having seen the Mountain as their refuge for centuries,[17] used it to build their distinctive home where they can finally find some sort of prosperity. This has led them to not only clash with surrounding communities and develop feelings of specialness and particularism but also to staunchly and vociferously defend whatever autonomy they could manage to gain when it comes to their political administration and the management of their members' personal and spiritual status.[18] The Druze, on the other hand, believe themselves to be descendants of tribes that migrated from the Arabian Peninsula,[19] which already put them on a slightly closer cultural footing with the surround Arab-identifying communities. While they valued their Emirate very highly,[20] the Druze are also known to incorporate *taqiyya*, a socio-political practice which has been translated as 'concealment' or 'dissimulation'.[21] This includes the concealment of the Druze faith and the willingness to accept (at least publicly) the dominant surrounding religion. While this is in no way the only explanation for lack of strong (or rather, one as strong as the Maronites') *public* political particularism from the part of the Druzes, it can certainly help with the understanding of the development of Druze 'nationalism' compared with the Christian counterparts. The final distinction that must be taken into consideration is the accusatory gaze with which the Druze viewed the Maronites. Having mostly been the feudal lords of the land on which the latter worked, the strong rise of the Maronites and the turning of the tables (with regard to power and influence) was always resented by the Druzes, and this was only aggravated by the somewhat grand ambitions of the Maronites, who were always quick to look outwards for foreign support and cooperation rather than seeking that of their Druze neighbours.

It is within this context of local tension and variation in the degree of foreign rule that forms of nationalism in Mt Lebanon emerged. The specific idea of nationalism is itself quite modern, and its roots didn't emerge in the Western world until the late eighteenth century with literature and thought surrounding events such as the French Revolution.[22] Not long after such a time in Europe, Bashir al-Shihabi II, a strong-willed emir – who was seen as fair by the Maronites yet accused by Druzes of having stripped them of their historical influence over the Lebanese Emirate[23] – was exiled by the Ottomans in 1840 for siding with Muhammad Ali in the Egyptian crisis of the time.[24] The political vacuum that followed allowed for the emergence of an actor that would become central to the development of Mt Lebanon (and Lebanese in general) nationalism: the Maronite Church. The head of the Church at the time, Mgr Yusuf Ḥubaysh, claiming to speak on behalf of 'inhabitants of Mount Lebanon', directed a request towards the 'Sublime State' in which he communicated requests for the reorganization for the sake of the 'Maronite community'.[25] Among the ten requests made in the communication, the first one stands out: the installation of a *Maronite* 'ḥākim' (i.e. ruler) of Mount Lebanon, one that only answers to the Porte itself.[26] In another attempt to show communal solidarity, Ḥubaysh gathered Maronite leaders and, together, they signed a pact that imposed on them to, from then on, 'form one body, act towards one sole aim and work as a single hand' in all community-related manners, specifically political issues.[27] This is seen by some as an opportunistic attempt by the Church to cover up any internal divisions among the Maronites with the view to gain more power and influence in the Mountain.[28] Regardless, there can be no doubt of the significance of such an endeavour by the Maronite Patriarch – an obvious leader in his religiously defined community – especially with regard to the origins of nationalism in Mount Lebanon. More importantly, while this was far from what would end up being a demand for full independence, the specific demand for self-rule (marked by the request for the 'ḥḤākim' of Mount Lebanon to be a Maronite[29]) is a substantial indicator of the birth of political self-consciousness and nationalism, at least among the Maronite community. The result of the vacuum[30] was the establishment of the Double (or Dual) Qaimaqamate in 1842, a quasi-federal system in which the Mountain was effectively divided into two administrative parts, one for the Maronites and one for the Druze.[31] This system did not last longer than two decades, as tension between the two sects grew to such a degree that in 1860, a civil war broke out in the Mountain.[32] The Double Qaimaqamate system was removed, and a brief vacuum reappeared, which allowed Mt Lebanon's nationalism to stretch its arms again, to see how far it can reach this time round.

Many other influential actors emerged during this short period between the Double Qaimaqamate and what would become known as the Mutasarrifiyya, both domestic and foreign, and all having some effects on nationalism in the Mountain. One such actor was General Beaufort, the head of the French Expeditionary Force (FEF).[33] Beaufort, a staunch French patriot who firmly believed in the protective role that France should have towards the Christians in the Orient, understood his mission to be the securing of a native homeland for the Christians of Lebanon, under the protection of France.[34] Beaufort's contribution to nationalism in Mount Lebanon, which at this point had started to truly take on a Christian character, was embodied in a report he made in 1861,[35] supposedly as a result of research and anecdotal evidence observed by himself and his officers.[36] Apart from calling for a virtually autonomous Christian Lebanon, and claiming local support for such a plan,[37] his most significant contribution to nationalism in the Mountain was the map he had drawn of the greatly exaggerated 'Lebanese territory'.[38] Beaufort had extended the territories of Lebanon, to what would eventually become the Republic of Lebanon, citing economic and security reasons.[39] Beaufort's plan not only encouraged nationalist sentiments by adding what would be considered strong empirical evidence, but it also drew literal lines around the vision of what Lebanon was desired and destined to be. In addition, it cemented, for the first time in centuries,[40] the political connection between France and the Lebanese Maronites, and turned the 'Franco-Lebanese dream' into something concrete. As for Beaufort's arguments (especially the historical ones revolving around a nostalgic view of the Emirate going back to the sixteenth century) and his map, they elevated Mt Lebanon nationalism to another level, as they added elements of Weber's traditional legitimacy as well as the incarnation of an accurately defined homeland for which such nationalism should aspire – in other words, a potential nation-state for this Mt Lebanon 'nation'.[41]

Other figures involved in Lebanism, as it has come to be known in the literature, by the end of the nineteenth century, included the new Maronite Patriarch Mgr Mas'ad, who continued the mission of his predecessor, and kept constant correspondence with many French political figures, all the way to head of the French state at the time, Napoleon III. As more French–Mountain contact was established during the late nineteenth century and maintained throughout the beginning of the twentieth century until the end of the First World War and the establishment of the French Mandate, there can be no doubt of the Christian character of nationalist sentiments in Mt Lebanon. Despite the Emirate historically having an almost-exclusively Druze character, the Maronites used their ascending socio-political influence to turn this historical particularism to their advantage, and developed a sense of community that started with demands for autonomy with regard to personal status and evolved into what would basically become a full-fledged nationalist ideology, one containing its own myths and figures, the historical existence of nation and a communal ambitious plan for a state in which they can fulfil their political potential.[42]

Surrounding Lebanese nationalism

Historically, there has been much less work on nationalism in the areas surrounding the Mountain that would become part of modern Lebanon. There are many reasons for this: firstly, there was no historical precedence for the existence of autonomous political entities in those specific areas, in the manner of the Emirate, which would have given rise to a feeling of *political* particularism. Part of what drove the surge of nationalism in the Mountain was what was perceived as an Ottoman ploy to take away Mt Lebanon's already-established autonomy. Secondly, the surrounding areas of Lebanese territory were overwhelmingly inhabited by Muslims, mostly Sunnis and Shī'as. While each community has undergone very different political experiences, neither (especially the Sunnis) were as far removed from the Ottoman official religion of Islam as the Maronites. This isn't to say that Christianity and the Druze religion were the *sole* reason for the evolution of political self-consciousness in the Mountain, but nationalist sentiments always involve feelings of 'the other', which would have been harder to develop with regard to co-religionists in the Sunni regions of the empire, for example. And thirdly, where feelings of separation *did* grow (such as preceding sentiments to what would become Arabism), this movement would not gain its intensive fervour until the First World War and, effectively, the period around (and after) the establishment of the Lebanese state. Therefore, it shall suffice for now to briefly examine the context in which both major Muslim communities lived in the areas of Lebanon surrounding the Mountain, before the establishment of Greater Lebanon.

The Shīʿa Not unlike the Druze, Shīʿas have also had a history of practising *taqiyya*, and theirs lasted much longer than the Druze who could on occasion openly practice their religion within the confines of the Mountain. It is therefore assumed that the Shīʿas continued to shield the 'true intent' of their faith and community throughout the Ottoman Empire, including its Lebanese regions, in order to avoid ostracization and persecution.[43] The fact that the Ottomans, whose millet system recognized special status for different confessions and religions, never officially accepted Shīʿism as a community separate from the 'umma'[44] can be seen as either a catalyst or a consequence of such widespread *taqiyya* practices.[45] With regard to their origins,[46] there is some disagreement about how the Shīʿas of Lebanon came to settle in their territories: their own traditional version includes the foundation of their community by Abu Dharr, a Companion of the Prophet and one of the first supporters of the claims of 'Ali to be his successor'.[47] External scholars such as Philip Hitti and Henri Lammens, however, argued that the Shīʿas of Lebanon are directly related to Persian immigrants. The evidence, however, seems to show that the Metawalis have links to South Arabian (possibly Yemeni) tribes.[48] Interestingly, the Metawalis themselves, according to 'Āmeli scholars,[49] have connected themselves both culturally and linguistically with an Arab identity.[50] The other area where Shīʿas are overwhelmingly present is the Biqāʿ Valley, specifically the norther part. There had been economic and political relations between the Valley and the Mountain since the days of the Emirate, and while there were instances of strong political connections,[51] the evidence usually shows a struggle for power, since the Biqāʿ was always seen to be a much-needed strategic location for the emirs and the nobles of the Mountain.[52] There is even less literature regarding the origin of *that* Shīʿa community, and while they could have the same origin as the dominant Shīʿas in Southern Lebanon, a feeling of disassociation and of being 'left behind' has lingered to this very day. Nevertheless, both 'factions' of the Shīʿa community in Lebanon have been marked by a characteristic social structure: kinship loyalty. For much of the nineteenth and twentieth centuries, in the period right before the creation of the Lebanese state which they found themselves in, the Shīʿas of the south and the Valley only valued allegiance for units of families and clans.[53] Histories and developments of communal allegiances and loyalty only truly developed *after* the French Mandate and the establishment of the Lebanese state.[54] In the period leading to the Mandate period, the Shīʿas were effectively made to choose the lesser of two evils: the Maronite-dominated vision for a Greater Lebanon or the Sunni-dominated vision for a greater Arab state, both of which neglected the Shīʿas as a distinct community with particular interests and concerns.[55]

Moreover, the Shīʿa's relationship with Arab nationalism was more problematic than the Arab nationalist literature would like to paint, considering the fact that even up until 1915 (only three years before the Ottomans would lose control over the Levant and state-building projects were proposed), only a minority of the Shīʿa community ʻadhered to proto-Arab nationalist sentiments'.[56] And yet, there were some scholars in Jabal ʿĀmel who were trying to reintegrate the Arab image of the Shīʿa into local loyalties and political self-consciousness, going so far as to critique the language with the hope of showing traces of Arabic influence that overwhelmed other roots – such as Persian.[57] The position of the Shīʿas between Lebanism and Arabism led to them being used by both sides to their respective advantages (mainly for human resources, support in armed clashes, etc.) yet almost completely deprived of power or influence in any resulting political system.[58] This feeling would eventually lead to the full-fledged *Harakat al-Mahrumin*, which literally translates to 'Movement of the Deprived'.[59]

The Sunnis Belonging to the majority religion of the Ottoman Empire,[60] the specific national sentiments that developed within the Sunni community in Lebanon are, firstly, tied to the same type of sentiments among the regional Sunnis and, secondly, are also a result of the development of a separate ethnic identity in relation to the Ottoman Sunnis.[61] The direct symptom of this perspective of ethnic difference between Sunnis in Lebanon and those at the centre of the Ottoman Empire[62] is the development of an Arab identity into Arab nationalist sentiments. Since Sunnis within current Lebanese territories were tied, before the creation of Greater Lebanon, to Damascus and accompanying Syrian entities, both culturally and politically, their nationalist sentiments were also linked to the sentiments within that region that is now outside Lebanese territories.[63] The development of Arab national sentiments was accompanied by typical nation-building tools such as origin myths developed by Sunni ʻulamas[64] in the Levant – particularly, that Arabs are direct descendants of the Abrahamic people, as well as of the Prophet himself.[65] In addition, that origin myth was substantiated by adding a religious element which meant that Arabs, through genealogy, were God's chosen people and Arabic was God's chosen language.[66] One can see how the religious element was crucial to the creation of special national sentiments among Sunnis in the Levant that could distinguish them from Ottoman Sunnis, and that could make them the *real* representatives of their religion,[67] allowing the feeling of pride and chosen-ness to spread and popularize itself through ʻulama teaching and popular belief. It is important to note that some ʻulamas such as ʻAbd al-Ghani al-Nabulusi showed a lot of compassion for non-Muslims (whether Christian or Jews) and included them in their Arab identifications.[68] On the other hand, scholars and thinkers such as Ebusuûd Efendi, another member of the Sunni ʻulama, usually preferred the separation of religious communities, which resulted in sporadic incidences of violence, but usually in general indifference towards non-Muslim issues, with a 'tinge' of contempt.[69] As for the population themselves, their feelings and sentiments changed with that of the dominant ʻulama thinking, and it was Effendi's separationist school of thought that would normally win out.[70]

The fact remains, nevertheless, that the Sunnis in the Levant were the majority ethno-religious community, and were always bound to feel in prime position to have a hand in the state-building projects that were to come after the fall of the Ottoman Empire. And while they were scattered and divided enough along ethnic, tribal and familial lines throughout the region, and were nowhere near as organized politically as, say, the Maronites were, there was an effort to unite them under the Arab flag, by both the ʿulamas and political leaders such as Sharīf Hussein, prince of Mecca, and his sons Abdullah and Faisal.

The state of Greater Lebanon

The nationalist sentiments that existed and evolved towards the end of the Ottoman period came to the fore and manifested themselves as state-building projects during and after the First World War. The following section will outline those projects as clearly as they can be, while highlighting the key figures.

The Maronites and the French

A historian might be tempted to merge French and Maronite interests into one project and policy. This is a result of their above-mentioned historical ties as well as the coordination of the actions and manoeuvres of the two actors. Despite this relationship, Maronite ambitions did not always align with those of the French, and while the latter worked to appease the former, France was well aware of its own interests and was not always so keen to grant Maronite wishes of enlargement – both literally and in terms of influence – of the Mountain, especially when such an expansion generated animosity among the surrounding communities (which it often did) and hindered peace in the region, peace that was crucial to the endurance of French governance of the Levant. The Lebanese state-building project, for the Maronites and those subscribing to their vision of what would become Greater Lebanon, was outlined first and foremost through diasporic associations of immigrants from the Mountain, most of whom had fled to Europe (and mainly France) during the last days of the Ottoman Empire. The purpose of this section is to outline the state-building project of the Maronites, and show how it reflected the ambitions of the Christian community in Lebanon; it was unrepresentative of the rest of the Lebanese population.

The Borders

The first and most essential component of the state-building project of those expatriates like Auguste Pasha, Yusuf Sawda and Michel Shīḥa was the expansion of the Lebanese borders. To be brief, this involved the addition of the surrounding territories to the Mountain, including those that were inhabited by the Sunni and Shīʿa communities. The reasons for this, first outlined by expatriate authors and then repeated throughout the formation of modern Lebanon, were historical, economic and natural.[71] French influence is very evident here, as Pasha and others referred to a map[72] drawn by General Beaufort of the FEF, a regiment of troops sent by France to guarantee security in the Mountain in 1860 after the bloody massacres that had occurred between Lebanese and Druzes – the FEF were part of an international peace plan devised at the time.[73] Beaufort had admitted, however, that he viewed his mission just as much a political as a military one: inspired by the French and Catholic historical ties to the land of 'the cradle of Christianity',[74] Beaufort made it his mission to restore the Emirate to its former glory with an even stronger foundation.[75] Through somewhat questionable petitions from various Christian villages and anecdotal evidence collected from his troops' interaction with the population within the Lebanese territories, Beaufort drew up the ambitious map with new Lebanese borders that would later become integral to the Lebanese state-building project of the Maronites, based on what was considered the confirmed wishes and opinions of the Lebanese Christian population.[76]

Pasha himself noted that 'the right to self-determination that he was invoking for the Lebanese might clash with the extension of the same right to the inhabitants of the territories that Lebanon wanted to annex and who might refuse to be joined to Lebanon'.[77] Pasha had argued for the expansion of the borders for Lebanon 'by virtue of the right to life, which cannot be denied to any people, large or small, strong or weak', arguing that the Mountain would be doomed to perish otherwise.[78] Pasha, and others who would advocate for such an enlargement based on self-determination, committed a fundamental contradiction, however, by arguing for the self-determination of one community over another. It is contrary to the principle of self-determination itself, firstly because it hinders the very same principle for another community, and secondly, because it is being extended to a people other than those for whom the principle was being invoked for in the first place. In other words, Pasha's project of state-building directly and self-admittedly involves the creation of a state around a somewhat united and coherent nation, and yet also includes other, possibly unwilling,[79] nations into that same state, through the will (i.e. self-determination) of the former, original nation. It is already very clear how this state-building project completely disregards the notion of representative legitimacy and confuses state-building with nation-building, since any hope of representative legitimacy must then inevitably rely on building a coherent nation, one that feels represented by and within the Lebanese state, a posteriori. This temporal relationship between state-building and nation-building was shown earlier to be most troublesome and unsustainable at best, or completely untenable at worst. This will also be shown to be the case through further analysis of the Lebanese case (Map 1.1).

Governance

While Beaufort was himself on a mission to enlarge the Lebanese territory, the Christians were reinvigorated by the arrival of the French and were petitioning the Sultan himself asking to abolish the existing dual government of the Mountain of the time and 'return' to a Mountain governed by the Christians.[80] They did not all, however, endorse Beaufort's scheme to restore the Shihabi Emirate through Majid Shihab, a grandson of Bashir II. Majid, a Christian, simply did not have enough

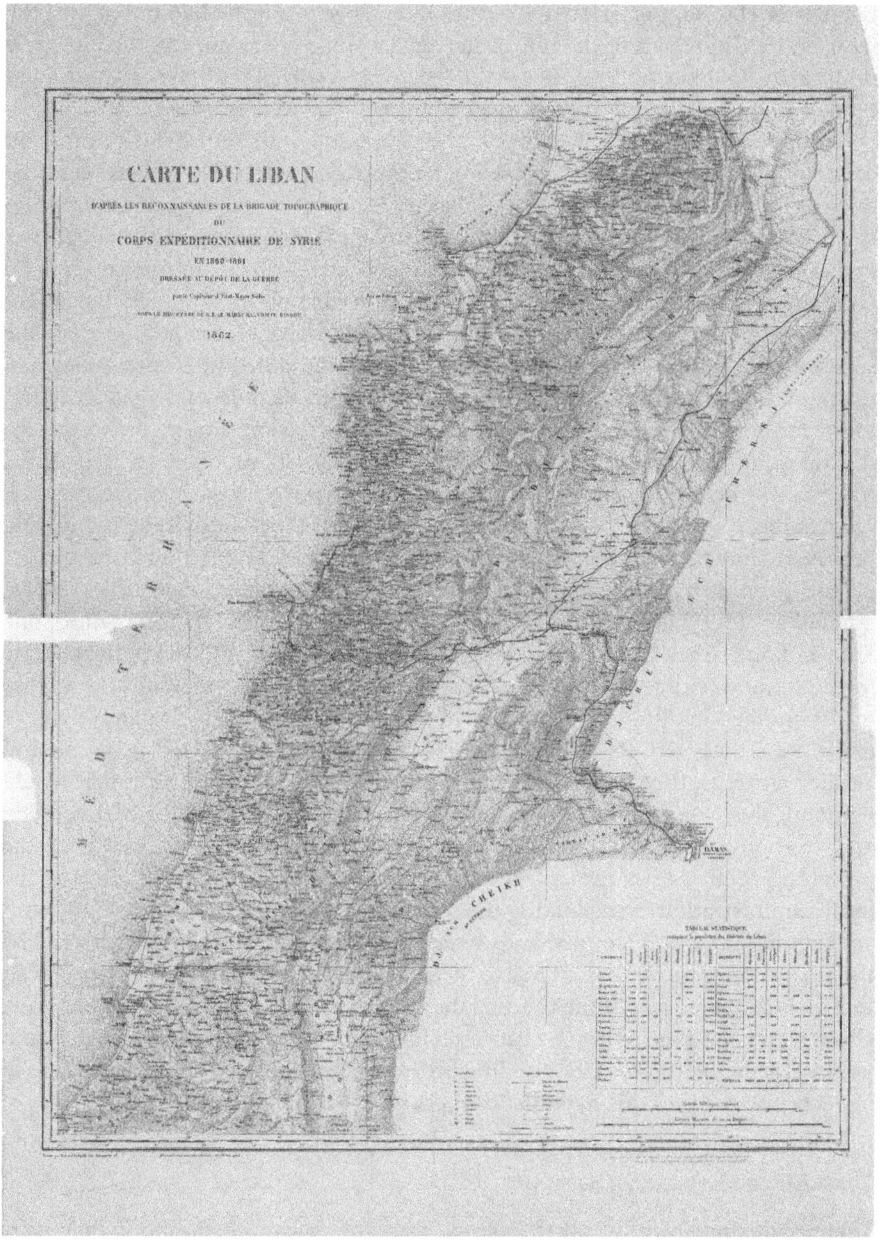

Map 1.1 Map drawn by the topographical brigade of the French Expeditionary Force in 1860–1.

Source: The Digital Library on International Research. Accessed on 10 July 2018: http://www.dlir.org/archive/orc-exhibit/items/show/collection/11/id/15888.

popular or elite support among the Maronites; specifically, he had not gained the trust of the Church or of the influential leader Youssef Karam, who had become provisional 'Qaimaqam'.[81] The issue, in 1861, was resolved with the establishment of the autonomous Mutsarrifiyya, headed by a Christian Mutasarrif.

By the end of the First World War, however, and with the obvious imminent defeat of the Ottomans, the Lebanese state-building project was revived, and the question of the political framework for Pasha's Beaufort-based project had come up again. It was clear, by this point, that the risk of an unrepresentative state project by Pasha could only be curtailed by allowing for the different communities to be represented in the prospective Lebanese state, on the political scale. By the end of the War, the Maronite Church and the Administrative Council had adopted the state-building project outlined by Pasha.[82] While the different communities had manifested their political ambitions during the war in various ways (it shall suffice to say for now that the majority within non-Christian communities did not adopt the Maronite state-building project in any way), it wasn't until the Ottoman retreat from Beirut on 30 September 1918 that substantial decisions and actions took place in the Mountain to secure the accomplishment of the Maronite state-building project, mainly through the Administrative Council and the Maronite Church.[83]

The Administrative Council of the Mountain had been made up of twelve members – four Maronites, three Druzes, two Greek Orthodox, one Sunni, one Shī'a and one Greek Catholic – and was technically the only elected political body in the Levant, and as such felt that it alone was eligible to represent the wishes of the indigenous population of the Mountain.[84] Apart from the ambitions of expansions that were based in Beaufort's plan and then reflected in Pasha and Sawda's writings, the Council had plans for an independent Lebanon that would be politically governed by an equally elected and representative legislative body and, crucially, with 'the help of the country of France for the realization of the preceding requests [of expansion and independence] and its assistance of the local administration in facilitating the spread of knowledge and education'.[85] Both geographical and political demands were formulated and were to be delivered by the delegations sent by the Council to the 1919 Paris Peace Conference, delegations that included members of the Council themselves as well as figures of the Maronite Church up to and including the Patriarch himself.[86] Thus, both geographically and politically, the Maronite state-building project included communities unwilling to be incorporated into this hypothetical Lebanese state (Map 1.2).

The other communities of Lebanon

There were, meanwhile, other members of the Lebanese diaspora that were outlining their vision of a state that incorporated the Mountain as well as the other Lebanese territories. Such bodies as the *Comité Central Syrien* (CSC) in Paris, the *Syria–Mount Lebanon League of Liberation* (SMLL) in New York and the *Conseil des Comités Libano-Syriens d'Egypte* (CCLS[87]) in Cairo had already begun planning and advocating for a Greater Syria that included the whole of Lebanon, with the addition of the Mountain.[88]

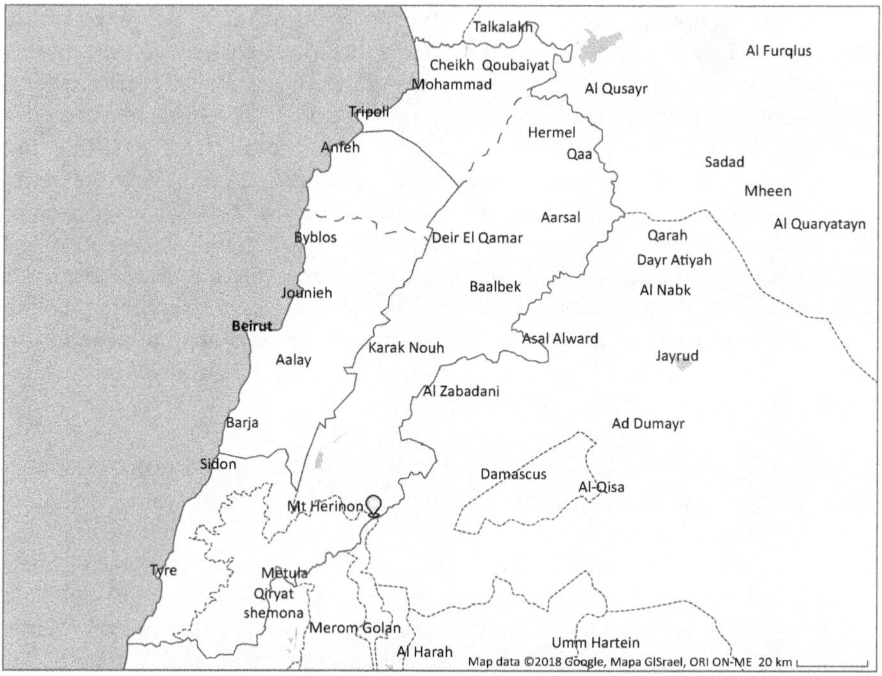

Map 1.2 Visualization of the expansion of the borders of Mount Lebanon, and the addition of Beirut, in the Maronite state-building project.

Comité Central Syrien For its part, the CSC sent a memorandum to Georges Clemenceau, the French prime minister and the president of the Peace Conference, outlining their ambitions and demands for a Greater Syria, rejecting any division of the historical land of Syria (meaning the territory comprising modern Syria and modern Lebanon) that would cause 'a mortal prejudice to the unity [of Syria], indispensable to the reconstruction of the country as well as to its moral, political and economic future'.[89] In addition to the call for independence for the whole Syrian territory including Lebanon, the CSC also demanded the 'mentoring' of France since 'a people cannot flourish without a long mentorship', and the choice of France presented itself as the natural filler of that role.[90] In fact, the CSC saw the role of France as the obvious answer for the question of which country the hypothetical Greater Syria would choose to ally itself with, on a political and administrative level. The CSC had already established contact with the Quai D'Orsay during the war,[91] urging France not to take the course of 'inaction' with regard to intervention in the Levant, and ascertaining a sphere of influence before the Arabs or the English establish political 'hegemony in the Orient'.[92] The CSC based its argument for the political unity of Syria on European experiences, arguing that diverging communities could be brought together in a Syrian state in the same way that they were in states such as France and Germany.

This was no doubt done to appeal to the sympathy of the Allied powers who, like the CSC, believed that communitarian and sectarian divisions were symptoms of a backward society, and unity under a secular state was the way forward for a people to develop and flourish, politically and economically. This is in fact a false analogy by the CSC since, unlike France and other European states, state-building through war-making and cultural integration was not achieved in any way in the Levant. Lebanon and Syria, for example, were to that and this day comprised of very closed and isolated communities which, despite geographical proximity, had never integrated enough to the point of the development of a national identity.[93] This was admitted by the CSC itself, as they conceded that no 'sentiment d'unité nationale' (sentiment of national unity) existed in Syria, hence the need for an 'arbitre' (referee) to oversee the rivalries that are very much alive, until those people, through progress, 'forget' their differences.[94]

Syria–Mount Lebanon League of Liberation The SMLL also had plans of its own which it conveyed to the president of the United States at the time, Woodrow Wilson, whose ideas of self-determination would come to play a central role in shaping the international political arena later on. The SMLL expressed their wishes of a united Syria, necessarily independent and, equally necessary, for such a Syrian state to be under the tutelage 'democratic Christian government'.[95] While the SMLL's plan reached high places,[96] all evidence points to such a state-building plan, like its proposed alternatives, lacking in the representative legitimacy needed for the corresponding state to function. That was first revealed, or rather not revealed, by the refusal of the SMLL to concede independence to a Lebanese state, whatever its borders be. Considering that the members of the SMLL were mostly Mountain-born or otherwise had close and familial ties to the Mountain, they were treated with contempt by those Maronites who were ready to endorse any plan that included a form of Lebanese independence.[97]

Lebano-Syrian Committees of Egypt Different committees of Syrians and Lebanese were created in Cairo, and their members moved between one and the other rather commonly depending on which project in the aftermath of the First World War they were convinced by, while the projects were developed around principled, ideological and circumstantial thought. A collection of them would eventually group themselves into the *Conseil des Comités Libano-Syriens d'Egypte*.[98] Different members, however, made efforts to convey their wishes and demands – ultimately their vision for a state-building project – to the Allied powers, mainly, and unsurprisingly, France. In a demand sent to the French minister in Cairo, asking him to relay that demand to the French president and government, a 'group of Syrians in Egypt' (as they identified themselves) presented a document signed by 201 of 'their compatriots'.[99] That document expressed the concern of those 201 'Syrians' over the 'entry of the Arab Tribes' to Damascus and 'the mixing of the Hejazians' in Syrian public affairs.[100] They demanded the complete separation of the Syrian question and the Arab question, showing again a clear clash with the Arab movement that was developing in and around Lebanon, and that group of 'Syrians'[101] clearly refused to identify with the Arab project, yet another alternative to the questions of the Levant. More importantly, however, here was yet another unrepresentative, and therefore societally illegitimate, state-building project that was being proposed.

Faysal and the Arab state-building project Throughout the war, different plans and agreements were being drawn up as to what would happen in the Middle East, most famously the Sykes–Picot agreement – a secret agreement between the French and the British to divide the conquered Middle East into respective spheres of influence – and, at the same time, the Hussein–McMahon correspondence.[102] Hussein bin Ali al-Hāshimi was Sharīf of Mecca, and a descendant of the Prophet Mohammad, who led the Arab revolt during the First World War and as a result of this cooperation with the Allied powers[103] and his direct contact with Sir Vincent McMahon, a lieutenant colonel in the British Army, had expected to be given control over the Hejaz post the World War.[104] Hussein would, in return, lead the Arab revolt and fight against Ottoman and Central Power forces.

As the war drew to a close, and the British forces under General Allenby were advancing further into the Levant, the city of Damascus's capture became imminent. By that point, most if not all of the city's traditional elite as well as any Syrian nationalist conspirators had either fled or been forced out. Those who had remained and were in control of various militias were confident enough in their abilities to secure the city and declared a government under Sa'id al-Jazā'iri. More importantly, the government that reigned increased its authority by claiming to be ruling under the Arab rule of Sharīf Hussein, and obtained the recognition of the Jamal Pāsha, the departing Ottoman commander.[105] A couple of days later, Hussein's son, Emir Faysal, who would become 'the embodiment of Arab-Muslim hopes', entered Damascus along with his Arab Irregulars, and the Greater Arab Syria state-building project was undertaken in the following months.[106]

The inclusion of Lebanon in the Greater Arab Syria project hinged on the promises made to the Sharīf, and this, along with the principles of self-determination that were formulated by President Woodrow Wilson, formed the basis of Faysal's argument for the realization of this project. Faysal, who maintained communication with the British and the French during and in the aftermath of the expulsion of the Ottomans from the Levant, had insisted on the whole region of Syria (including Lebanon) being part of the promises made to his father.[107] Operating under this assumption, he immediately put his plan into motion and ordered the mayor of Beirut, 'Omar al-Da'uq,[108] to establish an Arab government and hoist the Arab flag, declaring the allegiance of said government to the Sharīf, and in turn to Faisal and his Greater Arab Syria project.[109] This, along with establishment of the Arab government in Damascus,[110] only served to antagonize the French position towards Faysal, and they in turn acted quickly to restore the pre-agreed agreements that were conducted between themselves and the British.[111] The British, on the other hand, were more willing to stick to their more concrete arrangements with France than the somewhat ambiguous promises made to Faysal and his father:

> McMahon indeed reassured the Sherif that Britain would not conclude 'any peace … of which the freedom of the Arab peoples and their liberation from the German and Turkish domination do not form an essential condition'; and it is only in this context that the meaning of Arab 'independence' should be understood: liberation from their adversaries, not necessarily independence. Neither to Sherif Hussein nor to any other Arab leader did the British 'ever explicitly guarantee or even promise anything beyond liberation from the Turk'.[112]

After the French and the British had established military rule in the region, Faysal then proceeded to outline his plan at the Paris Peace Conference. In a memorandum sent on 29 January 1919 by Faysal to the Peace Conference, he explicitly stated that the 'aim of the Arab nationalist movements (of which my father became the leader in war after combined appeals from the Syrian and Mesopotamian branches) is to unite the Arabs eventually into one nation'.[113] The Arabs, according to Faysal, were all those peoples who were Arabic-speaking, from the Alexandretta-Diarbekir line southward,[114] were all united in their Arabic language as well as in their 'natural frontiers which ensure its unity and its future'.[115] The United States, whose principles of self-determination formed the basis for Faysal's and the others' arguments, were quite aware of this ambiguity with regard to how much of the population Faysal and the Arab movement truly represented. In a report presented by the intelligence section of the American delegation to the Paris Peace Conference, the following was recommended:

> The King of the Hedjaz and his sons should not receive support in an attempt to establish an artificial domination over tribes of about similar strength. If, however, it can be shown that the movement for Arab unity is natural and real, and that such unity can be developed without the use of force, the movement should be given encouragement and support. The proposal of the delegates of the King of the Hedjaz that a mixed commission be sent to Syria to learn the actual desires of the Syrians and report to the peace conference, is entirely fair and should receive support.[116]

Again, just like in Adib Pasha's and the CSC's projects, what is made explicitly clear is the acknowledgement that no coherent nation existed that corresponded to the territories and state which each of these projects strived for. Not only was the lack of one nation accepted by the different sides, but these different projects, representing the different desires of various communities, were evidently conflicting and mutually exclusive projects, meaning each of the projects was unrepresentative of the wishes of the population. That combined with the fervour with which each side was willing to fight for the creation of what they perceived to be the rightful state, and the degree to which each side refused to accept the realization of a state did not correspond to their view of an acceptable state. It was clear even at this point that any subsequent state created along the lines of each of these projects could not and would not be representative of the population, would lack a corresponding nation at its core and would therefore always be susceptible to societal illegitimacy. Its only option would then be to provide for institutions capable of garnering legitimacy in the institutional sense.

The King–Crane Commission

In accordance with US recommendations, the emir's desires and Dr Howard Bliss's request to determine the wishes of the populations in the region, a commission composed of the two Americans Henry King and Charles Crane was sent to Syria and Lebanon to try and ascertain what the communities wished in terms of their political future.[117]

The method that the King–Crane Commission (KCC) relied upon was quite simple: they would meet with individuals and delegations that would represent the different towns, regions and communities, and accepted petitions from various groups and sects.[118] The KCC was aware of the role of propaganda, influence and pressure that the different communities might be subject to, and believed that, with regard to the petitions, these elements would cancel each other out so long as the Commission covered the whole region and accepted petitions from all parts of the territories.[119] Nevertheless, the Commission was 'struck … with the large degree of frankness' they encountered upon their inquiries and were confident that this was a result of the Americanness of the KCC, as it had been made clear that, unlike Britain and France, the United States had no interest in gaining control or influence in either Syria or Lebanon.[120] The area of Mount Lebanon and the coastal regions (most of which would eventually be included in the Greater Lebanon state) was designated as O.E.T.A (West) which was estimated to be comprised of about 40 per cent Christians and 60 per cent Muslims,[121] and a total of 163 delegations were received from that area.[122] Figure 1.1 and Table 1.1 represent the data concerning the relevant petitions.

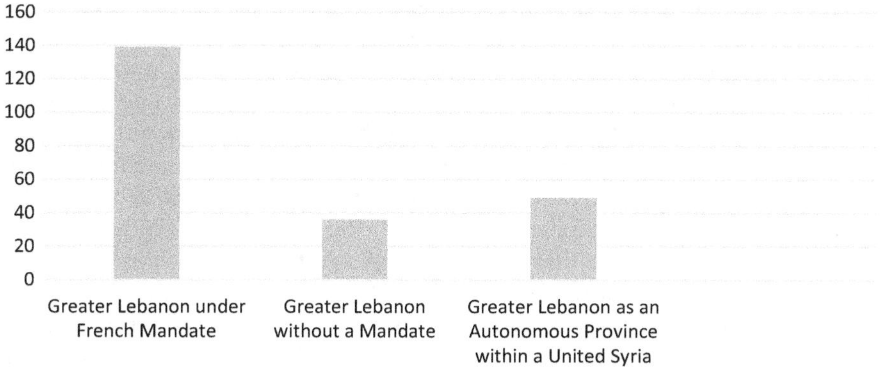

Figure 1.1 Number of petitions per project with regard to Lebanon.

Table 1.1 Petitions Received by the King-Crane Commission from the O.E.T.A (West) Region according to Political Programme

Political Programme	Petitions	Percentage of *Total* Petitions (446) (%)
For a United Syria	187	41.9
For an Independent Greater Lebanon	196	43.9
Against an Independent Greater Lebanon	108	24.2
For an Autonomous Lebanon within Syrian State	33	7.4
For the Inclusion of the Biqāʿ with Lebanon	7	1.5

Table 1.1 is an extract of the most relevant results published in the KCC report with regard to the O.E.T.A (West) region which, it must be noted, included areas that were either not a part of the Mountain at that time (e.g. Tyre, Tripoli) or areas that never even became part of Greater Lebanon (e.g. Alexandretta, Ladikiya). It must be noted that the results in the table do not reflect either/or, mutually exclusive, statements. In other words, some statements (e.g. those proclaiming opposition to Greater Lebanon) exist in some petitions but not in others, and those petitions themselves contain some statements that might fall into other categories.

While the O.E.T.A (West) results show an almost equal divide between those in favour of an independent Greater Lebanon and those for a United Syria, it would not be too speculative to suggest the following: had those towns and areas included in this set of data that would not be and were not ever involved in the Lebanist project removed, the statistics would show an increase in the percentage of those who favour a Greater Lebanon.[123] This point is further accentuated by the following statement from the KCC Report: 'In opposition also to a United Syria are the 203 petitions (10.9 per cent) asking for an independent Greater Lebanon. 196 of these came from Lebanon and 139 are copies of the French-Lebanon program.'[124] That statement shows how overwhelmingly in favour of Greater Lebanon the Mountain was, and hence, any opposition would have existed in those outside areas mentioned above.

However, far from confirming the validity of the Greater Lebanon project, this hypothetical simply highlights the disparity between the Mountain and the regions surrounding it. Similarly, this data set (of the coastal and mountainous areas that would ultimately be included in Greater Lebanon) would still be missing all the towns and areas east of the Mountain that were also part of Greater Lebanon (e.g. Biqāʿ, Rashaya, Hasbaya, Baalbeck, etc.), all of which were included in O.E.T.A (East) where 94.3 per cent of petitions were for a United Syria.[125] It can be concluded, hence, that the inclusion of these towns would rebalance the percentages to somewhat similar numbers as the original O.E.T.A (West) statistics.

It is important to note that in the O.E.T.A (East), which comprised of the area of modern Syria as well as the areas of modern Lebanon to the east of the Mountain, 954 (82 per cent) of petitions explicitly mentioned opposition to an independent Greater Lebanon.[126] It is also noteworthy that despite the clear contradiction that the Greater Lebanon programme would impose on the people it would involve, only thirty-three petitions out of 1,863 in the whole of the Syria, Lebanon and Palestine region accepted Lebanon as an autonomous province within a Syrian state.[127] This is crucial as it highlights the fact that the Lebanese majority wanted independence and enlargement, the Syrian majority wanted an independent Syria and harboured opposition to the independence of Greater Lebanon, and neither side accepted any sort of compromise on their position in the form of a Syrian Federation including an autonomous Lebanon. On one side, it is historically typical of the Lebanese, specifically those adhering to Lebanism, who had enjoyed political and administrative privileges that Syria hadn't, and had been striving for an independence that would protect them from the ever-looming majority, to reject any compromise on their claim for independence. As for the Syrians, it seems like the question of an autonomous Mountain was never put to them by the KCC, and it is therefore equally understandable why they would not be willing to part with a region (east of the Mountain) that has always been culturally and politically closer to Damascus than to Beirut. This refusal to compromise would end up looming over both countries' destinies. Similar refusal to compromise at any cost was observed in the King–Crane Commission Report concerning the choice of the Mandatory Power: The Maronites and other Catholic Christians were overwhelmingly in favour of a French Mandate, while the Druzes supported a British mandate; as a result of the division the Druses petitioned the KCC to explicitly request 'to be left out of the Lebanon in case it be given to France'.[128] The importance of such evidence, provided by the results of the KCC, for these contradictory state-building projects is only relevant to this book in its causal relations with regard to the early development of the state.

One can use Aristotle's causal model to understand where the different forms of nationalism in Lebanon fit into a resultant state-building project. Imagining a sculptor, for them to sculpt a marble statue X, four causes (or cause types) are necessary for the desired effect (or effect type) to occur. Firstly, a material cause (the marble). Secondly, a formal cause (the idea of a statue). Thirdly, an efficient cause (the act of sculpting). Fourthly, a final cause (the purpose for which the statue is being made).[129] Accordingly, aspirations in Lebanon for the state on the parts of the different communities help to serve as formal and final causes for why the early building of the Lebanese state was completely unrepresentative and therefore societally illegitimate. In other words, while the different state-building projects were always liable to be different, the fact that those projects were contradictory meant even less potential for national unification, and could only ever have resulted in an unrepresentative state. That, in the O.E.T.A (West) *alone*, 24.2 per cent of petitions to the KCC expressed a position of opposition to an independent Greater Lebanon speaks volumes: even if one were to take into consideration Lipset's form of passive legitimacy, this would clearly not apply here.[130] The combination of different state-building projects, the post-Ottoman vacuum for both state-building and foreign intervention, and the timing of the political decisions taken by the relevant actors such as the local communities, the neighbouring Arab movements and the great powers (particularly the French and British) serve to form a condition of causes that can explain the shape of the Lebanese state that would be created in 1920.

Notes

1 And certainly fought for, on certain occasions – see Samir Khalaf, *Civil and Uncivil Violence in Lebanon: A History of the Internationalization of Communal Conflict* (New York: Columbia University Press, 2002).
2 The people living within the current boundaries of Lebanon.
3 So dissimilar in some cases that they do not even intersect.
4 See, for example: Walker Connor, 'Nation-Building or Nation-Destroying?', *World Politics* 24, no. 3 (1972): 319–55; Shu-Yun Ma, 'Nationalism: State-Building or State-Destroying?', *Social Science Journal* 29, no. 3 (1992): 293–305; Jeffrey Ira Herbst, 'Responding to State Failure in Africa', *International Security* 21, no. 3 (1997): 120–44; Marina Ottaway, 'Nation Building and State Disintegration', in *State Building and Democratization in Africa: Faith, Hope, and Realities* (Westport, CT: Praeger, 1999), 83–98; Sherry Lowrance, 'Nationalism without Nation: State-Building in Early Twentieth-Century Palestine', *Middle East Critique* 21, no. 1 (2012): 81–99.
5 'Ali 'Abed Ftūnī, *Tarīkh Lubnān Al-Ṭaā'ifī* [Lebanese Confessional History] (Beirut: Dār al-Fārābī, 2013), 46.
6 Abdul Rahim Abu-Husayn, *The View from Istanbul: Lebanon and the Druze Emirate in the Ottoman Chancery Documents, 1546–1711* (London: I.B. Tauris, 2004), 8.
7 Massoud Daher, 'The Lebanese Leadership at the Beginning of the Ottoman Period: A Case Study of the Ma'n Family', in *Syria and Bilad Al-Sham under Ottoman Rule*, ed. Peter Sluglett and Stefan Weber. Trans. W. Matt Malczycki (Leiden: Brill, 2010), 331.
8 And their quite prominent differences that reflected their own identity-formation processes. See Daniel Meier, 'Borders, Boundaries and Identity Building in Lebanon: An Introduction', *Mediterranean Politics* 18, no. 3 (2013): 356.
9 See Charles Tilly, *The Formation of National States in Western Europe* (Princeton, NJ: Princeton University Press, 1975); Charles Tilly, 'Cities and States in Europe', *Theory and Society* 18, no. 5 (1989): 563–84; Charles Tilly, 'War Making and State Making as Organized Crime', in *Bringing the State Back In*, ed. Peter B. Evans, D. Rueschemeyer and T. Skocpol (Cambridge: Cambridge University Press, 1985), 169–91.
10 Such as the Shihāb Emirate, the Double Qaimaqamate or the Mutasarrifiya – see Meir Zamir, *Lebanon's Quest: The Road to Statehood 1926–1939* (London: I.B. Tauris, 1997).
11 The Druze and the Maronite confession, the influence and power of which also oscillated.
12 Kamal Salibi, *A House of Many Mansions: The History of Lebanon Reconsidered* (London: I.B. Tauris, 1988), 201.
13 Which generated the zenith of nationalism in the Mountain.
14 That is, historically accepted as fact in statistical studies – see Thibaut Jaulin, 'Démographie et Politique Au Liban Sous Le Mandat. Les Émigrés, Les Ratios Confessionnels et La Fabrique Du Pacte National [Demographics and Politics in Lebanon under the Mandate. Emigrants, Confessional Ratios, and the Fabric of the National Pact]', *Histoire et Mesure* 24, no. 1 (2009): 189–210.

15 Also see Penelope Zogheib, 'Lebanese Christian Nationalism: A Theoretical Analyses of a National Movement' [unpublished Masters thesis] (Northeastern University, 2013).
16 Hakim, *The Origins of the Lebanese National Idea, 1840–1920*, 39.
17 There are different theories with regard to the geographical origin of the Maronite community. These range between inner Syrian territories, regions within modern Turkey and the Arabian Peninsula.
18 This is confirmed even more later on when, seeing an opportunity to do so, they declare their intention for full Lebanese independence – see Hakim, 44.
19 Which might help explain their much less intense insistence on the distinction of ethnicity between Lebanon and surrounding Arabs (unlike the very strong insistence among Maronites).
20 In fact, there is a lot of evidence to show that the Druze showed, and have shown, more pride in Fakhr al-Din II's Emirate (1591–1635) than the Maronites do, as he is seen very much as a *Druze* leader, whereas Maronites usually find pride in Bashir II's Emirate (1789–1840), which was much more favourable to the Christians – see Yusri Hazran, 'Between Authenticity and Alienation the Druzes and Lebanon's History', *Bulletin of the School of Oriental and African Studies* 72, no. 3 (2009): 459–87.
21 Hazran, 479. See Obeid, *Druze and Their Faith in Tawhid*, 54, 127, 176. Also see Philip K. Hitti, *The Origins of the Druze People and Religion: With Extracts from Their Sacred Writings* (New York: Columbia University Press, 1928), 14.
22 See Anthony D. Smith, *Nationalism and Modernism: A Critical Survey of Recent Theories of Nations and Nationalism* (London: Routledge, 1998), 9.
23 Yet another example of disagreement over the history and importance of a figure between the Maronites and the Druzes.
24 Caesar E. Farah, *The Politics of Interventionism in Ottoman Lebanon, 1830–1861* (London: I.B. Tauris, 2000), 43.
25 Iliya F. Harik, *Politics and Change in a Traditional Society: Lebanon, 1711–1845* (Princeton, NJ: Princeton University Press, 1968), 290.
26 Harik, 290.
27 Hakim, *The Origins of the Lebanese National Idea, 1840–1920*, 33.
For full original text, see Tannus Al-Shidyaq, *Kitab Akhbār Al-A'yan Fi Jabal Lubnan* [Book on Dignitaries in Mount Lebanon] (Beirut: Publications de l'Université Libanaise, 1970), 324.
28 Hakim, *The Origins of the Lebanese National Idea, 1840–1920*, 33.
29 Along with the third request regarding the election 'by the votes of the people' of twelve councillors to serve the Hakim – see Harik, *Politics and Change in a Traditional Society*, 291.
30 As well as the inability of foreign powers, who had much influence in the matter, to come to an agreement with the Ottomans over how to reorganize the Mountain.
31 Yusri Hazran, *The Druze Community and the Lebanese State: Between Confrontation and Reconciliation* (New York: Routledge, 2014), 210.
32 The civil war also resulted in massacres against Christians in Damascus.
33 The FEF was sent to Lebanon as part of an international agreement with the mission 'of helping the Ottoman authorities re-establish law and order' – see Hakim, *The Origins of the Lebanese National Idea, 1840–1920*, 80.
34 Hakim, 83.

35 'Notes et renseignements sur le pays qui doit former le gouvernement du Liban' [Notes and Information on the Country that Should Form the Government of Lebanon] – see Hakim, 83.
36 Hakim, 83.
37 Which was followed up by a petition circled by Beaufort, the validity of which is hard to determine – see Hakim, 86–7.
38 See Map 1.2 for the map drawn by the FEF.
39 Economically, it was argued that the Mountain cannot be self-sustainable without ports for trade and the inner Biqāʿ plains for agriculture. Both those reasons would be extensively used later on by advocates of the establishment of such a large Lebanese state – see Hakim, *The Origins of the Lebanese National Idea, 1840–1920*.
40 Evidence of political interactions between the Maronites and France (or before that Franks) had existed since the eleventh century – see Kamal Salibi, 'The Maronites of Lebanon under Frankish and Mamluk Rule (1099–1516)', *Arabica* 4, no. 3 (1957): 288–303.
41 Weber's argument for traditional legitimacy (or traditional authority) implied that the state can maintain belief in its legitimacy through traditional and historic values, for example, religious authority, traditional, familial lineage and so on. See previous chapter.
42 Their state-building projects will be studied later on in the chapter. See Michael Selzer, 'Nation Building and State Building: The Israeli Example', *Phylon* 32, no. 1 (1971): 4–22, for more on the relation between nationalism and state-building.
43 Abdulaziz A. Sachedina, 'Activist Shiʿism in Iran, Iraq and Lebanon', in *Fundamentalisms Observed*, ed. Martin E. Marty and R. Scott Appleby (Chicago: University of Chicago Press, 1991), 423.
44 Which is the Arabic translation of 'nation', usually understood under Ottoman rule to mean the Sunni populations of the Empire.
45 Kais Firro, 'Ethnicizing the Shiʿis in Mandatory Lebanon', *Middle Eastern Studies* 42, no. 5 (2006): 741.
46 The origin-myth has been shown to be vital for establishing legitimacy to both nation and state and, certainly, nationalist sentiments – see Ronald Cohen, 'Legitimacy, Illegitimacy, and State Formation', in *State Formation and Political Legitimacy*, ed. Ronald Cohen and Judith D. Toland (Oxford: Transaction Books, 1988), 69–94.
47 The Shīʿas of Lebanon have been termed 'Metawalis', indicating a slight difference in identity from their co-religionists in Iran and the rest of the Middle East – see W. B. Fish, 'The Lebanon', *Geographical Review* 34, no. 2 (1944): 245.

Also see Albert Hourani, 'From Jabal ʿĀmil to Persia', *Bulletin of the School of Oriental and African Studies* 49, no. 1 (1986): 133.
48 See above footnote for 'Metawali'. Rodger Shanahan, *The Shiʿa of Lebanon: Clans, Parties and Clerics* (London: I.B. Tauris, 2005), 13–14.
49 ʿĀmeli being a demonym for people of Jabal; ʿĀmeli, the historical term for the region in Southern Lebanon that the Shīʿas have historically inhabited.
50 Rula Abisaab, 'Shiite Beginnings and Scholastic Tradition in Jabal Amil in Lebanon', *Muslim World*, 89 (1999): 4.
51 In fact, one of Fakhr-al Din II's daughters married the son of Yunus al-Harfoush, a member of one of the most influential families in the Shīʿa community of the Valley – see Shanahan, *The Shiʿa of Lebanon*, 20.
52 Shanahan, 20.

This struggle was mostly one-sided but there have been instances of Shīʿa control over non-Shīʿa inhabitants, such as the period after Fakhr al-Din's death (1635), when Hamadeh clan of Biqāʿ were given taxation powers over the north of Lebanon, including Christian and Sunni regions such as Bsharri and ʿAkkar – see Albert Hourani, 'Lebanon: The Development of a Political Society', in *Politics in Lebanon*, ed. Leonard Binder (New York: Wiley, 1966), 16–17.

53 Shanahan, *The Shiʿa of Lebanon*, 16.

54 Chalabi, *The Shiʿis of Jabal ʿAmil and the New Lebanon*, 14.

55 Chalabi, 73.

56 Chalabi, 52.

57 See Muḥammad Kāẓim Makki, *Munṭalaq Al-Ḥayat Al-Thaqāfiya Fi Jabal ʿĀmil* [The Beginnings of Cultural Life in Jabal ʿmil] (Beirut: Dār al-Zahra, 1991).

58 Though they did have a seat in the Administrative Council of Mount Lebanon that existed between 1860 and 1920 – see James A. Simon, 'The Creation of Greater Lebanon, 1918–1920: The Roles and Expectations of the Administrative Council of Mount Lebanon' [unpublished Masters thesis] (University of Utah, 1995).

59 Roschanack Shaery-Eisenlohr, *Shi'ite Lebanon: Transnational Religion and the Making of National Identities* (New York: Columbia University Press, 2008), 24.

60 And indeed, belonging to the majority religion since the ninth century AD, after the Muslim conquest of the Middle East – see David Nicolle, *The Great Islamic Conquests AD 632–750* (Essex: Osprey, 2009), 90.

61 Abdel Karim Rafeq, 'Social Groups, Identity and Loyalty, and Historical Writing in Ottoman and Post- Ottoman Syria', in *Les Arabes et l'Histoire Créatrice* [Arabs and Formative History], ed. Dominique Chevallier (Paris: Presses de l'Université du Paris-Sorbonne, 1995), 79–80.

62 That is, Sunni populace and elite of modern Turkey.

63 Najla Wadih Atiyah, 'The Attitude of the Lebanese Sunnis Towards the State of Lebanon' [unpublished doctoral thesis] (University of London, 1973), 71.

64 'Ulama literally meaning 'the learned ones' are considered, especially in Sunnism, 'the guardians, transmitters and interpreters of religious knowledge, of Islamic doctrine and law' – see Cl. Gilliot et al., "Ulama', in *Encyclopaedia of Islam, Second Edition*, ed. P. Bearman et al., 2nd edn (Leiden: Brill, 2012), X:801b, http://referenceworks.brillonline.com/entries/encyclopaedia-of-islam-2/ulama-COM_1278.
Cl. Gilliot, R. C. Repp, K. A. Nizami, et al. "Ulamā". Encyclopaedia of Islam, 2nd edn, ed. P. Bearman et al. Brill Reference Online. Web. 3 July 2018.

65 Steven Tamari, 'Arab National Consciousness in Seventeenth and Eighteenth Century Syria', in *Syria and Bilad Al-Sham under Ottoman Rule*, ed. Peter Sluglett and Stefan Weber (Leiden: Brill, 2010), 313–14.

66 Tamari, 315.

67 Or, to be precise, their branch of Islam.

68 A non-Muslim was referred to as 'dhimmi' during the Ottoman Period – see Sidney Harrison Griffith, *The Church in the Shadow of the Mosque: Christians and Muslims in the World of Islam* (Princeton, NJ: Princeton University Press, 2008), 16.

69 Bruce Alan Masters, *Christians and Jews in the Ottoman Arab World: The Roots of Sectarianism* (Cambridge: Cambridge University Press, 2001), 38.

70 Masters, 38.

71 It was argued that Fakhr al-Din II's Emirate, as well as Bashir II's rule that followed, had always enjoyed the autonomy that precedes independence. Additionally, that Emirate, at its height, once stretched to include part of or all these territories. It was also argued

that the Mountain has and will always need access to the seaports to its west (including Sunni-dominated Tripoli, and Shīʿa-dominated Tyre), as well as access to the Muslim-dominated Biqāʿ valley for agriculture and trade. And finally, it was argued that those borders were also natural and therefore justified (i.e. the Mediterranean to the west and the Anti-Lebanon to the east). See Auguste Adib Pacha, *Le Liban Après La Guerre* [Lebanon after the War] (Cairo: Imprimerie Paul Barbey, 1919).

72 The map is shown in Map 1.2.

73 Hakim, *The Origins of the Lebanese National Idea, 1840–1920*, 220.

74 Ordre general (No. 1) du Gl. Cdt. le Corps Exp., Marseille, 7 August 1860, in: Yassine Soueid, *Corps Expéditionnaire de Syrie: Rapports et Correspondance 1860–1861* [Syria Expeditionary Corps: Rapports and Correspondance 1860–1861] (Beirut: Naufal, 1998).

75 Soueid, 41.

76 See Ernest Louet, *Expédition de Syrie: Beyrouth - Le Liban - Jérusalem, 1860–1861. Notes et Souvenirs* [Expedition of Syria: Beirut - Lebanon - Jerusalem, 1860–1861: Notes and Souvenirs] (Paris: Amyot, 1862).

77 Pacha, *Le Liban Après La Guerre*, 132.

78 Pacha, 133.

79 The official stance of the surrounding communities will be made clearer in the following sections.

80 Pacha, 353. This was an erroneous (though probably intentionally so) request since, by this point, there had been no Christian governor of Lebanon, despite Bashir II's favouring of the Maronites.

81 Camille de Rochemonteix, *Le Liban et l'Expédition Française En Syrie, 1860–1861. Documents Inédits Du Général A. Ducrot.* [Lebanon and the French Expedition in Syria, 1860–1861. Unedited Documents of General A. Ducrot] (Paris: Picard, 1921), 180–1. Qaimaqam' is the Ottoman title of governor.

82 Pasha himself had initially left the question of the manner of governance for an enlarged Lebanon open, but later believed that a secular Lebanese republic headed by a proportionally represented parliament was the ideal answer. See Pacha, *Le Liban Après La Guerre.*

83 Simon, 'The Creation of Greater Lebanon, 1918–1920', 30.

84 The distribution of those seats was in accordance with the Organic Regulation on 6 September 1864. Reprinted in: Mounir Ismail, *Le Régime de La Mutasarrifiya Du Mont Liban 1861–1915* [The Regime in the Mutsarrifiya of Mount Lebanon 1861–1915] (Beirut: Edition des Oeuvres Politiques et Historiques, 2002), 239. Simon, 'The Creation of Greater Lebanon, 1918–1920', 49–51.

85 Georges Adib Karam, *L'Opinion Publique Libanais et La Question Du Liban (1918–1920)* [Lebanese Public Opinion and the Question of Lebanon (1918–1920)] (Beirut: Publications de l'Université Libanaise, 1981), 282–3. The legislative body would, also, be constituted based on proportional representation.

86 These decisions to allow members of the Church to head delegations to the Peace Conference were articulated in Administrative Council decisions such as the one on 28 February 1920 (reprinted and translated in: Antoine Hokayem, Da'd Bou Malhab Atallah and J. Charaf, *Documents Diplomatiques Français Relatifs à l'Histoire Du Liban et de La Syrie à l'Époque Du Mandat, 1914–1946* [French Diplomatic Documents Concerning the History of Lebanon and Syria at the Time of the Mandate, 1914–1946] (Paris: L'Harmattan, 2003), 102) and confirmed by letters from the Council itself to the French High Commissioner in Syria General Gouraud (reprinted in: Hokayem, Atallah and Charaf, 101).

87 All three of these organizations were formed by Syrian and Lebanese immigrants, Christian and Muslim. Corresponding organizations in different countries included the Syrian Committee in London and the Sociedad Sirio-Libanese in Mexico City.

88 Hakim, *The Origins of the Lebanese National Idea, 1840–1920*, 214–15.

89 Comité Central Syrien. 1919. La Syrie devant la Conférence. Mémoire à Monsieur Georges Clémenceau et à MM. les Délégués des Puissances Alliées et Associées à cette Conference [Syria Facing the Conference. Memorandum addressed to M. Georges Clémenceau and to the Delegates of the Allied and Associated Powers at this Conference]. Accessed from the Bibliothèque Nationale de France on 10 June 2018: https://gallica.bnf.fr/ark:/12148/bpt6k9399754.

90 Comité Central Syrien. 1919.

91 That is, The French Ministry of Foreign Affairs.

92 Letter from Ghanem, S. (1917), president of the CSC to the French Minister of Foreign Affairs on 8 November 1917. Reprinted in: Hokayem, Atallah and Charaf, *Documents Diplomatiques Français Relatifs à l'Histoire Du Liban et de La Syrie à l'Époque Du Mandat, 1914–1946*, 261.

93 Karam, *L'Opinion Publique Libanais et La Question Du Liban (1918–1920)*, 36.

94 Comité Central Syrien, 'La Syrie Devant La Conférence. Mémoire à Monsieur Georges Clémenceau et à MM. Les Délégués Des Puissances Alliées et Associées à Cette Conference [Syria Facing the Conference. Memorandum Addressed to M. Georges Clémenceau and to the Delegates of the Allie]' (Bibliothèque Nationale de France, January 1919), https://gallica.bnf.fr/ark:/12148/bpt6k9399754.

95 Letter of request from the Syria–Mount Lebanon League of Liberation to M. Woodrow Wilson, president of the United States on 10 May 1918. Reprinted in: Hokayem, Atallah and Charaf, *Documents Diplomatiques Français Relatifs à l'Histoire Du Liban et de La Syrie à l'Époque Du Mandat, 1914–1946*, 340–2.

96 Upon their request, President Wilson had proclaimed the United States' sympathy with the Syrian population, and the former's demand that 'security of life' and 'opportunity for autonomous development' be guaranteed for Syria. See Hokayem, Atallah and Charaf, 340.

97 Na'oum Moukarzel, the president of the Society of Lebanese Renaissance and an advocate of majority-Christian, independent Lebanon, called all seven members of the SMLL 'national traitors'. See John Daye, 'Syrianist Orientations in the Thought of Mikha'il Nu'ayma', in *The Origins of Statehood: Histories, Pioneers and Identity*, ed. Adel Beshara (London: Routledge, 2011), 204.

98 Hakim, *The Origins of the Lebanese National Idea, 1840–1920*, 214.

99 Letter from a Group of Syrians in Egypt to the French minister in Cairo on 25 October 1918. Reprinted in: Hokayem, Atallah and Charaf, *Documents Diplomatiques Français Relatifs à l'Histoire Du Liban et de La Syrie à l'Époque Du Mandat, 1914–1946*, 397–8.

100 Hokayem, Atallah and Charaf, 397–8.

101 Inverted commas are used to highlight the fact that some of them would later on officially become Lebanese citizens, but they chose to identify as Syrian.

102 See David Fromkin, *A Peace to End All Peace: The Fall of the Ottoman Empire and the Creation of the Modern Middle East* (New York: Henry Holt, 1989), 284–304.

103 On 26 September 1918, France and Britain both agreed that Hussein should be 'formally recognized as a member of the Allied camp'. See Jan Karl Tanenbaum, 'France and the Arab Middle East, 1914–1920', *Transactions of the American Philosophical Society* 68, no. 7 (1978): 21.

104 It was made clear in the correspondence between the two that the matter of 'limits and boundaries' was of 'vital and urgent importance' to the Sharīf (Found in 'The Mcmahon Correspondence of 1915–16', 1939, p. 8 published by the Royal Institute of International Affairs).

105 Malcolm B. Russell, *The First Modern Arab State: Syria under Faysal, 1918–1920* (Minneapolis, MN: Bibliotheca Islamica, 1985), 8–10.

106 Atiyah, 'The Attitude of the Lebanese Sunnis towards the State of Lebanon', 42.

107 Meir Zamir, 'Faisal and the Lebanese Question, 1918–20', *Middle Eastern Studies* 27, no. 3 (1991): 404.

108 To whom power had been relinquished by the retreating Ottoman governor. See Simon, 'The Creation of Greater Lebanon, 1918–1920', 31.

109 Simon, 31–3.

110 Beirut and Damascus were, after all, the two capitals and political hubs of Greater Syria.

111 Zamir, 'Faisal and the Lebanese Question, 1918–20', 405.

112 Isaiah Friedman, 'The McMahon-Hussein Correspondence and the Question of Palestine', *Journal of Contemporary History* 5, no. 2 (1970): 86.

113 David Hunter Miller, *My Diary at Conference of Paris – Volume IV – Documents 216–304* (New York: Appeal Printing Company, 1919), 297.

114 According to the Secretary's Notes of a Conversation Held in M. Pichon's Room at the Quai d'Orsay, Paris, on Thursday, 6 February 1919, at 3 pm, retrieved on 23 July 2018 from: https://history.state.gov/historicaldocuments/frus1919Parisv03/d61.

115 Secretary's Notes of a Conversation Held in M. Pichon's Room at the Quai d'Orsay.

116 Miller, 267.

117 Howard Bliss was the president of the Syrian Protestant College (later the American University of Beirut) during the war. He attended the Paris Peace Conference as a close friend of US President Wilson and Charles Crane. During the Conference, Bliss recommended consulting the population of the former Ottoman territories in the Levant, through a commission, 'as to what form of Government they desire and as to what power, if any, should be their Mandatory Protecting Power'. See *Secretary's Notes of a Conversation Held in M. Pichon's Room at the Quai d'Orsay, Paris, on Thursday, 13 February, 1919, at 3 p.m.* Paris Peace Conf. 180.03101/38. Papers Relating to the Foreign Relations of the United States, The Paris Peace Conference, 1919, Volume III.

The original plan was to have a commission which included delegates from all the Allied powers, but both Britain and France resisted, as they were confident in their unique role to solve the Syrian Question and believed any attempt to determine the wishes of the population would be ineffective. They were also wary of the possibility of an unfavourable result of such a commission. President Wilson eventually acted alone by sending an exclusively American commission. See Simon, 'The Creation of Greater Lebanon, 1918–1920', 75. Kaufman, *Reviving Phoenicia*, 84.

118 Simon, 'The Creation of Greater Lebanon, 1918–1920', 76.

119 King–Crane Commission Report (KCCR), 28 August 1919. Accessed on 15 June 2018: wwi.lib.byu.edu/index.php/The_King-Crane_Report.

120 King–Crane Commission Report.

121 No distinction was made between Sunni and Shīʿa.

122 King–Crane Commission Report (KCCR), 28 August 1919. Accessed on 15 June 2018: wwi.lib.byu.edu/index.php/The_King-Crane_Report.

123 Evidently, the rate of the increase is quite difficult to determine without going through each petition.

124 'Lebanon' here can be assumed to refer to the Mountain.
'French-Lebanon program' can be assumed to refer to the Lebanist project.
From *Report of the American Section of the International Commission on Mandates in Turkey*. Paris Peace Conf. 181.9102/9. Papers Relating to the Foreign Relations of the United States, The Paris Peace Conference, 1919, Volume XII. Accessed on 8 July 2018: https://history.state.gov/historicaldocuments/frus1919Parisv12/d380.
125 Report of the American Section of the International Commission on Mandates in Turkey.
126 Report of the American Section of the International Commission on Mandates in Turkey.
127 Report of the American Section of the International Commission on Mandates in Turkey.
128 Report of the American Section of the International Commission on Mandates in Turkey.
129 The four causes can then be subsequently divided into constitutive and non-constitutive causes: constitutive causes exist within X, and continue to exist within X after X comes to be. Non-constitutive causes are those that are 'superseded' once X comes to be and cease to exist. Milja Kurki modifies this by terming constitutive causes 'intrinsic' and contrasting that with 'extrinsic' causes that are not within X but 'lend an influence or activity to the producing of something'. Material and formal causes are then considered intrinsic, and efficient and final causes are taken to be extrinsic. See Milja Kurki, *Causation in International Relations: Reclaiming Causal Analysis* (Cambridge: Cambridge University Press, 2008).
See Kurki.
130 In the O.E.T.A (East), representing the areas of modern Lebanon east of the Mountain, as well as most of modern Syria, 82 per cent of petitions were against an independent Greater Lebanon.

Chapter 2

THE IMMEDIATE EFFECTS OF ILLEGITIMACY

It has been established so far that the state of Greater Lebanon, created on 1 September 1920, was neither fully formed, legally – not least because it was still under a French mandate – nor did it encompass a nation within its legally defined territory. As a result, Greater Lebanon hadn't achieved the standards of a nation-state, nor had it claimed the representative legitimacy it needed to function in a sustainable manner, as it would be expected to under the societal approach to state-building. The different communities comprising the Lebanese territory had been vocal about their positions towards the new state, some having an active hand in creating it, while others were so vehemently opposed to the idea that they were not willing to even recognize its existence. The state-building projects that were proposed a priori had to therefore evolve: the Lebanist project now had the opportunity to be put in effect *through* institutions of the state, while the opposing projects that had not come to fruition (e.g. Syrianism, Arabism) had to transform themselves and become nationalist movements with specific political agendas operating in an existent state. Consequently, the issue of nation-building that was in many ways ignored in those aforementioned projects had to now be addressed, while institutional legitimacy became a necessity if the institutional approach is to be followed. Additionally, the creation of central public institutions in Lebanon (as opposed to remaining a semi-autonomous portion of the Ottoman Empire) would allow for the emergence of multiple domestic actors whose decisions and interactions – with each other, with their communities and with the mandate power – would grow to play the crucial role that would equally affect the legitimacy of Lebanese state-building.

Overall, this chapter will highlight the interaction between state-building and nation-building that occurred during the mandate period of France over Lebanon, starting with the creation of Greater Lebanon until the country effectively achieved independence in 1943. It will show how those years of disillusion, instability and uncertainty were directly linked to the legitimacy or lack thereof of the Lebanese state, and how the dynamic between state-building and nation-building had been in play from the off, and ultimately where the theories fail to take into account the relation between legitimacy and stability in the Lebanese case. After having shown that societal legitimacy was practically absent by 1920, this chapter will emphasize the efforts by the state to claim legitimacy through institutional strength and democratic representativeness, though the ongoing lack of societal legitimacy will continue to be stressed in tandem.

Early prospects

While the creation of Greater Lebanon finally gave the Lebanists some confidence in their vision of an independent Lebanese state, the fact that a French mandate was very much looming meant that no political concessions were ruled out, in particular since France was dealing with Faisal and Syrian/Arab nationalists.[1] The Lebanists, fully aware of this, anticipated the possibility of their independence being used as a bargaining chip between the French and the Syrians.[2] The matter was exacerbated by the French not delineating a clear policy for their actions in the Levant, preferring instead to deal with each concerned party individually while keeping their cards close to their chest, a habit that would not be broken for some time when it comes to declaring broad mandatory policies.[3]

Initially, the policy adopted by the French was the division of Syria into four different regions, with a view of uniting them at some point in the future.[4] Colonel Georges Catroux, who was at the time the aide to the first French high commissioner of Syria and Lebanon, General Gouraud, believed that the latter had succumbed to his own prejudices when he decided to enlarge Lebanon at the expense of the Syrians.[5] The following will delineate the results of such an enlargement, the reactions from the parties involved and whether or not political stability in Greater Lebanon was attainable as a consequence.

The Syrian nationalists always looked at France's policy as one of 'divide and conquer', especially when faced with the somewhat contradictory decisions by the French to divide Syria into autonomous regions while failing to be consistent with the enlargement of the Mountain.[6] This was perceived, by the nationalists, as a clear matter of bias and favouring towards the French's old Catholic clients in Lebanon while Faysal and the Syrians themselves were treated as adversaries with whom there can be no compromise. This feeling quickly overflowed into Lebanon and increased any existing animosity, mostly among the Muslims, towards the state of Greater Lebanon, further cementing its illegitimacy within a significant portion of the population, especially among the citizens of Tripoli and the Muslim sectors of Beirut.[7] In fact, not only did most inhabitants of the newly annexed areas refuse to accept the fait accompli of Greater Lebanon, but scepticism was also festering among the Christians of the Mountain, who were wondering whether or not they had made a mistake in jeopardizing their much-needed demographical dominance.[8] Additionally, Robert de Caix,[9] regarded by many as the man responsible for the general French policy in the Levant throughout the mandate period,[10] believed that Beiruti Christians, especially Greek Orthodox, showed a lot of mistrust towards the Maronites and rejected the idea that relations between Greater Lebanon and Syria should be on an equal footing; they believed Greater Lebanon should, in one form or another, join a Greater Syria.[11]

There was no doubt about French and Lebanist awareness of the legitimacy problem that Greater Lebanon faced early on. Nevertheless, the Christian Lebanists, and specifically the Maronites, were not so willing to admit such shortages with regard to the legitimacy of Greater Lebanon. They decided to make their case for legitimacy by publicly arguing for how representative this new state was, in addition to adopting state-building policies that would make the state as representative as possible without giving up their own positions of privilege. The centre-point of those policies was the maintenance of the power-sharing system which had already been nominally in place in the Mountain, between the Druze and the Christians. The policy was also seen as a continuation of the Ottoman millet system, therefore guaranteeing representation and moving away from the 'exclusively Christian' tag for the new state.[12] Another sign of Lebanist awareness of this problem was the position of some of them (e.g. Emile Eddeh[13]) towards the possibility of ceding some territory (mainly Tripoli). People like Eddeh, Charles Corm and Marquis de Freige were more ready to address the issue of demographics and separatist sentiment than their co-religionists.

The French authorities were equally insistent of their fair rule with regard to the different communities in the Levant and their demands. Nevertheless, it wouldn't take long before French writers became aware of the differences in result of their mandates, and were quick to argue that those differences were the result of the existing dispositions of the various Lebanese and Syrian communities: Raymond O'Zoux, for example, analysed the different French policies in the Levant and argued that 'in Lebanon, we [the French] encountered a close moral connection due to religion and history. Our civilisation fits perfectly with that of the native population'. Meanwhile, he believed that 'the Muslim populations of this state [Syria] carry with them a civilisation … that is opposed to our own'.[14] He, like others, believed that the different French policies were justified and were a *result* of diverse attitudes as opposed to many (mainly local Muslims) that believed the policies themselves were the cause of antagonism towards the mandate.

Still, even though it was seldom publicly acknowledged, the awareness of the legitimacy problem – by both expansionists and isolationists – and the sense of urgency which it presented manifested itself in the nation-building efforts that were inevitably developed. Policies to produce a Lebanese nation were clearly the only way for the state to gain legitimacy, as it would allow a feeling of representation and involvement among all Lebanese people, old and newly incorporated. This would have to, and could only ever, be done through conventional nation-building efforts of producing national literature, origin myths such as the concept of Phoenicianism,[15] symbols of unity and so on as well as through actual state-building efforts, meaning the formation of representative state institutions that could also be effective.

From the off, there was a clear space for either approach to state-building: the institutional approach would argue that the construction of strong and effective institutions would successfully allow the state to claim legitimacy among the Lebanese population, while the societal approach would contend that, a nation being virtually absent, the Lebanese state would need to immediately embark on promoting 'the idea of the state' within the population so it can be given the legitimacy it needs from a developing 'nation'. Yet, the state cannot become effective institutionally when it is facing such a deep and fundamental opposition by such large parts of its population. Those feeling less represented will naturally refuse to cooperate, be liable to take advantage of opportunities to undermine the state when they arise, physically and forcefully rebel if they see fit. Meanwhile, those who are in positions of privilege will become more liable to develop animosity towards their co-citizens who refuse to cooperate or even show faith in the system in which they are all living, and they themselves will therefore be more liable to take advantage of the state, consolidate power, discriminate against those they feel are ungrateful and so on. The result is a vicious circle for the state, institutionally. Meanwhile, the state finds it just as hard to convince the society of its viability since it is neither representative nor effective. Legitimacy is therefore ultimately and perpetually lacking, from a state-building perspective. It will be shown that this is exactly what happened in the case of Lebanon, and that neither approach would have been realistically applicable (though degrees of both were tried).

Building the nation *through* state-building, though, makes for a virtually impossible task since the state, lacking legitimacy in the eyes of a significant part of the population, continuously fails to incorporate them *because* of that illegitimacy, as those communities refuse to recognize and accept a state that they do not feel a part of. The societal approach attempts to explain this problem, since it can show how legitimacy is ultimately tied to the feeling of national identity that is so crucially missing in the state of Greater Lebanon. However, the societal approach fails to adequately take into account the temporal element, since any nation-building endeavour embarked upon *after* the creation of an illegitimate state, with the objective of forming a nation for that specific state, especially when it is sponsored by that same illegitimate state, is unlikely to be successful, as will be shown in the case of Greater Lebanon. The only resort that was left for the Lebanese that allows for keeping the state intact is the redesigning of the institutions, specifically the political system, so as to become more representative and inclusive to the alienated communities. In this way, state-building and nation-building could occur simultaneously, where the state institutions are built *with the purpose* of nation-building,[16] even sacrificing efficiency and efficacy. Lebanon, already possessing a long history of proportional representation, was predisposed to do just that in the 1920s.[17]

The importance of the census

The necessity of nation-building-oriented institutions was recognized almost immediately by the first high commissioner, General Gouraud, as well as De Caix. In a letter to the Quai D'Orsay in April 1922, the latter maintained that the Lebanese did not yet develop the idea of 'patrie', which he described as 'the union of all under a common social or temporal ideal', as that union is impeded whenever it meets the 'barriers' of religious pluralism. The two main religious groups, he goes on, are divided into even smaller 'nations' that are clearly delineated and separated.[18] As a result of these conclusions, Gouraud immediately started by appointing members to a newly created, confessionally diverse 'Administrative Commission of Greater Lebanon' that included six Maronites (of ten Christians overall) out of fifteen members. Recognizing the sensitivity of the situation, Gouraud used the numbers available from previous censuses conducted by the Ottoman Empire,[19] the most recent one then being in 1913, to decide how to fairly divide the seats on the Commission, and establish it as Greater Lebanon's first native executive body.[20]

It wouldn't take long (twenty-one days), however, for Gouraud to reshuffle the seats in the Commission after a 'deeper examination of the … census',[21] adding two Sunni seats. In both decrees, he mentions the temporary nature of these institutions as well as their seat distributions, at least 'until a new census ensues' that would then be accompanied by elections. Six months later, a new census was confirmed by Gouraud, with its purpose as clear as can be: the census is 'necessary so as to assure an equitable basis of representation of the Lebanese state, as well as the distribution of taxes and public resources'.[22] The statement within Decree N° 763 effectively reveals how the societal approach was undertook straightaway: since the existence of the state itself did not represent the people's wishes,[23] its institutions had to be tailored to do so, otherwise there would be no hope of it attaining legitimacy. This implied, certainly for the non-Christian population, the distribution of every state resource, whether political, legal, fiscal or economic, equitably based on the demographic statistics of a census.

The significance of the demographic figures was not lost on the Lebanists – mainly Christians – as well as the French. Even before setting out the procedures and regulations of the census, both the Christians and French were well aware of the alarming number of Lebanese who had emigrated during the war, and they were equally cognizant of the fact that most of these expatriates were Christian. The French, ever mindful of this,[24] had already taken – somewhat unsuccessfully – measures to reduce and diminish the number of Lebanese leaving the country.[25] Consequently, it was decided that emigrants that are also registered taxpayers would be included in the census, which only helped to boost Christian numbers, and push their ratio from 50.8 per cent of the population to 53.4 per cent. Conversely, the Muslim ratio decreased from 47.7 per cent to 45.2 per cent. There is also evidence that shows that many Muslims (especially Sunni Syrian nationalists) boycotted the census, so as to avoid bearing Lebanese identity cards.[26] In fact, their rejection of the Lebanese identity was so strong that the high commissioner had to compromise and agree to remove the lower part of the identity card given to them where it stated that the holder is of Lebanese nationality.[27] Similarly, Muslim residents of Beirut had the 'Lebanese' section of their identity cards replaced with 'Beiruti' (Table 2.1).[28]

Still, because of boycotts and inaccurate registrations, these numbers are definitely questionable. For example, a report from the British consul general in Beirut to the Secretary of State gives the figures shown in Table 2.2 for the different religious groups in Greater Lebanon.[29]

So it was that, based on the 1921–2 census, the first national, elected institution of Greater Lebanon was formed: the Representative Council.[30] The name itself

Table 2.1 Results of the Census Conducted during 1921–2

Confession	Residents		Taxed Emigrants		Total	
	Total	%	Total	%	Total	%
Maronite	175,702	31.63	23,480	47.39	199,182	32.9
G. Orth.	64,416	11.59	12,993	26.22	77,409	12.8
G. Cath.	38,559	6.94	3,903	7.87	42,462	7.0
Protestant	3,730	0.67	485	0.97	4,215	0.7
Total C.	282,407	50.8	40,861	82.5	323,268	53.4
Sunni	121,917	21.94	2,824	5.70	124,741	20.6
Shīʿa	103,038	18.55	1,879	3.79	104,917	17.3
Druze	39,841	7.17	3,792	7.65	43,633	7.2
Total M.	264,796	47.7	8,495	17.1	273,291	45.2
Others	8,251	1.5	185	0.4	8,436	1.4
Total	555,454	100	49,541	100	604,995	100

Notes: The census officially started on 25 June 1921, and encompassed all of the mandated territories, finishing on 31 January 1922. See letter from R. de Caix, interim high commissioner to Aristide Briand, 15 April 1922.

Source: Himadeh, *Economic Organisation of Syria*, 1936, 410–11.

Table 2.2 Population Figures in Lebanon as Indicated in a 1922 Report from the British Consul General in Beirut

Total	609,069
Maronites	199,181
Sunni Muslims	124,786
Shīʿa Muslims	104,947
Greek Orthodox	81,409
Druzes	43,633
Greek Catholics	42,462
Protestants	4,215
Miscellaneous	8,436

gives an indication of the intention of this body, yet its existence immediately faced opposition from all directions. It was reported that many Sunnis completely boycotted the elections of March 1922, sticking to their belief of the illegality and unrepresentativeness of the state of Greater Lebanon.[31] Meanwhile, there was equal opposition from those supporting the state as they did not believe enough powers were given to the Representative Council, since it ultimately needed the approval of the governor of Greater Lebanon, who was himself appointed by and answered directly to the high commissioner.[32] In addition, due to the boycott of many Muslims and the resistance of some Christians, the French found themselves having to interfere in the elections in order to achieve a favourable result and avoid an early embarrassment at the start of its mandate.[33] This was such an open secret that even the British Consul reported that 'the Moslem representatives are practically nonentities' in terms of their actual representation of their community's wishes.[34] This presented a clear problem with theorizing about state-building early on: while the societal

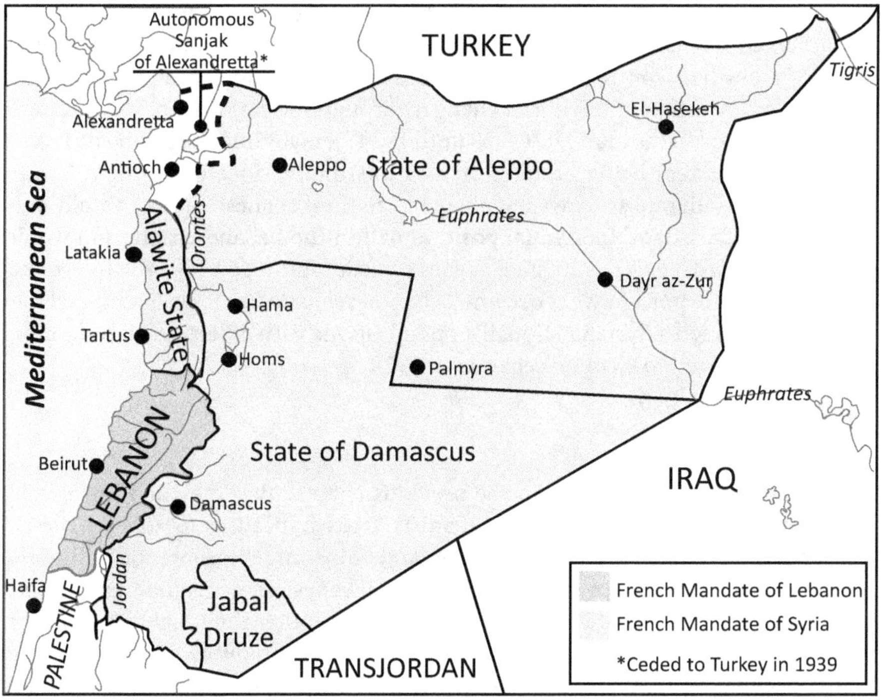

Map 2.1 Divisions of the first years of the mandate.
Source: Traboulsi, *A History of Modern Lebanon*, 2007, 89.

approach applies here and can be scrutinized as such, there is no evidence that it was being done validly, as the state could not, try as it may, become successful if many in the Muslim population simply refused to participate in its activities (Map 2.1).

Reactions to the new state

Between 1922 and 1926, the existence of Greater Lebanon was far from assured. Demands from different parts of the territory flooded in towards the high commission and, consequently, the Quai D'Orsay. Those demands came in the form of protests, petitions, personal letters and so on and the demands ranged between the rejection of Greater Lebanon, autonomy for certain regions, grants special status and unity with Syria. The following examples of uncertainty with regard to Greater Lebanon are meant to illustrate the doubts that surrounded the state in its early years as a result of its illegitimacy.

Even before the March elections, the agitations in Beirut by most Sunni Muslims and some Orthodox Christians caused the French to ponder the idea of turning Beirut into an autonomous municipality; De Caix believed that this model had proven to work with 'Mediterranean cities'.[35] Additionally, De Caix also claims that this would relieve many Christians: those Greek Orthodox that had not accepted Greater Lebanon and the Maronites who have looked at Beirut as more of a burden with regard to the governance of Greater Lebanon.[36] De Caix explored many different territorial changes throughout the time in which he was directly involved in the mandate (1920 until 1924[37]), including the ceding of Tripoli to Syria, which kept being brought up as a possibility, since giving up a Sunni-dominated city that has always felt alienated to the Lebanese project would only increase the Christians' influential position within the Lebanese state, and would deliver better prospects for the state to gain societal legitimacy.[38] Meanwhile, many Sunnis who were born in what became Lebanon relocated to Syria and joined – in some cases headed – Syrian nationalist organizations with objectives of reclaiming territories annexed to Greater Lebanon in 1920.

The Shīʿa

As for the Shīʿa, it was shown in the previous chapter that they had historically been overlooked, politically. The Lebanists tried appealing to this by, firstly, agreeing to their confession meriting a separate Muslim representation within the new institutions (unlike in the old Ottoman millet system which offered the Shīʿa no legal or political separation) and, secondly, accepting their rightful inclusion with the state itself through distribution of resources and public jobs.[39] The Shīʿa, whose population numbers were not as clear as other confessions because of the lack of recognition of their separateness under Ottoman rule, immediately felt alienated and under-represented. In addition, they had a historically antagonistic relationship with the French from the offset, mainly due to an issue of tobacco production that dated back to the end of the nineteenth century. The area of southern Lebanon known as Jabal ʿĀmel – the Shīʿa 'stronghold' – was mostly used by the Shīʿa peasants to cultivate tobacco, which was in turn produced, controlled and exported – exclusively – by the Régie Company, an Ottoman monopoly company that was itself formed by a group of European banks.[40] This exclusivity, which had expired in 1913,[41] was then transferred to the jurisdiction of the French high commission under the Lausanne treaty.[42] Aiming to update its standardization and efficiency, the Régie imposed even more numerous and restrictive regulations that hurt local, smaller, Shīʿa farmers, despite petitions and demands from ʿĀmelites.[43]

This, in addition to the arbitrary exile of many ʿĀmelite leaders such as Kāmil al-Asʿad, was one of the factors which pushed most Shīʿa to feel unrepresented by the new state which they could only perceive as a creation of France and its Christian clients from the Mountain. Additionally, the Shīʿa in the south felt that their territory was used by the French as a bargaining chip with both the Maronites and the Syrian nationalists. The ʿĀmelites, however, had already developed sympathies and close connections with Syrian nationalists by the time Greater Lebanon was formed. And, to further drive them in the direction of Damascus, the French failed to delineate Lebanon's southern borders with British-mandated Palestine, leaving the matter to subsequent treaties and agreements between the two European powers.[44] While the Ḥūla region was eventually reclaimed by the French, a similar incident happened in 1923 when, on 23 June, twenty-three 'Āmelite villages were transferred to the British-mandated territory, which only proved again to the 'Āmelites that their territory was only ever going to be regarded and used as a strategic bargaining chip.[45]

It was openly stated by Shī'a leaders that any decision made by the state of Greater Lebanon or its institutions was not worth cooperating with, and they rejected such decisions based on 'the lack of equality within the country, and the absence of a nation across the country'.[46] As a result of this feeling, the Shī'as of the South quickly developed an antagonistic view of the Lebanese state and, through official complaints, petitions, telegrams and journal articles, expressed their lack of recognition of the Lebanese 'creation' and demanded to join a Syrian Arab entity which they believed would protect their rights, even as a minority Muslim sect in a Sunni-dominated country.[47] This even led to some violent clashes between Christian gangs and 'Āmelites in the South.[48]

The Sunnis and the Syrians

Tripoli, the chief hub of the non-Christian sectors of the North of Lebanon, was also opposed to Greater Lebanon from the offset and, being Sunni-dominated, had historically felt much closer to Damascus than to the Mountain, or even Beirut for that matter. On 28 June 1922, the Syrian Federation was created with the exclusion of Greater Lebanon,[49] which the Representative Council showed complete unwillingness to join.[50] The creation of the Syrian Federation, however, did not appease the Syrian nationalists, nor did it stop Beiruti and Tripolitan anti-Lebanon movements.[51] Immediately, 'mazbatas'[52] were distributed in Tripoli (and, it was rumoured, Beirut) that called for agitation with the objective of being annexed to the Federation.[53] By that time, the attitude of Moslems towards Christians – and, it can be assumed, vice versa – was described as 'more or less' hostile.[54] On 24 January 1923, during a visit from the high commissioner to Tripoli, he was overcome with direct demands from citizens of the city to join the Syrian Federation or, failing that, to have the city as capital of its own 'sanjak'.[55] It was not the only Muslim-majority town to have such demands, as many groups and organizations in different coastal towns 'agitated unsuccessfully' for Lebanon to join the Syrian State.[56] Nevertheless, while some moderate Muslims in Beirut could be more easily convinced of the benefits of Greater Lebanon, Muslims in Tripoli were especially unified, regardless of class, in their mission to have it detached from Lebanon and join the Syrian state.[57] While small minorities of Greek Orthodox citizens of Tripoli showed loyalty to Greater Lebanon and to the high commissioner, they were much more overwhelmingly outnumbered than in the other coastal cities.[58] Meanwhile, there were reports of some resistance from Druzes gangs in Shūf and 'Aley with clear pro-Syrian messages.[59] In fact the Syrian revolt, that started in Jabal al-Druze around 1924 and expanded to the rest of Syria by 1925–6, did not take long to spill over to the Lebanon, all over the country in areas such as B'albak, Rashaya, the Litani, Mount Hermon, the Shūf and 'Aley.[60] During this time, Tripoli, Jabal 'Āmel, Sidon and B'albak all sent official requests and signed petitions asking to be annexed to Syria and threatening to boycott elections.[61]

The Syrians themselves were quite open about their affection and link to the Lebanese areas that want to join a Greater Syria. In 1926, then-new president of Syria Damad Ahmed Nami Bey (appointed by the high commissioner) made a proclamation in which he basically promised adding Tripoli to Syria as its own Mediterranean port. It was even believed by then that the French high commissioner at the time, Henri De Jouvenel, had agreed in principle to this concession.[62] All the while, Syro-Lebanese organizations and delegations promoting Syrian nationalism were doing everything they could, both domestically and internationally, to achieve the goal of a Greater Syria within which a Lesser Lebanon (i.e. the old Mountain) could play a part if it so desired.[63]

The French

In the meantime, the French were doing what they could to keep the national narrative one of unity, legitimacy and, naturally, one that was pro-France and pro-mandate. They did this by banning many anti-French newspapers,[64] reinforcing intersectarian conflict by sending rifles and supplies to the Christians with the objective of disarming Muslim rebels.[65] These flashes of conflict would usually start as personal disputes (land disputes being the most common) or 'unusually loud' religious celebrations that would exponentially escalate to violent levels, involving not only hand weapons but also rifles and, in some cases, bombs.[66] In addition, most elections were tarnished by reports of bribery, corruption and French interference.[67] The high commissioner also dissolved some municipal councils, such as the one in B'alabak for 'incessant requests to secede'.[68] And, in the worst-case scenarios, the commissioner would dissolve the Representative Council. The Council, when it could, would move straight away to proclaim Lebanese unity and independence, and establish institutions with the hope of cementing Lebanon's legal and political status.[69] Throughout this time there were also many other institutional adjustments, including territorial ones, but the latter were restricted to the Syrian territory (Map 2.2).[70]

The 1926 constitution

In 1926, a constitution for the Lebanese Republic was enacted. This was a result of the belief of Henri De Jouvenel, the first civilian high commissioner, that only through self-government and a show of trust for the native population could all disputes be finally resolved.[71] The Christians, now believing their fate was in their own hands, avoided any question over territorial changes to the country. They preferred to focus, however, on how state institutions can best represent the different communities in the country, and the question of whether state-building and nation-building should occur simultaneously was put forward again, under

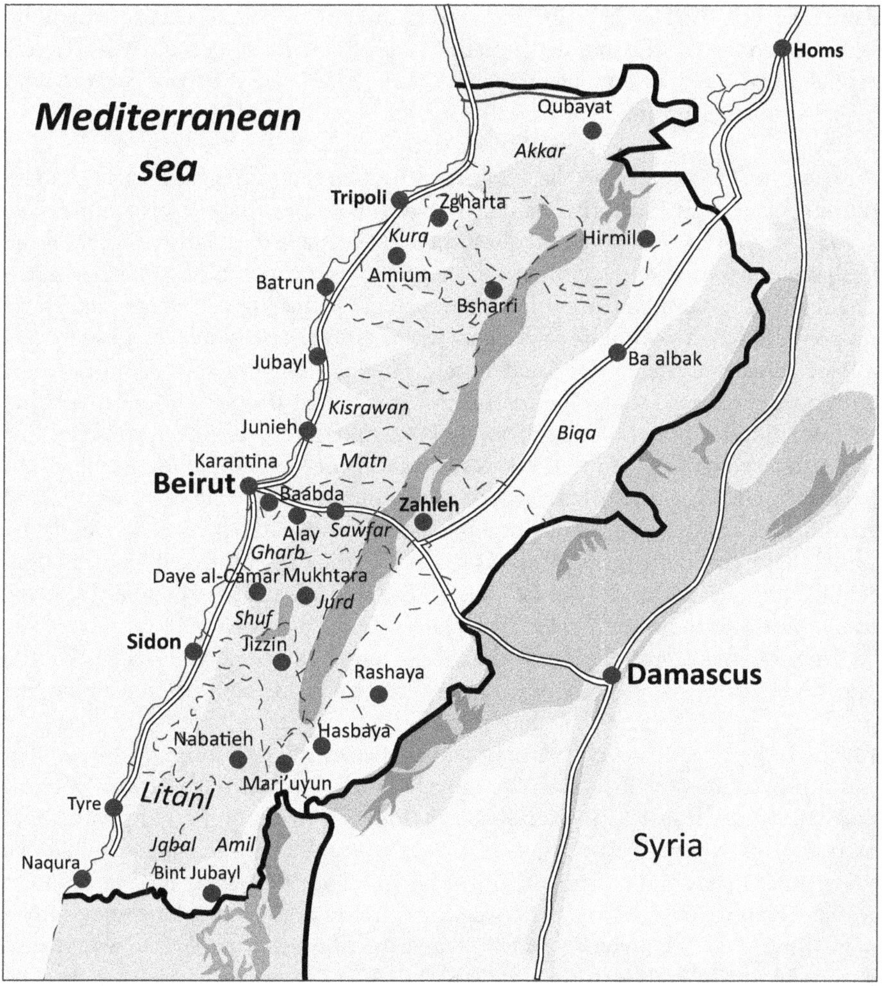

Map 2.2 Map of Lebanon.
Source: Traboulsi, *A History of Modern Lebanon*, 2007, xii.

the guise of 'sectarianism or secularism': should the state institutions be internally divided based on demographical proportions of the different confessions?

The Statute Commission,[72] charged with examining the draft prepared by the designated sub-committee,[73] decided, as part of the report it was supposed to then submit to the Representative Council, to send a questionnaire to the different communities of Lebanon.[74] Out of 189 persons to whom the questionnaire was sent, only 132 responses were received.[75] The groups and people that did not respond were almost all Muslims who disagreed with the existence of a Lebanese state and would therefore not be willing to recognize a constitution.[76] As for the questionnaire itself, a couple of questions (there were twelve in total) stand out: first among these was the question of a republic versus a monarchy: the majority opted for a parliamentary republic while twelve replies were for a monarchical regime, and these were all from Sunnis who believed in the legitimacy of Faysal's kingdom.[77] This fundamental difference in the type of regime desired and, more importantly, in the legitimacy that such a regime would represent (the Arab identity being an integral part of Faysal's old kingdom) was indicative of the type of difficulties that were to come. The second, equally as fundamental, question was in regard to the distribution of the parliamentary seats, and whether that should be made on a confessional basis. All 132 replies condemned the confessional system as a backward system, one based on prejudices that should be done away with as soon as possible. Yet, despite this, 121 believed that the confessional system *should* be the basis for representation within the Lebanese state. The reasons for this varied from tradition, to a belief that, for that time, *only* the confessional system could guarantee protection for minorities; some believed that it was necessary since a national identity had not been formed yet, while others argued that communities functioned as political parties in Lebanon and were therefore not so anti-democratic.[78] It should be noted that in his concluding remarks as head of the Constitutional Commission, Shibl Dammous remarked the following: 'The Lebanese has [*sic*] still not learned to put patriotic above confessional solidarity.'[79]

The obvious contradiction within these answers speaks for itself: for the Christians, ever wary of their regional circumstances, confessionalism meant protection and influence that they would never otherwise have, so long as they retained their valuable population within Lebanon. For those Muslims that did reply, confessionalism was the only hope they could have of any political participation within this foreign state, in addition to the hope that, with them attaining an eventual majority, Lebanon would ultimately be shaped to fit the wider Arab image and objectives. The decision to link confessional representation to state institutions would ironically endure throughout Lebanon's history, despite a unanimous 'repugnance' towards such a basis for a republic. It would also shape the rest of its history of state-building, tying the validity of institutions to legitimacy through representativeness.

There is not much that one could say about Lebanese institutional state-building up to the point of the constitution which would contradict many of the contemporary theories of how to create a successful state. Specifically, within the context of the mandate, those institutionalists that have analysed the possibility of external state-building would find it difficult to argue with the French policies in Lebanon. After all, by the end of 1926, the French had created a 'modern', previously absent, political system unheard of in the Levant and in Lebanon in particular. They had created an extensive administrative system and a political system which incrementally increased the degree of involvement and self-determination for the Lebanese (starting with a very limited Administrative Commission to the more powerful Representative Council and, by 1926, a bicameral legislative).[80] Crucially, as mentioned, they had maintained the principle of confessional distribution (albeit certainly not to the degree demanded by the non-Christian communities).

The mandatory power also created formal institutions for services such as justice, finance, policing, public works and so on. Finally, the French mandate ensured, certainly early on, that a significant sum of money was used to deal with the demands of these state-building endeavours and, despite early budget deficits, records from the years 1925 to 1927 show a healthy surplus.[81]

The institutions set up by the French mandatory power during the 1920s had undoubtedly been an organizational and functional improvement on the existing system in the Lebanese territories. For a theorist like Keohane, for example, this type of state-building would certainly not be far off his proposed trusteeship: a collection of rule-based, shared-sovereignty institutions which respected the existing ethno-religious divisions (*within* Lebanon, at least).[82] By all such accounts, one *should* be able to speak of a successful state-building experience in Lebanon during most of the 1920s, yet the following years would show otherwise.

Would the societal approach, then, fare better in explaining why, despite the creation of revolutionary public institutions in the Lebanon, the Lebanese state still suffered from chronic illegitimacy? Interestingly, 'societalists' would be content with the preservation of the power-sharing system, since the state was – up to that point – devoid of societal legitimacy. But through the combination of feeling under-represented and completely alienated from what they considered a foreign state, most in the Muslim communities (and many in the Greek Orthodox community) refused to cooperate with these new institutions. As a result, state institutions found it difficult to develop a track record of efficiency and positive performance. In fact, they had already faced opposition from the very communities they now aimed to represent. In other words, for those institutions to become valid, they would have to acquire legitimacy. But it was the societal *illegitimacy* of the state (i.e. its unrepresentativeness) from which those institutions originated that provided obstacles for this legitimacy. The identity of the state was not representative, so how could its institutions become so? The state decision-makers, composed mainly of the French and the Maronites, were thus left with one option: to use the state to develop an encompassing national identity. In other words, the Lebanese state would embark on a nation-building project (as all states are apt to do) that it would struggle with until, arguably, today.

Post-constitution

There was hope that the enactment of a constitution for what was thereafter the Lebanese Republic would lessen secessionist movements and calls, with the state and its territory being even more rooted in a legal and political basis.[83] Since state and nation were so intrinsically tied, legitimizing once meant the same for the other, and there was hope of that for those Lebanists who held firm in their belief of an enlarged Lebanon. De Caix, for his part as French delegate to the League of Nations, reminded the Lebanese as well as the Syrians that this wasn't his original vision for the region: his did not involve such an enlargement of Lebanon, and allowed for local autonomy but never to the point of 'pulverisation' of the whole region.[84]

For those that opposed the Lebanese state, however, the constitution did not change much. Opposition among the Sunnis was so strong that even government officials decided to voice their opinions;[85] they signed their name to petitions protesting the constitution and reiterating demands for Syrian unity.[86] Meanwhile, the Shīʿa's position was just as stern, although their demands were not as clear: most of them also refused to answer the questionnaire regarding the constitution, but their reply to the commission focused on their lack of representation within this 'Lesser Lebanon' and requested an independent administration for the ʿĀmelites.[87] The French, noticing the lack of demand – or rather, as strong a demand – for Syrian unity on the part of the ʿĀmelites, did what they could to appease the Shīʿa in the face of strong Sunni secessionism by allowing them autonomy over the personal status of their members.[88]

The issue of representation and identity would plague Lebanese institutions in the late 1920s, confounding state-building and nation-building. The perfect example of this is the school crisis of 1930. Emile Eddeh – a man perceived as a Christian fanatic and ardent supporter of the mandate – was appointed prime minister in 1929 and immediately tried to implement educational reforms both for the purpose of improving the efficiency of state-provided education and, more importantly, to cut expenditures and balance the budget.[89] As a result, he would shut down one hundred public schools, which were mostly attended by the poorer Muslim children; this immediately sparked protests and demonstrations from Tripoli, Beirut, Sidon, Jabal ʿĀmel and the Druze regions.[90] The issue then escalated and turned into what the Muslims perceive to be a move on the part of Eddeh to deprive the Muslims from an Arab education and to force them to become part of private schools, usually run by Catholic or Jesuit monasteries and the curriculum of which involved French and Western education.[91] There were even reports of the Lebanese government, backed by the French, pushing for the Latinization of the Lebanese language and the removal of the Arabic alphabet in the education system, which only made things worse in the eyes of the non-Christian communities.[92]

The school crisis which led to the ousting of Eddeh's government by a coalition Muslim and some opportunistic Christian deputies showed again the inevitably confessional character of state institutions in Lebanon. Regardless of whether Eddeh's reforms were specifically targeted against Muslims, the fact remains that a governmental reform could not and would not be allowed to work in the confessional system, for reasons other than its effectiveness. The state has to maintain fair representation, which the constitution had tied *not* to fair consideration but actual equitable distribution of funds based on the demography of the country. This meant that the state's legitimacy, which hinges on the fairness of its representation, would *always* win out, even when it was a question of the effectiveness of its institutions or, in the case of Eddeh's reforms, a balanced budget. Thus, as political crises occurred, it became clearer that societal legitimacy would trump institutional legitimacy in Greater Lebanon, and that nation-building as a policy (through the state's endorsement of equitable distribution) would be just as important, if not more so, than institutional state-building and the efficiency of public institutions.

The 1930s

Demands of one form or another of secession continued into the 1930s. The Sunnis did not ease up on their demands, and both them and the Shī'as became even more linked to – and therefore more strongly backed by – the Syrian National Bloc, Syria's nationalist party.[93] And while the ambivalence of 'Āmelites was not elucidated, their demands of secession remained constant: in 1931, the mufti of Tyre again requested the creation of an autonomous state during a visit from the high commissioner, citing unrepresentativeness as the main motivation.[94] Similarly, debates about true Lebanese identity and whether or not Arabness should become a part of it were still taking place within the Christian community.[95] Eddeh and his followers, on the one hand, still believed in the need to maintain a Christian character to Lebanon, which naturally meant an undisputable Christian demographic majority. In 1932, Eddeh argued that by turning Tripoli into an autonomous municipality, in the same way as envisaged by De Caix, and transforming the southern region into an autonomous sanjak, as advocated by the 'Āmelites, almost 140,000 Muslims would be removed from Lebanese territory which would give the Christians a majority of almost 80 per cent.[96] Eddeh pointed to the presidential crisis, which had occurred earlier that year when a notable Muslim from Tripoli, Muḥammad al-Jisr, decided to run. This created an atmosphere of panic among the Christians, while the Sunnis believed they had more than enough right to merit a presidential position, especially with rumours that Lebanon now had a Muslim majority.[97] The same debates and clashes over representation came up, which dragged state institutions into problems of nation-building, and while there was no legal or political reason for Jisr *not* to be elected, it was of utmost symbolic and sentimental importance to the Christians that the president be one of their own, unlike his Syrian counterpart that legally, under the Syrian Constitution, had to be a Muslim.[98] As a result, and to avoid making such a difficult decision, the high commissioner decided to suspend the constitution as well as the Chamber of Deputies, and appointed a Christian 'Head of State' of his choice.[99]

In a similar issue, during the month of October 1935, the Greek Orthodox community was agitated and was 'making every effort to secure the resignation' of 'Abdallah Bey Bayhum, the Muslim Secretary of State, because they believed the principles of proportional representation meant that they 'deserved' to claim that position. In fact, questions of representation led to many cabinet crises during the 1930s, the issue almost always being the need for an unanimous decision on behalf of the deputies with regard to the representativeness of the cabinet.[100] Throughout the early 1930s, secessionist groups popped up with offices in Lebanon, such as the ever-influential Syrian National Bloc in Syria, the Nādi al-Ahli, the League of National Action or the secret *Parti Populaire Syrien*, a Syrian nationalist underground party. Similarly, a number of conferences and meetings occurred with the goal of Syrian or Arab unity at the expense of the Lebanese Republic.[101] Additionally, by 1937, paramilitary groups such as the Christian Katā'ib or the Muslim Najjadis were periodically clashing, as tensions became so hostile that a presidential decree was issued banning all groups 'that have a paramilitary tendency'.[102] By this point, any stances that proclaimed or exposed any bias on the part of citizens, organizations or even members of state towards any community were immediately banned and suppressed, regardless of the accuracy of their claims, in an effort by the state to keep a mainstream message of unity.[103]

By the late 1930s, the issue of tobacco reared its troublesome head again. The Régie monopoly had expired and the French adopted a 'banderole system' which focused on taxing individual packs and granting licences of cultivation and manufacturing to smaller private companies.[104] This raised hope among the different communities, including the 'Āmelites, of a more lenient and forgiving structure.[105] This system, however, combined with the economic recession of the early 1930s, led to a massive overproduction as well as smuggling. This, in addition to the continued inequality in taxation between regions,[106] led to new protests across Lebanon. As a result, in an effort to control production and prices, the Compagnie Libano-Syrienne de Tabacs, a private French–Lebanese consortium, had been granted the monopoly and was setting somewhat arbitrary prices.[107] This led to Jabal 'Āmel strikes throughout the late 1930s.[108] Crucially, however, the monopoly did not distinguish between Mount Lebanon and the rest of the Lebanese territory with regard to taxation,[109] which suddenly put the Christians, particularly the Maronites, in the same boat as the rest of the Lebanese against the high commission. The Maronites then sought help and refuge at the place where they had historically done so: the Patriarchate. Tobacco-growers, politicians, businessmen and affected citizens all pleaded with Mgr 'Arīḍa, the Maronite Patriarch, to resolve the issue in one way or another.

Some Maronites, mainly the Constitutional Bloc of Bishāra al-Khūrī – traditional enemies of Eddeh's Lebanese National Bloc – had also been annoyed and fed up with all the changes made by the high commission and had already come to see France as an obstacle to Lebanese prosperity as opposed to Eddeh's view of the need for France to ensure Christian predominance and security.[110] By this point, Khūrī had already established relations with Syrian nationalists – especially through childhood friend Riāḍ al-Ṣulḥ, a staunch nationalist in his own right – and was much closer to them than Eddeh ever was or became.[111] Similarly, Mgr 'Arīḍa had established contacts with Syrian nationalists through visits that had been made to Bkerke.[112] He advocated for cooperation between Maronites and Sunnis, and became so critical of the high commission that he was accused of being anti-French.[113]

The 1936 treaty

By the time the 1936 presidential elections came around, tensions within the Maronite camp were already quite high, and the two eventual candidates Emile Eddeh and Bishāra al-Khūrī could not be further apart on issues such as the mandate, cooperation with Syrian nationalists, Lebanese identity and particularism, the tobacco monopoly and – this can be assumed from their previous stances – the borders of the Lebanese territory. Although Emile Eddeh won, his election was attributed less to his support in the Chamber of Deputies (where the vote takes place) and more to his being the favourite of both the high commissioner (Damien de Martel) and the former Head of State Ḥabīb Pāsha al-Sa'd (who was himself appointed by the high commissioner, not elected).[114]

In early 1936, strikes and manifestations in Syria resulted in an uprising that demanded a treaty that secures full Syrian independence.[115] That, in addition to another Conference of the Coast that took place around that time,[116] meant that another campaign to return the annexed areas to Syria took place, this time by the Syrian National Bloc as well as an invigorated group of Lebanese Syrian nationalists.[117] Meanwhile, negotiations between the Syrians and the French were being facilitated and conducted by Lebanese middle-men including Riāḍ al-Ṣulḥ and Khalīl Abi al-Lama', who both had close ties with Khūrī.[118]

On 3 March 1936, Khūrī's Constitutional Bloc presented a memorandum – sponsored by Mgr 'Arīḍa – in which it demanded a similar treaty between France and Lebanon that would replace the mandate system as well as fully restore the constitution.[119] The memorandum and its impact immediately tied the Constitutional Bloc and supporters of Mgr 'Arīḍa (i.e. the 'Treaty camp') with the Syrians and, by association, the Syrian National Bloc in their fight for full independence. According to Khūrī himself, Lebanon's political scene completely changed with that memorandum, suddenly splitting the country in two: 'the Lebanese asking for cooperation with the Arab countries, and others holding on to isolationism'.[120] De Martel initially refused to accept the Constitutional Bloc's demands, as he believed that negotiations with Syria over a treaty needed to be concluded before one with Lebanon could be initiated.[121] This resulted in more anti-French feelings in Lebanon, especially among the Christians who were eager for a show of commitment to prove Lebanon's equal status with Syria.[122] By the summer, the Syrian delegation in Paris had been negotiating with France and had requested the return of the annexed territories,[123] while Tripoli became an integral part of the Syrian nationalists' campaign and demands of Syrian unity were again issued by Lebanese areas all around the Mountain.[124] The French did what they could to alleviate Lebanist fears with regard to the annexed areas, assuring Eddeh that the Lebanese borders would not be changed and that Franco-Lebanese negotiations would also take place.[125] They would fulfil that promise, and the resulting Franco-Syrian treaty had no mention of Lebanon which, conversely, allowed the Syrians *not* to recognize Lebanon as an independent state and therefore simply postpone their ambitions for that time.

No sooner was this promise of a Franco-Lebanese treaty given than another rift within the Lebanese state occurred, concerning the representativeness of the delegation which would conduct negotiations with the French: while Eddeh believed it should be in the hands of the executive to conduct such negotiations, Khūrī believed that a more widely representative delegation should be sent, which included the Constitutional Bloc. Eventually, Khūrī was elected by parliament as chairman of a committee that would take part in the negotiations, along with the president and his Secretary of State.[126] Khūrī would not pull any punches, and started off by demanding the full restoration of the constitution of 1926 *before* any negotiations took place. This would plunge Lebanon into another political crisis, in which the constitution itself was debated; Eddeh believed it was inadequate and needed revision (ones that would strengthen the presidential office) while the Constitutional Bloc argued for a stronger legislative.[127] Bitter rivalries and personal ambitions would take over the Lebanese political scene during those few years, all while questions of confessionalism and representativeness remained unanswered.

When Eddeh tried to contact religious leaders, notable businessmen, local people of influence and organizations to obtain their thoughts on a Lebanese constitution, the Syrian National Bloc and the Constitutional Bloc launched a campaign against Eddeh personally, and contacted those same people to pressure them not to answer his request.[128] Some, however, replied: one of them was the Sunni Grand Mufti Muḥammad Toufiq Khāled who expressed his views and demanded unity with Syria based on plebiscite.[129]

Change of stance

Because of what became at stake, many (mostly Beiruti) Sunnis decided to provide an olive branch to the Christians, and called for unity in the face of the French colonizer, while arguing that the annexed areas give Lebanon its Arab character and, in any case, the independence of those areas could only be one step towards Syrian unity.[130] In fact, some of the Muslim deputies now openly supported the independence of Lebanon within its current borders. This attitude, however, seems to have been constricted to Beirut and the more prosperous, moderate Muslims while the rest maintained their negative perception of the Lebanese state and did not let up on the calls for immediate Syrian unity.[131] Beiruti openness to conciliation and cooperation, even with the question of Lebanon joining a federation still being proposed, spread to certain parts of Lebanon such as Jabal ʿĀmel. Feudal ʿĀmelite leaders who had historically benefited from aligning themselves with the dominant power started leaning towards acknowledgement of Lebanon and its distinctiveness. And in this way they exerted their influence over other ʿĀmelites.[132]

On 23 October 1936, a Muslim Conference in Beirut was held because many felt they were unrepresented in the delegation sent to negotiate Treaty (not in numbers but in delegates chosen). It was attended by four hundred representatives from across Lebanon, and it seemed to perfectly summarize the views – though somewhat contradictory – of the Muslims during the treaty negotiations. The conference's resolution agreed to some patience with regard to Syrian and eventual Arab unity, but Lebanon was expected to have a federal link to Syria, and this should be included in the treaty.[133] The independence of Lebanon as a goal was recognized, and expressions of friendship were extended and cooperation was cited as a reason why a more decentralized system would be accepted so long as the different Cazas in Lebanon shared equal administrative power: this should also be mentioned in the treaty. Additionally, the resolution requested that the Franco-Syrian treaty should also be taken in consideration during negotiations.[134]

Messages of openness and cooperation became included in most petitions and telegrams sent to the high commission by Muslims across Lebanon,[135] apart from Tripoli where there remained violent protests and manifestations. For the rest of the Muslim areas, calls for secession slowly transformed into calls for administrative and legal independence, demanding a certain degree of decentralization in a recognized, independent Lebanon.[136] Thus a significant portion of the Muslims and the Christians were united in their demands for independence. Fighting the common enemy, they both saw independence as an indispensable first step in their ultimate projects of state-building: the Muslims had a Syrian/Arab confederation in mind while the Christians of the Constitutional Bloc imagined an independent Lebanon as a country built on cohabitation and cooperation, occupying a very special and particular position *within* the wider Arab region, not outside it.[137] Kāzim al-Ṣulḥ, an Arab nationalist who participated in the Conferences of the Coast, summarized what Muslim thinking would develop into by the early 1940s in a statement published the day after the 1936 Conference. In it, Kāzim argues that there can – and should – be a separation of the concepts of politics and nationalism. From that perspective, one can accept an independent Lebanon if it adopts a form of Arab nationalism, in the same way that one can accept Syria and Iraq being two independent countries united under this overarching Arabist umbrella. So long as that is the case, there will be progress towards an eventual Arab unity, which means that those goals would no longer be contradictory.[138]

Post-treaty

After these different crises of 1936, Lebanon's political landscape changed to become, somehow, even more complicated. The rise of personal rivalries between Khūrī and Eddeh left the Christian camp thoroughly divided, while the Muslims were still unsure of how much they should buy into the Lebanese venture, with thoughts of Syrian and Arab unity still tugging at their political heartstrings.[139] This, once again, meant that many state-building measures were undertaken while the country was trying to figure out an adequate political system. Different institutions underwent many changes in both their characters and their compositions: most notably, different governments were tried and given up on because of issues of misrepresentation. On the one hand, rivalries and personal ambitions meant that certain parties refused to collaborate at all with post-treaty governments.[140] On the other hand, it was argued that a government of national unity is the only one of its kind that can fairly represent the Lebanese communities, and this, in turn, was experienced with, and failed. Additionally, the question of which community should hold the position of prime minister was put forward, and the Sunnis made the strongest claim. Similarly, the position of the president was debated, and the extent of his powers was contested; eventually it was agreed that the president, usually a Maronite, should not exert any influence over a national unity government, while his term should be extended to six instead of three years.[141] In addition, the high commissioner would end up enlarging parliament in order to distribute seats even more fairly, while the Shīʿa demanded a guarantee of the position of speaker of the parliament as their own.[142] These decisions would prove to be crucial, as they would end up shaping the National Pact of 1943, which in turn moulded the Lebanese Republic as we know it today, while reinforcing the Lebanese system of nation-building institutions, where state-building and nation-building would be perpetually tied together.

The National Pact

By 1939, the new dynamics of politics in Lebanon were becoming clearer. The narrative of the divide had become less about who supported the Lebanese state and who didn't, and more about who supported the president (Eddeh) and his backers (the French), versus those claiming to be supporters of Lebanese independence and cooperation with the Arab world. The issue of a representative state, however, remained the focal point of any cooperation, especially between Christians and Muslims.

It was in this climate that, on 21 September 1939, twenty days after the German invasion of Poland, Gabriel Puaux – then high commissioner – suspended the constitution and most forms of political life, and instituted what was basically martial law in anticipation of war across the Mediterranean.[143] This, however, would not stop Khūrī and Eddeh's bitter feud and, while the Lebanese waited for the outcome of another European war, they both continued to manipulate any situation to their advantage, trying to lay the groundwork for a post-war Lebanon that matched their incompatible sketches. Messages of cooperation and Arabness then started to become much more prevalent among the Christian communities, in addition to the creation of popular parties that openly supported regional cooperation and interaction.[144]

In December 1941, General Catroux – then high commissioner after the Free French reclaimed control over the Levant – formed a new cabinet, which was immediately met with opposition. Earlier that year Catroux had promised, for both Syria and Lebanon, a path that would end with the termination of the mandate and independence for both states.[145] As the Constitutional Bloc proclaimed its obvious dissent, so did the Arab nationalists, as well as some of Eddeh's disheartened allies. Notable disproval, however, came from the British, who were trying to both fulfil their commitments to the Arabs and keep the region in its favour in the midst of the war.[146] Fuelled by this 'coalition' against the French mandate, the calls for independence became overwhelming, and unified plans of mobilization were put in place against the government, especially by the Maronite camp. 'Ārīda and Khūrī, along with other members of the Maronite clergy and Maronite leaders, combined their powers and, by Christmas 1941, they had adopted a resolution in the name of the Lebanese, demanding for full independence.[147] By the summer of 1942, Khūrī had garnered the sponsorship of Britain, Egypt and Syria to pursue the Christmas resolution to its end, and seek an independent, enlarged Lebanon.[148]

As 1943 progressed, Britain's involvement in Lebanese politics had reached a high, and their pressure on the French resulted in the re-establishment of the constitution on 18 March 1943. Ayūb Tābet was installed as head of state and elections were promised to occur in the coming months.[149] Immediately, bitter rivalries were revived and questions of representativeness and divisions of power sparked traditional resentments and accusations.[150] In fact, that year saw the emergence of contradictory trends that showed that Christian–Muslim animosity was still very much alive, with the same protests of unrepresentativeness still taking place. Some of these objections, however, differed in nature in that they now seemed more inclined to fix this issue within the Lebanese state, as opposed to outside of it. Nevertheless, communities refused to recognize governments, ministers, regional governors, simply because they felt unrepresented or under-represented across state institutions. A particular Muslim outrage happened when Ayūb Tābet issued a decree which increased the ratio of Christian seats in the Chamber of Deputies. The issue of seat distribution would cause yet another crisis in 1943 which revived feelings of separatism among the Sunni population.[151] It should be noted, as well, that while some Lebanese leaders were finding common ground, the more radical sections of the communities were still engaging in volatile rhetoric and occasional incidents of violence. Examples of these are the supposedly fascist-inspired groups: the Christian Katā'ib, the Muslim Najjada and the pan-Syrian SSNP.[152]

Eventually, Ayūb Tābet would be replaced by another appointee, Petro Trād, a Greek Orthodox lawyer. Under his tenancy, negotiations would continue between all parties involved (which by then included Britain, France, Syria, Egypt, and all the Lebanese communities). It was the relationship between Riad al-Ṣulḥ and Khūrī, seen as a duo of pragmatic compromise between the two forms of nationalism, that was central to the negotiations and agreements that occurred. Eventually a ratio of six Christians to five Muslims with a parliament based on multiples of eleven was agreed to, and on that basis, the parliamentary elections of September 1943 took place, in which the Ṣulḥ-Khūrī alliance prevailed and obtained a majority. A few weeks later, Khūrī was elected president and al-Ṣulḥ was tasked with forming a government.[153]

Thereafter, what became known as the unwritten 'National Pact' was crafted, in which the Christians supposedly agreed not to rely on foreign – specifically, Western – support and accept Lebanon's 'Arab face', while the Muslims would accept Lebanon's complete independence and the traditionally special status of the Christians, and with that acceptance was supposed to come the abandonment of Syrian unity. In addition, the different influential positions within the state would be distributed fairly among the different communities so as to always ensure a representative state. The main points of the agreement involved the president being Maronite and the prime minister being Sunni.[154] In fact, while the National Pact was meant to be a pragmatic agreement of cohabitation and cooperation between the different Lebanese communities, it was also the ultimate reinforcement of the combination of nation-building and state-building with the Lebanese state. Not only did representativeness become instilled within state institutions that lacked legitimacy, but a certain *type* of representation (i.e. based on numbers and state positions) was cemented within the Lebanese state, which meant that a change in demographics – which is inherently flexible – would not necessarily result in a change in the make-up of the state, especially if, as implied, it would mean that one camp would have to agree to a loss of representation. Therefore, the state set itself up to where it could not be representative on the long term, and whatever societal legitimacy it had achieved with the creation of the National Pact would not take long to be put into question again, as was the case a few years later.[155] Additionally, while the numerical representativeness of the state was dealt with, the issue of its identity had still to be settled, and for that reason, a new nation-building movement would have to take place, not only promoting cooperation and openness but also settling the question of Lebanon's role within the wider Arab world.

This nation-building movement did not take long to begin, with al-Ṣulḥ declaring straightaway in his ministerial statement of October 1943 that 'Lebanon is a country whose features are Arab but which desires to extract what is best from occidental civilization.'[156] Meanwhile Khūrī went on to make similar, if not symmetric statements, in which he recognized the Muslims' wishes to remain an integral part of the Arab world and expressed the acceptance of Christians to no longer look towards the West for assistance.[157] Immediately, the government, with the confidence of the Chamber of Deputies and the support of the president, announced its intention to reflect this new unity among the Lebanese people, and this inevitably meant the removal of some clauses of the 1926 constitution that recognized the mandatory's existence and its prerogatives.[158] al-Ṣulḥ also declared his intention to institute Arabic as the only official language of the country.[159]

The amendment to the constitution took place later that October, which resulted in an aggressive reaction by the French that included the imprisonment of Khūrī, al-Ṣulḥ, three ministers and a deputy. Strikes and demonstrations across all communities took place within the two weeks after that, including the closure of Beirut for more than 48 hours.[160] Letters from both Arab nationalists and Lebanists in different countries flooded into the White House, Downing Street and the Quai D'Orsay.[161] Britain, which had then become more concerned with the situation than ever, gave its support to the imprisoned politicians and effectively secured their release on 22 November 1943, the day celebrated as Lebanon's Independence Day.[162] It was seen as a symbolic day that pushed the French thereafter to begin negotiations that put an end to the mandate and give Lebanon its official and complete independence.

The chain of events from 1920 to 1943 showed again and again how the Lebanese state had struggled to achieve the legitimacy it needed to function as a nation-state. This began by the event that was not societally legitimate itself: the creation of the state. The subsequent events followed (and were themselves linked) from that illegitimacy and the unrepresentativeness of the state, which was reflected in the actions of both the latter and the Lebanese communities in their efforts to achieve their political goals.

Not only was the lack of societal legitimacy the reason for the different actions of the actors involved, but those actions themselves would reinforce that illegitimacy in two ways. From the standpoint of the population, the different groups that refused to recognize the state or asked for secession only strengthened the opinions of their followers that they were living in an alien state with which they could never identify. As for the state itself, and those that were in power, they strove to ensure fair representation within the state, even at the expense of the credibility, effectiveness and durability of state institutions, thus putting aside institutional legitimacy while still not having addressed the question of the 'idea of the state'. This would in turn further alienate those communities that could not identify with the state to begin with. Evidence shows that there was outright opposition to the creation of Greater Lebanon by a major part of the population: most of the Sunni community, parts of the Shīʿa community, parts of the Druze community and even some parts of the Christian community such as the Beiruti Greek Orthodox Christians and a minority of Maronites. This led to obstructions to state institutions throughout the 1920s. The attempt to create a fair constitution for Lebanon was met with equally strong opposition, and was hence not able to achieve its goal of representativeness and nation-building. The results of such a failure were clear: amendments, suspensions and violations of the constitution became a recurring thing. Similarly, the legislative and executive institutions were subject to constant change and reshuffling with the hope of achieving the same outcome: representativeness for all the major Lebanese communities.

Put simply, political stability was unattainable during the early years of the Lebanese state. A societal approach to legitimacy would indicate that this is because, despite the constitution striving to ensure fair representation, the state had still not succeeded in familiarizing the different communities with the idea of the state. Meanwhile, an institutional approach points to the inefficiency of public services, the constant involvement of French mandatory powers, and the high level of corruption and political feudalism as the sources of state institutional illegitimacy, and thus political instability. As such, the argument is easily made that the major cause for the survival of the Lebanese institutions until the 1940s was the presence of the French mandatory power.[163] After the events of 1943 and the initiation of the independence process, however, it would be up to the new Republic of Lebanon to figure out a way to survive the institutional and societal illegitimacies, and the National Pact – which created institutions that encouraged consensus but did not address the possible outcome when consensus could not be achieved – was placed at the heart of such a task.

Notes

1 Russell, *The First Modern Arab State*, 117–20.

2 Meir Zamir, *The Formation of Modern Lebanon* (Leiden: Dover, 1985), 62. The risk of being inserted between the Syrians and the French had already been felt by the Lebanese. In fact, on 10 July 1919, before the mandate had even begun, the Administrative Council in Mount Lebanon had adopted a resolution (albeit signed by seven out of thirteen members) that was sent to Faysal in Damascus. In it, they

agreed to give up wishes of a French mandate in exchange for the recognition of an independent Lebanon. See Zamir, 90.

3 Anne-Lucie Chaigne-Oudin, *La France et Les Rivalités Occidentales Au Levant 1918–1939* [France and the Oriental Rivalries in the Levant 1918–1939] (Paris: L'Harmattan, 2006), 213–70.

4 Central File: Decimal File 890E.00, Internal Affairs of States, Lebanon, Political Affairs, 15 March 1933–15 November 1943. Records of the Department of State Relating to Internal Affairs of Lebanon, 1930–44. U.S. National Archives. Archives Unbound. Web. http://go.galegroup.com.ezphost.dur.ac.uk/gdsc/i.do?&id=GALE%7CSC5111817027&v=2.1&u=duruni&it=r&p=GDSC&sw=w&viewtype=Manuscript. Accessed on 17 October 2018.

5 Georges Catroux, *Deux Missions En Moyen-Orient: 1919–1922* [Two Missions in the Middle East: 1919–1922] (Paris: Plon, 1958), 26–8.

Catroux on Gouraud: 'He had obeyed as much to his own tendencies as he did to the pressures put on his by the Christian communities, notably the Maronites, being too "voracious" in taking away from the Muslims their revenge for the past and their safety net for the future.' See Catroux, 29.

6 Wajīh Kawtharānī, *Al-Ittijāhāt Al-Ijtmā'iyya Al-Siyāsiyya Fī Jabal Lubnān Wa Mashriq Al-'Arabi* [Socio-Political Objectives in Mount Lebanon and the Arab Levant 1860–1920] (Beirut: Ma'had al-Inmā' al-'Arabi, 1978), 350.

7 Reports were made of Muslims throughout Lebanese territory refusing to be treated as citizens of Greater Lebanon and only ever identifying as Syrians and never as Lebanese. For example, see *al-'Ahd al-Jadīd* newspaper, issue 150, 23 December 1925.

See in *al-Mihmāz* newspaper on 28 December 1922, published op-eds and letters by citizens and notables of Tripoli of opposition towards Greater Lebanon and requests to join Syria.

For the political reaction of the major confessions to the establishment of Greater Lebanon and the Mandate, see Muḥammad F. Al-Khālidi, *Al-Mu'āmara Al-Kubra 'ala Bilād Al-Shām: Dirāsat Taḥlil Lil-Nosef Al-Aqal Min Al-Qurn Al-'Ashrin* [The Great Conspiracy Against the Levant: An Analysis of the First Half of the Twentieth Century] (Beirut: Dār al-Rāwī lil-Nasher wal-Tawzi', 2000), 390–9.

Also see 'Issām Kamāl Khalīfeh, *Abḥāth Fī Tārīkh Lubnān Al-Mu'āṣer* [Studies in Lebanese Contemporary History] (Beirut: Dār al-Jalīl, 1985), 127–47.

For an idea of the number of Muslims in Beirut, see the results of the 1921 census (only the major confessions are included):

Sunnis	32,884	42.3%
Shiites	3,274	4.2%
Druzes	1,522	2%
Maronites	17,763	22.8%
Greek Orthodox	12,672	16.3%
Greek Catholic	4,256	5.5%
Total	77,820	

Source: Marwan R. Buheiry, *Beirut's Role in the Political Economy of the French Mandate, 1919–39, Papers on Lebanon* (Oxford: Centre for Lebanese Studies, 1986), 408–9.

For the positions of Muslims and Greek Orthodox Christians in Beirut, see: Résumé du rapport de M. De Caix sur l'organisation de la Syrie du 9 mars 1921 [Summary of Mr. De Caix's report on the Organisation of Syria on 9 March 1921], in: Khoury, *Une Tutelle Coloniale: Le Mandat Français En Syrie et au Liban* [Colonial Guardianship: French Mandate in Syria Lebanon], 344.

8 Kawtharānī, *Al-Ittijāhāt Al-Ijtmā'iyya Al-Siyāsiyya Fī Jabal Lubnān Wa Mashriq Al-'Arabi*, 352–3.

The 'newly annexed areas' refers to the Biqā' valley, Rashaya, Hasbaya, Tripoli, Sidon, Tyre and 'Akkār.

9 'Robert de Caix' was the first secretary general and civilian aide to Gouraud, and would remain influential in mandatory policy for most of the 1920s.

10 See David Hunter Mizrahi, 'La France et Sa Politique de Mandat En Syrie et Au Liban (1920–1939) [France and Its Mandate Policy in Syria and the Lebanon (1920–1939)]', in *France, Syrie et Liban 1918–1946: Les Ambiguïtés et Les Dynamiques de La Relation Mandataire* [France, Syria and Lebanon 1918–1946: Ambiguity and the Dynamics of the Mandatory Relationship], ed. Nadine Méouchy (Damascus: Presses de l'IFPO, 2002), 35–71, http://books.openedition.org/ifpo/3162.

11 De Caix, 'L'Organisation Donnée à La Syrie et Au Liban: De 1920 à 1923 et La Crise Actuelle [The Set Organisation for Syria and the Lebanon: From 1920 to 1923 and the Current Crisis]', in *Une Tutelle Coloniale: Le Mandat Français En Syrie et Au Liban* [Colonial Guardianship: The French Mandate in Syria and the Lebanon], ed. Gérard D. Khoury (Paris: Belin, 2006), 343–4.

12 See 'The Foundations of the Modern State', in Helena Cobban, *Lubnān: 400 Sana Min Al-Tā'ifiya* [Lebanon: 400 Years of Confessionalism], ed. Samīr 'Atalla (London: Highlight, 1985).

13 Emile Eddeh was a Francophile Maronite who grew up outside Lebanon, and returned in 1912 with a staunch view of the need for a Lebanese Christian state. He would grow to become one of the most influential politicians during the mandate. See Zamir, *Lebanon's Quest*, 71.

14 Raymond O'Zoux, *Les États Du Levant Sous Mandat Français* [The States of the Levant under the French Mandate] (Paris: Larose, 1931), 299.

15 Phoenicianism was a nation-building movement that espoused to claim an origin myth that the contemporary Lebanese population were descendants of the ancient Phoenicians, and with that came a sense of pride due to the Phoenicians' infamous trading achievements, contributions to culture and invention of the early alphabet. This Lebanese origin myth found itself completely opposed by a majority of the Muslims who felt it was taking away from their Arab identity, which was the main source of pride for their community. See on Phoenicianism: Asher Kaufman, 'Phoenicianism: The Formation of an Identity in Lebanon in 1920', *Middle Eastern Studies* 37, no. 1 (2001): 173–94; Kaufman, *Reviving Phoenicia*; Kais Firro, 'Lebanese Nationalism versus Arabism: From Bulus Nujaym to Michel Chiha', *Middle Eastern Studies* 40, no. 5 (2004): 1–27; Salameh, *Language, Memory, and Identity in the Middle East*.

Also see Cohen, 'Legitimacy, Illegitimacy, and State Formation', on origin myths and their relation to state legitimacy.

16 See Firro, *Inventing Lebanon*, 42.

Also see Dominique Chevallier, 'Comment l'Etat a-t-Il- Été Compris Au Liban? [How Was the State Understood in the Lebanon?]', in *Lebanon: A History of Conflict and Consensus*, ed. Nadim Shehadi and Dana Haffar Mills (London: I.B. Tauris, 1988), 210–23.

17 See Hakim, *The Origins of the Lebanese National Idea, 1840–1920*, for a history of nation-building in Lebanese politics before 1920.

18 Robert de Caix, 'Lettre à M. Le President Du Conseil, Ministre Des Affaires Étrangères', in *Une Tutelle Coloniale: Le Mandat Français En Syrie et Au Liban* [Colonial Guardianship: The French Mandate in Syria and the Lebanon], ed. Gérard D. Khoury (Paris: Belin, 2006), 384.

19 See Karpat, *Ottoman Population 1830–1914: Demographic and Social Characteristics* (London: University of Wisconsin Press, 1985).

20 Arrêté N° 336, p. 73, in: Receuil des Actes Administratifs du Haut-Commissariat de la Republique Française en Syrie et au Liban. Années 1919–20. Vol. I.

21 Arrêté N° 369, in: Receuil des Actes Administratifs du Haut-Commissariat de la Republique Française en Syrie et au Liban. Années 1919–20. Vol. I.

22 Arrêté N° 763, p. 39 in: Receuil des Actes Administratifs du Haut-Commissariat de la Republique Française en Syrie et au Liban. Année 1921. Vol. II.

23 As was shown in the previous chapter.

24 See p. 1144 in: Central File: Decimal File 890D.01, Internal Affairs of States, Syria, Government. Mandates, Recognition, 13 June 1930–29 September 1933. Records of the Department of State Relating to Internal Affairs of Syria, 1930–44. U.S. National Archives. *Archives Unbound.* http://go.galegroup.com.ezphost.dur.ac.uk/gdsc/i.do?&id=GALE%7CSC5111835599&v=2.1&u=duruni&it=r&p=GDSC&sw=w&viewtype=Manuscript. Accessed on 10 October 2018.

25 Eastern Affairs. Further Correspondence Part VI. 1921. [Government Papers]. At: The National Archives, Kew. FO 406/45. Available through: Adam Matthew, Marlborough, Archives Direct. http://www.archivesdirect.amdigital.co.uk/Documents/Details/FO406_45 Accessed on 10 October 2018.
French authorities prohibited emigration from Lebanon (somewhat unsuccessfully) 21 December 1920, p. 192.

26 Muḥammad J. Bayhum, *Lubnān Bayna Mashriq Wa Maghreb: 1920–1969* [Lebanon, in between East and West: 1920–1969] (Beirut: Author, 1969), 24.
Also see Muḥammad J. Bayhum, *Qawāfil Al-'Urūba Wa Mawākibouhā Khilāl Al-'Uṣūr: Al-Juz' Al-Thānī* [The Procession of Arabism and Its Convoys throughout the Ages: Part Two] (Beirut: al-Kashāf Press, 1948), 96–7.
In addition, many Lebanese purposefully ignored the census and did not register as instructed, the reason for this being that the Ottomans would use census results for conscription purposes – see de Caix, 'Lettre à M. Le President Du Conseil, Ministre Des Affaires Étrangères', 383.

27 Bayhum, *Lubnān Bayna Mashriq Wa Maghreb*, 25.

28 See *Lisān al-Ḥāl* newspaper on 14 January 1921.

29 FO 371/7846/E 324/274/89, 13 March 1922.

30 The resulting distribution of seats was: sixteen Christians, thirteen Muslims and one seat reserved to represent minorities, although this would usually end up being occupied by a Christian of some small confession (e.g. Protestant). See Landau, *Middle Eastern Themes*, 1973, chapter 11, p. 5.

31 Atiyah, 'The Attitude of the Lebanese Sunnis towards the State of Lebanon', 107–8. Also see Traboulsi, *A History of Modern Lebanon*, 88.

32 Arrêté N° 1304, in: Receuil des Actes Administratifs du Haut-Commissariat de la Republique Française en Syrie et au Liban. Année 1922. Vol. III.

33 See Bishāra Khūrī, *Ḥaqā'iq Lubnāniyya, Al-Jiz' Al-Awal* [Lebanese Truths, Part One] (Beirut: 'Awrāq Lubnāniyya, 1961), 116.

See also Bayhum, *Qawāfil Al-'Urūba Wa Mawākibouhā Khilāl Al-'Usūr*, 97, who quotes Youssef Mirzā, director of the Lebanese Ministry of Finance: 'If you asked them [the members elected in 1922] who voted for them most would say the [French] government through different means, and it would be beneficial to pull back the curtains on them.'

34 FO 371/7847/E 5994/274/89 dated 1 June 1922.

35 Robert de Caix, 'Lettre Au Général Gouraud [Letter to General Gouraud]', in *Une Tutelle Coloniale: Le Mandat Français En Syrie et Au Liban* [Colonial Guardianship: The French Mandate in Syria and the Lebanon], ed. Gérard D. Khoury (Paris: Belin, 2006), 372.

36 de Caix, 373.

37 He would remain involved in French foreign policy as the French delegate to the League of Nations' Permanent Mandate Commission until 1939.

38 Zamir, *Lebanon's Quest*, 5–10.

Emile Eddeh, in particular, was accused (by all sides) of being in favour of Tripoli being ceded. See Meir Zamir, 'Emile Eddé and the Territorial Integrity of Lebanon', *Middle Eastern Studies* 14, no. 2 (1978): 232–5.

39 See Cobban, *The Making of Modern Lebanon*. Chapter 3.

In addition, many Shī'a feudal lords such as Youssef al-Zein and Kāmel al-'As'ad were won over by promises of gaining or retaining local spheres of influence – see 'Omar K. Ramadān, Al Inqisām Al-Waṭani Al-Lubnāni Fī 'Ahd Al-Intidāb 1920–1943 [National Division in Lebanon during the Mandate 1920–1943]', *Majallat Dirāsāt Tārīkhiyya* 16 (2014): 219.

40 Murat Birdal, *The Political Economy of Ottoman Public Debt: Insolvency and European Financial Control in the Late Nineteenth Century* (London: I.B. Tauris, 2010), 129–30.

41 A fifteen-year extension was agreed but never officially ratified by the Ottoman government.

42 Which made it that all treaties and contracts in place before 1918 in the territory of the Ottoman Empire were to be held and continued under the responsibility of the Occupying power. See: Lausanne Peace Treaty Part II – Financial Clauses. From Turkish Ministry of Foreign Affairs: http://www.mfa.gov.tr/lausanne-peace-treaty-part-ii_-financial-clauses.en.mfa. Accessed on 7 September 2018.

43 Ali A M Sha'ib, *Maṭāleb Jabal 'Āmel: Al-Waḥda, Al-Mousāwāt Fī Jabal Lubnān* [Demands of Jabal 'Āmel: Unity, Equality in Mount Lebanon] (Beirut: Al Mu'assasa al-Jāmi'iyya Lil-Dirāsāt wal-Nashir, 1987), 12–14.

44 On 29 July 1920, an agreement was reached between Britain and France that the Ḥūla region – on the inner slopes of Jabal 'Āmel – became part of the British territories. This immediately provoked a negative reaction from the inhabitants of Ḥūla who sent a telegram expressing their refusal to live under 'Jewish rule' and a request to be joined to Jabal 'Āmel – see Fāyez Al-Rayyes, *Al-Qura Al-Junūbiyya Al-Sabe'* (Beirut: Mou'assasat al-Wafā', 1985), 71–2.

45 Sha'ib, *Maṭāleb Jabal 'Āmel*, 90–1.

46 See *al-'Irfān* journal on 5–6 April 1921.

Al-'Irfān, founded in 1909, was an 'Āmelite journal that had Shī'a-targeted educational and reformist objectives as its basis, but grew to become the mouthpiece of Shī'a Arab nationalism in the south of Lebanon. See Naef, 'La Presse en tant Que Moteur Du Renouveau Culturel et Littéraire: La Revue Chiite Libanaise Al-'Irfàn

[The Press as a Motor for Cultural and Literal Renewal: The Lebanese Shiite Journal Al-'Irfān]'.

47 See MAE, Serie E-Levant, Syrie Liban vol. 262. 12 Septembre 1923.

48 The gangs were, according to some 'Āmelite historians, supplied and encouraged by the French authorities. There is also mention of truces between other sections of the Christians and the Shī'a, and even some declarations of unity. It should be noted that the early opposition to the French mandate culminated with an attempted – but failed – assassination of General Gouraud in Qunaytra, on the foothills of Jabal 'Āmel on 23 June 1921. See Eastern Affairs. Further Correspondence Part VII. 1921. [Government Papers]. The National Archives, Kew. FO 406/46. Available through: Adam Matthew, Marlborough, Archives Direct, http://www.archivesdirect.amdigital.co.uk/Documents/Details/FO406_46. Accessed on 15 October 2018.

49 This Federation merged the states of Damascus, Aleppo and Alaouites into one unit. Arrêté N° 1459 bis found in: *Receuil des Actes Administratifs du Haut-Commissariat de la Republique Française en Syrie et au Liban.* Année 1922. Vol. III. Also see for exclusion of Greater Lebanon: Journal officiel de la République française. Débats parlementaires. Chambre des députés: compte rendu in-extenso. Impr. du Journal officiel (Paris). 1923-11-15. https://gallica.bnf.fr/ark:/12148/bpt6k62174208. Accessed on 3 February 2018.

50 Eastern Affairs. Further Correspondence Part VI. 1921. [Government Papers]. The National Archives, Kew. FO 406/45. Available through: Adam Matthew, Marlborough, Archives Direct, p. 224. http://www.archivesdirect.amdigital.co.uk/Documents/Details/FO406_45 Accessed on 13 October 2018.

51 Eastern Affairs. Further Correspondence Part XII. 1923. [Government Papers]. The National Archives, Kew. FO 406/51. Available through: Adam Matthew, Marlborough, Archives Direct, http://www.archivesdirect.amdigital.co.uk/Documents/Details/FO406_51. Accessed on 14 October 2018.

52 A 'mazbata' was the Ottoman reference for a written protocol.

53 Eastern Affairs. Further Correspondence Part XII.

54 Confidential Correspondence 1922 File No. 800 Consular Posts Beirut, Lebanon Volume 461, [2 of 2]. 1922. Record Group 84: Records of Foreign Service Posts of the Department of State, U.S. Consulate, Beirut, The Lebanon, Confidential Files. National Archives (U.S.). Archives Unbound. http://go.galegroup.com.ezphost.dur.ac.uk/gdsc/i.do?&id=GALE%7CSC5108641889&v=2.1&u=duruni&it=r&p=GDSC&sw=w&viewtype=Manuscript. Accessed on 15 October 2018.

55 Confidential Correspondence 1922 File No. 800 Consular Posts Beirut, Lebanon Volume 461.

56 Eastern Affairs. Further Correspondence Part XV. 1924. [Government Papers]. The National Archives, Kew. FO 406/54. Available through: Adam Matthew, Marlborough, Archives Direct, http://www.archivesdirect.amdigital.co.uk/Documents/Details/FO406_54. Accessed on 14 October 2018.

57 Memorandum in 1925. Confidential Files 1925 Consular Posts Beirut, Lebanon Volume 465, [1 of 4]. 1925. Record Group 84: Records of Foreign Service Posts of the Department of State, U.S. Consulate, Beirut, The Lebanon, Confidential Files. National Archives (U.S.). *Archives Unbound.* http://go.galegroup.com.ezphost.dur.ac.uk/gdsc/i.do?&id=GALE%7CSC5108639696&v=2.1&u=duruni&it=r&p=GDSC&sw=w&viewtype=Manuscript. Accessed on 15 October 2018.

58 Confidential Files. 1925. Consular Posts Beirut, Lebanon, Volume 465.

59 See Amīn Sa'īd, *Al-Thawra Al-'Arabiyya Al-Koubra* [The Great Arab Revolt] (Cairo: 'Īsa al-Bābi al-Ḥalabi and Co. Press, 1934), 259. Also see Eastern Affairs.

Further Correspondence Part XIV. 1924. [Government Papers]. The National Archives, Kew. FO 406/53. Available through: Adam Matthew, Marlborough, Archives Direct, http://www.archivesdirect.amdigital.co.uk/Documents/Details/FO406_53. Accessed on 14 October 2018.

60 For the B'albak region, see Sa'īd, 259. Additionally, there was such a clear link between the Druzes of Lebanon and Jabal al-Druze (literally meaning 'the mountain of the Druze') that the French had to ask their neighbouring mandatory power, the British, for the supply of additional troops to prevent the arousal of more Lebanese Druzes. See Eastern Affairs. Further Correspondence Part XVII. 1925. [Government Papers]. The National Archives, Kew. FO 406/56. Available through: Adam Matthew, Marlborough, Archives Direct, http://www.archivesdirect.amdigital.co.uk/Documents/Details/FO406_56. Accessed on 14 October 2018.

61 Sa'īd, 411–15.

62 Eastern Affairs. Further Correspondence Part XVIII. 1926. [Government Papers]. The National Archives, Kew. FO 406/57. Available through: Adam Matthew, Marlborough, Archives Direct, http://www.archivesdirect.amdigital.co.uk/Documents/Details/FO406_57. Accessed on 14 October 2018.

63 This included setting up meetings not only with local leaders in the region but also with British, American and representatives of the League of Nations. See Eastern Affairs. Further Correspondence Part XI. 1922. [Government Papers]. The National Archives, Kew. FO 406/50. Available through: Adam Matthew, Marlborough, Archives Direct, http://www.archivesdirect.amdigital.co.uk/Documents/Details/FO 406_50. Accessed on 15 October 2018.

64 See Eastern Affairs. Further Correspondence Part XI.

65 Examples of these incidents of violence include Marja'youn and Kawkaba. See: *Confidential Files 1925 Consular Posts Beirut, Lebanon Volume 465, [1 Of 4]*. 1925. Record Group 84: Records of Foreign Service Posts of the Department of State, U.S. Consulate, Beirut, The Lebanon, Confidential Files. National Archives (U.S.). *Archives Unbound*. http://go.galegroup.com.ezphost.dur.ac.uk/gdsc/i.do?&id=GALE%7CSC5108639696&v=2.1&u=duruni&it=r&p=GDSC&sw=w&viewtype=Manuscript. Accessed on 15 October 2018.

66 See Eastern Affairs. Further Correspondence Part XVII. 1925. [Government Papers]. The National Archives, Kew. FO 406/56. Available through: Adam Matthew, Marlborough, Archives Direct, http://www.archivesdirect.amdigital.co.uk/Documents/Details/FO406_56. Accessed on 14 October 2018.

In fact, those 'flashes' became so common that, during the Druze revolt of 1925, the British consul general in Beirut Satow, in a letter to the Foreign Secretary M. Austen Chamberlain, suggested the urgent need for disarming Beirut *before* disarming the revolutionary Druze.

67 See Eastern Affairs. Further Correspondence Part XVII.

68 Sa'īd, 417.

69 See Eastern Affairs. Further Correspondence Part XVII.

70 Arrêté N° 2980 found in: *Receuil des Actes Administratifs du Haut-Commissariat de la Republique Française en Syrie et au Liban*. Année 1924. Vol. V. The state of Syria initially comprised of the state of Aleppo and the state of Damascus, with the Alaouite state being eventually annexed to it, as well as the Jabal Druze. The sanjak of Alexandretta would become part of Turkey.

Also see O'Zoux, *Les États Du Levant Sous Mandat Français*.

71 Zamir, *Lebanon's Quest*, 10–12.
72 Composed of twelve members: six from the Representative Council and six high functionaries appointed by the high commission – see Jean Lapierre, *Le Mandat Français En Syrie: Origines, Doctrine, Exécution* [The French Mandate in Syria: Origins, Doctrine, Execution] (Paris: Librairie du Recueil Sirey, 1936), 119.
73 The sub-committee was made up of three members chosen by the Representative Council.
74 This included religious leaders, municipal and local councils, high magistrates, notable corporations and so on.
75 Lapierre, 119.
76 For example, Sunnis in Beirut and Tripoli refused to respond – see Chalabi, *The Shi'is of Jabal 'Amil and the New Lebanon: Community and the Nation-State, 1918–1943*, 129.

Similarly, the 'Āmelites and the notables of Sidon refused to answer the questionnaire and replied instead with another request to be annexed to Syria – see Sha'ib, *Maṭāleb Jabal 'Āmel*, 98. Also see Atiyah, 'The Attitude of the Lebanese Sunnis towards the State of Lebanon', 122.
77 Faysal, by this point, was appointed as king of Iraq under the British Mandate – see Russell, *The First Modern Arab State*. Also see Lapierre, *Le Mandat Français En Syrie*, 119–20.
78 Lapierre, 120–2.
79 Quoted in Rondot, 'Lebanese Institutions and Arab Nationalism', 43.
80 By 1927, for example, the Lebanese government included over 3,700 employees. See Marun Yusef Kisirwani, 'Attitudes and Behavior of Lebanese Bureaucrats: A Study in Administrative Corruption' (Bloomington: Indiana University Press, 1971), 56.
81 See O'Zoux, *Les États Du Levant Sous Mandat Français*, 153.
82 These are conditions in Keohane's argument. See Keohane, 'Political Authority after Intervention: Gradations of Sovereignty', in *Humanitarian Intervention: Ethical, Legal, and Political Dilemmas* (Cambridge: Cambridge University Press, 2003), 275–98.
83 Although the constitution still recognized and relinquished a lot of power to the French (Giannini, 1931).
84 Georges Samné, 'Questions Orientales [Oriental Questions]', *Correspondance D'Orient*, April 1928, 146–7.
85 In fact, one of the Beiruti Sunnis who decided after a meeting to reject was a member of the drafting committee ('Omar al-Da'uq) Al-'Ahd al-Jadid, No.159, v.1, 6 January 1926.
86 See Beirut newspaper on 16 and 17 August 1936.
87 Chalabi, *The Shi'is of Jabal 'Amil and the New Lebanon*, 129.
88 The Shī'as were allowed to administer their own personal status under their Ja'fari law as of January 1926. See Atiyah, 'The Attitude of the Lebanese Sunnis towards the State of Lebanon', 123; Sha'ib, *Maṭāleb Jabal 'Āmel*, 98. Also see *al-'Ahd al-Jadīd* newspaper on 17 and 18 January 1926.
89 Zamir, *Lebanon's Quest*, 72.
90 Zamir, 77.
91 Kaufman, 'Phoenicianism', 177.
92 Firro, *Inventing Lebanon*, 111.
93 Shanahan, *The Shi'a of Lebanon*, 52.
94 Chalabi, *The Shi'is of Jabal 'Amil and the New Lebanon*, 129.

95 A famous back and forth took place between the two leading Christian newspapers at the time: Gebrån Tueyni's *Aḥrār* and Gabriel Khabbāz's Orient over the identity of the Lebanese and the extent of their Arabness – see Gebrān Tueynī, *Fī Waḍe' Al-Nahār – Maqālāt Moukhtāra* [In the Nahār's Situation – Selected Articles] (Beirut: Dār al-Nahār, 1939), 1–2. Also see Al-Ḥallāq, *Tārīkh Lubnān Al-Mou'āṣir 1913–1952*, 123.

96 Zamir, 'Emile Eddé and the Territorial Integrity of Lebanon', 232–3. It is not mentioned where Eddeh gets these numbers from, but, according to the 1932 census, the removal of 140,000 Muslims would turn the Christians into a majority of about 67 per cent. That census also took into account Lebanese emigrants which, for the Christians, added 215,844 while for the Sunnis, Shī'as, and Druze, the emigrants would add a meagre 28,706. See Rania Maktabi, 'The Lebanese Census of 1932 Revisited. Who Are the Lebanese?', *British Journal of Middle Eastern Studies* 26, no. 2 (1999): 219–41.

97 See Maktabi.

98 See Constitution De L'etat De Syrie Promulguée par Arrêté du Haut Commissaire de la République Française N° 3111, du 14 Mai 1930. Chapter 1, Article 3. In: Bulletin Officiel des Actes Administratifs du Haut-commissariat. 15 January 1930.

99 Central File: Decimal File 890E.00, Internal Affairs of States, Lebanon, Political Affairs, 25 August 1931–29 September 1939. Records of the Department of State Relating to Internal Affairs of Lebanon, 1930–44. U.S. National Archives. *Archives Unbound*. http://go.galegroup.com.ezphost.dur.ac.uk/gdsc/i.do?&id=GALE%7CSC5111816249&v=2.1&u=duruni&it=r&p=GDSC&sw=w&viewtype=Manuscript. Accessed on 26 September 2018. This also would be one of many times that the Lebanese Constitution would be suspended under the French Mandate.

100 Central File: Decimal File 890E.002, Internal Affairs of States, Political Affairs, Lebanon, Cabinet. Ministry, 6 November 1929–21 January 1939. Records of the Department of State Relating to Internal Affairs of Lebanon, 1930–44. U.S. National Archives. *Archives Unbound*. http://go.galegroup.com.ezphost.dur.ac.uk/gdsc/i.do?&id=GALE%7CSC5111816622&v=2.1&u=duruni&it=r&p=GDSC&sw=w&viewtype=Manuscript. Accessed on 26 September 2018.

101 These included conferences called for by Lebanese notables such as Riāḍ al-Ṣulḥ, the many 'Conferences of the Coast' or the Blūdan Conference of 1937 for which the Lebanese government prevented any official attendance. See Central File: Decimal File 890E.00, Internal Affairs of States, Lebanon, Political Affairs, 25 August 1931–29 September 1939. Records of the Department of State Relating to Internal Affairs of Lebanon, 1930–44. U.S. National Archives. *Archives Unbound* Also see Sha'ib, *Maṭāleb Jabal 'Āmel*.

102 Presidential Decree found in: Central File: Decimal File 890E.00, Internal Affairs Of States, Lebanon, Political Affairs, 25 August 1931–29 September 1939. Records of the Department of State Relating to Internal Affairs of Lebanon, 1930–44. U.S. National Archives. *Archives Unbound*.

103 For example, the *al-Nahār* newspaper in August of 1938 for quoting then president Eddeh as having called Lebanon 'a Christian island' in an interview conducted during a visit to France. See Central File: Decimal File 890E.00, Internal Affairs of States, Lebanon, Political Affairs, 25 August 1931–29 September 1939. p. 319.

104 Zvi Yehuda Hershlag, *Introduction to the Modern Economic History of the Middle East* (Leiden: Brill, 1980), 252.

105 Max Weiss, *In the Shadow of Sectarianism: Law, Shiʿism, and the Making of Modern Lebanon* (Cambridge, MA: Harvard University Press, 2010), 190.
106 Tobacco companies in Mount Lebanon only paid 25 per cent of tax while the rest of the country was paying 45 per cent – see Hershlag, *Introduction to the Modern Economic History of the Middle East*, 252.
107 Philip Shukry Khoury, *Syria and the French Mandate: The Politics of Arab Nationalism, 1920–1945* (Princeton, NJ: Princeton University Press, 1987), 452.
108 Central File: Decimal File 890E.61331, Internal Affairs of States, Agriculture. Field Crops. Seeds, Alkaloidal Plants, Lebanon, Tobacco, 21 July 1930–2 May 1936. Records of the Department of State Relating to Internal Affairs of Lebanon, 1930–44. U.S. National Archives. Archives Unbound. Web. 17 October 2018. http://go.galegroup.com.ezphost.dur.ac.uk/gdsc/i.do?&id=GALE%7CSC5111814952&v=2.1&u=duruni&it=r&p=GDSC&sw=w&viewtype=Manuscript.
109 Up to that point, the Mountain had enjoyed different tax rules with regard to Tobacco – see Zamir, *Lebanon's Quest*, 164.
110 Khūrī, *Ḥaqā'iq Lubnāniyya, Al-Jiz' Al-Awal*, 189–200. Between 1922 and 1934, there had been five different forms of legislative bodies (Khūrī, 1961, pp. 322–6). In addition, the constitution had been suspended in May 1932 for a period of eighteen months (Arrêté N° 55 L/R on 9 May 1932). It was partially reinstated in 1934 (Arrêté N° 1/LR; N° 2/LR; N° 3/LR; N° 4/LR; N° 8/LR during January 1934), with the exception of the office of the president, which became an appointed 'head of the executive'. The presidential elections would not be reinstated until two years later (Arrêté N° 1/LR on 3 January 1926). It wouldn't be until 1937 that the full constitution would be reinstated (Arrêté N° 1/LR on 4 January 1937).
111 Walīd 'Awād, *Aṣḥab Al-Fakhāma: Rou'asā' Lubnān* [Masters of Luxury: Presidents of Lebanon] (Beirut: al-Ahliyya lil-Nashr wal-Tawzī', 1977), 211–12.
112 For example, a visit was paid by Fakhri al-Barūdi in 1934 – see Zamir, *Lebanon's Quest*, 154. Also see el-Solh, *Lebanon and Arabism*, 17.
113 MAE, Syrie Liban 1930–40, vol. 500, 1 April 1935, 137.
114 Central File: Decimal File 890E.001, Internal Affairs of States, Political Affairs, Lebanon, Chief Executive. Sovereign. Visits, 17 March 1932–28 August 1939. Records of the Department of State Relating to Internal Affairs of Lebanon, 1930–44. U.S. National Archives. Archives Unbound. Web. http://go.galegroup.com.ezphost.dur.ac.uk/gdsc/i.do?&id=GALE%7CSC5111816589&v=2.1&u=duruni&it=r&p=GDSC&sw=w&viewtype=Manuscript. Accessed on 18 October 2018.
115 Khūrī, *Ḥaqā'iq Lubnāniyya, Al-Jiz' Al-Awal*, 199.
116 The Conference, for the first time, was decisively split between those that stuck to a more traditional Syrian nationalism and other radicals that now shifted their focus to Syrian unity being a step towards a wider Arab federation. See el-Solh, *Lebanon and Arabism*, 23–6.
117 Daniel Pipes, *Greater Syria: The History of an Ambition* (Oxford: Oxford University Press, 1990), 63–4.
118 Khūrī, *Ḥaqā'iq Lubnāniyya, Al-Jiz' Al-Awal*, 199.
119 el-Solh, *Lebanon and Arabism*, 19.
120 Khūrī, *Ḥaqā'iq Lubnāniyya, Al-Jiz' Al-Awal*, 200.
121 Zamir, *Lebanon's Quest*, 193.
122 Zamir, 193–4.
123 MAE, Paris, Syrie et Liban, vol. 478 'Délégation de la république syrienne: études critiques des projets français', Paris, 11 June 1936.

124 Sha'ib, *Maṭāleb Jabal 'Āmel*, 147–50.
125 Eastern Affairs. Further Correspondence Parts XXXVIII & XXXIX. 1936, pp. 243–5 [Government Papers]. The National Archives, Kew. FO 406/74. Available through: Adam Matthew, Marlborough, Archives Direct, http://www.archivesdirect.amdigital.co.uk/Documents/Details/FO406_74. Accessed on 18 October 2018.
126 Zamir, *Lebanon's Quest*, 204.
127 el-Solh, *Lebanon and Arabism*, 38–9.
128 Zamir, *Lebanon's Quest*, 201–2.
129 See *Beirut* newspaper on 14 August 1936.
130 Atiyah, 'The Attitude of the Lebanese Sunnis towards the State of Lebanon', 148–50. Also see in Firro, *Inventing Lebanon*, 149: declaration by 'Ādil Arslān, a Druze Arab nationalist, arguing for the need to keep Muslim districts that protect Lebanon's Arab 'cachet'.
131 The disagreement between the Beirutis and the other Muslims was discussed in the 'Beirut' newspaper – a mouthpiece for Beiruti Muslims: it came out and defended the calmness and patience of the Beirutis over the constant protests that had been occurring in Sidon and Tripoli. See *Beirut* newspaper on 2 September 1936.
132 Sha'ib, *Maṭāleb Jabal 'Āmel*, 151.
133 See *al-Nahar* newspapers on 25 and 26 October 1936.
134 Sha'ib, 153–56. 'Caza' is the term for the different Lebanese administrative divisions (i.e. counties).
135 See *al-Qabas* newspaper on 3 November 1936.
136 Khalīfeh, *Abḥāth Fī Tārīkh Lubnān Al-Mu'āṣer*, 147.
137 It was telling that such a short-term, crucial, unifying goal as independence was shown to be very temporary in Syria since, as soon as the Franco-Syrian treaty was ratified and guaranteed independence, even a body as strong as the Syrian National Bloc found itself divided into what eventually became two distinct parties – see Khoury, *Syria and the French Mandate*, 623.
138 Ḥassān Al-Ḥallāq, *Mu'tamar Al-Sāḥil Wal-Aqḍiya Al-Arb'a, 1936* [The Conference of the Coast and the Four Districts, 1936] (Beirut: Dār al-Nahār, 1983), 77–80.
139 The differences between those that advocated Syrian unity as a step towards a form of Arab union, and those that sought Syrian unity as an end in itself became even more striking, and it led to the development of rival parties that would exhibit some tendencies to violence and paramilitarism. One of the most prominent ones that would become stronger by the end of the 1930s was the pan-Syrian SNP (Syrian Nationalist Party), founded by the Orthodox Christian Antoine S'ādeh, that espoused for a strictly Syrian nation-state. See Salibi, *A House of Many Mansions*, 54.
140 The Constitutional Bloc declared its refusal to deal with the 1936 government post-treaty negotiations and put 'personal ambitions' over 'public interest', despite the Franco-Lebanese treaty that reinstituted the constitution and promised a place in League of Nations. See Eastern Affairs. Further Correspondence Parts XL-XLI. 1937. [Government Papers]. The National Archives, Kew. FO 406/75. Available through: Adam Matthew, Marlborough, Archives Direct, http://www.archivesdirect.amdigital.co.uk/Documents/Details/FO406_75. Accessed on 18 October 2018. The Constitutionalists would stick to their position until Khūrī struck a deal with de Martel and formed a national unity government – see Zamir, *Lebanon's Quest*, 232.

141 Khūrī would reluctantly agree to these stipulations. His agreement is due in no small degree to the fact that in 1937, he was basically promised the presidency of 1942 in a meeting between the chief of the opposition and himself. See: Central File: Decimal File 890E.00, Internal Affairs of States, Lebanon, Political Affairs, 15 March 1933–15 November 1943. Records of the Department of State Relating to Internal Affairs of Lebanon, 1930–44. U.S. National Archives. *Archives Unbound*. Web. Accessed on 18 October 2018. http://go.galegroup.com.ezphost.dur.ac.uk/gdsc/i.do?&id=GALE%7CSC5111817027&v=2.1&u=duruni&it=r&p=GDSC&sw=w&viewtype=Manuscript. Also see Zamir, 235–6.
142 Ftūnī, *Tarīkh Lubnān Al-Ṭaā'ifī*, 88–91.
143 Khūrī, *Ḥaqā'iq Lubnāniyya, Al-Jiz' Al-Awal*, 235–6.
144 Fadia Kiwan, 'La Perception Maronite Du Grand-Liban [Maronite Perception of Greater Lebanon]', in *Lebanon: A History of Conflict and Consensus*, ed. Nadim Shehadi and Dana Haffar Mills (London: I.B. Tauris, 1998), 143.
145 Eastern Affairs. Further Correspondence Parts LVI-LIX. 1944. [Government Papers]. The National Archives, Kew. FO 406/82. Available through: Adam Matthew, Marlborough, Archives Direct, http://www.archivesdirect.amdigital.co.uk/Documents/Details/FO406_82. Accessed on 21 October 2018.
146 el-Solh, *Lebanon and Arabism*, 155–7.
147 Firro, *Inventing Lebanon*, 192.
148 Farid el-Khazen, *The Communal Pact of National Identities: The Making and Politics of the 1943 National Pact, Papers on Lebanon* (Oxford: Centre for Lebanese Studies, 1991), 18.
149 Firro, *Inventing Lebanon*, 201.
150 Eastern Affairs. Further Correspondence Parts LLI-LV. 1943. [Government Papers]. The National Archives, Kew. FO 406/81. Available through: Adam Matthew, Marlborough, Archives Direct, http://www.archivesdirect.amdigital.co.uk/Documents/Details/FO406_81. Accessed on 21 October 2018.
151 See Central File: Decimal File 890E.00, Internal Affairs of States, Lebanon, Political Affairs, 15 March 1933–15 November 1943. Records of the Department of State Relating to Internal Affairs of Lebanon, 1930–44. U.S. National Archives. Archives Unbound. Web. http://go.galegroup.com.ezphost.dur.ac.uk/gdsc/i.do?&id=GALE%7CSC5111817027&v=2.1&u=duruni&it=r&p=GDSC&sw=w&viewtype=fullcitation. Accessed on 21 October 2018.
152 Firro, 196.
153 Youssef Chaitani, *Post-Colonial Syria and Lebanon: The Decline of Arab Nationalism and the Triumph of the State* (London: I.B. Tauris, 2007), 16.
154 See Hassan Saab, 'The Rationalist School in Lebanese Politics', in *Politics in Lebanon*, ed. Binde (New York: Wiley, 1966), 275–7. Later on, the position of the speaker of the parliament would be put aside for the Shī'a, who were somewhat overlooked in 1943 – see Salibi, *A House of Many Mansions*, 186.
155 The National Pact of 1943 would be elevated to become essentially a constitutional norm, one that has not been altered to this day. One must also not forget, though, that there were still many sectors of the Lebanese population that were against it, although admittedly it can be assumed to be a minority.
156 Chaitani, *Post-Colonial Syria and Lebanon*, 16.
157 el-Khazen, *The Communal Pact of National Identities*, 38.
158 Chaitani, *Post-Colonial Syria and Lebanon*, 16.
159 French had been the co-official language.

160 Chaitani, 17.

161 Central File: Decimal File 890E.00, Internal Affairs of States, Lebanon, Political Affairs, 15 March 1933–15 November 1943. Records of the Department of State Relating to Internal Affairs of Lebanon, 1930–44. U.S. National Archives. Archives Unbound. Web. 21 October 2018. http://go.galegroup.com.ezphost.dur.ac.uk/gdsc/i.do?&id=GALE%7CSC5111817027&v=2.1&u=duruni&it=r&p=GDSC&sw=w&viewtype=fullcitation.

162 For Britain's increased involvement, see Central File: Decimal File 890E.00, Internal Affairs of States, Lebanon, Political Affairs, 15 March 1933–15 November 1943. Records of the Department of State Relating to Internal Affairs of Lebanon, 1930–44. U.S. National Archives. Archives Unbound. Web. 17 October 2018. http://go.galegroup.com.ezphost.dur.ac.uk/gdsc/i.do?&id=GALE%7CSC5111817027&v=2.1&u=duruni&it=r&p=GDSC&sw=w&viewtype=Manuscript.

163 'Indeed, France held Lebanon together until the political, social, and economic forces that would help integrate the annexed areas into the state began to take effect.' See Zamir, *Lebanon's Quest*, 241.

Chapter 3

Compromise and Ensuring the Survival of the State

By 1947, the issue of full independence from France and the end of the mandate had been officially resolved – the last French soldier had left Lebanese territory on 31 December 1946.[1] The Lebanese state was about to enter a new stage in its development, with the National Pact of 1943 marking the foundation of a state-building endeavour based on power-sharing between the different Lebanese communities. While the Pact had 'bound' the different communities to each other and had discouraged them from seeking external support, it was still unclear how different Christian and Muslim communities, which had established ties with external factions for decades, were going to react going forward.[2] What was certain, however, was that the creation of the National Pact and an alliance formed between the Khūrī and the Ṣulḥ camps opened a new page for the nascent Lebanese state within its expanded borders. The issue of the societal legitimacy of the state was believed to have been resolved: each community was now guaranteed representation and a voice in the national, political arena.

It was earlier shown how the Lebanese state could not attain internal legitimacy during the mandate, both in its societal and its institutional form. The result was multiple periods of political instability, though the state itself somehow managed to survive despite much adversity. Both approaches to state-building explain this illegitimacy by focusing on the French influence during the mandate period as well as the Christian tendencies to turn Lebanon into an unrepresentative, Christian homeland. Would the National Pact be enough, however, to provide an adequate foundation for state legitimacy? In essence, the Pact was an attempt at both state-building and nation-building, and its creators hoped that it would solve the question of Lebanese identity and, with it, the idea of the state across Lebanese society. One could therefore project, societally, favourable odds for its success. However, not all the communities saw it as such: some continued to regard it as a pragmatic and temporary agreement, the purpose of which was to drive out the French mandatory forces.[3] And while the Pact functioned as a foundational aspect of the state, political instability persisted: by the end of the 1950s, the constitution would already be amended multiple times, parliament would be dissolved and its structure changed, and no fewer than sixteen prime ministers would form an even bigger number of cabinets, in the search to find a working formula compatible with the unbreakable National Pact. Additionally, challenges to 'true' state representativeness were brought up again and again while the idea of the state, crucial to societal legitimacy, was rarely, if ever, realized.

A study of the implementation of the Pact will shed light on the reasons for its inability to achieve stability while also uncovering its shortcomings in the face of the institutional approach. Particular events that challenged state legitimacy during the term of Bshāra al-Khūrī (1943–52) – Lebanon's first post-Pact president – will be highlighted. These events will be analysed through the institutional and the societal approach to explain the legitimacy crises that resulted therefrom. Those specific instances in Lebanon's early political history have been chosen because, they represent a perfect point to which one can apply both approaches to legitimacy. The major events that will be studied are: the creation of the League of Arab States, the genesis of the Arab–Israeli issue, the 1947 elections which resulted in the re-election of the president, the attempted coup on the state in 1949 and the resignation of the president in 1952.

The first test

It was not only the Pact but the results of the 1943 elections that also sparked another essential change in the Lebanese state apparatus. In fact, the legislative situation painted a very different picture to the one shown by the November crisis of the same year. The latter situation which resulted in the National Pact would suggest a form of rapprochement between the more moderate camps within the Christian and Muslim communities, but it was in fact Eddeh's more Lebanist National Bloc party which had recouped eleven of the seventeen seats in the Christian-dominated Mountain, while Khūrī's Constitutionalists (members of his Constitutional Bloc) acquired their seats from surrounding areas where more mixed populations lived.[4] On the other hand, the Arab nationalist lists of Riāḍ al-Ṣulḥ and 'Abd al-Ḥamīd Karāmī were dominated the southern and northern constituencies, respectively, and ended what was, until then, an exclusion of Arab nationalism from parliamentary life (this was due to a combination of a self-imposed policy of non-recognition from these nationalists and various campaigns from the state itself). These election results provide an indicator of the atmosphere within which the National Pact was signed and are themselves indicative of the concessions made for the creation of the Pact.[5]

If Eddeh's Lebanists were the majority within the Christian hub and Arab nationalists dominated the different Sunni (and to an extent Shī'a) hubs then the window within which Khūrī and his moderates operated did not provide enough leverage for many concessions to be made. Nevertheless, the Arab nationalists (some of them Syrian nationalists) – led at this point by Riāḍ al-Ṣulḥ – were looking for reconciliation and most importantly the removal of the mandate, and were looking to use their leverage in parliament to bring about an appropriate president who is sympathetic to their political outlooks. They were able to obtain promises of Arab cooperation (excluding any political unification) from both Eddeh and Khūrī,[6] who in the meantime attempted – reluctantly – to find a compromise candidate but failed.[7] Eventually, through his own political manoeuvring and rapprochement with the Sunni community,[8] the support of the Egyptian and Syrian governments, and partly because of Eddeh's failure to deliver on his pro-Arab policies, Khūrī managed to obtain forty-four out of fifty-five votes in parliament to become the president of the Lebanese Republic.[9] His alliance with Ṣulḥ would go on to spur this new government to push for an amendment of the Lebanese Constitution, removing all references to the mandate and sparking the November crisis of that year.

Indeed, the environment in which the National Pact was drafted helps understand the events that followed Lebanon's independence, as it establishes two very important factors. Firstly, the National Pact was very much a pragmatic agreement, a compromise resulting from bargaining for the predetermined goal of achieving independence and presenting a unified front against the mandatory power. This was especially shown to be the case when Ṣulḥ had approached Eddeh, a historical and ideological enemy, to propose a similar formula of compromise for the sake of achieving full independence. In this sense, the National Pact does not represent a set of principles or a unifying ideology – or even identity – and this is shown by the contingent nature in which it was born. Secondly, understanding the context of the time highlights the fact that Khūrī did not necessarily have an elected mandate from his own community. The fact that Eddehists still obtained a clear electoral majority in the Christian-dominated Mountain indicates that most Christians – specifically those politically motivated enough to vote – were still harbouring Lebanist sentiments,[10] and it is unclear just how much they were willing to compromise with and accommodate Arabist tendencies.[11] Incidentally, their will would be put to the test in the months following the election of both parliament and the president, as the Lebanese government, now united under the National Pact and driven by the momentum of independence, would ready itself to participate in the preliminary talks that aimed to form a regional Arab organization.

On the whole, the objective of the Pact was not only to reconcile the two major communities but to establish a foundation for a widespread Lebanese identity and with it an equally-as-widespread 'idea of the state'. The challenge was for the Pact to achieve this through state institutions that had not achieved any form of legitimacy, and within a society that was still as divided as ever with regard to nationalist aspirations. The arbitrary and pragmatic nature in which the Pact was formed indicates that this new 'idea of the state' was not as widespread as its participating elites liked to claim. This immediately put the state's ability to attain societal legitimacy at a handicap, since the rapprochement between communities was not as significant as advertised, and thus the communal differences that existed before the Pact were, for the most part, still present after its creation.

It is thus unsurprising that Lebanese involvement in Middle Eastern regionalism and the eventual creation of the League of Arab States was one of the, if not the, first political tests of the new state. After all, Lebanese foreign policy would have to be a reflection of where its people saw themselves in relation to their immediate surroundings, and with regard to their relationship with the West after the end of a divisive mandate period. As such, the multiple events that arose from Lebanon's early relations with its Arab neighbours were directly related to the National Pact and particularly its societal legitimacy, since they immediately affected, and shaped, the 'idea of the state'. For the Pact's proponents, Lebanese involvement with Arab issues would highlight the success of the Pact and the emergence of a new Lebanon with its 'Arab face'. Nevertheless, there were still many who had not yet accepted the state's new identity. The events of 1944 and 1945 that preceded and culminated in the creation of the League of Arab States would form the first challenge to the societal legitimacy of the Lebanese state.

The National Pact implied a sort of neutrality with regard to foreign policy, and many looked to Switzerland as a perfect model for the Lebanese state. However, the Pact did not *explicitly* establish a neutral foreign policy, and neither political side was ready to give up its external ties or international ambitions. The Arabists still had high aspirations of immersing the new state into a form of Arab unity: many of the earlier advocates for such a unity maintained their transnational ties and ambitions despite the new character of the state. On the other hand, pro-Western Christians had foregone the direct protective role that France (or the West general) could play in an independent Lebanese state, but were still not ready to relinquish the particularism which they believed defined Lebanon, especially in the face of its Arab neighbours.

Having shunned Eddeh, the figurehead of pro-mandate Christian nationalism, from political life as punishment for his acts during the November crisis,[12] the Khūrī–Ṣulḥ alliance was now fully in control of the state, with Khūrī as president and Ṣulḥ as prime minister. The former was able to further strengthen his position in parliament thanks to two new vacant seats acquired by his Constitutional Bloc,[13] while Ṣulḥ consolidated his own power within the Sunni community. Such was the momentum with which the Lebanese government approached the preliminary talks for the League of Arab States that took place between the Arab countries in late 1943 and early 1944.[14]

On the regional level, different camps were forming within the context of Arab unity: the Hashemite scheme was being put up against an Egyptian-led project of strong Arab unity which had been gaining strong momentum in Syria, while Saudi Arabia had its own Western interests to protect as well as its special Islamic status to consider, so it advocated – along with Yemen – a less-integrated form of Arab cooperation that excluded any form of political union.[15] In the face of pressure from both of these currents, the new Lebanese state had to tread carefully so as to conserve a neutral position and maintain the now-necessary internal balance between the different aspirations of the communities.

Negotiations and contradictions

That balance proved particularly hard to strike during the preliminary talks for the creation of the League of Arab States. In fact, there is no evidence that it was struck at all; instead, two different rounds of talks occurred, with a different Lebanese delegation being present each time. The first round, in early January 1944, was conducted by Riāḍ al-Ṣulḥ and Salīm Taqla, who was a member of Khūrī's Constitutional Bloc. The attitude they presented was consistent with the policies of the National Pact, while also leaning towards a more Arabist view.[16] Firstly, they reiterated their desire for close cooperation with the Arab states. Secondly, they blamed the lack of cooperation and past Lebanese reservations towards the matter on 'foreign interests that worked to distance Lebanon from Syria'. Once those interests had been eradicated, Lebanon had shown that it was willing to cooperate with Syria and in turn with the rest of the Arab world. When the question of the nature of an Arab organization was put to him, Ṣulḥ kept an official commitment to the Pact: he emphasized recognition of Lebanese independence and tried to rid the talks of any ambiguity with regard to unity; Lebanon would only accept cooperation with other states, not a union.[17]

In spite of this, Ṣulḥ's performance during the talks did not sit well with many Lebanese. The commitments he received from the other Arab delegates were seen as papering over the cracks, the cracks being the concealed objective of Arab unity.[18] An opposition coalition therefore formed in Lebanon against Ṣulḥ during that time; it included 'Abd al-Ḥamīd Karāmī of Tripoli (who had been, like most Tripolitans, a Syrian unionist), many of Eddeh's Lebanists and some members of Khūrī's Constitutional Bloc that considered themselves 'Mediterraneanists' and opposed such an accelerated relationship with the Arab states.[19] The fact that many members of the opposition came from Khūrī's own party is good indication that, only a few months after its creation, questions about the National Pact's regional implications were already being raised.

The first round of negotiations resulted in the Alexandria Protocol, an outline of the framework for an Arab organization, and established the basis for further talks that would draft an official charter for the League of Arab States. The Protocol especially faced opposition in Lebanon from those Christians who still refused to accept such a close Arab link.[20] The Maronite Patriarch, Antūnios 'Arīḍa, tasked Yusuf al-Sawda (a prominent contributor to Maronite historiography and nation-building) to study the Protocol and find any conflicts between it and true Lebanese independence.[21] Sawda arrived to many conclusions that reflected Christian fears of the time: he argued that the Protocol and its preceding negotiations bore a worrisome Islamic character.[22] He also believed that the special resolution recognizing Lebanon's current borders was too contingent on Lebanese policies aligning with Arab ones, and was thus not a true and guaranteed recognition that could be relied on.[23] Additionally, he was too sceptical of the resolution which, theoretically, could bind Lebanon to the Anglo-Iraqi treaty that was still in effect.[24] Sawda's study, coupled with agitation on the part of Eddehists and Mediterraneanists, drove Khūrī to ask Ṣulḥ to push for an amendment to the resolution on foreign policy during the next round of talks establishing the charter.[25]

By early 1945, tension was on the rise again in Lebanon, to the point where the British minister remarked in February that 'pro-French sentiments are on the increase' and that the 'French have recovered much of the ground lost in November

1943'. He also theorized that many of the Lebanese would 'not object' to living under a French umbrella: 'The Christians would mostly welcome it, the Metwalis (Shīʿa) would be relatively indifferent and only the Sunni Moslems would resent it implacably.'[26] The extent to which this assessment is true, however, is debatable. It was clear by then that a significant portion of the Christians demanded complete independence, while the number of Shīʿa that would be 'indifferent' was also questionable, as many of them had become affiliated with either Arabism or Syrianism.[27] But Eddeh's influence, it seems, was as strong as ever, taking advantage of Khūrī's absence to strengthen his own position among the cabinet. He met with the Patriarch himself as well as the head of the Katāʾib party Pierre Jmayyil to reassure them that Lebanon would be gradually dropped 'out of the Arab orbit'.[28]

A few months later, the Lebanese cabinet took on a very different shape: Khūrī had fallen seriously ill and had to take a break from his presidential duties, which made him answer to opposition demands by removing Ṣulḥ from his ministerial duties and appointing Karāmī instead. Given Karāmī's Arab nationalist past and his perception among extreme Lebanist circles as a 'Muslim fanatic', his government, which still comprised of pro-National Pact politicians, was even more delicate than its predecessor.[29] As such, it was heavily criticized internally for the weakness of its policies and its equally limited implementations. These were early signs of the shortcomings of the Pact: it necessitated the amalgamation of two contradictory perspectives towards Lebanese state identity, which resulted in both institutional and societal pitfalls. Henri Far'ūn, one of the Mediterraneanists who balanced the National Pact with his belief in Lebanese Christian identity, was appointed as foreign minister and immediately took steps to alleviate Lebanist fears regarding Arab unity.

The first meetings of the political sub-committee that was charged to create the charter for the League of Arab States occurred on 14 February 1945. The Lebanese delegation was headed by Far'ūn and his contributions would show a stark divergence from his predecessors' positions and highlight the contradictory nature of the ideas derived from the National Pact. This second phase of the negotiations – led by the Christian moderate Far'ūn – will show itself in stark contrast to the earlier rounds which presented a certain idea of the Lebanese state both internationally and to the Lebanese public. This idea was best exemplified by the phrase 'Arab face' which Ṣulḥ made famous, implying a degree of identification with Arabism and Arab unity while also allowing for the rest of the Lebanese 'body' to maintain its particularities. The round of negotiations in February 1945, however, showed that not only was this idea very uninfluential within the Lebanese population, it was also not consistently upheld within the Lebanese state itself.

This was immediately apparent when the Lebanese delegation arrived to the negotiations having created its own draft of the charter, prepared by Far'ūn and Chīḥa, both Mediterraneanists.[30] This draft was pitted against an Iraqi one, and the difference between the two was very telling. The Lebanese draft presented a very minimal Arab organization, one that did not emphasize Arab identity, insisted on total state sovereignty and only accepted a strong intervening role of the League when a state had requested for such.[31] The latter point was especially emphasized by

Far'ūn with regard to interstate aggression, showing the more reserved Christian thought which he represented, and he insisted that sovereignty and independence should not be relinquished or threatened in any way. The representativeness of Far'ūn's scepticism was felt during the negotiations, when 'Abd al-Raḥman 'Azzām, an Egyptian delegate, interjected and highlighted the issue behind Lebanon's repetitive objections: 'We always aspire for the text of this Charter to be for the benefit of all and not only Lebanon. … The Charter has become very clear on this point [sovereignty] and the remaining valuable is Lebanese public opinion.'[32]

The significance of the League charter was apparent to everyone within the Lebanese political arena. Seen as the country's first step into true independence,[33] the path which it chose to embark upon became a representation of the idea that the state wished to espouse of itself. Societal state-building was very much expected to occur, yet an idea of the state was both too ambiguous and ultimately non-existent on the social level. In fact, the different communities saw in the League charter diverging declarations of the long-term policy and idea of the Lebanese state. For the Arabists, they had finally achieved their goal of being rejoined to a common Arab destiny, even if the League was not as integrated as they would've hoped. This attitude was characterized by Karāmī's speech in celebration of the charter. He struck a very different tone to Far'ūn, speaking on behalf of an 'Arab Lebanon' and declaring the League a 'huge and important step' towards what the different Arab populations wanted: Arab unity. Others who had sought Arab unity for decades looked at Arab attachment as a condition for their accepting of this new Lebanese 'nation', and believed that such closeness was a natural consequence of the National Pact. On the other hand, reserved Christians looked at the charter as an establishment of a bilateral relationship between a neutral Lebanon and its Arab surroundings: a satisfactory status quo in which Lebanon had accepted its 'Arab face' without being assimilated into Arab identity.

Not only are those two ideas incompatible and are in themselves a source for confessional instability among the Lebanese population, the two perspectives were just as present within the power-sharing system of the Lebanese state, which stopped the state itself from promoting a coherent idea across the different communities. Scepticism had not disappeared internally however, and Karāmī's particular wording in his statement was brought up by the Maronite deputy Joseph Karam during the subsequent parliamentary session. Karam asked Karāmī what he meant by his statement and declared his refusal of any pact that is merely a 'step' and not an end in itself.[34] This was immediately followed by objections from other Christian members of parliament. Similarly, the government was challenged for what was perceived to be an ambiguous position with regard to the projects of a 'Greater Syria' which was still very much being discussed by Syrian and Jordanian leaders.[35] Whether it was those that viewed themselves as non-Arab or those that leaned towards the 'Arab face' formula, Lebanists believed that the National Pact was what guaranteed the existence of a Lebanese nation which only had to accept minimal cooperation with the surrounding Arab states.

Eventually, the question of Lebanese 'Arab' identity was settled in a similar manner to the creation of a National Pact: a balanced relationship between two contradictory outlooks was maintained, with an overall ambiguity as to the direct implications on the Lebanese state. As the League was created and different opinions voiced their displeasure with its implications on Lebanese national identity, the state maintained its official line of argument: the charter was the embodiment of the Pact on the international arena. Ultimately, Arab cooperation was not restricted to a matter of foreign policy and became a key aspect of the societal state-building project which the Pact had tried to set in motion.

Yet, the fact that the two main Christian and Muslim communities did not perceive this crucial political phenomenon in the same manner implied that the Pact was not gaining the ground it needed to become the foundation of a legitimate Lebanese state. Instead, the Pact could only realize the minimal achievement of keeping the Lebanese under the same state apparatus, elevating itself to a norm higher than the constitution itself.[36] As traditional divisions reared their head, the issue of the League charter was the first sign of the inadequacies of the Pact as a state-building tool in the societal sense. While not much time – relatively – had elapsed for the Pact to properly implement an idea of the state, the negotiations with the Arab states show that even those who endorsed the Pact had not yet agreed on an idea which would shape both the state and its identity-based relationship with its neighbours. These disagreements not only meant unfavourable prospects for the success of the Pact in achieving societal legitimacy, but this contradiction *within* the state also hinted at obstacles in achieving institutional legitimacy through strong and united public institutions.

The Arab–Israeli conflict

Khūrī resumed his tenure as president on 31 March 1945 and, as the Lebanese achieved further and more complete independence,[37] more and more divisive issues forced the communities to deal with the stark reality of the deeper divisions that remained unresolved within the country. Christian–Muslim tension remained and fluctuated between benign and explosive, as the mid-1940s were characterized by demonstrations and conflicts on most religious observances and holidays.[38]

The state had fully sponsored the Pact by this point and took on a totally confessional nature, employing public positions based not on competence but on confessional belonging, being forced to maintain a balance across the entire apparatus in order to comply with the spirit of coexistence and cohabitation. Subsequently, the feeling of being bound by confessionalism was promoted across the communities, especially in the areas with lingering characteristics of feudal loyalties, that one's confessional loyalty was what earned them a position within the state, and their ideological tendencies were almost irrelevant.[39] That feeling only served to reinforce the clientelism that was already rampant throughout urban and rural Lebanon, as individuals kept flocking towards local feudal and economic leaders who had enough sway to guarantee representation within the state.

Within this context, a second foreign policy issue tested the division between the main Lebanese communities, and the disparities in identity that had not been – and possibly could not have been – addressed by the National Pact: the Jewish migration to the Middle East and the eventual creation of the Israeli state. The antagonism with which both those events were received within Arab circles once again forced the Lebanese society to choose sides, and although the state declared war on Israel, many in the Christian community simply didn't recognize such a decision, and executed their own relationships with the new Jewish state.[40] As is attested by many theorists, chief among them Charles Tilly, war-making and the development of the 'other' is a crucial element to both approaches to state-building.[41] Hence, the 1948 Arab–Israeli war represented an opportune way for the state to consolidate its legitimacy through a unified idea. However, the following incidents show how the state was not able to use this war to its advantage, as disregard for its policies continued to exist within the Maronite community, indicating continuous lack of societal legitimacy. This was even more problematic when taking into consideration that the Maronites looked at themselves as the founders of modern Lebanon.

Maronite–Zionist relationships

Lebanese Muslims, in general, were united with regard to an anti-Zionist position. The Arab nationalists all agreed in one way or another with League policy and looked at any Arab–Zionist relationship in a very antagonistic manner. And while there was some belief within the Jewish Agency that the Shīʿa of southern Lebanon were not as adamant in their opposition to Zionism as the Sunnis, and that there was some chance of appeasing them, evidence seems to suggest that this was possibly the case for only a few minorities, while most Shīʿa – whether notables or local populations – were opposed to any sort of Zionist project south of the border.[42] The Christians, however, were not as clear in their stance with regard to the creation of the state of Israel.

Throughout the 1930s and 1940s, many Maronite figures had developed relations with Zionist figures: Emile Eddeh had already shown pro-Zionist tendencies throughout his political career, while the Church, through the Maronite Patriarch ʿArīḍa and the archbishop for Beirut, Ignatius Mubārak, was known to be sympathetic to Jewish migration.[43] In fact, earlier in the 1930s, an idea began circulating in international political circles of settling around fifty-thousand German Jews in Lebanon, as a response to the rise of Hitler and Nazism. According to Guy Bracha, those rumours were generally met with four distinct reactions from the Lebanese society. City-dwelling merchants – both Muslim and Christian – and landowners welcomed the influx of money in the country as well as the potential profits to be made from selling and renting land. A second attitude also developed among professionals and the working class who feared a takeover of the employment market. A third group, mainly composed of Arab nationalists (but also French officials), saw in the possible settlement an extension of Zionism into Lebanon and Syria, and thus vehemently opposed it. This was especially true for the Arab nationalists, who believed that the French were part of this conspiracy to remove Arab–Muslim elements in the Levant. And finally the fourth attitude, espoused by Lebanists and particularly Maronites, supported the possible Jewish settlements with two objectives in mind: 'to increase the non-Muslim element in Lebanon, and to strengthen their connections with the Zionist movement'.[44] This last position would continue to characterize many Christian politicians in the coming decade.

By 1946, the combination of the League's existence and the rising urgency of the Palestinian issue provided a lot of ground for the Lebanists to gain. Eddeh had started to re-enter the political scene after his expulsion from parliament. He began a strategy of 'rapprochement' with the League itself in order to show that he was willing to cooperate with Arab aspirations while doing the same with the British government from which, as a known Francophile, he had distanced himself.[45] Whether his approach towards the League was more to do with showing Britain that he could play along than a matter of actual personal conviction was up for debate, but once again a divide among the Christian – especially the Maronite – community was brewing.

The Church, whose power and influence had been waning since the Mandate period, started to stretch its legs into the political arena as well. Direct contact was established, though covertly, between 'Arīḍa himself and David Ben-Gurion.[46] In fact, ties between the Jewish Agency and the Church eventually developed so much that a secret 'treaty' was signed between the two on 30 May 1946, establishing formal contacts and establishing mutual support with regard to the Jewish aspirations for a state in Palestine and the 'independent Christian character of Lebanon'.[47] Nevertheless, 'Arīḍa insisted on the covert nature of the treaty and refused to openly support Zionism, not unlike most pro-Zionist Christians of the time.[48] This wasn't the case for Mubārak, the archbishop for Beirut, who sent a letter to the UN Special Committee on Palestine (UNSCOP) in which he openly backed 'freedom for the Jews in Palestine' and dismissed the Arab claims to the land.[49] He then went to the press and declared that 'Lebanese Christians … realize that Zionism is bringing civilization to Palestine and to the entire Middle East'.[50] Meanwhile, another party that would develop contacts with the Jewish Agency was the Katā'ib.[51] In fact, both Eddeh and Elias Rabābi – a representative of the Katā'ib – met in secret with Israeli officials during the events of 1948, and the possibility of a 'Christian revolt' with the support of Israel was discussed during said meetings.[52] However, neither the treaty nor any semblance of a direct coup would occur in Lebanon, due to many factors ranging from the diminishing political standing of pro-Zionists (let alone the Church's generally weakening political influence) to the lack of resources or capabilities to effect such a revolution.

Still, the Palestinian issue continued to highlight the lack of legitimacy of the state among key Maronite circles, as many of their key figures did not develop the same feeling of antagonism towards Jewish immigration and Israel in particular. After all, historically, the main threat to the Maronites had been the different forms of Muslim persecution. This prompted many of them to not only *ignore* official state rhetoric against the creation of Israel but also to establish ties with Jewish and Israeli officials in a manner that went *against* state policy. This division in commitment to the 'Palestinian cause' between Christians and Muslims in general was evident throughout the war.

Khūrī, on the other hand, and most of the other Constitutionalists, were – at least officially – uncompromising when it came to any pro-Zionist policies.[53] They stuck to their Pact-driven positions and, believing in the need for Christian–Muslim cooperation within an independent Lebanon, considered Zionism as a hindrance and a threat to this alliance. The general Christian position to Zionism seemed to parallel their earlier one towards France: some saw in it a method of guaranteeing the protection of the Christian minority in either a 'Lesser Lebanon' or a Lebanon in which Christians had a privileged political position. Others looked at it as another obstacle to 'true' Lebanese independence which inevitably involved coexistence and trust between Christians and Muslims.[54]

Lebanon's role in the war

While the Christian camp seemed, on the surface, divided with regard to Zionism and the creation of Israel, there was nevertheless a reluctance to engage in warfare across the Christian political landscape. Both Khūrī and General Fu'ād Shehāb, the head of the new and underdeveloped Lebanese army, lobbied for Lebanon to play a defensive role in the war, even managing to ignore some of the orders coming from the Arab League's Arab Liberation Army (ALA) command.[55]

It took a special kind of political balancing to maintain such hesitant positions while having the government take an unwavering stand alongside the Arab League against the state of Israel. In 1947, the foreign minister Ḥamīd Frangieh had declared officially, in front of the UN General Assembly, Lebanon's support for the Palestinian people's right to self-determination and affirmed the Lebanese opposition towards a Jewish state as well as 'unlimited' Jewish migration to Palestine based on Zionist beliefs.[56] Subsequently, the government declared war on Israel, along with the rest of the League, on 15 May 1948, while many Lebanese individuals and groups rushed to voluntarily join the ALA.[57] The government was more than happy to allow such volunteers, backing them up with a very active and vocal diplomatic role within the domestic and the international arena in declaring its opposition to the Israeli state.[58] In the meantime, the Lebanese Armed Forces were made sure to play an almost negligible war in the Arab–Israeli conflict, justified through militaristic weakness, but also clearly affected by the lack of a strong enough political will for the war.[59] This allowed the state to perfectly appease both sides.

And though the state maintained its opposition on Israel, the difference in commitment between Christians and Muslims was strong enough to affect the role of the army. In fact, the Lebanese army in 1948 was very much seen as a 'Christian Army' by the Muslim population within the country, and relative indifference was perceived to be widespread among the Christians compared to the passion with which many of the Muslim communities were willing to go to war.[60] This difference in commitment, coupled with General Fu'ād Shehāb's insistence on maintaining a separation between the army and politics in order to preserve institutional neutrality, also allowed for a very minor military role for Lebanon in the Arab–Israeli war of 1948.[61]

The state was not only paralysed by societal divisions but was also visibly ignored when it came to the Palestinian issue. Its legitimacy was called into question again by Christian groups dealing directly with Israeli officials, making them effectively 'traitors' both in the eyes of Arabists and in an official manner once war was declared. On the other hand, the state was also bypassed by those Arabists that supported an anti-Israel stance but simply did not have faith in the state to carry out such policies. One example of this was Prime Minister Riāḍ al-Ṣulḥ himself, who set up an Association of Anti-Zionist Lebanese Parties to participate in the war on the creation of Israel. The events surrounding the 1948 war with Israel serve to show the similar, and related, trends that had been present during the creation of the League of Arab States. Hence, the consequences for legitimacy were also similar: both societally and institutionally, legitimacy remained absent.

The 1947 elections

While Lebanese foreign policy became an opportunity for the state to consolidate an 'idea of itself' among the population and bolster its societal legitimacy, there continued to be internal obstacles that it also needed to face. The 1947 parliamentary election was an essential test of Lebanese legitimacy: the election was presented as a public vote on the Khūrī–Ṣulḥ alliance itself and the nature of the National Pact. Earlier, elections had been rife with corruption and political interference, so many were looking to these elections to mark the start of a new institutional era: though the issue of identity had remained unsettled, there was still hope for institutional integrity and effectiveness. In other words, the elections also served as a test for the Lebanese state's institutional state-building.

At the beginning of the year, elections were brought forward so as to avoid having them during the summer of that year. This required parliament to amend the constitution to allow for a dissolution of itself and the conducting of new elections.[62] Khūrī, meanwhile, had already become quite the provoking figure and, during the statement made in parliament prior to his resignation as prime minister, Sāmī al-Ṣulḥ mentioned how he felt he was blindsided (by the sudden resignation of a couple of his ministers) through 'manoeuvres' from 'behind the scenes'.[63] He would also write in his memoirs of a 'corrupting virus' in the presidential palace, where statesmen would go to become 'slaves to the owner'.[64]

By this point, Khūrī's policy of appeasing Sunni leaders on a rotational basis in order to ensure consent and balance of the position of prime ministership was becoming clear. It was also already a sign of the lengths to which he would go to protect the equilibrium of the Pact, seeing that the repeated change and overdiversity only served to hinder those governments in their policies: the only benefit to such instability was the protection of internal balance and the obvious acquisition of personal power (since he remained the only constant throughout). Additionally, there were demographic issues to deal with, mainly the general census that was presumed necessary before the first independent general elections took place. Earlier that decade, a census was meant to take place through a decree by the French high commissioner in March of 1943, yet it never materialized.[65] Afterwards, Riāḍ al-Ṣulḥ had also mentioned conducting a census in his ministerial statement of that same year, labelling it a 'guarantor of true popular representation'; this, again, did not materialize.[66]

In the run-up to the elections, Khūrī's personal motivations were attacked from all sides of the opposition, and the British first minister believed that Khūrī's 'main ambition [was] to be re-elected President' while his fear was being 'replaced' by Eddeh.[67] Houstoun-Boswall also believed that Khūrī himself, while a 'shrewd politician', carried 'little weight with the public in large'.[68] This perception of Khūrī reinforces the image of him playing feudal and communal leaders against each other while maintaining the balance he needs to remain the most appropriate man for the presidency. The timing of the 1947 elections, however, seemed to push him to overplay his cards, as it was only two years after that a presidential election was due, and the only way to ensure re-election for himself was to obtain a majority in parliament strong enough to amend the constitution as a president was not allowed to serve successive terms.[69]

Results

Accusations of fraud and tampering were rampant throughout the country, and became especially strong in the Mountain. Khūrī himself admitted to his intervention in the formation of lists for candidates to run on but understated the effect of the government's influence and believed that 'presidential culture' in Lebanon dictated the overinvolvement of the president in all political matters.[70] What he meant by that remains unclear, but the rest of his thoughts and policies indicate that he was only too aware of the responsibility that he bore in order to ensure not only a balanced parliament but also one that would not openly call into question the legitimacy of the state or the Pact.

Claims against the validity of the election included purposeful miscounting of votes, voting in the names of deceased or emigrated persons, pressurizing voters, bribery and corruption of election officials and those in charge of vote counting, and not allowing party representatives to oversee vote counting.[71] Khūrī's brother, Salīm,[72] who had run on an independent list, was also showered with accusations of fraud from within and without parliament, which eventually led to his resignation a few days after the election.[73] Kamīl Sham'ūn and Kamal Junblāṭ ran on Khūrī's list – in spite of their previous calls for governmental reform – and both, despite winning their seats, openly denounced the results and acknowledged fraud on behalf of the government; Junblāṭ even declared parliament invalid and demanded another election.[74] Eddeh, who by this point had become so disenchanted with this 'new' Lebanon that he had flirted with the idea of cooperating with advocates of 'Greater Syria' to attain the goal of an autonomous 'Lesser Lebanon' within their scheme, did not win a seat; nor did anyone on his list.[75] His National Bloc party even published a book detailing the corrupt actions that occurred in different districts, mentioning the concerns raised by both Sham'ūn and Junblāṭ as well as 'Arīḍa who also publicly contested the vote.[76]

On 30 May, a day before the second round of elections, a mass protest in Beirut was attended by members of the opposition, including Karāmī, Mubārak, Eddeh's National Bloc and others.[77] Meanwhile, in the following weeks, a number (a 'majority', according to Houstoun-Boswall) of newspapers sent a letter directly to the president threatening to boycott parliament completely while also demanding a re-election.[78] These protests could not achieve much as Khūrī's supporters won a majority in the Mountain while government-sponsored lists also managed to sweep victories in the north and the south of the country.[79] In Beirut, the government list also won but by Khūrī's own admission, election fraud made it so that the victory was 'total'.[80] As a way to appease those calls for re-election, Khūrī issued a decree[81] calling for parliament to set up a committee to look into these allegations of fraud, as Article 30 of the Constitution stated that the 'deputies alone have competence to judge the validity of their mandate'.[82] As such, an Appeals Committee was formed and its report judged three deputies to have gained their seat through incorrect results. The fate of those three deputies was then put to a parliamentary vote and all three of them kept their seats as the Committee's report was downvoted.[83]

As a result of corruption on such a massive scale, the Lebanese state was left with a parliament the validity of which was openly questioned by most members of the society. This did not improve the prospects of all communities internalizing an idea of the state which they all agreed upon. Crucially, though, institutional legitimacy was also openly questioned on a large scale. Because of the nature of the National Pact and the fact that it formed such a fundamental character of the early Lebanese state, the state had to intervene in order to protect itself and, by extension, the Pact. Khūrī and Ṣulḥ were both openly aware of the threats to the fragile institutions that had been created through their agreement: these included, firstly, the Christian nationalists who were still against or undecided on Arab relations, the Palestinian issue and the identity of the state itself. Secondly, many Arab nationalists and Islamists in the Sunni community were still unsatisfied with the unfair influence Maronites held on Lebanese institutions. Thirdly, many members of the rural Shī'a, especially those opposed to their local feudal leaders, gravitated towards leftist and nationalist organizations that continued to resist the existence of the Lebanese state.[84] Additionally, there were those, like Junblāṭ, who had accepted the Lebanese entity but were so vehemently against its confessional make-up. Plus, Antūn S'ādeh's Syrian nationalist party had still been growing and gathering momentum that would peak within the coming years. After the elections, all of these groups openly questioned the legitimacy of state institutions (such as parliament) or, in some cases like S'ādeh's, the state itself.

It was indeed not a coincidence that the 1947 elections, one of the most tampered-with election processes in Lebanese history,[85] were described by Ṣulḥ in his subsequent ministerial statement as a 'plebiscite of [state] policy of this [independent] era'.[86] The elections were not simply legislative ones; rather, it was the idea of the 'Pact' state itself which was faced with an existential risk. Thus, societal legitimacy became directly linked with institutional legitimacy through the Pact.

Re-election

Having 'stacked' parliament with enough supporters who can elect him, Khūrī's path to re-election became clear. There were many factors for why Khūrī was able to remain president, but the clearest one among them was his ability to appease enough leaders in each of the Lebanese communities. Among the Muslim deputies, he had spearheaded the movement of Christians towards a more pro-Arab position while also being just as strong-headed on the issue of Palestine. He had also succeeded – as mentioned previously – in appeasing Sunni leadership in general by allowing each leader to 'have a go' at the prime ministership. On an individual level, he had the full backing of Riāḍ, who would only accept Khūrī as president, even threating to run himself in contradiction to the Pact if an alternative option was chosen.[87] Karāmī, on the other hand, met with the prime minister and declared that the Palestinian issue would take precedence over domestic affairs and in that regard, Khūrī had satisfied Muslim demands.[88] So even though he did not have any real oppositional influence within parliament itself, even Karāmī had come to accept Khūrī's prolonged presidency. Ironically, Riāḍ al-Ṣulḥ, Khūrī's longest serving prime minister and his natural ally, would employ a similar tactic (with Khūrī's blessing) with regard to the Shī'a of the country. Ṣulḥ, being from the south, incorporated different Shī'a leaders into the government – starting with Aḥmad al-As'ad, a member of the historically prominent al-As'ad family – in order to appease them despite local rivalries.[89] Meanwhile, other families such as the Ḥamādehs and the 'Oseyrān had been 'won over' to the idea of a Lebanese state since the Mandate period, and the Pact represented a perfect compromise for them. Specifically, Sabri Ḥamādeh had been more than satisfied in the guaranteed position of speaker of parliament, a position which he used to his personal benefit. 'Ādil 'Oseyrān would also become speaker during Sham'ūn's term. The Shī'a tribes in the B'albak province were also incorporated into political institutions, but their historical detachment from the state as well as their history of ḥashīsh trade meant repeated altercations with the weak Lebanese security forces.[90]

Otherwise, there were no real satisfactory alternatives from the Maronite side either. Khūrī himself argued that he was the best guarantor for the trajectory of Lebanon's independent policy (i.e. the National Pact) and his reign as president was needed for stability to be properly embedded, while he also used the Palestinian issue as another justification for his re-election.[91] Other candidates like Sham'ūn had already had disputes with Ṣulḥ; Far'ūn would be prevented to run anyway as per the Pact (he was not a Maronite); Frangieh, the foreign minister, had not acquired the political prestige needed while Eddeh or anyone still an ardent Lebanist was out of the question. As for Jmayyil, leader of the Phalange party, he and his party had not yet broken through the glass ceiling that separated the Christian politicians from the populists – the Phalangists themselves did not have any deputies and they were still seen as too unorthodox.[92] As for the president's brother, Salīm, he seemed to be satisfied with the local influence he had acquired and in any case would be less inclined to oppose his own brother. Khūrī, through the Pact, became the perfect compromise candidate. There was also an institutional argument to be made for Khūrī's re-election. Under his first few years, the state did manage to develop its capabilities through the acquisition of previously mandated powers, and enlarged its scope as well. Examples of this include the expansion of the education system,[93] the postal and telephone services, and the agricultural sector, among others.[94] Whether or not this expansion was a direct result of the state taking over many of the relevant public institutions, and creating other new ones, as opposed to Khūrī himself playing a role, is up for debate.

Still, on 22 May 1948, after a petition by the required number of deputies, a constitutional law was passed that sanctioned an exceptional 'one-time' amendment to the constitution that allowed Khūrī to be re-elected 'for the sake of stability' and the work that he had done for the country.[95] Five days later, Khūrī was unanimously elected for a second term as president, although nine deputies did abstain from voting.[96] A few weeks later, yet another cabinet resignation came and a new government was established, still under Riāḍ al-Ṣulḥ, on 3 August 1948.[97]

The late 1940s

Throughout the 1940s, the issue of the Pact and a confessional system was being contested by some politicians, yet most political leaders – either for personal or for pragmatic reasons – were unwilling to reopen the conversation on the durability of the 'Pact' state. Kamāl Junblāṭ, who evolved to become the main Druze leader during this time, remained very much against what he considered to be the 'illusion of a confessional and religious nation'.[98] Similarly, the Katā'ib party, which was becoming more and more influential among the Maronites, also denounced confessionalism, arguing like Junblāṭ that it was being manipulated to pit religions against each other at the expense of the nation.[99] Nonetheless, the Katā'ib would, throughout most of their political history, show a strong tendency to ensure a Maronite 'image' for Lebanon. Correspondingly, Junblāt would remain for most of his political life a leader of an almost Druze-exclusive party despite espousing a leftist ideology. Meanwhile, within parliament, a proposition by deputy 'Abdallah al-Yāfi in February 1944 to begin removing confessionalism from the state could not even gather the required number of signatories to be put on the parliamentary agenda.[100] This in itself indicated the unwillingness of members of the state to challenge the status quo, even though many had at some point agreed that confessionalism was more of a burden and that the Pact should be eventually let go.

Khūrī's solution for the diversity of views, on the other hand, was to integrate each of them into state positions on a periodic basis. This was especially the case when it came to rivalries within the Sunni community which were exploited by Khūrī throughout his presidential tenure to maintain the status quo.[101] Additionally, dissenting figures like Junblāṭ, Sham'ūn and Karāmī were allowed to participate in governments to 'have their go' at reform. By June 1947, Riāḍ al-Ṣulḥ's cabinet had to be reshuffled after the elections caused it to come under a lot of scrutiny.[102] The new government, which excluded some of the old opposition members such as Far'ūn and Junblāṭ, became Lebanon's sixth cabinet in four years of independence. Karāmī, meanwhile, set up a National Liberation Body as an effort to unite the opposition under one umbrella, with its main goal being the dissolution of parliament which he still considered to be illegitimate.[103]

The later years of the 1940s would continue the trend of Lebanese politics being mostly centred around foreign issues. In June, the Palestinian problem would change the dynamic of government–opposition relations as Ṣulḥ and his cabinet stepped up their commitment to helping the Palestinians gain exclusive independence within their territory. The amalgamation of demands from the opposition was quite telling, and was also a main reason for the lack of impact on the character of the state. Most of the opposition was extra-parliamentary, and different factions had different demands that were equally as contradictory and fundamental: Mubārak, the Church, the Phalangists and the National Bloc were all – albeit to different degrees – looking to ensure the special Christian character of the Lebanese state. Junblāṭ, wary as ever of Maronite tendencies for political ascendancy, strongly stood for his cause of separating confessionalism from the state.[104] Karāmī had no faith in parliament or the president and, being a Tripolitan, always flirted with forms of Arab nationalism that did not recognize the Lebanese state.

All three of these movements within the opposition were unsatisfied with the state as it was. The 1947 elections added to that mixture the fact that many of the opposition members simply refused to recognize the parliament's mandate. In fact, the distinction between parliamentary opposition and those who refused to accept the legitimacy of the state (i.e. refused to recognize either parliament or the state) was made within parliament itself, by then deputy Amīn Nakhleh.[105] An example of the nature of the opposition is an incident in February 1948, where a group of peasants (mostly Druze) were instigated by Nihād Arslān to attack a police base in Sawfar, with the intention of instigating a revolution. The attack was ultimately quelled and nothing came of the incident, despite the fact that Mubārak was rumoured to be a co-conspirator of Nihād's.[106] The fact that Nihād was released a few days later shows a perfect example of the weakness of the Lebanese state at the time, as it had inherently opened itself up to illegitimacy and weakness through its obligations to the different communities. The state was in its ever-binding need to maintain confessional balance and keep a stable status quo, and it could simply not afford to upset the Druze community, so as a result it did not react to an act of open aggression against it.

The coup

The next time an open attack on state institutions would occur, however, in July of 1949, the state reacted much differently. Antūn S'ādeh's Syrian Social Nationalist Party (SSNP) or Parti Populaire Syrien (as it was known then) was, as suggested by its name, a Syrian nationalist party that had always been at odds with the Lebanese state, naturally. This resulted in many incidents of 'back and forth' between members of the party and those of the government as well as a ban on the SSNP during the French mandate. As a result of the party's objectives and the location of its main operations (i.e. the Mountain), the SSNP often clashed with the Phalangists who were seen as their natural enemies because of their staunch Maronite Lebanese Nationalism. Crucially, the SSNP had developed a very strong base in Syria.

Throughout the mid-1940s, relations between the Lebanese and the Syrian state were developing and amicable, even complementary at times, after the 'Pact' regime had decided to cooperate with Syria on issues of independence, relations with the French, the Arab League and the Palestine issue.[107] That friendly relationship, however, was seen as both pragmatic and personal (i.e. between specific members of the respective governments), and turned out not to be as stable as both governments would have liked to think.[108] In fact, that relationship was tested when Ḥusni al-Za'īm, then Syrian chief of staff, led a coup d'état on Jamīl Mardam's government at the end of March 1949.[109] Initially, al-Za'īm was perceived in Lebanon to be loyal to the Hashemite dynasty, and by extension susceptible to be part of their Greater Syria scheme, which pit him against both Muslim–Arab nationalists in Lebanon (that were for the most party anti-Greater Syria) and Christian Lebanese nationalists. So while the Lebanese government recognized the new Syrian regime at the time of the coup, most of the Muslim community maintained an uncooperative position while Riāḍ himself was perceived by Za'īm as an enemy.[110]

Over the next few months, many incidents would serve to augment the antagonistic atmosphere between the two regimes, including an incident where Syrian forces intruded on Lebanese territory in order to arrest a Lebanese national thought to be involved in smuggling arms and provisions to Israel. Those forces were subsequently arrested by the Lebanese police, and Lebanese officials decided to try them in Lebanon as there was no extradition treaty in place between the two countries. A few days later, Za'īm enraged at the Lebanese government's actions, put a food embargo in place, and later on began planning an economic separation from Lebanon.[111] Seeking to once again increase Syrian influence within Lebanese politics, Za'īm also started cultivating a relationship with S'ādeh, who by June of 1949 had fled to Syria after a violent clash with the Katā'ib which resulted in a police raid of SSNP headquarters.[112] As clashes between party members and the police ensued, S'ādeh proclaimed a general rebellion on the radio from Syria.[113]

A few weeks later, on 8 July, S'ādeh was unexpectedly[114] handed over to the Lebanese police, charged with treason (among other things), tried in a military court and sentenced to death the next day. The government's involvement in the charging and sentencing of S'ādeh for his actions – but more importantly for his anti-Lebanon ideology[115] – was apparent. Neither Khūrī nor Riāḍ were ready to accept responsibility for what was perceived to be an unjust and political trial, and they would lay the blame on the other's doorstep with regard to the decisions that led to S'ādeh's execution.[116] In any case, there was no doubt of the implication of the government's actions in the S'ādeh affair: firstly, the idea of a coup was greatly exaggerated, not least since Mubārak and Arslān had issued similar calls for revolution and civil disobedience that went unpunished. Secondly, the swift and seemingly improper trial and execution of S'ādeh was clearly a reaction of a government that had been faced with external pressure from all sides, and was once again confronted with a threat that did not even recognize the state's right to exist. In many ways, the state perceived S'ādeh as a threat to itself and acted to try and consolidate power by defending the idea of the state and its 'Pact' character.

Once again, the state had been trapped in a vicious circle of illegitimacy: it was attacked by a prominent political movement that deemed it societally illegitimate, which pressured it to circumvent its own institutions in order to protect itself. This, in turn, only served to diminish both its societal and its institutional legitimacy. The failure of S'ādeh's execution to help the state acquire legitimacy was apparent soon after, both by the internal reactions to the trial and by the repercussions that resulted in the assassination of Riāḍ al-Ṣulḥ a few years later.

Khūrī's resignation

The abrupt end to Khūrī's term epitomizes the illegitimacy of the first years of the state: the manner in which he would resign showed the institutional instability that had been the norm up to that point, while the reasons for which he did so – and the reaction from his opponents – symbolize the struggle between political parties to agree on an idea of the state that could bring about societal legitimacy.

The last few years of Khūrī's presidency were not dissimilar to the rest of his term; they were also marked by accusations of personal motives within the government,[117] public resignation to state corruption,[118] and the continuation of the prime ministerial carousel which Khūrī had learned to employ excellently to his benefit.[119] Confessional tension did not decrease either,[120] and the presence of about 140,000 Palestinian refugees (who were mostly Muslim) only served to increase pressure on the very fine balance that had been established.[121] Regionally, the same rivalries were still existent, and the schemes for a regional union (mainly the Hashemite plan for a Greater Syria) were still very much alive. Syria experienced further coup d'états and each new government flirted with different proposals of regional unions, mainly one between Syria and Iraq.[122] Additionally, the Egyptian revolution which would signify Jamāl 'Abd al-Nāṣer's ascendance occurred in July, and the establishment of Israel was seen as a political threat by most Muslims while many Christians saw in it an economic threat to Lebanon's commercialism in the region.[123] A momentum of revolution and change had swept the Middle East since the perceived loss of the Arab–Israeli war in 1948 that even resulted in the assassination of King 'Abdallah of Jordan in 1951.[124]

Two internal factors, on the other hand, pushed tensions within Lebanese politics to the extreme. The first and main event was the assassination of Riāḍ al-Ṣulḥ by members of the SSNP in Jordan in July of 1951.[125] His killing was perceived by many Lebanese as an orchestrated act by Syrian officials who had been amicable to the SSNP, even more so after Za'īm's removal from power. The second, which also contributed to Khūrī's downfall, was the increasing power of his brother Salīm, whose 'sinister influence' kept growing and was becoming more and more representative of the corruption of Khūrī's regime.[126] The elections of 1951 were intended and perceived to be a significant improvement on the ones in 1947, due in no small part to the 'neutral' government – headed by Ḥussein al-'Uweynī and reduced to three technocratic ministers – installed by Khūrī in a bid to restore some credibility to his term. Another measure to appease the opposition was the enlargement of parliament from fifty-five to seventy-seven members, in order to allow for more diversity in members and opinions.[127] Despite the more positive image of the 1951 elections, the majority of the new parliament was still perceived to be pro-Khūrī and this continued the trend of having an extra-parliamentarian opposition.

Both the opposition and the government grew to be dissatisfied with Khūrī.[128] Such multifaceted opposition in the power-sharing system was only ever going to mean the end of his term. The government's displeasure with Khūrī was most highlighted a few days before his resignation, when Sāmī al-Ṣulḥ – who had regained the prime ministership – openly attacked Khūrī's interference and influence on government ministers and state corruption in general.[129] As Sāmī resigned during that same session, Khūrī scrambled to find a replacement but failed. He also received a letter calling for his resignation signed by opposition members of parliament and, sensing that he had lost the delicate balance of power on which he heavily relied, resigned on 18 September 1952.[130]

The sudden end of Khūrī's term, which was legally supposed to last until 1955, was hailed as a 'white revolution' by the opposition, specifically by Junblāṭ and Sham'ūn, who had together come to represent the struggle against old feudal and corrupt politics.[131] Many factors have been named as reasons for Khūrī's downfall, such as his rift with long-term partner Riāḍ al-Ṣulḥ, but it was ultimately his upsetting of the balance of different communal interests that led to the end of his tenure, especially when it resulted in the disenchantment of the Maronite and the Sunni communities – the main constituents of his support – and the increasing hope for reform among the opposition.[132] A few days later, on 22 September, Kamīl Sham'ūn was elected with seventy-four of seventy-six votes, and delivered a speech in which he proclaimed his goal to be the establishment of a peaceful and content Lebanon in which its 'one people' are not separated by confession, living within a unified country 'supported' by the National Pact.[133] The endurance of the Pact,[134] despite its failure in garnering either form of legitimacy for the state, was highly significant. Many have argued that its permanence remained in the interest of the Lebanese elites who could use clientelism to their advantage. Nevertheless, there was widespread and clear conviction that Lebanese state-building could only be successfully carried out *through* the Pact.

The persistence and survival of the Pact – without any changes – is not consistent with either approach to state-building. The societal approach points to the clear inconsistencies present therein, since the Pact wasn't nearly as representative and coherent as it needed to be: the Christian community continued to dominate politics through the presidency, while the idea of the state remained very much ambiguous. The institutional approach, on the other hand, points to the obvious obstacles that the Pact presents for effective state institutions: clientelism, corruption and an anti-meritocratic bureaucracy could hardly lead to effective distribution of resources, while the personal relations developed by elites served to maintain politics at the highest level in the hands of the few. Both approaches point to the need to change the Pact itself or alter the foundation for the state, yet the events of the 1950s would prove them both wrong, as the Pact continued to survive one crisis after another, unchanged.

So what *can* explain the survival of the Pact, and thus of the state? On the one hand, one can make an institutional argument by looking at the equation of power-sharing and the role of the Christians, particularly the Maronites, who held the main positions of power in the state: the presidency, the highest executive position; a majority in parliament, the highest legislative body; and the position of head of the army, the highest security authority. One example of the way those actors took actions to 'save' the state is Fu'ād Shehāb's refusal to have the army involved in the 1952 revolution, or his reluctance to take on the role of temporary prime minister which was reserved for a Sunni. Shehāb specifically cited the risk of national division as the reason for these reservations.[135] These positions, combined with the Maronites' enduring feeling of Lebanese particularism, meant that there was a much bigger will to compromise on the part of the Christians so as to maintain the existence of the state under the Pact: after all, the Pact still provided them with a country 'of their own', and it protected their authority within its state.

On the other hand, there is also a more societal argument to be made, particularly with regard to the other communities. While the state was not as representative as many of the Muslim communities would like it to be, it was still the case that the Pact elevated many of the Sunni leaders to positions of power (the biggest example being the prime ministership), positions that would not be as attainable otherwise (in a greater Syrian state, for example). This was especially effective through Khūrī's policy of appeasing elite Sunni families – the most popular and influential ones – by giving them ministerial posts. Furthermore, there were two other societal reasons which can explain the survival of the state, from the point of view of the Muslim communities, specifically the ones that lived in mixed-confession areas. The first one is more technical, and revolves around the electoral process. In those mixed areas where Christians were guaranteed seats, their candidates 'could not hope to be elected unless they had Muslim support'.[136] This gave Muslims in many regions an important 'veto' over Christian candidates to parliament. The second societal reason is the ability of the Pact to give the Lebanese Muslims space to argue for Arabism and to protect Lebanon's 'Arab face'. Those in legislative and executive power (like Riād al-Ṣulḥ) could have a significant impact on both the national dialogue and the actual degree of Lebanese participation in Arab matters. After all, despite historical threats to secede, many Muslims still recognized that an isolated, fully Western Lebanon would prove to be problematic for Arabist aspirations.

The combination of these elements created a strange phenomenon: the state was illegitimate, both institutionally and societally, yet was also protected, to an extent, on both fronts. This protection was enough to ensure the state's survival, at least for the first decade or so after its independence. One would be tempted, in light of this circumstance, to argue for *some* form of legitimacy for the Lebanese state. Yet the developments examined above show no conventional legitimacy of any kind. The extremely difficult and delicate balance that the Pact required for the state to exist meant that inaction as opposed to neutrality became the norm, since any action risked alienating a certain community and thus tipping the balance within and against the state. In fact, the only times action was taken were in protection of that balance itself, either in the example of the elections when the risk of incorporating the opposition into the state presented itself, or in the event of the physical attack on state institutions during the attempted coup of 1949. Thus, on an institutional level, the Lebanese state was effectively built to protect the source of its own weakness, and the Pact's main accomplishment was a minimum framework for state institutions to exist, but not one for them to become legitimate. On a societal level, the already-existent tendencies to refuse the idea of the state, espoused by the Pact, were only exacerbated through the constant disillusion of key members of the Lebanese communities. This was either due to the aforementioned state inaction, as was the case for the Arabists during the Arab–Israeli war, or because of self-preserving action, as was the case for reformists during the 1947 elections. In either case, the Pact failed to create a general and englobing framework for an idea with which the communities could recognize the state. Both action and inaction were perceived as unjust by some, while the image of neutrality which the Pact was built upon was never fully produced – or defined – to the satisfaction of Lebanese society as a whole.

As a result, neither state-building nor nation-building attempts were successful during Khūrī's term as president, though his personal efforts to use the Pact to ensure his own (and by extension the state's) survival set a precedent that would grip Lebanese politics for decades. Day to day, this meant continuous instability in the form of political crises and, in some cases, overt refusal to cooperate with the state. But the Pact itself survived and quickly became the most – if not the only – stable institution of the state, contradicting what either approach to state-building would expect. This survival flies in the face of conventional conceptions of legitimacy. Thus, the only resort if one is to accept that the state was neither legitimate nor *so* illegitimate to break down (not yet anyway) is a concept of 'negative legitimacy'. If legitimacy is the acceptance of the state's right to rule, the phenomenon in Lebanon could, at best, be described as: the toleration of the state's existence. That would be the Pact's main achievement: ensuring the Lebanese state's survival *despite* its illegitimacy.

Notes

1 See: *Taqī al-Dīn, al-Jalā': Wathā'iq Khatīra Tunsharu li-'Awal Marra* [The Evacuation: Important Documents Published for the First Time] (Beirut: Dār Beyrūt, 1956).

2 In fact, the French were trying to push for a treaty by using the removal of their troops as leverage and, through a patient strategy of mediation, the British supported them. Ironically, Khūrī and Ṣulḥ were also playing both sides against each other to achieve full independence. See Zisser, *Lebanon*, 88.

3 For the stances of the different communities towards the Pact, see: Bāsem Al-Rā'ī, *Mīthāq 1943: Tajadhur Al-Hawiya Al-Waṭaniya Al-Lubnāniya* [1943 Pact: Genesis of Lebanese National Identity] (Zouk Mosbeh: al-Markaz al-Mārūnī lil-Tawthīq wal-Abḥāth, 2009).

4 el-Solh, *Lebanon and Arabism*, 202–3.

5 Unlike previous elections which were marred by tampering on the part of the French, the 1943 elections were shown to be a 'healthy sign', and were in general a 'marked improvement' over earlier ones conducted during the mandate. Specifically, in the Mountain, the achievement of the British first minister to Syria and Lebanon Major General Spears's work was highlighted in impeding French intervention. So while results have to be taken with a grain of salt, the wins of Arab nationalists over French-sponsored lists in the north and south of the country can show that the results are able to serve as some sort of indicator for public opinion.
See: Central File: Decimal File 890E.00, Internal Affairs of States, Lebanon, Political Affairs, 15 March 1933–15 November 1943. Records of the Department of State Relating to Internal Affairs of Lebanon, 1930–44. U.S. National Archives. Archives Unbound. Web. http://go.galegroup.com.ezphost.dur.ac.uk/gdsc/i.do?&id=GALE%7CSC5111817027&v=2.1&u=duruni&it=r&p=GDSC&sw=w&viewtype=Manuscript. Accessed on 18 October 2018.

6 In fact, Ṣulḥ himself preferred an ideal cooperation with Eddeh as he was perceived to be the more popular of the two Maronite leaders and any unity between Arab nationalists and France's strongest Maronite ally would strike a much deeper blow to the mandatory power. See Sāmī Al-Ṣulḥ and Salīm Wakīm, *'Aḥtakim Ila Al-Tārīkh* [An Appeal to History] (Beirut: Dār al-Nahār, 1970), 61–2.

7 See Ḥassān Al-Ḥallāq, *Al-Tayārāt Al-Siyāsiya Fī Lubnān 1943–1952* [Political Currents in Lebanon 1943–1952] (Beirut: Ma'had al-'Inmā' al-'Arabi, 1982), 100. Also see Bishāra Khūrī, *Ḥaqā'iq Lubnāniyya, Al-Jiz' Al-Thānī* [Lebanese Truths, Part Two] (Beirut: 'Awrāq Lubnāniyya, 1961), 258.

8 For example, an Islamic Conference was convened on 20 September 1943, a day before the presidential elections, in which it was decided that Khūrī was the candidate to back. See Atiyah, 'The Attitude of the Lebanese Sunnis towards the State of Lebanon', 173.

9 Aḥmad Bayḍūn, *Riād Al-Ṣulḥ: Fī Zamānihi* [Riād Al-Ṣulḥ: In His Time] (Beirut: Dār al-Nahār, 2011), 182–3. Also see minutes of the Parliamentary session on 21 September 1943. Retrieved from: http://www.legallaw.ul.edu.lb/PeriodSessionLandingPage.aspx?TextID=16553. Accessed on 16 February 2019.

10 In the small Mountain constituency, Eddeh's list won seven out of eight seats. See: Central File: Decimal File 890E.00, Internal Affairs of States, Lebanon, Political Affairs, 25 August 1931–29 September 1939. Records of the Department of State Relating to Internal Affairs of Lebanon, 1930–44. U.S. National Archives. *Archives Unbound.* http://go.galegroup.com.ezphost.dur.ac.uk/gdsc/i.do?&id=GALE%7CSC5111816249&v=2.1&u=duruni&it=r&p=GDSC&sw=w&viewtype=Manuscript. Accessed on 26 September 2018.
In addition, the Maronite Patriarch himself called for voters to vote against any that called for Arab unity and even called for Khūrī to explain himself after the names of

many of his Bloc came up as signatories to a leaked document of an Arab Economic Pact. See Al-Ḥallāq, *Al-Tayārāt Al-Siyāsiya Fī Lubnān 1943–1952*, 317–18.

11 The internal split within the Maronite community was again highlighted in the by-election on 27 April 1944, held because of the death of a Maronite deputy, in which the pro-French Joseph Karam won. His swearing-in resulted in an incident of armed violence between French and Lebanese officer during which his supporters hoisted French flags as well as those of mandatory Lebanon – see Zisser, *Lebanon*, 109.

12 It was mostly through the intervention of Maronite leaders that Eddeh escaped more severe punishment, as many members of Khūrī's and the Muslims' camp desired to have him tried for treason. See Zisser, 105.

13 Those seats were respectively due to Eddeh's expulsion and his own elevation to the presidency.

14 Specifically, the talks united representatives from Egypt, Syria, the Kingdom of Transjordan, the Kingdom of Iraq, Saudi Arabia, Yemen and Lebanon – see Ahmad Tarabein, *Al-Waḥda Al-'Arabiyya Fī Tārīkh Al-Mashriq Al-Mou'āser 1800–1958* [Arab Unity in the Contemporary History of the Near East 1800–1958] (Damascus: University of Damascus, 1970), 425. Also see: Gomaa, *The Foundation of the League of Arab States: Wartime Diplomacy and Inter-Arab Politics, 1941 to 1945* (London: Longman, 1977).

15 The two Hashemite kings 'Abdallah and a very young Faisal II (grandson of Faisal I who ruled Syria for a brief period of time before the start of the French mandate) were respectively kings of Transjordan and Iraq by this point and the former had strived to unite the two kingdoms since the 1930s. Part of this overall ambition included the plan for a Syrian-Jordanian union under King 'Abdallah although he oscillated between the inclusion of Lebanon and Iraq, sometimes excluding one or both from his plans. See Pipes, *Greater Syria*, 74. Egypt, on the other hand, spearheaded by Prime Minister Mustafa al-Naḥās, had been the one to invite the different countries to participate in these talks regarding 'Arab unity', proclaiming himself personally concerned with the realization of 'Arab hopes for freedom and independence' – see 'Abd al-Ḥamīd Muhammad Al-Muwāfi, *Maṣr Fī Jāmi'at Al-Duwal Al-'Arabiyya: Dirāsa Fī Dawr Al-Dawla Al-Akbar Fī Al-Tanẓīmāt Al-'Iqlīmiyya 1945–1970* [Egypt within the League of Arab States: A Study in the Role of the Greatest State in Regional Oganisations 1945–1970] (Cairo: al-Hay'a al-Maṣriya al-'Āma lil-Kitāb, 1983), 80. He had also been the one to invite Khūrī along with then-Syrian prime minister Jamil Mardam for talks on Arab cooperation during the summer of 1943 – see Ḥamlāwi Jalāl Youssef, 'Musṭafa Al-Naḥas Basha Wa Dawrahu Fī Al-Ḥaraka Al-Waṭaniyya Al-Maṣriyya 1879–1952 [Mustafa Al-Naḥas Basha and His Role in the Egyptian National Movement 1879–1952]' [unpublished Masters thesis] (University of Biskra, 2017), 63. Also see Tarabein, *Al-Waḥda Al-'Arabiyya Fī Tārīkh Al-Mashriq Al-Mou'āser 1800–1958*, 434–5.

16 Ṣulḥ himself was a staunch Arabist during the mandate.

17 See Aḥmad Khalīl Maḥmūdī, *Lubnān Fī Jāmi'at Al-Duwal Al-'Arabiyya, 1945–1958* [Lebanon in the League of Arab States, 1945–1958] (Beirut: al-Markaz al-'Arabi lil-Abḥāth wal-Tawthīq, 1994), 60–2. The reason given by Ṣulḥ was more than indicative of the domestic situation in Lebanon: Ṣulḥ argued that pushing for Arab unity would endanger the Pact as well as the alliance that had been struck between the Constitutional Bloc and the Arab nationalists. That, combined with the ongoing external pressure to sign a treaty with France, made Ṣulḥ reluctant to commit to any federation or confederation in the name of his country.

18 One particular resolution discussed in Alexandria stating that 'in no case will the adoption of a foreign policy which may be prejudicial to the policy of the League or an individual member state be allowed' was accused of being too vague in an attempt to formulate a common Arab foreign policy. It caused an uproar when, on 5 February 1945, Kamīl Sham'ūn, then Lebanese minister plenipotentiary to Britain, declared that Lebanon would not recognize any privileged position for France, due to the commitments of the resolution. This provoked much unrest among Lebanist circles. See el-Solh, *Lebanon and Arabism*, 262. See: *Basic Documents of the League of Arab States*. The Arab Information Center. New York, 1955.

19 el-Solh, 227–8.

20 George Ḥanna, *Min Al-Iḥtilāl ... Ilā Al-Istiqlāl* [From Occupation ... to Independence] (Beirut: Matba'at Dār al-Funūn, 1946), 229–30.

21 The Patriarch was notorious for his reservation and hesitancy to enter into any pact that he perceived could endanger the Christian presence in Lebanon. He was always wary of Muslim schemes that he believed were made to 'erase' the Christians. See Ghāzī Ja'ja', *Al-Batriark Mār Anṭūn Butrus 'Arīḍa, 1863–1955* [The Patriarch Mār Antūn Butrus 'Arīḍa, 1863–1955] (Beirut: Dār Bshāriā lil-Nasher, 2006), 239.

22 'Abd el-Raḥman 'Azzām, who would become the first secretary general for the League of Arab States, had mentioned during the talks in Alexandria his belief that Arab culture was founded in Islam and even advocated for the Qur'an to form the constitution of the League, see Salāḥ Abu Jawdeh Al-Yasū'y, *Hawiyat Lubnān Al-Waṭaniya: Nash'atuhā Wa 'Ishkāliyātihā Al-Ṭā'ifiya* [Lebanese National Identity: Origin and Confessional Issues] (Beirut: Dār al-Mashriq, 2008), 80–1.

23 The argument made by the opposition was based on the fact that the 'Special Resolution Concerning Lebanon' in the Protocol was really one of recognition of the current government and not the Lebanese state, since the resolution called for respect of Lebanon's sovereignty in consequence of Lebanon's adoption of an independent policy, which the government of that country announced in its programme of 7 October 1943, unanimously approved by the Lebanese Chamber of Deputies. Other questions posed to the government included the extent of the League's internal influence on its individual members and the reason why the Saudi and the Yemeni delegations refused to sign the Protocol. See Maḥmūdī, *Lubnān Fī Jāmi'at Al-Duwal Al-'Arabiyya, 1945–1958*, 66. See: Arab Information Center, *Basic Documents of the League of Arab States* (New York: Arab Information Center, 1955).

24 el-Solh, *Lebanon and Arabism*, 251–3.

25 Khūrī, *Ḥaqā'iq Lubnāniyya, Al-Jiz' Al-Thānī*, 110.

26 See FO 406/82/43-65 (2) Eastern Affairs. Further Correspondence Parts LX–LXIII.

27 See previous chapter on political positions of Shī'a population and leaders.

28 See FO 406/82/43-65 (2) Eastern Affairs. Further Correspondence Parts LX–LXIII.

29 el-Solh, *Lebanon and Arabism*, 259.

30 el-Solh, 265.

31 For example, the Lebanese draft did not require a state to be 'Arab' in character in order for it to be eligible for League membership. While this step seems quite progressive, it is also arguably a great indicator of Lebanon's hesitance to accept a fully 'Arab' identity, seeing as this issue had neither actually come up previously nor been brought up again by any other member state. See Maḥmūdī, *Lubnān Fī Jāmi'at Al-Duwal Al-'Arabiyya, 1945–1958*, 69.

32 Maḥmūdī, 74.

33 The ratification of the eventual Charter for the League of Arab States would become the Lebanese state's first ever international document.

34 The election of Joseph Karam resulted in a clash between the French and Lebanese forces. See earlier footnote.

35 Maḥmūdī, 82.

36 For example, the constitution would be modified multiple times within the next few years, whereas the Pact would remain untouched and, in 1958, would be added into the swearing-in of Lebanese presidents.

37 This was very much achieved in conjunction with the Syrian government as both states claimed more and more institutions from the French such as the Common Interests and the Special Troops, which would become the fulcrum of the Lebanese army. The Lebanese government also had to deal directly with its Syrian counterpart on economic and trade issues. And finally, more and more states had started to recognize Lebanese independence and established diplomatic presence in the country. See: Chaitani, *Post-Colonial Syria and Lebanon*. Also see: FO 406/84/44-53 Eastern Affairs. Further Correspondence Parts LXIV-LXVII, pp. 80–3.

38 'Every time the Christians would get excited and ring their church bells, they were met by louder speakers on the mosques' – see George Ḥanna, *Al-'Aqda Al-Lubnāniyya* [The Lebanese Tangle] (Beirut: Dār al-'Elm lil-Malāyīn, 1957), 49. The end of the Second World War also sparked some tension, as many Christians proceeded to raise French flags on their balconies and cars, while proclaiming slogans of loyalty to France and De Gaulle – see Ḥanna, *Min Al-Iḥtilāl … Ilā Al-Istiqlāl* 233–4. Also see Al-Ḥallāq, *Al-Tayārāt Al-Siyāsiya Fī Lubnān 1943–1952*, 223–5.

39 Al-Ḥallāq, 193. Also see 'Omar Farrūkh, *Difā'an 'An Al-'Elem Difā'an 'an Al-Waṭan* [In Defence of Knowledge, in Defence of the Country] (Beirut: Beirut Arab University, 1977), 35–6. Farrūkh published his *Difā'an 'an Al-'Elem* in 1945 and followed it up with *Difā'an 'an al-Watan* in 1946. He criticized confessionalism and those who take advantage of it in both.

40 Both the Alexandria Protocol and the Charter for the League of Arab States included special texts on the Palestinian issue. Apart from the formal implications of these texts, the charter also put the Palestinian 'cause' firmly within the League's policy: it was clearly considered to be an Arab issue, and the Palestinian population to be an Arab one. Achieving independence and sovereignty for the Palestinians became part of the League's mission and it openly opposed Jewish migration into Palestinian territory, for example, the 'Annex Regarding Palestine' in the Charter allows for the League itself to 'take charge' of Palestinian representation within its framework. See 'Pact of the League of Arab States' and 'The Alexandria Protocol' in: Arab Information Center, *Basic Documents of the League of Arab States*.

41 See Charles Tilly, 'War Making and State Making as Organized Crime', in *Bringing the State Back In*, ed. Peter B. Evans, D. Rueschemeyer and T. Skocpol (Cambridge: Cambridge University Press, 1985), 169–91; and Charles Tilly, *Coercion, Capital, and European States, AD 990–1992* (Cambridge: Blackwell, 1990) Also see Anthony D. Smith, 'Nations before Nationalism? Myth and Symbolism in John Armstrong's Perspective', *Nations and Nationalism* 21, no. 1 (2015): 165–70.

42 See Akram Z'aytir, *Yawmīyāt Akram Z'aytir: Al-Ḥaraka Al-Waṭanīya Al-Filastīnīya, 1935–1939* [Diaries of Akram Z'aytir: The Palestinian National Movement, 1935–1939] (Beirut: Mu'assasat al-Dirāsāt al-Filastīnīya, 1980).
The evidence seems to point to a fluctuation of positions among Shī'a leaders with regard to the Jewish population, especially before the war when many of them had

established economic and trade relationships, including the sale of land to Jews – see Omri Nir, *Lebanese Shi'ite Leadership, 1920–1970s: Personalities, Alliances, and Feuds* (Cham: Palgrave Macmillan, 2017), 41.

43 Laura Zittrain Eisenberg, 'Desperate Diplomacy: The Zionist-Maronite Treaty of 1946', *Studies in Zionism* 13, no. 2 (1992): 148–9. Also, for Eddeh's positions, see: See: Bader Al-Ḥāj, *Al-Judhūr Al-Tārīkhiya Lil-Mashrū' Al-Ṣahyūnī Fī Lubnān* [Origins of the Zionist Project in Lebanon] (Beirut: Dār Muṣbāḥ al-Feker, 1982), 47.

44 Guy Bracha, '"The Germans Are Coming!": The Jewish Community of Beirut Facing the Question of Jewish Immigration from Germany', *Leo Baeck Institute Year Book* 61 (2016): 46–7.

45 See: FO 484/1 Correspondence Respecting Lebanon – part I.

46 At the time, Ben-Gurion was chairman of the Jewish Agency. He would later become Israel's first prime minister.

47 Laura Zittrain Eisenberg, *Lebanon in Early Zionist Imagination, 1900–1948* (Detroit, MI: Wayne State University Press, 1994), 10–11.

48 Any pro-Zionist activity from members of the Lebanese population was covert, and some was done from abroad. There were also reports in European newspapers about Lebanese smugglers having helped Jews out of Europe and into Palestine. See: Minutes of the Parliamentary session on 3 September 1945. Retrieved from: http://www.legallaw.ul.edu.lb/PeriodSessionLandingPage.aspx?TextID=16990. Accessed on 16 February 2019.

49 Eisenberg, 'Desperate Diplomacy', 159.

50 See *Beirut Archbishop Refutes Moslem Claims* in The Palestine Post. 21 March 1946. vol. 21, N° 6055. Mubārak's letter sparked a lot of reaction from all communities. Those who either agreed with or were indifferent to his views did not openly back him. He was seen as betraying the National Pact and the Palestinian issue was directly linked to Lebanese system itself: there is no doubt that being pro-Zionist was perceived as being both anti-Arab and anti-Muslim, as Mubārak was accused of being during the parliamentary session in September 1947. The Maronite deputies issued a statement in parliament refuting his letter as well as his position to speak in the name of his co-religionists. They declared him and those who agreed with him a 'pack of opportunistic deceivers' waging a war against Lebanese independence and internal cooperation. See minutes of the Parliamentary session on 29 September 1947. Retrieved from: http://www.legallaw.ul.edu.lb/PeriodSessionLandingPage.aspx?TextID=17822. Accessed on 16 February 2019.

51 Irene L. Gendzier, *Notes from the Minefield: United States Intervention in Lebanon and the Middle East* (New York: Columbia University Press, 2006), 59.

52 Avi Shlaim, 'Israeli Interference in Internal Arab Politics: The Case of Lebanon', in *The Politics of Arab Integration*, ed. Giacomo Luciani and Ghassan Salamé (New York: Croom Helm, 1988), 236. Eddeh did not believe the Christians were organized or united enough to succeed in such a coup. Also see Eugene L. Rogan and Avi Shlaim, eds, *The War for Palestine: Rewriting the History of 1948* (Cambridge: Cambridge University Press, 2007); Eyal Zisser, 'The Maronites, Lebanon and the State of Israel: Early Contacts', *Middle Eastern Studies* 31, no. 4 (1995): 889–918; Kristen E. Schulze, *Israel's Covert Diplomacy in Lebanon* (Basingstoke: Palgrave Macmillan, 1998); Benny Morris, 'Israel and the Lebanese Phalange: The Birth of a Relationship, 1948–1951', *Studies in Zionism* 5, no. 1 (1984): 125–44.

53 Khūrī was particularly proud of being one of the first leaders of the Arab world to speak publicly in 'defence of Palestine' and to argue for the differentiation between

Judaism and Zionism, when he gave a speech in Zgharta in Northern Lebanon in 1945 – see Khūrī, *Ḥaqā'iq Lubnāniyya, Al-Jiz' Al-Thānī*, 165–6.

54 Eisenberg, *Lebanon in Early Zionist Imagination, 1900–1948*, 123.

55 Matthew Hughes, 'Collusion across the Litani? Lebanon and the 1948 War', in *The War for Palestine: Rewriting the History of 1948*, ed. Eugene L. Rogan and Avi Shlaim (Cambridge: Cambridge University Press, 2007), 211.

56 See United Nations Archives. A/364/Add.2 PV.38. Official Records of the Second Session of the General Assembly. Supplement No. 11. 22 July 1947. https://unispal.un.org/DPA/DPR/unispal.nsf/c17b3a9d4bfb04c985257b28006e4ea6/15d51d0d80adc17f85256e9e006f0501?OpenDocument. Accessed on 12 February 2018.

57 Other than declaring war, two complementary laws were passed by parliament: one censoring the press with regard to Palestinian operations and the other adding a special tax in order to help the Palestinian cause. See: minutes of the Parliamentary session on 28 April 1948. Retrieved from: http://www.legallaw.ul.edu.lb/PeriodSessionLandingPage.aspx?TextID=18330. Accessed on 16 February 2019.

58 See Jāsem Muḥammad Al-Jabūrī, 'Mawqaf Lubnān Fī Jāmi'at Al-Duwal Al-'Arabiyya Min Al-Qadiya Al-Filastiniya [Lebanon's Position within the League of Arab States on the Palestinian Cause]', *Majallat Abḥāth Kulliyat Al-Tarbiya Al-Asāsiya* 6, no. 2 (2007): 76–106. Also see United Nations Archives. A/364/Add.2 PV.38. Official Records of the Second Session of the General Assembly. Supplement No. 11, 22 July 1947: https://unispal.un.org/DPA/DPR/unispal.nsf/c17b3a9d4bfb04c985257b28006e4ea6/15d51d0d80adc17f85256e9e006f0501?OpenDocument. Accessed on 12 February 2018.

59 Matthew Hughes, 'Lebanon's Armed Forces and the Arab-Israeli War, 1948–49', *Journal of Palestine Studies* 34, no. 2 (2005): 27–8.

60 R. D. McLaurin, 'Lebanon and Its Army: Past, Present, and Future', in *The Emergence of a New Lebanon: Fantasy or Reality?*, ed. Edward E. Azar (New York: Praeger, 1984), 84. Also see Hughes, 'Lebanon's Armed Forces and the Arab-Israeli War, 1948–49', 27–8; FO 484/3 Further correspondence respecting Lebanon – part 3.

61 Stéphane Malsagne, 'L'Armée Libanaise de 1945 à 1975: Du Socle National à l'Effritement [The Lebanese Army from 1945 to 1975: From National Bedrock to Disintegration]', *Vingtième Siècle. Revue d'histoire* 124 (2014): 22.

62 See Law issued on 21 January 1947 concerning the amendment of the constitution. Published in the Lebanese Official Gazette N° 5, 29 January 1947, 58. Retrieved from: http://www.legallaw.ul.edu.lb/Law.aspx?lawId=244752. Accessed on 16 February 2019.

63 See minutes of the Parliamentary session on 18 May 1946. Retrieved from: http://www.legallaw.ul.edu.lb/PeriodSessionLandingPage.aspx?TextID=17637. Accessed on 16 February 2019.

64 See Sāmī Al-Ṣulḥ, *Mudhakarāt Sāmī Bek Al-Ṣulḥ, Ṣafaḥāt Majīda Fī Tārīkh Lubnān* [Memoirs of Sāmī Bek Al-Ṣulḥ, Glorious Pages of Lebanese History] (Beirut: Maktabat al-Fikr al-'Arabi wa Maṭba'atihā, 1960), 142–3.

65 See *The Lebanese Official Gazette*, N°4074, 31 March 1943, 11011 http://www.legallaw.ul.edu.lb/SearchOfficialJournal.aspx. Accessed on 16 February 2019.

66 See minutes of the Parliamentary session on 17 June 1947. Retrieved from: http://www.legallaw.ul.edu.lb/PeriodSessionLandingPage.aspx?TextID=17771. Accessed on 16 February 2019.

67 See FO 484/1.

68 See FO 484/1. William Houstoun-Boswall was Envoy Extraordinary and Minister Plenipotentiary at Beirut from 1947 to 1951.
69 Per Article 77 of the Lebanese Constitution, a two-thirds majority is needed to revise the constitution. See *The Lebanese Constitution as Promulgated on May 23, 1926 with Its Amendments*. The Constitutional Council. Retrieved from: http://www.cc.gov.lb/en/constitution.
70 Bishāra Khūrī, *Ḥaqā'iq Lubnāniyya, Al-Jiz' Al-Thāleth* [Lebanese Truths, Part Three] (Beirut: 'Awrāq Lubnāniyya, 1961), 30–1.
71 See Report of the Appeals Committee on the General Elections of 1947 in: minutes of the Parliamentary session on 1 July 1947. Retrieved from: http://www.legallaw.ul.edu.lb/PeriodSessionLandingPage.aspx?TextID=17804. Accessed on 16 February 2019.
72 Known locally as 'Sultān Salīm' for his feudal-like social standing in Furn al-Shebbāk. He was widely believed to have used his brother's position to his advantage in order to aggressively gain authority in the Mountain. See Eyal Zisser, 'The Downfall of the Khuri Administration: A Dubious Revolution', *Middle Eastern Studies* 30, no. 3 (1994): 487.
73 Zisser, *Lebanon*, 135.
74 Zisser, 136.
75 The call for a Greater Syria was still very strong at this state, both internally through Antūn S'ādeh's Syrian Social Nationalist Party and externally through Hashemite claims. See FO 484/1.
76 See Georges Akl, Abdo Ouadat and Edouard Hunein, eds, *The Black Book of the Lebanese Elections of May 25, 1947 (An Account Translated from the Arabic Original)* (New York: Phoenicia Press, 1947).
77 See Akl, Ouadat and Hunein, 51.
78 See FO 484/1.
79 In Tripoli, the Sunni hub of the north, Karamī – an opposer to both Riāḍ and Khūrī – decided not to stand and paved the way for a pro-government victory while Ṣulḥ managed to get his name on both lists running against each other in the Shī'a south which also guaranteed pro-government support (Zisser, 2000), 129, 132.
80 Khūrī, *Ḥaqā'iq Lubnāniyya, Al-Jiz' Al-Thāleth*, 41.
81 Decree N° K/9147 as found in the Minutes of the Parliament Session on 9 June 1947. Retrieved from: http://www.legallaw.ul.edu.lb/PeriodSessionLandingPage.aspx?TextID=17748. Accessed on 16 February 2019.
82 Per Article 30 of the Lebanese Constitution, a two-thirds majority is needed to revise the constitution. See *The Lebanese Constitution as Promulgated on May 23, 1926 with Its Amendments*. The Constitutional Council. Retrieved from: http://www.cc.gov.lb/en/constitution.
83 See Minutes of the Parliamentary session on 8 July 1947. Retrieved from: http://www.legallaw.ul.edu.lb/PeriodSessionLandingPage.aspx?TextID=17827. Accessed on 16 February 2019.
84 Roschanack Shaery-Eisenlohr, *Shi'ite Lebanon: Transnational Religion and the Making of National Identities* (New York: Columbia University Press, 2008), xiii.
85 It was labelled 'the black elections' by some. See: Antūn Sarufīm, *Wazīfat Al-Intikhābāt Al-Niyābiya Fī Lubnān* [The Role of Parliamentary Elections in Lebanon] (Beirut: Dār al-Fārābī, 2015), 127.
86 Minutes of the Parliamentary session of 17 June 1947. Retrieved from: http://www.legallaw.ul.edu.lb/PeriodSessionLandingPage.aspx?TextID=17771. Accessed on 16 February 2019.

87 Yūsif Sālim, *50 Sana Min Al-Nās* [50 Years of People] (Beirut: Dār al-Nahār, 1998), 317.
88 FO 484/3.
89 Nir, *Lebanese Shi'ite Leadership, 1920–1970s*, 38–9. This policy towards the Shīʿa community was simply a continuation of the old Mandatory policy of the French, which they used in order to gain popular support for the existence of the Lebanese state.
90 Nir, 46–7. In some cases, the army would get involved in such quarrels. In December 1948, for example, 'the army was again heavily involved in ongoing battles with bandits in the Ras Baalbek area, where it performed badly, provoking an official inquiry into the defeat and deaths of army personnel'. See Hughes, 'Collusion across the Litani? Lebanon and the 1948 War', 208.
91 Khūrī, *Ḥaqā'iq Lubnāniyya, Al-Jiz' Al-Thāleth*, 122.
92 See John P. Entelis, 'Party Transformation in Lebanon: Al-Kata'ib as a Case Study', *Middle Eastern Studies* 9, no. 3 (1973): 325–40.
93 The number of schools itself nearly tripled between 1943 and 1947 (248 to 623), the number of students essentially doubled (22,844 to 52,422) and the number of teachers drastically increased (421 to 1,332) in that time. See N.a., *Lubnān Fī 'Ahd Al-Istiqlāl*, 76, a report presented at the Arab Conference for Culture in 1947.
94 See N.a., *Lubnān Fī 'Ahd Al-Istiqlāl*, 76, a report presented at the Arab Conference for Culture in 1947.
95 See minutes of the Parliamentary session on 22 May 1947. Retrieved from: http://www.legallaw.ul.edu.lb/PeriodSessionLandingPage.aspx?TextID=18279. Accessed on 16 February 2019. Also see: Temporary Constitutional Law Authorising the Re-election of the President of the Republic in Lebanese Official Gazette N° 21, 26 May 1948, 359. Retrieved from: http://www.legallaw.ul.edu.lb/Law.aspx?lawId=175059. Accessed on 16 February 2019.
96 See minutes of the Parliamentary session on 27 May 1947. Retrieved from: http://www.legallaw.ul.edu.lb/PeriodSessionLandingPage.aspx?TextID=18280. Accessed on 16 February 2019.
97 See minutes of the Parliamentary session on 3 August 1948. Retrieved from: http://www.legallaw.ul.edu.lb/PeriodSessionLandingPage.aspx?TextID=17973. Accessed on 16 February 2019.
98 Junblāṭ, *Rubʿ Qarn Min Al-Nidāl* [A Quarter-Century of Struggle] (al-Mukhtāra: Dār al-Taqadumiya, 1987), 110–11. Junblāṭ would go on to become the main Druze leader, forming his Progressive Socialist Party which opposed the Khūrī government as it saw in it the representation of the old feudal system – see Junblāṭ, 25.
99 See *al-'Amal* journal, vol. 124, 29 July 1944.
100 See *al-Nahār* newspaper, vol. 2842, 17 February 1944.
101 Zisser, *Lebanon*, 111.
102 FO 484/2.
103 FO 484/2.
104 Junblāṭ believed that confessionalism and traditional feudal loyalty were at the heart of corruption in the Lebanese state. After an incident in Zahle in 1947 where a peaceful protest escalated into an armed conflict that eventually resulted in the government asking the military to step in, the result was many casualties and a very bad hit on Ṣulḥ's cabinet's reputation. Junblāṭ delivered a speech in parliament where he went into detail on the individuals he believed were accountable both for the Zahle incident and state corruption in general: 'If we intend to build a state

then every man needs to be given certain responsibilities, and he should be held accountable and rewarded accordingly.'
See minutes of the Parliamentary session on 24 November 1947. Retrieved from: www.legallaw.ul.edu.lb/PeriodSessionLandingPage.aspx?SessionID=1696. Accessed on 16 February 2019.
Junblāṭ had seemingly lost all confidence in the new parliament, missing most chamber meetings and going so far as getting kicked out of one, then proclaiming that he would 'come back armed'.
See minutes of Parliamentary session on 25 November 1947. Retrieved from: http://www.legallaw.ul.edu.lb/PeriodSessionLandingPage.aspx?SessionID=1697. Accessed on 16 February 2019.

105 See minutes of the Parliamentary session on 25 September 1948. Retrieved from: http://www.legallaw.ul.edu.lb/PeriodSessionLandingPage.aspx?TextID=17783. Accessed on 16 February 2019.

106 Al-Ḥallāq, *Al-Tayārāt Al-Siyāsiya Fī Lubnān 1943–1952*, 249–50.

107 In July of 1948, an Economic Agreement between the two countries was also signed that set up a framework for amicable trade.
Additionally, a Financial Agreement was signed with France in August of that year which settled the last hurdles left over from the mandate. Syria refused to sign such an agreement with France and relations with Syria were threatened, much to the dismay of the Muslim community in Lebanon. See FO 484/3.

108 Specifically, relations were strong between Khūrī and al-Ṣulḥ on the one hand and Shukri al-Quwaytli and Jamīl Mardam on the other hand. The four cooperated extensively in their respective fights for independence and during the early years of the Arab League.

109 Philip K. Hitti, *Syria: A Short History* (New York: Macmillan, 1961), 252.
The main catalyst for the coup seems to have been the Palestine 'disaster' in which it was discovered that Mardam's government had virtually made no provisions for the war and as such lost all credibility among the public – see Chaitani, *Post-Colonial Syria and Lebanon*, 129.

110 Chaitani, 130–1.

111 He would even act to prevent Syrian citizens from spending their vacations in Lebanese resorts – see Chaitani, 133.

112 Zisser, *Lebanon*, 184.

113 On 3 July, it was believed that S'ādeh issued a resolution to his party members calling for them to consider themselves part of the 'Social Nationalist forces in Lebanon' and asking of them to 'obstruct all works and measures' taken by the current Lebanese regime. See Bayḍūn, *Riād Al-Ṣulḥ: Fī Zamānihi*, 379.

114 Za'īm remained elusive as to why he decided to deliver S'ādeh to the Lebanese state, denying any involvement publicly while internally blaming external pressures – see Nadhīr Fanṣa, *Ayām Ḥusni Al-Za'īm* [The Days of Ḥusni Al-Za'īm] (Beirut: Dār al-'Āfāq al-Jadīda, 1982), 77.

115 It was generally believed that S'ādeh was tried as much on his Syrian nationalism as his call for civil disobedience. One of the charges levied against him was cooperation with Israel, an accusation that was highly doubted as S'ādeh was an ardent anti-Zionist.

116 Junblāṭ was one of the most outspoken critics of S'ādeh's trial – see Al-Ḥallāq, *Al-Tayārāt Al-Siyāsiya Fī Lubnān 1943–1952*, 270.

Riāḍ later confessed that one of his biggest regrets was consenting to S'ādeh's death in order to 'satisfy' Khūrī – see Khāled Al-'Aẓem, *Mudhakarāt Khāled Al-'Aẓem, Al-Jeld Al-Thānī* [Khāled Al-'Azem's Memoirs, Volume Two] (Beirut: al-Dār al-Mutta7ida lil-Nasher, 1973), 42. Khūrī, on the other hand, distanced himself from the matter and implicitly placed S'ādeh's arrest and trial under Ṣulḥ's supervision – see Khūrī, *Ḥaqā'iq Lubnāniyya, Al-Jiz' Al-Thāleth*, 240–1.

117 FO 484/4.

118 FO 484/4.

119 In fact, Khūrī met with Riāḍ al-Ṣulḥ before the 1951 elections, convinced him to resign for political reasons (presumably to give off the image of neutrality for the elections) and presented a plan in which the next four prime ministers were already chosen, so that 'each Sunni [leader] can bear his part of ministerial responsibilities'. See Khūrī, 339–40.

120 Both the Prophet's birthday (which occurred on 22 December) and Christmas eve of 1950 were respectively characterized by demonstrations from members of the Muslim and Christian communities which involved gunfire and explosions. See FO 484/5. Khūrī believed the instigators on the Moslem part to be supporters of Riāḍ executing a show of strength and support for the latter as rumours grew of Khūrī's intention to appoint a new prime minister – see Khūrī, 340.

121 FO 484/5.

122 Tarabein, *Al-Waḥda Al-'Arabiyya Fī Tārīkh Al-Mashriq Al-Mou'āser 1800–1958*, 552–3.

123 Zisser, 'The Downfall of the Khuri Administration', 495.

124 George Britt, 'Lebanon's Popular Revolution', *Middle East Journal* 7, no. 1 (1953): 4.

125 Despite Ṣulḥ's efforts to relieve himself of any responsibility leading to S'ādeh's execution, which even involved reaching out to party members and offering compensatory measures, the SSNP always regarded Ṣulḥ's government as the ultimate conspirator in attacks on the party in general, including S'ādeh's death. See three following documents:

'Riyad al-Ṣulḥ and Reconciliation with the Parti Populaire Syrien', 1951, History and Public Policy Program Digital Archive, Emir Farid Chehab Collection, GB165-0384, Box 2, File 62F/2, Middle East Centre Archive, St Antony's College, Oxford, https://digitalarchive.wilsoncenter.org/document/176602.

'Internal Party Declaration', 5 September 1954, History and Public Policy Program Digital Archive, Emir Farid Chehab Collection, GB165-0384, Box 2, File 25F/2, Middle East Centre Archive, St Antony's College, Oxford, https://digitalarchive.wilsoncenter.org/document/176558.

'Plan to Assassinate Officials', 8 March 1954, History and Public Policy Program Digital Archive, Emir Farid Chehab Collection, GB165-0384, Box 2, File 18F/2, Middle East Centre Archive, St Antony's College, Oxford, https://digitalarchive.wilsoncenter.org/document/176554.

126 FO 484/6.

127 See Law issued on 10 August 1950 concerning the election of members of parliament. Published in the Lebanese Official Gazette N° 33, 16 August 1950, pp. 523–39.

The ratio of Muslims to Christians within parliament was kept at 5:6.

128 As did the general public, and the British media. Specifically, *The Economist* heavily critiqued the 1951 elections and portrayed Khūrī as a dictator.

See 'The Lebanon Follows the Fashion'. *Economist*, 4 October 1952, p. 38. *The Economist Historical Archive*. Accessed on 28 February 2019.
Also see A. Lebanese. 'Lebanon at the Polls'. *Economist*, 9 June 1951, p. 1369. *The Economist Historical Archive*. Accessed on 3 February 2019.

129 Minutes 9 September 1952 http://www.legallaw.ul.edu.lb/PeriodSessionLandingPage.aspx?TextID=19420. Accessed on 16 February 2019.

130 Interestingly, Khūrī appointed the commander of the army Fu'ād Shehāb as interim prime minister until the next presidency, believing in his ability to maintain order and neutrality. The latter, known for his distaste for politics (though he would ironically later become president), immediately rid himself of the post when the next president was elected a few days later.
See Stéphane Malsagne, *Fouad Chéhab, 1902–1973: Une Figure Oubliée de l'histoire Libanaise* [Fu'ād Shehāb, 1902–1973: A Forgotten Figure of Lebanese History] (Paris: Karthala, 2011), 141–4.

131 'Abed al-Raḥman Maḥmūd Al-Ḥoṣ, *Lubnān Fī 'Ahd Al-Ra'īs Kamīl Sham'ūn* [Lebanon under President Kamīl Sham'ūn]. (Beirut: Maṭba'at al-Hilāl, 1953), 7.
See Junblāṭ, *Rubʿ Qarn Min Al-Niḍāl*, 166–7.

132 Zisser, 'The Downfall of the Khuri Administration', 498.

133 See minutes of the Parliamentary session on 23 September 1952. Retrieved from: http://www.legallaw.ul.edu.lb/PeriodSessionLandingPage.aspx?TextID=19421. Accessed on 16 February 2019.

134 Which did not represent the wishes of all the members of the opposition, especially the anti-Pact Junblāṭ.

135 His decisions during the 1952 crisis were explicitly commended by Khūrī himself (despite his slight disappointment in the outcome) and by the opposition – specifically the Sunni leaders. See Khūrī, *Ḥaqā'iq Lubnāniyya, Al-Jiz' Al-Thāleth*, 476. Also see Al-Ḥallāq, *Tārīkh Lubnān Al-Mou'āṣir 1913–1952*, 429, 452.

136 Rondot, 'Lebanese Institutions and Arab Nationalism', 44.

Chapter 4

THE FIRST SIGNS OF DISINTEGRATION

The early years of Lebanese independence were marked by institutional corruption, inefficiency and political manipulation. Equally, the lack of social cohesion was evident; while a majority of the different communities had been able to come together to put an end to the French mandate, it proved much more difficult to achieve such national unity with regard to issues of internal distribution of resources, matters of foreign policy and degrees of autonomy within and between the different confessions.

The National Pact of 1943, aimed at ensuring representativeness, had proved insufficient in increasing the institutional strength of the state and in satisfying the pre-existing political aspirations of the different Lebanese communities. In this sense, both the state-building and nation-building potential of the National Pact had clearly not been reached. Internal instability unsurprisingly followed: sectarian clashes, clandestine actions, attempted coups and widespread abuse of power were ubiquitous during the time of Khūrī's term and were especially apparent during certain key events of that period. And yet, for most political leaders, the Pact itself was not perceived to be the problem at the time, as blame was laid on Khūrī's doorstep and he was forced to resign not soon after.

The regime, as opposed to the state, was held accountable for the instability that had got in the way of development, and its removal was seen by its opponents as a peaceful revolution. Nevertheless, other than the removal of the president from office, no other characteristic of the Lebanese state was modified by the time of Khūrī's resignation. Still, much of the hope was placed on his successor, Kamīl Sham'ūn, to undergo reforms to the political bureaucracy and ultimately modernize state institutions, in an attempt to eradicate corruption. On a societal level, the Pact was still expected to gradually develop a sense of belonging to an overarching Lebanese identity that would cut across all the communities. A neutral Lebanon with an 'Arab face' but a close relationship with the West was still expected to be projected, both inwardly and outwardly, but whether or not such neutrality would be possible to maintain in the face of growing antagonism between the West and the Arab leader, Jamāl 'Abd al-Nāṣer, would prove to be key.

The objective of this chapter is to analyse the state-building efforts during Sham'ūn's presidential terms, to look at their effects and shortcomings, and establish why Lebanese state-building during the 1950s cannot be examined through the existing theories. The first section of the chapter will therefore focus on state-building endeavours, both institutional and societal, under Sham'ūn's early term. By doing so, the chapter will uncover further evidence that the Pact itself, and not a specific regime, remained at the heart of the illegitimacy of the Lebanese state, despite its representativeness and the steady support it received from Lebanese communities. Thus, as the necessity of the Pact became further entrenched into the Lebanese political system, its ability to bestow the state with both societal legitimacy and institutional legitimacy remained deficient. The second part of this chapter will move on to look at the specific events linking Lebanese state-building to the crisis of 1958. It will be shown that, as instability and sectarian tensions endured, the conflict of 1958 became a direct result of political illegitimacy. Finally, the effects of the crisis on the state itself will also be touched upon.

Legitimacy under Sham'ūn

After spearheading the 'White Revolution' against the Khūrī regime in 1952, Sham'ūn was expected by his co-revolutionaries to provide an unimpeded path towards reform. Many optimistic politics envisioned him going so far as to remove confessionalism from the state; they would be disappointed, however. The following will look at the institutional and societal state-building endeavours that occurred under Sham'ūn's term, and assess their performances against some of the theoretical literature.

Institutional state-building under Sham'ūn

Considering himself a more pragmatic politician, however, Sham'ūn assembled a first government which did not meet the standards of the reformists (who had expected members of the opposition to form most if not all of the ministerial cabinet), and he reamended the electoral law to reduce the number of deputies to forty-four (even lower than it was under Khūrī[1]). This reduction coupled with a lower barrier of entry (the new law decreased the fee for candidacy), and the implication that a Senate would be established in the near future, was argued to be in the aim of diminishing political feudalism. In fact, the number of electoral districts was increased from nine to thirty-three, with twenty-two of those districts containing just one seat up for grabs.[2]

Sham'ūn also executed other administrative reforms early on during his term, and while the first government that was assembled was not to the liking of members of the opposition, it was purposefully made up of non-parliamentarians whose main task was to enforce the new electoral law which was seen as a fundamental step towards improvement. On the other hand, his organizational reforms were mostly based on recommendations by a number of workers within the respective ministries and public sectors, and were rooted in personal experiences. Even when specific – mostly foreign – experts were contracted to study developmental needs and give suggestions, they were virtually ignored.[3]

Economic growth and the policy of inactivity Sham'ūn's early changes – and the obstacles they faced – have been argued by many[4] to have been failed attempts at modernization. For Sham'ūn, there was no question as to the nature of his reforms: he embarked upon a modernizing state-building programme which was intended to strip power from the traditional and feudal leaders while accelerating economic growth through increased liberalism, which meant minimal state intervention.[5]

The figures show that this policy was successful in achieving general growth,[6] though how much of it was an actual policy is still debatable: the term 'policy' itself might be somewhat inapplicable since it was just as much 'what wasn't done' as 'what was done' that shaped Lebanon's economic development at the time.[7] Additionally, there is enough evidence that Sham'ūn's economic 'non-policies' were pushed for by those in the commercial and financial sector, especially once discussions over a customs union with Syria had tapered off. It was argued then that Lebanon's only manageable economy would have to centre around low tariffs and a free flow of capital. Henri Far'ūn, who was so influential during the Khūrī regime, and who 'has [*sic*] long represented Lebanon's community of high finance', was a perfect example of those who argued for 'a politics of inactivity'.[8] For those like Far'ūn, the role of Lebanese politics was severely restricted to confessional balance as the equilibrium between the different communities and their interests was too fragile for the state to risk embarking upon real reform and development.[9]

On the other hand, the lack of state interference allowed many of the more influential members of the society, who were usually either those with pre-existing feudal influence or those owning the means of production, to abuse the economic system. One example of such loopholes taken was the employment of Syrian or Palestinian immigrants for much cheaper wages; that coupled with the lower rate of growth in the industrial and the agricultural sector meant that rural unemployment began to rise, though the ability of employment figures to reflect the reality at the time has been contested.[10] While most of the members in this growing commercial class were Christians, the Sunni bourgeoisie – specifically in Beirut – also managed to expand their political influence at the expense of traditional families. The amount to which the state disassociated itself from the economy was highlighted in 1959, when a poll asked '170 persons, primarily Beirutees [*sic*], from the middle and upper income brackets' what they believed was the main reason for poor standards of living in the Middle East.[11] Of the responses given, 'irresponsible and corrupt governments' and 'underdeveloped economic institutions' formed a combined 52.5 per cent of the answers, unlike 'low levels of social consciousness', the second-most popular answer which fell at 30.9 per cent.[12]

Still, most of the Sunni middle class, especially those in the periphery, continued to regard the Lebanese state as 'a Christian institution controlled by a Maronite Catholic President'.[13] This was largely due to two main factors: firstly, the belief among the Muslims that since the last census of 1932, the Muslim population had overwhelmingly outgrown their Christian counterparts but were still under-represented in the legislative institutions. Secondly, the perception that the policy of inactivity under Shamʿūn mainly benefited educated Christian businessmen with historical ties to Western capital, who were mostly looking for short-term money-making endeavours at the expense of long-term benefits for the lower uneducated classes, who were for the most part Muslims, specifically from the periphery (i.e. in those areas annexed during the creation of Greater Lebanon).[14] Even when state policy did benefit Sunnis in Beirut, the outer rural and agricultural areas – and even Sunni-dominated Tripoli – were left without any benefits from this flow of capital as most of it was siphoned through the capital, which remained the focal point of the general economic boom.[15]

While economic growth was certainly associated with growing political modernization and did lead to short-term stability (in terms of sectarian tensions), the underlying issues raised by many in the (mostly) Muslim communities were ignored, and the crisis of 1958 showed that the Shamʿūn regime only succeeded in papering over the cracks for a short period of time. Its failure in effective institutional state-building is based on two main factors: the inability of governments to agree on strong policies due to confessional and traditional differences, and the subsequent choice of Shamʿūn to remain inactive and ignore the confessional nuances of Lebanese society, believing that economic growth would pave the way for national reconciliation. If one were inclined to remove Shamʿūn's personal ambitions aside, the ultimate Shamʿūnist goal can be described as follows: previous loyalties to feudal and traditional leaders would transition to individualism and the progression of a bourgeois middle class would replace communal leadership with power being based on intellectual and business acumen. In the meantime, politics would be reduced to Farʿūn's vision of a minimal stratum the primary function of which is making sure that transition goes smoothly while fading traditional leaders are preoccupied with petty political squabbles. State institutions would also gain more strength through bureaucratic reforms and the diminishing influence of corrupt tribalism. In the context of the Cold War, such economic state-building was only encouraged by Western powers whose pre-existing relations with Beirut drove them to shape it as the liberal outpost of the Middle East in the face of Nasserism and communism.

Public administration While economic organization is a central part of the institutional approach to state-building, there is an equally important organizational element which must also be taken into consideration.

Despite early administrative reforms by Shamʿūn, the Lebanese state continued to be plagued by ineffectiveness. Institutional strength was as absent as ever, especially in the executive and security branches, as described by the British ambassador at the time: there is 'no civil service worthy of the name, and no effective police force'.[16] In 1952, Shamʿūn issued legislative decrees establishing educational prerequisites and competitive examinations for several civil service positions.[17] Those examinations applied to all applicants for civil service positions, and were meant to ensure a selection process whereby the most qualified applicants were selected for public jobs. However, due to the growing pressure for confessional representation within these positions, the selective exams had to be scrapped.[18]

In particular, representation was threatened since a majority of the well-educated, well-informed and well-connected applicants were from the Christian community, or from the middle-class Sunni community in Beirut. Hence, the replacement was a pass/fail exam that simply allowed the applicant to be considered for specific posts. Once the exam was passed, an 'examining committee' from within the ministry was mandated to select the best candidates while ensuring, *at the same time*, proportional confessional representation.[19] That committee was directly appointed by the relevant minister.[20]

In the confessional context of Lebanon, this system of recruitment presents immediate and obvious drawbacks that show how confessionalism and the Pact can operate in direct contradiction with institutional strength. This contradiction would manifest itself as follows: in every government formed under Sham'ūn, the Pact dictated that there be a certain amount of representation guaranteed for each community in the form of ministerial appointments. In some cases, the *type* of minister is also guaranteed to be of a certain confession.[21] Thus, the competition for these posts moves from inter-confession to intra-confession, with factions on the sub-confessional level competing for who can 'best represent' their community on the governmental level. Instead of official elections, unofficial political influence is what guarantees accession to these positions, in a system not dissimilar to an electoral 'first past the post' one. Thus, governmental 'input' remains sectarian, in that the competition of who 'best represents' each sect remains purely the business of that sect.[22] Meanwhile, ministers are expected to act on a national level, thus dictating that governmental 'output' remain on the national scale. As a result, promises to act nationally become somewhat irrelevant for communities that are looking for their own betterment. The best way, then, to compete for political influence is by promising future favours and growing the social base of one's clientele within their own community since, unlike actual elections, a 'candidate' cannot promise to execute official policies that benefit only their community.[23] To that end, actual employment in the civil service became one of the biggest favours a politician can offer to his clientele, and the system of 1955 allowed each minister to have direct involvement in the recruitment process. As a result, within each sect, whoever wins political influence and the ministerial position will then decide which members of *their* community can be employed within that ministry. Additionally, they could also offer similar favours for members of other communities where they are trying to gain favour with their leaders.

Vicious circles such as the one outlined above highlight more ways in which the state gets in its own way, since, in its mission to ensure full representativeness (and therefore legitimacy), it sacrifices institutional strength and embeds sectarian cleavages. Coincidentally, in an attempt to ensure an accurate representation of confessions, and with the pressure on politicians to continue to ensure employment for their clientele, the number of civil servants continued to increase on an unprecedented scale, growing to more than 11,000 in 1954 (from about 3,000 in 1933). In contrast to that growth of over 260 per cent, the number of Syrian civil service employees had grown by about 125 per cent.[24] In France, on the other hand, the number of civil service employees grew by 43 per cent between

1936 and 1946.[25] Both Syria and France were somewhat centralized states, neither of which involved any confessional or power-sharing system. Yet, it was Lebanon that was centralizing at an accelerated rate, while not improving its institutional performance. Such an increase in size would preferably, from an institutionalist perspective, correspond with an increase of functional scope as per Fukuyama's theory of state-building, except that the state, as shown above, had embarked on a policy of non-interference, and 'its attention and efforts [had] been limited to enforcing the law in the narrowest sense'. It thus came as no surprise that Louis Roché, appointed French ambassador to Lebanon in 1956, declared the following about the state: '[its] depth is but an illusion'.[26] And as a result of this hollow make-up, 'official channels [were] avoided unless no other avenues are open'.[27]

For institutionalists like Fukuyama, the explanation is simple enough: clientelism and 'neopatrimonial' networks are 'often threatened' by a modern, Weberian-style bureaucracy. Thus, it is unsurprising to find the Lebanese state in the position where both its scope and its strength were narrow and weak respectively, while confessional politics remained strong and formed the basis for institutional flaws. One can infer that an institutionalist solution would be the eradication of the confessionalist system through the supply of a different set of institutions, and the evolution of societal relations from pre-modern and feudalistic to interest-based, modern social groups (e.g. Western-style political parties). Fukuyama argues, however, that such profound institutional changes rarely occur without 'a crisis of one sort or another', since states are more likely to remain bound by path dependencies.[28] Thus, the crisis of 1958, itself driven by calls for profound change, can serve as an indicator to the extent that the Lebanese (or a significant portion among them) were ready to rid the state of confessionalism. On the other hand, Fukuyama also allows for a *demand* for modern institutions (i.e. the removal of confessionalism) as 'the product of crisis or extraordinary circumstances that create no more than a brief window for reform'.[29] On this, the 1958 crisis will also shed light.

Societal state-building under Sham'ūn

It has been made clear how, institutionally, the Pact hindered the state in its objective to reach adequate institutional strength, and burdened by the need to ensure proportional distribution, the state's administrative reforms were insufficient in attaining widespread belief in its institutional legitimacy. The question remains whether or not the state achieved political legitimacy on the societal level, through forms of representative state-building and parallel nation-building that aim to achieve a sense of national unity. The following will look at the effects of Sham'ūn's policies in these two areas.

A representative state Sham'ūn's term started with much optimism among the 'revolutionaries' since supporters of reform viewed his election as the first step towards altering an archaic, weak and divisive Lebanese state. By removing feudal and traditional loyalties, there was hope that the Lebanese communities could rally around the new political identity of the state. This feeling was only augmented by Sham'ūn's popularity not only internally but also abroad.[30]

One argument for making the state more representative was the abolishment of confessionalism itself. For Junblāṭ, Sham'ūn's main accomplice in the revolution and by this point the most influential Druze leader, reform started with the removal of traditional feudal leaders and the ultimate goal of abolishing confessionalism within the Lebanese state. There was no question for Junblāṭ that the National Pact was simply not a 'sufficient basis for a state',[31] since he viewed it as nothing more than a remnant of the old feudal system which has its roots in the backward days of the Ottoman Empire. This tradition of confessionalism now stood in the way of modernization and individual emancipation as well as state effectiveness – in other words, he saw in the National Pact an insufficient attempt at state-building.[32] Nevertheless, Junblāṭ's aspirations were seen by many as too ambitious in such a short time scale: it was better for change to come gradually.

Two days before Sham'ūn's elections, on 21 September, the main opposition group[33] had met and decided on a number of reforms that the new president would undertake. These reforms included the abolition of feudalistic elements within the state, the amendment of the election laws and the dissolution of parliament (which was to be re-elected), and a new role for the president which limited his interference in governmental affairs and his personal relations with ministers; it was claimed that Junblāṭ, Pierre Eddeh and Sham'ūn were among the signatories of this document.[34] The latter, however, did not feel as bound by this document by the time he became president, and while he affected some reforms (as shown above), they were much more incremental and nowhere near as drastic as the more radical oppositionists desired.

Junblāṭ wasn't the first nor the last that would publicly argue for the abolition of confessionalism, however. But how real was this demand? It has been noted in earlier chapters how, many times prior to Sham'ūn's term, the issue of power-sharing came up in parliament and any possible change failed to gain the necessary traction: despite the rhetoric from politicians for the need to move on from confessional loyalties, there was simply not enough will – nor personal benefit for many of them – to effect any change.[35] In fact, the argument for a state 'for all Lebanese' became a recurrent rhetoric from most members in the political sphere in the 1950s, and 'overt confessionalism' was 'definitely frowned upon'. Yet, 'when opportunities for the abolition of confessionalism [were] presented, they [were] approached, sampled, but rejected as too precipitous'.[36] Few actors were ready to discard the advantages presented to them by confessionalism, while others were still deeply concerned for the threats that secularism could pose to the socio-cultural rights of Lebanese communities. Even Junblāṭ, who remained the strongest opponent to confessionalism, remained exclusively supported only by his Druze community and there was no guarantee of his political ascendancy if confessionalism was abolished. Meanwhile, other progressivists also judged Lebanese society to have been unready for such an immediate and drastic change to their political system. Hence, the Lebanese were clearly unwilling to forego confessional loyalty yet.

Instead, Sham'ūn tried to conduct reforms which would make the state more representative *within* the confessional system itself, while also attempting to rid public institutions from the influence of feudalistic elements. After setting up a new government, Sham'ūn dissolved parliament only a few months later and announced new elections scheduled for July 1953 complemented by the new electoral laws that were designed to be more inclusive.[37] Those elections, however, were marked by claims of government involvement and general corruption, especially by deputies like Kamāl Junblāṭ, Kāmil al-As'ad and Ghassān Tuweynī who blamed Sham'ūn himself.[38] The subsequent chamber was a mixture of old and new faces, containing nineteen deputies out of forty-four that retained their places, a few others that only replaced family members and a dozen or so truly new voices. By the time the elections came around, however, Sham'ūn had already reshuffled the government, and it was becoming too obvious that he was struggling to achieve balance between his commitments to reform and the political 'game' by which Pact-sponsored confessionalism had bound his predecessor. Subsequently, his new cabinet (and subsequent ones) would be headed by familiar faces (e.g. former prime ministers Ṣā'ib Salām,[39] Sāmī al-Ṣulḥ and 'Abdallah al-Yāfi), yet also included members of opposition parties such as the Phalanges or the National Bloc. This internal mixture of contradictory views, however, served to paralyse those governments, and often forced Sham'ūn to reshuffle cabinet positions time and again, just as Khūrī was compelled to do: in the first three years of Sham'ūn's term, he formed five governments which remained paralysed by internal contradictions.[40]

Because of the state's lack of solidarity, sub-state political and traditional leaders stepped in to fill the void, convinced that the state was not representative of their communities' demands. In 1953, a pamphlet with the title of *Moslem Lebanon Today* was published by a group claiming to represent a large section of Lebanese Muslims, and included the following: firstly, the demand for 'confessional redistribution of resources'; and secondly, accusations of 'false Christian majorities' and presidential corruption.[41] Similarly, in 1954, a 'congress representing "Muslim parties, associations and organizations"' issued a letter to the government demanding a general census, an 'equitable' distribution of public jobs, financial decentralization and an 'immediate implementation of the plan of economic union between Syria and Lebanon'.[42] And yet, unfairness within the state was not an accusation exclusive to the under-represented Muslim community. In the same year, Pierre Jumayyil, leader of the Phalanges, issued a statement in which he proceeded to claim: 'If the law is to be applied equally as required by individual rights, then the Christians must not pay 80% of taxes while others pay 20%. And if the distribution of treasury funds is to be revised, then let it [the money] not go to certain confessions while denying others.'[43] He would also respond to the demand for an updated census, by insisting on the inclusion of Lebanese immigrants (which, historically, had been mostly Christian).

Nation-building On the other hand, as was explained in earlier chapters, the Pact itself necessitated a certain degree of nation-building. This is not uncharacteristic of a state-building project that clearly falls within the societal approach through its insistence on power-sharing. As such, the 'idea of the state' had to be, as Migdal put it, naturalized, and a Lebanese identity had to be permeated in parallel to the creation of representative institutions. The Christians, holding both the highest executive position (i.e. the presidency) and the highest cultural and influential positions (due to their historically higher socio-economic standing) put them in a position to continue the expansion of their Lebanist ideas through both public and private institutions.

During this time, debates – both implicit and explicit – over what it means to be Lebanese had not diminished. In particular, Phoenicianism as a literary and cultural movement remained strong in many Christian intellectual circles. Christian writers and cultural figures like Charles Corm, Michel Shīḥa and Saīd 'Akl continued to argue for pre-Arab roots for the Lebanese identity, emphasizing ancient Phoenician hegemony over the Mediterranean coast while also engendering a geographical link between the Mountain and the Lebanese people. Corm had already begun to do this since the early years of Greater Lebanon, and was very much a Lebanist in the days before 1943.[44] But once the Pact was in place, Phoenicianism shifted from the political stratum to the cultural one: writers now argued that it is precisely *because* of its Phoenician legacy that Lebanon can only have an Arab 'face', retaining a special character within the Arab world that prevents it from fully integrating with the rest of the 'body'. At the time, this reservation manifested itself in the saying: 'There are no camels in Lebanon.'[45]

As time went on, however, Phoenicianism came to mean different things. Shīḥa, for example, has been labelled a Mediterraneanist as opposed to a Phoenicianist. While he was in no small way affiliated with Corm's early ideas, Shīḥa developed his own interpretation of Lebanese national identity. Though geography obviously played its part in Shīḥa's thought, inhabiting the eastern Mediterranean also implied a type of mentality for the Lebanese: it meant an open exchange of cultures, ideas and, most importantly, trade.[46] Both Phoenicianism and Mediterraneanism faced opposition from many writers from different communities, such as various Christian Orthodox thinkers that were affiliated with Syrianism and S'ādeh's thought, but mostly from Arabists that were in majority Muslim. One of the best examples of this opposition was Muḥammad Jamīl Bayhum's, who in 1957 criticized Lebanese *Shu'ūbiyat* for their 'fabricated' links to ancient Phoenicia, which in his opinion were born through foreign influence in the nineteenth century and encouraged by the French authorities during the mandate.[47]

Nevertheless, Shīḥa's particular perception of Lebanon as a Mediterranean, merchant republic where capital can flow as freely as thought resonated both with Sham'ūn's thought and his policies (in no small part because of their close personal relation[48]). His perspective – and that of similar-minded, middle-class Lebanese merchants – was by far the most influential on the state, as his economic prowess gave him an exceptionally influential social standing.[49] An example of those cultural policies is the state-organized Baalbeck International Festival which occurred yearly after its foundation in 1955. In addition to the city's classical heritage, the festival itself was held in and around the temples of

Baachus and Jupiter, and the performances thereof openly emphasized Lebanon's historical lineage as envisaged by advocates like Shīḥa.[50] As Christopher Stone put it, for those involved in the festival, 'their Lebanon boasted not only of a glorious past, but also of a past that was very much connected, through its folklore, to its present'.[51] Additionally, the state itself used imagery to promote these links between Lebanon and Phoenicia, one example being the Phoenician ship minted on the '10 Piastres' coin in 1955.[52]

These forms of state-sponsored nation-building were placed in stark contrast to their Arab-centric counterparts in neighbouring states. In Egypt, for example, the Nāṣer regime strived to reinforce the belief in Arab nationalism through various methods such as school curricula and even through state influence on the film industry, the press and Egyptian historiography.[53] Even the country's flag showed a great disparity between Lebanese and Arab nation-building: while Lebanon's flag retained the cedar tree at its centre, the surrounding countries of Syria, Jordan and Egypt all adopted a combination of the pan-Arab colours of red, green, black and white.[54] Lebanese insistence on particularism within and through state symbols and celebrations only continued to alienate Arab-identifying Muslims and strengthened the perception of a Christian state, despite the Pact's insurance of representation within public institutions.

Non-governmental organizations With the state's nation-building efforts being overtly one-sided and therefore potentially problematic, one would be forced to look in non-state sectors to discover if more promising nation-building endeavours existed.

One of these sectors which would prove useful to study is education. According to the Lebanese constitution, the different communities retained their rights to 'have their own schools provided they follow the general rules issued by the state regulating public instruction'.[55] These provisions naturally hindered the prospects of national uniformity with regard to education, something which could strengthen inter-communal ties. Accordingly, over 60 per cent of students still attended private education organizations throughout the 1950s.[56]

Despite making the Arabic language compulsory for private schools in 1950,[57] most Christian schools continued to teach the majority of their material in French (or English) while using foreign textbooks.[58] And while, according to the law of 1950, schools had to stick to state-issued material on Lebanese history, geography and civic education, they were given the freedom to add to this curriculum, teach complementary foreign history and geography, and even issue their own certificates. As a result, private schools indirectly reinforced sectarian differences as students from different communities went through what was virtually a contradistinctive educational formation.[59] Additionally, since most private schools were rooted in religious history (e.g. Christian schools set up by missionaries in the eighteenth century), they also taught religious studies that were exclusive to that community.[60] Subsequently, sectarian divisions continued to subsist throughout other non-governmental organizations which often find their roots in school environments. These include the Boy Scouts which were also divided along sectarian lines, and the Red Cross that operated as a distinct Red Crescent in Muslim regions.[61]

These differences were also linked to another cultural debate within Lebanon over the possibility of bilingualism. After the end of the mandate, the updated Lebanese Constitution removed French as an official language, but its spread among the Christian community had already been extensive. Thus, it remained taught in many educational establishments. Since the Pact itself officially linked politics and communal culture, attacks were levied by many in the Muslim community (and some in the Christian community) over the fact that Christian schools insisted on teaching in the French language as well as familiarizing students with French culture. Such criticism was levied, for example, by Zaki Naccache, who was at one point a director of the Makassed school in Lebanon, from which many Muslim social figures graduated.[62] Another notable example is ʻOmar Farrūj, who associated the imposition of the French language with neo-colonialism. Some criticisms even came from Maronite literary figures, notably Kamāl Yūsif al-Hajj.[63] Most of the accusations levied by 'Arabophones' involved the superficiality of bilingualism, its destruction of the 'proper' use of either language and its role in sustaining ambiguity when it comes to national identity.[64] For the most part, however, Christians argued that bilingualism was the perfect embodiment of the Pact, whereby students embraced both the Arab-centric state curriculum taught in Arabic while also preserving their cultural, Western-centric, educational heritage.[65] In 1953, for example, Shīḥa declared that 'Lebanon cannot but remain forever invested in its congenital polyglotism.'[66] The issue of bilingualism grew to become such a factor of national identity that one article in 1965 proclaimed that 'one's attitude to bilingualism can be taken roughly as an indication of one's faith, or lack of it, in "Arabism"'.[67]

Moreover, personal laws continued to be under the jurisdiction of each confession, with the state finding itself in awkward situations when internal communal conflict arose over these issues. For example, in 1952, the election of a Yazbeki sheikh to the Highest Druze Court of Appeal[68] was accused by the Junblatis of being tampered with. As a result, the Junblatis refused to accept the government-recognized Yazbeki sheikh and, despite some efforts at reconciliation, the Court of Appeal ceased to operate for many years. In other words, many Druze were left without proper legal rights as court cases went without litigation for years.[69] The fact that these religious authorities have to be given government recognition to function within the confessional system means that intra-communal dispute became impossible to handle without an escalation of the conflict, as the government is forced to recognize certain religious authorities over others. While such intra-confessional conflict might allow for a vacuum to be filled by a more encompassing identity which could override such differences, the power-sharing system forced the state to intervene, thereby alienating a section of the concerned confession, pushing it away from loyalty to the state and in the hands of local leaders who are powerful enough to resolve such issues on the ground. In this sense, the power-sharing introduced further obstacles to nation-building on the social level.

Similarly, marriage was another institution governed by each confession. Because of sectarian tensions, inter-religious marriage produced more obstacles: not only was the consent of the two individuals required, it also involved the consent of families and/or communities as the ceremonies themselves involved traditions and laws of the other confession. Another result of this autonomy was that domestic affairs were referred to religious authorities. For example, if a divorce was based on domestic assault, it usually bypassed the state and a ruling on the severity of domestic violence is left to the discretion of the relevant religious authorities. In other words, the institution of marriage remained in the societal realm and only aggravated tensions as the state refused to intervene in most cases, and intersectarian marriage remained frowned upon. The level of state non-interference is evidenced by the lack of laws on marital and domestic issues. Indeed, one of the few rulings on marriage issued by the state was a law in 1951 whereby civil – as opposed to religious – marriages occurring within Lebanon that involved Jews or Christians were declared invalid.[70]

In conclusion, nation-building efforts by the state ultimately proved fruitless, since they usually served to sponsor a certain type of national identity which alienated communities that did not endorse it. And while open endorsement of the state remained the mainstream narrative among political leaders who believed that officially upholding the Pact was paramount, sectarian tensions remained the norm in Lebanese society, and any potential for nation-building on the social level remained equally unsuccessful. As a result, societal legitimacy continued to elude the state since most Lebanese sought solutions within the framework of their own communities, and avoided interaction with the state except as a last resort. Lebanese identity, meanwhile, continued to be drastically different depending on where a 'citizen' happened to grow up, which community they belonged to, which education they received, which traditional leaders they followed and which personal decisions they took in their lives.

It was also evidenced that, whenever the state needed to intervene in social disputes, the power-sharing system stood in its way with regard to both nation-building and engendering an 'idea of the state' in cross-sectarian terms. Throughout the 1950s, the state remained officially representative,[71] yet its representativeness got in the way of both institutional effectiveness *and* its ability to develop an idea of the state which most (if not all) Lebanese could rally around. Instead, the power-sharing system itself, seen by both the Lebanese and theorists of pluralism as the best way to ensure a representative state, resulted in the very illegitimacy it tried to prevent. Thus, a lacuna shows itself within the societal approach to state-building. Can it provide an answer for a case where the representative state gets in the way of its own legitimacy? One argument could be made that, despite the state being representative on the legislative level, and that it was somewhat (though not fully) representative on the administrative level, it was in fact *not* representative on the executive level, since the Maronite president retained most of the executive power. In that sense, official state representativeness did not hinder its policies of nation-building since it was *not*, in fact, officially representative. Two counter-arguments can be presented here: firstly, that the opposition specifically demanded the resignation of the pro-Western Sham'ūn, and not the removal of a Maronite from the position of president. Indeed, Khūrī and Sham'ūn's successor faced more societal problems from the Christian communities than the Muslim one. And secondly, the opposition also specifically demanded a *return* to the National Pact, which had enshrined the position of the president to the Christians, in an attempt to safeguard the 'special' character of Lebanon. Thus, while one could argue, with the increasing change in demographic circumstances, that the Lebanese state was not officially as representative as it needed to be, one must also respect the context within which Sham'ūn's term took place, an environment in which the Muslim communities had not yet challenged the position of the presidency yet. Such a challenge would occur later on during the development of the state. For now, it was the *policies* of the president, and not the president himself, that were being called into question.

Political developments

It has thus far been shown that in Sham'ūn's early years, the state failed – to different degrees – in both its institutional and its societal state-building, while nation-building had not shown signs of success in either national or communitarian spheres. Subsequently, legitimacy, both institutional and societal, continued to elude the state. So what did this mean for the stability of both the state and the Pact? An answer to this question requires a focus on the political events that occurred in the mid- to late 1950s. These include domestic and regional affairs, while taking into consideration the international context of the time and the state of the overarching Cold War. The following will trace those events and link them together in an effort to explain how the issue of illegitimacy affected the development of the state during the latter part of Sham'ūn's term. The relation between those events can explain how the conflict erupted in 1958, how it is directly linked to the issues of political legitimacy outlined above and, crucially, what can explain how the state was able to endure without undergoing significant changes to both its make-up and its policies.

The regional context

Some historians have argued that, early in the 1950s, in the midst of regional turmoil in which Palestinian refugees fled to adjacent territories, Egyptians had abolished their monarchy, and Syrians were undergoing multiple coups in only a few years; Lebanon's relatively peaceful political transition and stability was an indicator of positive things to come. Indeed, by 1955, the Lebanese were thought to be living 'in a state of enjoyable chaos'.[72] What surrounded that chaos, however, was a different matter – one that deserves its own analysis, and a look at the wider context in which Lebanon existed.

In the Arab world, two main factions were forming that would threaten the stability of the Lebanese state: on the one hand, Iraq and Jordan, backed by the

United States and Britain, began pressurizing Lebanon to sign a defence treaty as a response to the communist 'threat'. On the other hand, the rise of Jamāl 'Abd al-Nāṣer in Egypt brought with it an enormous wave of Arab nationalism, particularly characterized by national socialism and an increase in antagonism towards the United States. As had happened before, these external issues found themselves at the forefront of internal Lebanese politics. An example of the degree to which Lebanese politics were caught up in regional and international relations occurred in 1954, when a manifestation was headed by a Syrian student at the American University of Beirut, in protest to rumours of Iraq signing a pact of cooperation with Turkey and Pakistan.[73] Subsequent violence and armed confrontations with police forces resulted in shootings at the students and a scandal for al-Yāfi's government.[74]

The issue of foreign policy, as always, dominated internal political debates, and the question of where Lebanon stood in the context of the Cold War, both regionally and internationally, was brought to the fore.[75] Additionally, the internal balance of the state itself was starting to be questioned, and with no census to show definite numbers that could shed light on confessional distribution of posts, many among the Muslim communities started to feel like they might be owed more influential positions due to their increase in demographical proportions.[76] In an effort to maintain neutrality and to adhere to the 'spirit' of the Pact, contradictory actions were being taken: for example, the government was mostly willing to follow suit in the Arab League with regard to its antagonistic policy towards Israel and its Western ally. And yet, Sham'ūn remained personally close with US officials and in April 1955, parliament voted on 'co-operation with the West' during a secret session.[77]

Within the regional context, differences between Arab countries had resulted in factions, just as it had done during the end of the Second World War. Nasserist Egypt had begun to lead a coalition opposing the US-oriented Iraq and its allies, which involved the likes of Syria and Yemen. It soon became clear that Muslim communities tended to be much more sympathetic to Nāṣer as a symbol of Arab nationalism, while most Christians remained tied to their traditional allies in the West. Since both sides shared power, the result once again was a paralysed state, the policy of which could only ever be one of equilibrium through weakness and inactivity. In fact, he degree to which the Lebanese state was unable to stop external intervention[78] on the political level would become another indicator that institutional legitimacy was absent, as institutionalists such as Charles Tilly and Mohamed Ayoob have argued. The following will uncover the extent of such foreign influence on the weakness of state decision-making.

Internal divisions

As regional and international developments became more and more central to Lebanese politics, parliament itself became more divided. In part, this was because the parliament of 1953 was different to the one elected in 1947: the latter was a collection of handpicked men, loyal to the 'Pact' regime and the

Khūrī-Ṣulḥ alliance through which the country became independent. In that case, the opposition, while present in the chamber, was mostly extra-parliamentary. The 1953 parliament, on the other hand, included many new faces, and not all were loyal to Sham'ūn or his policies in the same way that its predecessor was to Khūrī.[79] Governments under Khūrī never failed to gain the vote of confidence from parliament as the president made sure to distribute power among multiple Sunni leaders while also distributing ministerial positions among all communities in order to ensure the appeasement of all.[80] Governments formed by Sham'ūn, however, were gaining parliamentary confidence but often through smaller margins; and at one point in September 1955, the government came under so much scrutiny during a parliamentary session that most of its ministers resigned by the end of the meeting.[81]

The divide within the state was becoming more and more apparent. In October 1955, Rashīd Karāmī (then-prime minister and son of 'Abed el-Ḥamīd Karāmī) issued a very pro-Nāṣer governmental statement, which resulted in parliament issuing a declaration of 'appreciation' for Nāṣer and his armament policies 'against the [Tripartite] aggression', doing so with what was described as an 'ecstasy of national pride'.[82] Sham'ūn, meanwhile, had refused to either align himself with the pro-US Baghdad Pact (which included Iraq and Turkey) or sign a mutual defence pact with Nāṣer's Egypt which Syria and Saudi Arabia had done in 1955,[83] despite external and internal pressure to choose a side in the 'Arab Cold War'. Generally, Sham'ūn was perceived to have been favourable to joining a US-sponsored defence pact but had not publicly declared these intentions in the face of overwhelming opposition from those that were either pro-Nāṣer or those that argued that Lebanon should maintain a neutral stance.[84] Nevertheless, rumours grew of Sham'ūn's Western preferences and his standing among the Muslim community began to sharply decline.[85]

In 1956, the Suez Crisis, which resulted in the nationalization of the Suez Canal by Nāṣer, thrust Nasserism onto the Lebanese arena. During the crisis, Sham'ūn called for a meeting of Arab leaders to discuss the issue; that meeting resulted in many Arab countries cutting diplomatic ties with France and Britain, but Sham'ūn refused to do so. While he wasn't the only leader among Arab countries to take a differing stand (Iraq and Jordan, e.g., were still bound by treaties with Britain and only cut diplomatic ties with France), his decision caused more divide between Nasserists within the Lebanese state (that were predominantly Muslims[86]) and those who agreed with the president's positions (mostly Christians) as questions of Arab Unity were brought up again and the character of the Lebanese state was once again called into question.[87] This was in no small part due to Nāṣer himself enforcing a propaganda policy across the Middle East.[88]

Sham'ūn had seen first-hand how Khūrī was able to balance Arab and Western interests both internally and externally, and believed that he should, and could, do the same. In his eyes, it was only Nāṣer's propaganda which painted him as pro-Western.[89] Hence, Sham'ūn continued to argue for a united Arab front, convinced that the real divisions lay in the ideologies among the Arab countries themselves rather than within Lebanon. He believed that he was upholding the Pact-inspired foreign policy that had characterized independent Lebanon when he refused to cut ties with the West. He argued that only an Arab policy sponsored by the League of Arab States would be one worth following. At the same time, he also assumed that Lebanon's position meant that it could play the perfect role of mediator in this conflict, and thus his calling for a meeting of Arab leaders was meant to show Muslim communities that he had not forgotten Lebanon's place in the Arab world as prescribed by the Pact.[90]

His stance, however, was proving to be untenable as it became clear that two positions espoused by the West and Nāṣer were too contradictory, particularly during the crisis that pit them against each other. On the second day of the conference of Arab leaders in Beirut,[91] the issue of diplomatic ties with Britain and France came up again. Yāfi – then-prime minister – and Salām – minister of state – informed the president of their intention to resign unless Lebanon followed suit with its diplomatic relations. Despite the conference being successful in presenting a united – albeit somewhat moderate – Arab position on the Egyptian issue, the resignations of Yāfi and Salām indicated that this would not be satisfying to many in the Muslim community.[92] As a result, the aftermath of the conference showed an escalation in tensions between the Muslim-majority opposition and the president's supporters. While the Egyptian embassy in Beirut had already served as a kind of propaganda machine,[93] November 1956 was marked by a particularly high number of armed violence. During that month, bombs were set off near the French and British embassies, and a police investigation found members of the Egyptian diplomatic corps to be directly involved.[94]

Nāṣer's aggressive policy on what he perceived to be a Christian-run, anti-Arab, Lebanon forced Sham'ūn – who had for so long shown indecisiveness – to finally start choosing sides. The government he formed that month – which would prove to be his final one – would be headed by Sāmī al-Ṣulḥ who, unlike Karāmī and Yāfi before him, did not take a pro-Nāṣer or anti-West stance, while its foreign minister was Charles Mālik, an ardent supporter of the United States and its Middle Eastern policies.[95]

The Eisenhower Doctrine

In January of 1957, President Eisenhower issued a proclamation containing a special message to Congress, in which he declared that the United States would 'assist any nation or group of nations in the general area of the Middle East' with economic and political development, as well as authorize the use of forces 'to secure and protect the territorial integrity and political independence of such a nation' if the latter requests such aid.[96] This policy became known as the Eisenhower Doctrine, and it fuelled the Cold War in the Middle East, facing opposition from countries like Egypt and Syria while receiving support from the likes of Saudi Arabia and Iraq. In March, Lebanon became the first country in the Middle East to formally accept US aid and receive Eisenhower's special envoy.[97] Only a month later, though, seven opposition deputies resigned in protest of the Doctrine, six of whom were Muslim deputies,[98] and on 30 May, a demonstration broke out in protest against the government's policies – chiefly the acceptance of the Eisenhower Doctrine – and a clash with Lebanese security forces resulted in many deaths and tens of injuries, including the former prime minister Salām.[99] In the midst of such clashes, opposition leaders such as the journalist 'Abdallah al-Mashnūq began to call for 'revolutionary protests'.[100] These public debates over Lebanon's foreign policy rarely made any mention of the benefits of alignment with the West and instead focused more on the symbolic meaning and the purpose of Sham'ūn's stand. This was clearly another debate over the 'idea' and identity of the Lebanese state, and Sham'ūn was accused by his opposers of having 'destroyed the National Pact'.[101]

The debate was once again – as it had been during the creation of the Arab League in 1945 – framed as that between those who were ready to cooperate with their Arab brethren in the face of aggression and in the name of 'positive neutrality', and those who were willing to cling on to old ties to the West at the expense of regional relationships. Nāṣer himself fuelled that fire during one of his speeches, when he accused the 'isolationists',[102] and specifically the Phalanges, of wishing for the destruction of Egypt.[103]

The 1957 elections

As a national divide was taking place, the 1957 elections were scheduled to be held in June and debates centred mainly on the government's foreign policy and Sham'ūn's supposed bid for re-election, which also grew to become a main focus of attack for the opposition.[104] The latter issue only grew worse when Sham'ūn refused to openly rule out the option of his re-election, and decided to remain silent on the issue. At the same time, he reamended the electoral law to increase the number of deputies to sixty-six and was personally involved in drawing electoral constituencies.[105]

While the opposition continued to focus on the issue of re-election to the presidency, it was clear that the real debate revolved around national identity and the idea of the state. This can be evidenced by the fact that, while there were certainly those that openly opposed the possibility, most politicians and their communities were not as incensed by Khūrī's re-election as the potential for Sham'ūn's. In other words, the issue of constitutional amendment on its own had not been previously opposed by Lebanese politicians. Interestingly, it would be supported years later during Fu'ād Shehāb's term when he was pushed to run for re-election. Thus, one cannot realistically argue that re-election lay at the heart of the 1958 crisis, as many in the opposition did at the time. There was a clear clash between what the idea of the state was for two factions that, for the most part, coincided with confessional lines of divide in Lebanese society and, even still, aligned with the same divides that separated the different nationalist projects prior to the creation of the state in 1920.

For all intents and purposes, the elections became as much a battleground between external forces as one between the government and the opposition, since the process was framed as a referendum for Lebanese foreign policy.[106]

In particular, Sham'ūn enjoyed strong political and financial backing from the United States while the likes of Russia, Egypt and Syria provided support to the opposition.[107]_Subsequently, reports of bribery, corruption, intimidation and incidents of violence on behalf of almost all parties involved were rampant.[108]

The result of the elections was a parliament that was overwhelmingly supportive of the president, with core members of the opposition (who had maintained parliamentarian positions for years) ousted. In fact the opposition, united under the name 'United National Front' (UNF), only secured eight seats. This meant that for the first time since the end of Khūrī's term, opposition to the government was almost-exclusively extra-parliamentary.[109] The last time such a phenomenon occurred was when Khūrī's government manipulated parliamentary elections in 1947 and 1951.[110] During Khūrī's term, his attempts to take over state institutions resulted in a situation ripe for revolution, only avoided through his decision to step down three years into his term. It was not a surprise, then, when Sham'ūn's regime faced a similar crisis a few months after the elections.

Insurrection

The fall of 1957 was mostly marked by a stand-off between opposition and 'loyalist' forces, with the issue of Syria's Soviet relations and Sham'ūn's possible re-election dominating the political headlines. Both topics fostered polarization among Lebanese society: whenever the opposition would become 'overenthusiastic in their pro-Syrian sentiments, this … had the effect of rallying the loyalist forces in support of the Government'.[111] This tension was only exacerbated by the regional context, in particular the antagonistic relationship between Sham'ūn's government and the one in Syria.[112] To make matters worse, Sham'ūn declared in a speech on New Year's eve 1957 that he was only opposed 'in principle' to the amendment of the constitution which would allow for his re-election. He stated, however, that he would reconsider this position should no candidate appear, which can assure the 'total continuity' of his policies.[113] Naturally, this did not satisfy the opposition.

In February of 1958, the United Arab Republic (UAR) was formed – with Nāṣer as its president – by merger of Egypt and a Syria dominated by Arab nationalist groups like the Ba'th party.[114] Unsurprisingly, creation of the UAR only served to further exacerbate tensions between the Lebanese factions. Political leaders both regionally and within Lebanon immediately realized the importance of this new political entity: it left Sham'ūn to benefit from fearmongering among the Lebanese Christians and his loyalists, whereas it allowed opposition Muslims and Arab nationalists to gain momentum in the hope that the ultimate dream of Arab unity was much closer to realization. Thus, many opposition figures within the state came out and declared both support and loyalty to the UAR – and sometimes to Nāṣer himself – with some going as far as demanding Lebanon to join the Republic.[115]

Likewise, sub-state actors were equally as quick to react.[116] Instances of fighting between government forces and local opposition sprung up in areas like the northern Biqā', the Shūf region, areas in the south and certain sections of Tripoli and Beirut.[117] In addition, bombs had gone off in 'Akkār, near the presidential palace in B'abda, and near the house of the minister for public works and transport.[118] It wasn't until 8 May, though, that an open insurrection started taking place with the clear aim of removing Sham'ūn from power.[119] The assassination of opposition journalist Nasīb al-Matnī on that day provided the spark for a period of turmoil as the blame was placed right at the regime's doorstep, and the month of May proved to be the beginning of the end for Sham'ūn's regime.

Broadly, divisions were formed along confessional lines, as had been the case before. The Phalanges had effected the bulk of paramilitary activities along with the help of government forces, while the Najjada had become the main force on the ground for the opposition (along with local armed groups).[120] A 'Third Force' had also emerged at the time, including the likes of Henri Far'ūn, journalist Ghassān Tuweynī, former head of state Alfred Naccāsh and deputy Taqī al-Dīn al-Ṣulḥ. Many of the members of the Third Force personally sympathized with one side or the other, but they all agreed on the need for Sham'ūn to step down and the necessity of the cessation of violence.[121]

There were some exceptions to the overall confessional division, however, and some unusual alliances took place. For example, both the Communist Party and the Maronite Patriarch sided with the opposition and demanded that Sham'ūn step down and that the state disassociate itself from Western alignment. The communists were completely against the Eisenhower Doctrine, while the Patriarch M'ūshī – who was elected in 1955 – had become a staunch advocate of reconciliation between Christians and Arab Nationalism, going so far as to argue that, unless the Maronites can find a way to cooperate with regional Muslim goals, they might as well 'pack up and leave'. That last comment sparked much anger among Maronite circles and resulted in an unprecedented protest march against the Church.[122]

On the other hand, the SSNP – historically anti-Western – was staunchly against Nasserism and the spread of a version of Arab nationalism that not only rivalled their own regional aspirations but was also too ideologically aligned with communism for their liking. Hence, they sided with the pro-Western government and the Phalanges, despite an historically bitter rivalry with the two.[123] Shī'a leaders, for the most part, were either part of the opposition or sympathized with the UNF. Specifically, speaker 'Ādil 'Oseyrān had already declared his support for the UAR and Nasserism, and pursued his own agenda in the face of the president's.[124] Additionally, Aḥmad al-As'ad, who was considered the most influential leader of the Shī'a of the south, had also been an opponent of Sham'ūn's and joined the rebellion in 1958. As always, though, many of the political loyalties among Shī'a were also based on personal relations. For example, Kāzim al-Khalīl, al-As'ad's opponent in the South, who had been supported by Sham'ūn and even named minister, remained a loyalist at the expense of his own safety.[125]

These ideological or personal alliances gave indication that there were other dimensions to the conflict, and there probably were. During such a time of regional and international tension, many individuals and groups forewent traditional or ideological principles, and focused instead on protecting their most fundamental assets and power bases. Nevertheless, one of the most telling indications that the crisis in 1958 was just as confessional, and nationalistic, as any other in Lebanese history was the decision taken by Shehāb – general of the Armed Forces at the time – to refuse interfering on the side of the state against the rebellious forces. Apart from having a famous distaste for what he considered to be a political battle, he insisted that it was 'likely' that the army would split between Christians and Muslims were he to intervene.[126]

There was no doubt at this point that the state had not achieved societal legitimacy, as a debate over policy went from a debate over the idea of the state, to an armed battle for control of institutions and territory. Sham'ūn's alienation of many sections of Lebanese society – and in particular most Muslim communities – had served to completely undermine the idea of the pluralist, neutral Lebanese state in which power was shared. And yet, the ambiguous nature of the National Pact – upon which that state was supposedly built – meant that both sides accused the other of undermining the foundation of the Lebanese state. As a result, the debate remained around what the National Pact *meant* as opposed to the ability of the Pact itself to remain at the foundation of the state.[127] The traditional debate of Lebanism versus Arabism manifested itself through the idea of East versus West, United States versus USSR, despite the fact that, ideologically, most Lebanese Christians had shown a much higher degree of conservatism than Western liberalism might allow and the Arab nationalist movement had proven itself to be the enemy of most, if not all, local communist parties in the Middle East. The deeper level of division among the Lebanese communities was not lost on some of the actors involved at the time. For example, on 19 April 1958, Ghassān Tuweynī – a member of the Third Force – argued in his op-ed that despite the debate over the country's policies, there seemed to actually contain 'two countries', that the state itself comprised two states and that the people themselves formed two enemies who are each 'waiting for the day of reckoning'.[128]

As time went on, both the UNF and the Third Force changed their arguments from Sham'ūn's re-election to the need for him to step down immediately. Hence, discussions turned to who would be his replacement, and Fu'ād Shehāb – chief commander of the Lebanese Armed Forces – quickly became the frontrunner. Not only respected for his good standing among both Christian and Muslim communities, Shehāb was also commended for his militaristic achievements and his insistence on keeping the army non-aligned during the civil conflict, despite demands from Sham'ūn to involve the Armed Forces. Shehāb had declared many times before that he was not interested in politics, but this served to bolster his honourable image even more. In fact, he even had the support of Nāṣer when it came to the presidency. Generally, he became a symbol of neutrality.[129]

Internationalization

While a 'sharp decline [had] taken place in the general authority of Government' by the end of 1957,[130] the government was struggling even more for control during the spring and summer of 1958, as opposition rebels became more and more hostile to the state. In April alone, there were reports of incidents in the northern towns of ʿAbdah, Ḥalba and Tripoli. In the south, the city of Sidon witnessed many occurrences of violence and clashes with government authority, while the same was true of the northern and middle Biqāʿ valley.[131] Subsequently, the government lost even more ground during the month of May.

Sensing the growing danger of the opposition, Shamʿūn turned abroad for a resolution to the conflict. He insisted – both privately and publicly – that the ongoing troubles were in fact a result of infiltration on the part of the UAR and the wider reaching arm of the Soviet Union. The latter's involvement was particularly emphasized to US officials as Shamʿūn worried that he could not invoke the Eisenhower Doctrine without proof of a communist threat.[132] On 13 May, Shamʿūn contacted the US administration and inquired into the possibility of US troops landing in Lebanon. Having finally been faced with a request for actual military assistance, US officials – not affording to ignore Shamʿūn – informed him of their conditions for accepting his demands: 'that he accept UN help in resolving the crisis, that he obtain support from at least one other Arab state, and that he renounce his own candidacy for a second term'.[133]

Thus, on 21 May, the Lebanese government lodged an official complaint to the League of Arab States against the UAR for 'unfriendly acts of intervention in the internal affairs of Lebanon, which constitute a threat to its independence, territorial integrity and constitutional forms of government', and called for an urgent meeting of the League Council.[134] The next day, the Lebanese representative at the UN submitted a similar complaint to the president of the Security Council, with the additional clause that the situation in Lebanon represented a potential danger to the 'maintenance of international peace and security'.[135] Within the League, a draft resolution which was unanimously approved by League members called upon reconciliation both within Lebanon and between the latter and the UAR, and requested the withdrawal of the government's complaint. That resolution was rejected by the Lebanese government as it was regarded too passive, unspecific and non-obligatory.[136] The UN Security Council, on the other hand, found enough weight in the complaint to form an observer group.[137] The first reports of the United Nations Observer Group in Lebanon (UNOGIL), however, submitted during the month of July argued that 'no substantiated or conclusive evidence of major infiltration at that point' could be found, though the group also noted that they had faced resistance and, in some cases, open fire on border regions where the opposition was in control.[138] Unsurprisingly, the Lebanese government contested the early UNOGIL reports since they considered them incomplete, while US officials argued that instances of infiltration had been reduced by the simple presence of UNOGIL.[139] Still, while the accuracy of the reports themselves could be debated, it has been argued that, had they shown clear signs of foreign infiltration, the scope of the crisis itself could have been significantly enlarged. Accordingly, one could see how the UNOGIL played a crucial role in containing the conflict as it failed to provide international credibility to the Lebanese complaint at the UN.[140]

The result

As loyalists continued to frame the ongoing conflict in international terms, insisting that the Lebanese crisis was one of liberalism against communism, and of Lebanon against UAR infiltration,[141] many were already planning for an end to the Lebanese crisis. It had been clear that Sham'ūn's term had not succeeded in harbouring legitimacy – neither socially nor institutionally – for the state. The ultimate question was thus implicitly asked: was it because of Sham'ūn's particular policies? Or was the state itself not built to allow for the achievement of durable political legitimacy? This book has argued for the latter, and showed how theories of state-building which demand certain policies or adjustments to the state are not in themselves capable of accounting for the vicious circle of illegitimacy which has surrounded the Lebanese state since its formation. Henri Far'ūn, a man so pivotal to the shape of the state in the 1940s and, crucially, to the interpretation of the Pact which had been adopted during Khūrī's presidential term, declared the following on 5 June: 'the solution to the crisis demands that there be no victor and no vanquished'.[142] Those words would prove to be at the heart of the resolution of the 1958 conflict, and would shape the form that the state would take as a result. The following will briefly delineate the events of the crisis which led to that point.

In early July, many in the international sphere (specifically UN Secretary General Dag Hammarskjöld) became hopeful of an end to the conflict: it was reported that US and UN officials had been able to convince Sham'ūn to step down as president while agreeing with the opposition for 'a cooling off period during which a compromise might be prepared'.[143] On 14 July, however, a military coup in Iraq resulted in the killing of the pro-Western monarchy and the establishment of a republic with a regime at the helm that was sympathetic to the UAR. The same day, Sham'ūn called for military assistance from the United States as the situation escalated and the Lebanese conflict came to present a potentially wider, regional struggle.[144] Despite the ambiguity as to the application of the Doctrine to the nature of the Lebanese crisis, Sham'ūn's request was accepted and US Marine troops landed on Lebanese shores the next morning.[145] For the opposition, who had already been opposed to the Doctrine, US intervention was seen as the ultimate conspiracy,[146] and was heavily criticized by pro-opposition figures and outlets.[147] The fact that the UN Security Council also met that day and did not openly denounce the troop landings only exacerbated the feeling of conspiracy, and resulted in a total lack of cooperation from opposition forces with the UNOGIL mission.[148]

By the end of July, civil violence had reached such a point that, on the 25th, an attack on the presidential palace was launched, wherein Sham'ūn claimed to have participated himself in its defence.[149] But, despite conspiratorial accusations, the fact that US troops coordinated with Lebanese Armed Forces (under Shehāb's command) and refrained from engaging in combat meant that they could play the role of mediator while also holding a 'stick' that could threaten both sides.[150] After deciding to withdraw their unconditional support for Sham'ūn – at the expense of much anger from the latter and his loyalists – it became clear that US diplomatic officials in Lebanon had gained favour among some of the opposition leaders such as Karāmī and Junblāṭ, and discussions soon began for both a cessation of hostilities and a post-war plan which would include a delineation of Lebanese neutrality.[151] Despite attempts by both Sham'ūn and some oppositionists,[152] the United States – now endorsing Shehāb – pressed on with negotiations and ensured that presidential elections took place on 31 July.[153] Opposition deputies, against whom arrest warrants were issued, were allowed to participate in the voting and Shehāb was declared the winner by forty-eight votes of fifty-six total ballots.[154] It was then agreed that Sham'ūn would remain in office until the end of September.[155]

The period between Shehāb's official election and the first government that he would form proved to be the most unstable. During those two months, the state only retained nominal control over Lebanese territory, while instances of bombings, violence, kidnappings and murder continued to occur.[156] Meanwhile, the UNF's headquarters in Basta (a Muslim-dominated neighbourhood in Beirut) continued to serve as a stronghold for the more extreme members of the opposition, as many of them continued their fight until autumn.[157] The United States, in the meantime, carried on playing a crucial role in institutional state-building as McClintock practically took on the roles of official mediator and special advisor to Shehāb 'in a manner that made the political autonomy of the Lebanese presidency a mockery'.[158] Eventually, after much negotiating and reshuffling, a four-man government was formed on 14 October, in which two loyalist Christians (Raymond Eddeh and Pierre Jumayyil) and two opposition Muslims (Karāmī and 'Uwaynī) served. Karāmī, acting as prime minister, declared it a 'government of national salvation', and it adopted the motto uttered a few months earlier by Far'ūn: no victor, no vanquished.[159]

The implications of such a formula for Lebanese state-building were clear: the end of the crisis did not mean that one idea of the state overcame the other. Sham'ūn was seen as an aberration, not a natural outcome of the 'Pact' state, and his policies were painted as those of an opportunistic fanatic. In that sense, this new formula indicated a return to a status quo in which the 'true' neutrality dictated by the Pact would be restored. The previous chapters have shown, however, that such a clear idea of the state and its neutral identity was never a reality. In fact, one could clearly see the link between earlier crises and the conflict of 1958. What had changed, then? The most direct explanation would be that Sham'ūn, unlike his predecessor, refused to keep the state on the sidelines and to have it act as a neutral referee, especially when it came to foreign policy. Another argument could be made that both the regional and the international context made absolute neutrality a somewhat impossible position to hold. And yet, it was also just as clear that Sham'ūn had a particular vision of the idea of the state, one that undoubtedly coincided with a vast majority of Lebanese Christians and that the Pact, as ambiguous and unclear as it had ever been, allowed for such an interpretation. Thus, the most sufficient explanation for the 1958 crisis is that it was a direct result of the inability of the state to achieve institutional and societal legitimacy. Thus, once the state shifted from being inactive and somewhat irrelevant, it became a hindrance to the confessional or communal interests and ambitions.

Instead of state and confessional institutions being mutually exclusive (and even complementary in some cases), Sham'ūn's attempt to enforce a certain idea of the state allowed both sets of institutions to clash within certain communities, thus creating a situation ripe for insurrection by a portion of the population.

Despite the agreement of both sides to participate in power within a post-war formula, the crisis had also clearly shed light on deeper and more dormant ambitions from both sides that were left unaddressed: how attached had the more extreme Christians remained to the idea of Western protection? How willing were ideological Muslims to forego the ultimate dream of Arab unity in the face of Lebanese sovereignty and independence? As Fahim Qubain wrote only three years after the 1958 conflict, 'The Lebanese crisis … was fundamentally caused by a division in the soul of Lebanese society. All other factors are either external manifestations or subsidiary derivatives.'[160] The 'no victor, no vanquished' formula – in typical Far'ūnist fashion – left too many questions unanswered, and once again confined the Lebanese state to the role of balancing confessionalism, despite the inadequacies that such a state had shown prior to the crisis of 1958.

Summary

A brief summary is needed here to understand the development of events in Lebanon during this time. It was shown, in the first section of this chapter, how Sham'ūn's term was marked by both institutional and societal state-building endeavours. Institutionally, Sham'ūn looked to push the state out of the way of economic growth, thus partaking in a policy of inactivity (whether willingly or otherwise). Without state intervention, though, the evolution of the Lebanese economy created a level of inequality that overlapped with confessional lines. Lebanese Christians, due to their historical advantages, greatly benefited while most Muslim communities were forced to settle for lower gains. On the other hand, Lebanese public administration continued to be bound by confessionalism as levels of corruption and nepotism grew to become as high as ever, while the sheer size of the state increased to an unnecessary level since institutions were neither strong nor effective enough to sustain such responsibilities. In this sense, confessionalism was a clear hindrance to the institutional development of the state, yet it was also just as clear that there was no demand for the removal of power-sharing, or for the revision of the National Pact.

In terms of societal state-building, the state remained bound by the Pact to be as representative as possible. And yet, with no unified idea of the state, the result of power-sharing was the amalgamation of contradictory views on the role and identity of the state, thus resulting in a culture of opportunism and backstabbing within state institutions themselves. Subsequently, early governments under Sham'ūn continued to be paralysed by internal disputes while policies enacted were rarely solid enough to gain wide popular support. Thus, feudalism and clientelism remained the norm in Lebanese politics as communities continued to look inward for institutions and services that they could identify with and accept as their own. In this sense, representativeness – a staple of the societal approach to state-building – was the very reason for the illegitimacy of the state.

Similarly, efforts of nation-building – both within and outside of the state – created more division as the different views of what it meant to be Lebanese remained as contradictory as ever. Many Muslims stayed as tied as ever to the idea of Arab unity or, at the very least, a vision of Arab fraternity that binds the state to certain policies in relation to its Middle Eastern neighbours. Meanwhile, the Christian communities were not as ready to forego their historical relations with the West, insisting that the Pact allowed them to continue to identify with Western values. The natural result was, then, exclusive socio-cultural institutions that emphasized different if not contradictory beliefs between communities, with the issue of bilingualism being a significant and representative example of such communal cleavages. Additionally, the fact that the state under Shamʿūn endorsed, and adopted, some Phoenician – that is, pre-Arab – symbols and celebrations only served to weaken its already-frail societal legitimacy as most Muslims continued to feel alienated.

The regional and political events at the time only served to exacerbate the strong tensions present within the Lebanese state and society. The 1956 Suez Canal crisis, the enaction of the Eisenhower Doctrine and the heavy external involvement in the Lebanese politics all served to make the contradictory views of Christians and Muslims clash. Within the context of the Cold War, Shamʿūn was forced to definitively choose sides. Even neutrality was no longer tenable, as evidenced by Shamʿūn's efforts to play the role of mediator during the 1956 crisis. Consequently, his acceptance of the Eisenhower Doctrine and the government's overt intervention in the 1957 elections resulted in the rise of an armed opposition, the goal of which became the removal of Shamʿūn from power.

As a violent insurrection began to take place, the internationalization of the crisis in May 1958 and the landing of US Marine troops that summer brought the conflict between government and opposition to its peak.[161] Still, as the United States withdrew its unconditional support for the president, talks between Shamʿūn 'loyalists' and the opposition began to take place. Eventually, the election of Fuʾād Shehāb was agreed upon and occurred, as he was seen to be a neutral figure; thus the new government of Lebanon adopted the motto: no victor, no vanquished. Despite a relatively successful resolution to the conflict, however, a crucial question was left unaddressed: was a change of policy needed? Or, as shown throughout the chapter, did a more fundamental question of the legitimacy of the Lebanese state needed addressing, one that could be traced back to the formation of the state? The unfolding of the events of 1958 shows that the Lebanese opted for the former, believing that a truly neutral president can succeed in achieving state legitimacy, both institutionally and societally. As Ghassān Tuweynī warned in June 1958, the 'true crisis' would occur after the cessation of hostilities, that crisis being 'the problem of deciding the future of a country which we have made a state, but which we have not known how to make into a nation'.[162]

Notes

1 See Legislative Decree N° 6 issued on 4 November 1952 concerning the amendment of the electoral law previously issued on 10 August 1950 Published in the Lebanese Official Gazette N° 46, 12 November 1952, 927–34. http://www.legallaw.ul.edu.lb/Law.aspx?lawId=194819.

The new law prohibited many from running for elections depending on their public positions while also reorganizing constituencies. It was argued that this new electoral law would promote quality over quantity. See Attié, *Struggle in the Levant*, 51.

Critics such as Junblāṭ believed the new constituencies were arbitrary and not representative of demographical and geographical distributions. See 'Azīz Al-Matni, *Kamāl Junblāṭ: 'As'ila Wa Ḥaqā'iq* [Kamāl Junblāṭ: Questions and Truths] (al-Mokhtāra, al-Shūf: Dār al-Taqadumiya, 2010), 143.

It should also be noted that Sham'ūn had been planning to revive the Senate, a second chamber which formed part of the Lebanese constitution but had been dissolved during the Mandate and had yet to be revived. See FO 484/8.

Other reforms that followed Sham'ūn's philosophy included the restriction of 'political journals' by limiting the number of licenses for daily and weekly newspapers.

2 Ralph E. Crow, 'Religious Sectarianism in the Lebanese Political System', *Journal of Politics* 24, no. 3 (1962): 503.

3 Ralph E. Crow and Adnan Iskandar, 'Administrative Reform in Lebanon 1958–1959', *International Review of Administrative Sciences* 27, no. 3 (1961): 296–7.

4 For a 'modernizationist' outlook on the Lebanese state in the 1950s, see Elie Adib Salem, *Modernization without Revolution: Lebanon's Experience* (Bloomington: Indiana University Press, 1973); Hudson, *The Precarious Republic*. Also see Gendzier, *Notes from the Minefield*.

5 See: Camille Chamoun, *Crise Au Moyen Orient* [Crisis in the Middle East] (Paris: Gallimard, 1963).

6 For example, the 'Lebanese national income' was estimated to have increased from LL1,090 m in 1952 to LL1,465 m in 1956. Similarly, exports increased by over $70 m over those years while imports only increased by about $19 m in that time.

See: Statistical Office of the United Nations Department of Economic and Social Affairs, *Statistical Yearbook 1958* (New York, 1958).

Also see William Persen, 'Lebanese Economic Development since 1950', *Middle East Journal* 12, no. 3 (1958): 277–94.

7 Roger Owen, 'The Economic History of Lebanon, 1943–1974: Its Salient Features', in *Toward a Viable Lebanon*, ed. Halim Isber Barakat (London: Croom Helm, 1988), 38.

8 Hudson, *The Precarious Republic*, 138–9.

9 Far'ūn was very much a reflection of his predecessors and peers. His brother-in-law, for example, was Michel Shīḥa, who participated in the drafting of the Lebanese Constitution of 1926 and was regarded as the epitome of Maronite aspirations for a liberal Greater Lebanon at the time. See Hudson, 138.

Also see Fawāz Ṭrābulsī, *Ṣilāt Bilā Waṣl: Mishāl Shīḥa Wal-'Īdiyōlōjiya Al-Lubnāniya* [Connections without Association: Michel Chiha and the Lebanese Ideology] (Beirut: Riad El-Rayyes Books, 1999).

10 For example, the IFRED report of 1961 showed how, despite the low percentage of 'active population' (28–36 per cent), these numbers fail to reflect the Lebanese custom of women and children working with the husband or father without being

given a salary as an employee. Similarly, many employees had second 'jobs' or sources of income which usually involved an investment of some kind (e.g. plot of land, plantation, etc.). These secondary jobs are also not regarded in the numbers.

See Institut de Recherche et de Formation en Vue du Développement Harmonisé, *Besoins et Possibilités de Développement Du Liban; Étude Préliminaire. Mission IRFED-Liban, 1960–1961. Tome I* [Requirements and Possibilities of Development in Lebanon; A Preliminary Study. IRFED-Liban Mission, 1960–1961. Volume I], ed. Louis-Joseph Lebret (Beirut: Wizārat al-Taṣmīm al-ʿĀm, 1963).

Another issue that has been brought up is one of disguised unemployment, which was fairly present across the Middle East at the time.

Also see Amin A. Galal, *The Modernization of Poverty: A Study in the Political Economy of Growth in Nine Arab Countries, 1945–1970* (Leiden: Brill, 1974).

11 The questioners argued that this question would work as an indicator of local theories on economic causation – see Lincoln Armstrong, 'A Socio-Economic Opinion Poll in Beirut, Lebanon', *Public Opinion Quarterly* 23, no. 1 (1959): 27.

12 Armstrong, 27.

It must be noted that there is no mention of confessional differences among the participants in the poll, simply that they were middle- to upper-class Beirutis, 134 of who were males and thirty-six were females. The following statement was the only indication on their confessional nature: 'The interviewing team felt that the respondents were reasonably representative as far as the religious structure of Beirut is concerned.' See Armstrong, 19.

13 Michael Johnson, *Class & Client in Beirut: The Sunni Muslim Community and the Lebanese State, 1840–1985* (London: Ithaca Press, 1986), 117.

14 This perception of the unequal effect of policies was not limited to one of Christian bourgeoisie versus Muslim proletariat. Even the same occupations and professions resulted in different standards of living. For example, the Christian peasantry in the Mountain lived much more comfortably than their Muslim counterparts in the Biqāʿ where many lived with 'no pure water and poor medical and social services'. See Fahim I. Qubain, *Crisis in Lebanon* (Washington, DC: The Middle East Institute, 1961), 31.

For a representation of Muslim perception of Shamʿūn's policies, see Farrūkh, *Difāʿan ʿan Al-ʾElem, Difāʿan ʿan Al-Waṭan*, 33.

For an overview of Lebanese economic growth in the 1950s, see A. J. Meyer, 'Entrepreneurship and Economic Development in the Middle East', *Public Opinion Quarterly* 22, no. 3 (1958): 391–6.

15 Atiyah, 'The Attitude of the Lebanese Sunnis towards the State of Lebanon', 233.

16 FO 484/8.

17 For example, see Decree N° 7525 issued on 5 February 1952 concerning entrance exams for the Ministry of Foreign Affairs Published in the Lebanese Official Gazette N° 7, 13 February 1952, 127–8. Retrieved from: http://www.legallaw.ul.edu.lb/Law.aspx?lawId=203964.

Also see Decisions 210, 216 and 253 to amend the 'Employee System' of 1943. Published in the Lebanese Official Gazettes N° 8, N° 10, N° 28 in 1952. Retrieved from: http://www.legallaw.ul.edu.lb/Law.aspx?lawId=205168; http://www.legallaw.ul.edu.lb/Law.aspx?lawId=166438; http://www.legallaw.ul.edu.lb/Law.aspx?lawId=203964.

18 See Halim Faris Fayyad, 'The Effects of Sectarianism on the Lebanese Administration' [unpublished Masters thesis] (American University of Beirut, 1956), 83, https://schol

arworks.aub.edu.lb/bitstream/handle/10938/5000/t-161.pdf. Retrieved from: http://hdl.handle.net/10938/5000.

19 Fayyad, 83.

20 See Legislative Decree N° 14 issued on 7 January 1955 concerning the Employee Regulations. Published in the Lebanese Official Gazette N° 2, 12 January 1955, 56–154. Retrieved from: http://www.legallaw.ul.edu.lb/Law.aspx?lawId=244070.

21 For example, the position of foreign minister was held by a Christian in all governments except one from 1943 until 1955 (nineteen overall). See Fayyad, 78–80.

More evidence of this deterministic employment occurred in 1953, where an editorial in *L'Orient* argued that the allocation of ministerial positions was easy to predict, as the confession for each ministership was pretty much determined. The editorial was almost completely accurate in its prediction. See *L'Orient* newspaper, on 12 August 1953.

22 This itself is imbedded in the Lebanese system, as each sect maintains autonomy over issues of personal status, education, religious beliefs and so on.

23 See Nizar A. Hamzeh, 'Clientalism, Lebanon: Roots and Trends', *Middle Eastern Studies* 37, no. 3 (2001): 167–78.

24 Steven Heydemann, *Authoritarianism in Syria: Institutions and Social Conflict, 1946–1970* (Ithaca, NY: Cornell University Press, 1999), 59.

Also see Ralph E. Crow, 'The Civil Service of Independent Syria, 1945–58' [unpublished doctoral thesis] (University of Michigan, 1964).

25 Ruiz, É, 'Trop de Fonctionnaires? Contribution à une Histoire de l'État par ses Effectifs (France, 1850–1950).' Retrieved on 20 March 2019 from: https://tel.archives-ouvertes.fr/tel-00863780/file/THESE_EMILIEN-RUIZ_SEPT-2013.pdf.

26 Roché went on to say, 'One frequently has the impression of facing a pseudo-government, a pseudo-parliament, a pseudo-justice, a pseudo-police force.' See Stéphane Malsagne, *Sous l'oeil de La Diplomatie Française: Le Liban de 1946 à 1990* [In the Presence of French Diplomacy: Lebanon from 1946 to 1990] (Paris: Geuthner, 2017), 63.

27 Crow and Iskandar, 'Administrative Reform in Lebanon 1958–1959', 294.

28 Francis Fukuyama, 'The Imperative of State-Building', *Journal of Democracy* 15, no. 2 (2004): 32.

29 Fukuyama, 35.

30 See *Le Monde* newspaper. 25 September 1952. *M. Chamoun jouit d'une immense popularité*. Sablier, Édouard.

Sham'ūn had developed very close relationships with Britain ever since his diplomatic work there which began in 1943. That year, Sham'ūn's name had been submitted as a compromise candidate between Eddeh and Khūrī before the November crisis, but after an agreement could not be concluded, Sham'ūn ended up serving as ambassador to the UK in what was considered to be political exile. His affinity with the British even led to widespread rumours that the British government played a significant role in ensuring a broad majority for his election.

31 See: interview with Moḥsen Dalūl, former deputy head of the Progressive Socialist Party in: Aḥzāb Lubnān [Lebanese Political Parties]. Directed by Farīd 'Assāf. al-Sharika al-Wataniya lil-Intāj [National Production Company]. 2003.

32 Al-Matni, *Kamāl Junblāṭ*, 137.

Also see Yusri Hazran, 'Lebanon's Revolutionary Era: Kamal Junblat, The Druze Community and the Lebanon State, 1949 to 1977*', *Muslim World* 100, no. 1 (2010): 161–2.

33 By this point the opposition had united under the banner of the 'National Socialist Front'.

34 Al-Matni, *Kamāl Junblāṭ*, 140–1.

35 Clyde G. Hess and Herbert L. Bodman, 'Confessionalism and Feudality in Lebanese Politics', *Middle East Journal* 8, no. 1 (1954): 24–5.

36 Hess and Bodman, 26.

37 See Decree N° 2062 issued on 30 May 1943 concerning the dissolution of parliament. Published in the Lebanese Official Gazette N° 22, 3 June 1953, 1167–9. http://www.legallaw.ul.edu.lb/Law.aspx?lawId=175536.

38 Layla Ra'd, *Tārīkh Lubnān Al-Siyāsī Wal-Iqtiṣādī, 1958–1975* [Lebanese Political and Economic History, 1958–1975] (Tripoli: Maktabat al-Sā'iḥ, 2005), 39–40.

39 Salām had served towards the end of Khūrī's tenure yet his appointment was seen as somewhat reformist since it was his family that rivalled the Ṣulḥs more than any others, and the latter was seen as a predominant symbol of the old corrupt regime (Attié, *Struggle in the Levant*, 46). Nevertheless, subsequent appointments to the prime minister position showed that Sham'ūn succumbed to the same manoeuvres as Khūrī, mainly the rotation of the prime ministership to appease different Sunni leaders.

40 The earliest example of this paralysis and its effects on the government's popularity was when Salām's cabinet proclaimed its statement in parliament while Lebanon and Syria were conducting negotiations for potential economic unity (in the forms of an official customs union). Confidence in Salām's government was earned only by a slight margin of six (which was much lower than the usual majority that governments enjoyed). In particular, many deputies hopeful of Lebano-Syrian economic unity were sceptical of the government's ability to negotiate so long as it included two Maronite ministers who had already declared their opposition to such a unity. This issue of economic relations with Syria was a particularly inflammatory one. Minutes of Parliamentary session on 12 May 1953. Retrieved from: http://www.legallaw.ul.edu.lb/PeriodSessionLandingPage.aspx?SessionID=1916.

41 See Johnson, *Class & Client in Beirut*, 129–31.

The pamphlet also cited unfair policies such as the freezing of rent prices in Beirut, for properties built before 1944. This particularly affected Muslims since they formed the majority of proprietors before 1944. Meanwhile, Christians, who became the majority of proprietors after Lebanese independence drove the rural exodus, benefited from the increase in rent.

42 Qubain, *Crisis in Lebanon*, 32.

The letter also demanded the abolition of confessionalism, though the extent to which this was a realistic demand compared to the others can only be judged in the context of the time, where there was no strong will for a real removal of the confessional system, as is shown in this chapter.

43 Suleimān Taqī al-Dīn, *Al-Taṭawur Al-Tārīkhī Lil-Mushkila Al-Lubnāniya* (Beirut: Dār Ibn Khaldūn, 1977), 82–3.

This formed part of a statement in which Jumayyil addressed 'Islamic organisations [that] desire "the achievement of social justice and equal distribution" for confession.' He argued for 'this demand to be realised in the next twenty four hours, on the condition that it be applied properly, making ethical and technical competence the basis of such job distribution'.

44 See Asher Kaufman, '"Tell Us Our History": Charles Corm, Mount Lebanon and Lebanese Nationalism', *Middle Eastern Studies* 40, no. 3 (2004): 21.

45 Josephine Crawley Quinn, *In Search of the Pheonicians* (Princeton, NJ: Princeton University Press, 2018), 5.
46 Kaufman, *Reviving Phoenicia*, 166.
47 See Muḥammad J. Bayhum, *Al-'Urūba Wal-Shu'ūbiyāt Al-Ḥadītha* [Arabism and the Modern Shu'ūbiyāt] (Beirut: Maṭābi' Dār al-Kishāf, 1957).
A *Shu'ubi* (the agent-noun of the plural *Shu'ūbiyāt*) evolved to denote a non-Arab who objected to Arab pride and who supported separatist groups within the Arab–Muslim world – see Kaufman, *Reviving Phoenicia*, 220.
48 They had both been affiliated with Khūrī's Constitutional Bloc during the 1940s. See earlier chapters.
49 See Georges Hakim, 'The Economic Basis of Lebanese Polity', in *Politics in Lebanon*, ed. Leonard Binder (New York: Wiley, 1966), 57–69.
Also see Nadim Shehadi, *The Idea of Lebanon: Economy and State in the Cénacle Libanais 1946–54* (Oxford: Centre for Lebanese Studies, 1987).
Also see: 'The Merchant Republic', in Traboulsi, *A History of Modern Lebanon* (London: Pluto Press, 2007).
50 Kaufman, '"Tell Us Our History"', 21.
51 Christopher Stone, 'The Ba'albakk Festival and the Rahbanis: Folklore, Ancient History, Musical Theater, and Nationalism in Lebanon', *Arab Studies Journal* 11, no. 2 (2003): 20.
52 Quinn, *In Search of the Pheonicians*, 12.
53 See Mona Arif, 'Constructing the National Past: History-Writing and Nation-Building in Nasser's Egypt', *Shorofat 1*, 11 December 2017. Retrieved on 20 May 2019 from: https://www.bibalex.org/Attachments/Publications/Files/2017121114173047484_ShorofatEnglish1.pdf.
Also see Jack Jr. Crabbs, 'Politics, History, and Culture in Nasser's Egypt', *International Journal of Middle East Studies* 6, no. 4 (1975): 386–420.
54 See Elie Podeh, 'The Symbolism of the Arab Flag in Modern Arab States: Between Commonality and Uniqueness', *Nations and Nationalism* 17, no. 2 (2011): 419–42.
55 See Article 10 of the *Lebanese Constitution as promulgated on May 23, 1926*. Retrieved from World Intellectual Property Organization on 23 May 2019: https://www.wipo.int/edocs/lexdocs/laws/en/lb/lb018en.pdf.
56 The expansion of state schools did not effectively commence until the later 1960s and 1970s. In fact, a public school with a full programme – one including primary, secondary and upper secondary levels – was only established in 1952 and the state university established in 1951 only had one department up until the end of the decade. See Munir Bashshur, 'The Role of Education: A Mirror of a Fractured National Image', in *Toward a Viable Lebanon*, ed. Halim Isber Barakat (London: Croom Helm, 1988), 48–9.
57 See Decree N°1436 issued on 23 March 1950 concerning the regulations for private schools. Published in the Lebanese Official Gazette N°13, 29 March 1950, 172–6. http://www.legallaw.ul.edu.lb/Law.aspx?lawId=168800.
58 Crow, 'Religious Sectarianism in the Lebanese Political System', 498.
59 For more on the development of Lebanese education in relation to sectarian politics, see Nemer Frayha, 'Education and Social Cohesion in Lebanon', *Prospects* 33, no. 1 (2003): 77–88.
Also see Munir Bashshur, 'Higher Education and Political Development in Syria and Lebanon', *Comparative Education Review* 10, no. 3 (1966): 451–61.
60 Crow, 'Religious Sectarianism in the Lebanese Political System', 499.

61 Crow, 499.
62 Officially the 'Jam'iyat al-Maqāsid al-Khayriya al-Islāmiya' [Islamic Society of Benevolent Intention], the Makassed school was originally founded in 1878 as a non-profit organization to provide education for Beirut's poorer Sunni population. During the twentieth century, it grew to become 'the most important Sunni Muslim organisation in Lebanon'.
See Michael Johnson, 'Factional Politics in Lebanon: The Case of the "Islamic Society of Benevolent Intentions"', *Middle Eastern Studies* 14, no. 1 (1978): 56–75.
63 al-Hajj was himself an ardent believer in the National Pact and the role it could play in nation-building.
See Ghassān Fawzī Tah, *Hawiyat Lubnān ('ind Al-Kiyāniyīn – Al-Qawmiyīn – Al-Islāmiyīn)* [Lebanese Identity (in Lebanism – in Nationalism – in Islamism)] Beirut: al-Markaz al-Islāmī lil-Dirāsāt al-Fikrīyah, 2009.
64 Jacques Benjamin, 'La Minorité En Etat Bicommunautaire: Quatre Études de Cas [Minorities in Bicommunal States: Four Case Studies]', *Canadian Journal of Political Science/Revue Canadienne de Science Politique* 4, no. 4 (1971): 486.
65 In particular, Sélim Abou developed an elaborate argument for the positive role of bilingualism in relation to Lebanese identity.
See Sélim Abou, *Le Bilinguisme Arabe-Français Au Liban: Essai d'Anthropologie Culturelle* [Arab-French Bilingualism in Lebanon: An Essay on Cultural Anthropology] (Paris: Presses universitaires de France, 1962).
His arguments, however, have been accused of being ideologically driven.
See, for example, Rosemary Sayigh, 'The Bilingualism Controversy in Lebanon', *World Today* 21, no. 3 (1965): 120–30.
66 Michel Chiha, *Visage et Présence Du Liban* [The Face and Presence of Lebanon] (Beirut: Editions du Trident, 1984), 162.
67 Sayigh, 'The Bilingualism Controversy in Lebanon', 121.
68 The Highest Druze Court of Appeal is formed by the religious heads (Sheikh al-Aql) of the Junblati and the Yazbeki factions. The two clans are historically opposed – see Hazran, 'Lebanon's Revolutionary Era', 162.
69 Crow, 'Religious Sectarianism in the Lebanese Political System', 509–10.
70 See Law issued on 2 April 1951 concerning the terms of reference for members of the Christian and the Jewish religion. Published in the Lebanese Official Gazette N° 15, 11 April 1951, 253–9. http://www.legallaw.ul.edu.lb/Law.aspx?lawId=258197.
71 The use of 'officially' here serves to indicate that the executive and legislative institutions remained committed to proportional representation. The issue of the compatibility of those proportions with demographical reality would be brought up during the 1958 crisis.
72 Attié, *Struggle in the Levant*, 40.
73 Turkey and Pakistan had signed a Pact of Mutual Cooperation in early 1954, and the eventual Baghdad Pact of 1955 would include all three countries.
74 Minutes of the Parliamentary Session on 30 October 1954. Retrieved from: http://www.legallaw.ul.edu.lb/PeriodSessionLandingPage.aspx?TextID=21457.
75 FO 484/8.
76 FO 484/9.
77 FO 484/9.
78 According to Wolfram Hanrieder, a political system is penetrated when, firstly, its decision-making process is influenced by external events – specifically on allocation of resources and in garnering support for its goals – and secondly, the relevant

decision-makers are willing to adapt and change according to those external events. See Wolfram Hanrieder, *West German Foreign Policy, 1949–1963: International Pressure and Domestic Response* (Stanford, CA: Stanford University Press, 1967), 230.

79 In fact, a letter sent to Khūrī by fifty-six deputies a few days before his resignation shows that he even enjoyed the support of a parliamentary majority when he resigned. See Malsagne, *Fouad Chéhab, 1902–1973*, 144.

80 This became somewhat of a norm in Lebanese politics, as governments were supposed to represent most if not all the communities.

81 Minutes of the Parliamentary Session on 13 September 1955. Retrieved from: http://www.legallaw.ul.edu.lb/PeriodSessionLandingPage.aspx?TextID=21762.

82 Minutes of the Parliamentary Session on 4 October 1955. Retrieved from: http://www.legallaw.ul.edu.lb/PeriodSessionLandingPage.aspx?TextID=21774.
Also see FO 484/9.

83 See The Jewish Telegraph Agency, vol. XXII, N° 203, 21 October 1955.
Retrieved on 10 March 2019 from: https://www.jta.org/1955/10/21/archive/egypt-syria-sign-mutual-defense-pact-against-israel.

For texts of both pacts, see Egyptian–Syrian Mutual Defense Pact (20 October 1955). Egyptian–Saudi Arabian Mutual Defense Pact (27 October 1955). *Middle East Journal*, 10, no. 1 (1956): 77–9.

Retrieved from: http://www.jstor.org/stable/4322774.

84 Sham'ūn had been favourable to the proposed Middle East Defence Organisation (MEDO) in 1952 – see Attié, *Struggle in the Levant*, 73. He also expressed his desire to the British ambassador to have Lebanon join the Baghdad Pact. See FO 484/10.

85 Sami E Baroudi, 'Divergent Perspectives among Lebanon's Maronites during the 1958 Crisis', *Critique: Critical Middle Eastern Studies* 15, no. 1 (2006): 12.

86 For example, students of the Islamic Makassed school declared themselves ready to be conscripted and to fight for Egypt – see Ra'd, *Tārīkh Lubnān Al-Siyāsī Wal-Iqtiṣādī, 1958–1975*, 56.

87 Maḥmūdī, *Lubnān Fī Jāmi'at Al-Duwal Al-'Arabiyya, 1945–1958*, 228–9.

88 See Elie Podeh, 'The Struggle over Arab Hegemony after the Suez Crisis', *Middle Eastern Studies* 29, no. 1 (1993): 91–110.

89 Chamoun, *Crise Au Moyen Orient*, 292.

90 Chamoun, 285–6.

91 13 November 1956.

92 Attié, *Struggle in the Levant*, 104.

93 For example, it was reported that the embassy was distributing portraits of Nāṣer for people to hang in place of Lebanese symbols or, in some cases, in place of Sham'ūn's own portraits in schools – Desmond Stewart, *Turmoil in Beirut: A Personal Account* (London: Wingate, 1958), 14–15.

94 Attié, *Struggle in the Levant*, 104.

95 FO 484/11.

96 Recording of Dwight D. Eisenhower speech, 5 January 1957. 'A Special Message to Congress on the Situation in the Middle East' provided by the Miller Center of Public Affairs.

Retrieved from: https://millercenter.org/the-presidency/presidential-speeches/january-5-1957-eisenhower-doctrine.

97 Later that year Mālik declared that the United States had agreed to assist the Lebanese state by providing 'the most modern defence equipment' while also promising

'unlimited economic aid' dedicated to the development of the country. Tensions were reaching a boiling point both within and outside the state. See FO 484/11.

98 Minutes of the Parliamentary session on 9 April 1957. Retrieved from: http://www.legallaw.ul.edu.lb/PeriodSessionLandingPage.aspx?TextID=23835.

The Christian deputy who resigned was Ḥamīd Frangieh who remained a staunch member of the opposition throughout Sham'ūn's term, though his motivations were questioned as he had presidential aspirations of his own.

99 Karol R. Sorby, 'Lebanon: The Crisis of 1958', *Asian and African Studies* 9, no. 1 (2000): 82–3.

Another reason given to the protest was the arrest warrant issued to 'Abdallah al-Mashnūq, who days prior had called for a 'revolutionary protest' against the government and accused Sham'ūn of abusing the Pact, and of leading the country to 'American colonialism'. See Ra'd, *Tārīkh Lubnān Al-Siyāsī Wal-Iqtiṣādī, 1958–1975*, 67–8.

100 Ra'd, 67.

101 Al-Tāhiri, *Siyāsat Al-Ḥokm Fī Lubnān*, 488.

102 'Isolationist' became an often-used term by Lebanese and Arab politicians to describe the extreme Lebanists without having to directly attack the Christian community.

103 Maḥmūdī, *Lubnān Fī Jāmi'at Al-Duwal Al-'Arabiyya, 1945–1958*, 229.

104 Attié, *Struggle in the Levant*, 141.

105 Attié, 132.

See Law issued on 24 April 1957 concerning the amendment of the electoral law. Published in the Lebanese Official Gazette N°18, 25 April 1957, 426–38. http://www.legallaw.ul.edu.lb/Law.aspx?lawId=172013.

106 Ra'd, *Tārīkh Lubnān Al-Siyāsī Wal-Iqtiṣādī, 1958–1975*, 69.

107 FO 484/11.

For details including US policies on the elections and direct payments to Sham'ūn, see Wilbur Eveland, *Ropes of Sand: America's Failure in the Middle East* (New York: W. W. Norton, 1980).

The US ambassador at the time – Donald Heath – got personally involved, making it his mission to ensure the defeat of those deputies that resigned, 'as punishment no matter what the cost'. In fact, US plans involved bringing about 'a 99.9 percent-pure pro-US parliament', and particularly strove to ensure the election of Foreign Minister Charles Mālik despite his lack of popularity among the electorate. See Eveland, 248–50.

108 Sham'ūn, in particular, was perceived to have gone even further than Khūrī had previously done with regard to government involvement: Fu'ād Shehāb, then commander of the armed forces and future president, claimed that the 'corruption, bribery, and general skulduggery during the [1957] elections had been a scandal and … had reached proportions never before seen in the Lebanon'. Junblāṭ, who had inexplicably lost his seat within a newly drawn constituency, could not believe that Sham'ūn would go as far as to personalize the elections and ensure opposition members would lose, since even Khūrī had not dared to do so. See Al-Matni, *Kamāl Junblāṭ*, 178. Even Sāmī al-Ṣulḥ, prime minister during the elections, later admitted that the president was involved in gerrymandering. See Sāmī Al-Ṣulḥ, *Lubnān: Al-'Abeth Al-Siyāsī Wal-Maṣīr Al-Majhūl* [Lebanon: Political Futility and the Unknown Destiny] (Beirut: Dār al-Nahār, 2000), 266.

109 This lack of support outside parliament as opposed to the backing that Sham'ūn enjoyed within the chamber is also highlighted by Sir George Humphrey Middleton, then-ambassador of Great Britain (see FO 484/11).

110 Interestingly, Sham'ūn was perceived as more of an ardent Arabist than Khūrī at the beginning of his tenure, much to the dismay of many in the Christian community who were worried that he might push the country too far in the direction of Arab unity. See Attié, *Struggle in the Levant*, 70.

111 See FO 484/11.

112 In 1956, the Syrian government – headed by the National Party – signed multiple economic and military agreements with the Soviet Union. By Charles Mālik's own admission, it was 'impossible' for both Western-oriented Lebanon and Soviet-oriented Syria to exist; 'sooner or later, one of them must disappear'. See Muḥammad Ḥussein Haykal, *Sanawāt Al-Ghilyān, Al-Jiz' Al-Awal* [The Boiling Years, Part One] (Cairo: Markaz al-'Ahrām lil-Tarjama, 1998), 843.

113 See Le Jour newspaper on 31 December 1957.

114 Adeed I. Dawisha, *Arab Nationalism in the Twentieth Century: From Triumph to Despair* (Princeton, NJ: Princeton University Press, 2003), 194–5.

A union with Egypt had also become the wish of most of the Syrian population. As Syria's chief of staff at the time put it, 'Who at that hour could dare say we do not want unity? The people would tear their heads off.'

115 In a speech in late February, former prime minister Rashīd Karāmi declared to Nāṣer that 'the Lebanese people … believe in [Nāṣer's] principles and mission', and added that 'when the hour strikes [the Lebanese] will all leap up as one man to hoist the banner to which all the Arabs will rally'.

Weeks later, a protest in Karāmi's city of Tripoli resulted in calls for union with the UAR, 'contrary to promises given to the authorities' that demanded no such appeals occur (see *L'Orient* newspaper on 25 March 1958). A few months later, the Speaker of Parliament 'Ādil 'Oseyrān visited Cairo and declared that it was in Lebanon's interest to join the United Arab States (a confederation established between the UAR and the Kingdom of Yemen), and demanded 'even more than this'. Equally, Sunni deputy Taqī al-Dīn al-Ṣulḥ declared in parliament that the UAR was as much a Lebanese phenomenon as an Arab one, since the 'dream for Arab Unity was formed as Lebanon was formed'.

See M. S. Agwani, *The Lebanese Crisis, 1958: A Documentary Study* (London: Asia Publishing House, 1965), 45–53.

See minutes of Parliamentary session on 25 March 1958. Retrieved on 1 June 2019 from: http://www.legallaw.ul.edu.lb/PeriodSessionLandingPage.aspx?SessionID=2231.

116 The Phalanges criticized the union as 'unrealistic' and the Syrian Social Nationalist Party (SSNP) openly denounced it. Meanwhile, organizations like the 'Arab National Youth Party' condemned the Sham'ūn regime for its lackadaisical attitude in recognizing UAR and issued a statement speaking directly to the 'Arab public' in Lebanon who 'consider confessionalism as a threat to Lebanese independence', arguing that the UAR is a progressive idea that represents the pure will of the people which it governs, and reassuring that it will not endeavour to force itself upon the Lebanese unless they equally desire it. See Ra'd, *Tārīkh Lubnān Al-Siyāsī Wal-Iqtiṣādī, 1958–1975*, 74–5.

A few days later, a celebration for the creation of the UAR occurred in Muslim-dominant Tyre where there were reports of Lebanese flags being torn and burnt.

Additionally, communication between Nāṣer and the leader of the Najjad party was immediately established with discussions focusing on the potential of Lebanon joining the UAR. See Attié, *Struggle in the Levant*, 158.

117 Nādia Karāmi and Nawāf Karāmi, *Wāqi' Al-Thawra Al-Lubnānīya* [The Reality of the Lebanese Revolution] (Beirut: Maṭba'at Karam, 1959), 54.

118 This last bombing in particular showed that the opposition was not solely discriminating along confessional lines, as the minister in question – Khalīl al-Habrī – was a Sunni Beiruti who was described as an 'Arab nationalist'. And yet, the combination of his support for Sham'ūn and the fact that he made 'no secret of his belief in cooperation with the British' is presumed to have made him a target for the opposition.

See FO 484/11.

119 As Salām declared on 16 July, 'Its [the opposition's] only aim is to get rid of Camille Sham'un's dictatorship, tyranny, and corrupt regime, and to save the Lebanon from the foreign influence under which Camille Sham'un has placed it.' See Agwani, *The Lebanese Crisis, 1958*, 295.

120 M. S. Agwani, 'The Lebanese Crisis of 1958 in Retrospect', *International Studies* 4, no. 4 (1962): 334.

121 Arnold Hottinger, 'Zu'amā' and Parties in the Lebanese Crisis of 1958', *Middle East Journal* 15, no. 2 (1961): 139–40.

122 Ra'd, *Tārīkh Lubnān Al-Siyāsī Wal-Iqtiṣādī, 1958–1975*, 76.

There were also some in Maronite circles who believed that M'ūshī's differences with Sham'ūn were more personal, and that he even had his eye on the presidency. Retrospective analyses of his political stances post-1958 seem to indicate that he was more of an opportunist than an ideological or principled 'politician'. And despite his significant role in the opposition to Sham'ūn, he would later end up allying with him against Shehāb's presidential term which he deemed as too close to Arab nationalist aspirations. See Hudson, *The Precarious Republic*, 128–9.

Similarly, others argued that the fact that M'ūshī was former president Khūrī's second cousin also influenced his political decisions. In fact, according to Ephraim Frankel, M'ūshī suggested the return of Khūrī to the presidency before supporting Shehāb as Sham'ūn's successor. See Ephraim A. Frankel, 'The Maronite Patriarch: An Historical View of a Religious Za'im in the 1958 Lebanese Crisis', *Muslim World* 66, no. 4 (1976): 254.

123 Robert D. Little and Wilhelmina Burch, *Air Operations in the Lebanon Crisis of 1958* (Washington, DC: USAF Historical Division Liaison Office, 1962), 6.

124 Omri Nir, 'The Shi'ites during the 1958 Lebanese Crisis', *Middle Eastern Studies* 40, no. 6 (2004): 113.

125 Shanahan, *The Shi'a of Lebanon*, 69.

126 K. S., 'The Lebanese Crisis in Perspective', *World Today* 14, no. 9 (1958): 379.

127 While the opposition had argued that the Eisenhower Doctrine violated the spirit of the Pact, the loyalists accused members of the opposition of plotting for Syrian unity or a merger with the UAR, which *they* argued violated the Pact. Indeed, Pierre Jumayyil himself made this explicit accusation in June.

See L'Orient newspaper on 1 June 1958.

128 Tuweynī also observed than an internal arms race was occurring between these two 'countries'.

See *al-Nahar* newspaper on 9 April 1958.

129 Malsagne, *Fouad Chéhab, 1902–1973*, 144.
Also see Chapter 3: Towards the Presidency in Malsagne, *Fouad Chéhab, 1902–1973*.
130 According to Sir George Humphrey Middleton, see FO 484/11.
131 See al-Nahar newspaper on 20 April 1958.
132 Douglas Little, 'His Finest Hour? Eisenhower, Lebanon, and the 1958 Middle East Crisis', *Diplomatic History* 20, no. 1 (1996): 40.
133 Little, 38–40.
While initially, Robert McClintock, US ambassador to Lebanon at the time, described Fu'ād Shehāb as 'a neutral legume who would require careful pruning to in the right direction', the United States accepted the inevitably of his acquisition of the presidency.
134 Hussein A. Hassouna, *The League of Arab States and Regional Disputes* (Dobbs Ferry, NY: Oceana Publications, 1975), 61.
135 Letter Dated 22 May 1958 from the Representative of Lebanon Addressed to the President of The Security Council. 23 May 1958. S/4007.
Retrieved on 28 May 2019 from: https://unispal.un.org/DPA/DPR/unispal.nsf/0/57E3CABA858324B5052566CE006A45A2.
136 Hassouna, 65.
137 UNOGIL's official mission was to 'ensure that there is no illegal infiltration of personnel or supply of arms or other *matériel* across the Lebanese borders'. See UN Security Council Resolution of 11 June 1958. S/4023 Retrieved on 1 June 2019 from: https://undocs.org/S/RES/128(1958).
138 Walter A. Dorn, *Air Power in UN Operations: Wings for Peace* (Farnham: Ashgate, 2014), 136–7.
139 Dorn, 136–7.
140 Gerald L. Curtis, 'The United Nations Observation Group in Lebanon', *International Organization* 18, no. 4 (1964): 762.
141 As Jumayyil put it, 'Any compromise formula would be nothing but a concession.' See L'Orient newspaper on 5 June 1958.
142 L'Orient newspaper on 5 June 1958.
143 Little, 'His Finest Hour? Eisenhower, Lebanon, and the 1958 Middle East Crisis', 43.
144 Chamoun, *Crise Au Moyen Orient*, 423–4.
145 Gendzier, *Notes from the Minefield*, 308.
146 A declaration from an opposition group compared the landing of American troops to the 'colonial' presence of French mandatory forces, and called for the opposition to 'kill any foreigner'. See Karāmi and Karāmi, *Wāqiʿ Al-Thawra Al-Lubnānīya*, 290–1.
Similarly, Ṣā'ib Salām warned on 15 July of the return of imperialism 'in a hideous plot hatched with the traitor agent Camille Sham'un and his criminal gang'. See Agwani, *The Lebanese Crisis, 1958*, 293.
147 Attié, *Struggle in the Levant*, 198–9.
148 Curtis, 'The United Nations Observation Group in Lebanon', 757.
For the UN Security Council meeting, see Repertoire of the Practice of the Security Council, Chapter 8 – Part II. Retrieved on 3 June 2019 from: https://www.un.org/en/sc/repertoire/56-58/Chapter%208/56-58_08-12-Complaint%20by%20Lebanon-%20Complaint%20by%20Jordan.pdf.
149 Chamoun, *Crise Au Moyen Orient*, 412.
150 Special Envoy Robert Murphy, for example, claims to have brought up the ability of US equipment to 'destroy all of Beirut in a matter of minutes' in his discussions with

opposition leader Salām, which, according to him, had the desired effect of reducing shootings in Beirut during night-time. See Robert Murphy, *Diplomat among Warriors* (Garden City, NY: Doubleday, 1964), 405.

151 Gendzier, *Notes from the Minefield*, 343.

152 Sham'ūn blamed Shehāb for his losses, both politically and militarily, while many in the opposition denounced Shehāb for cooperating with the United States, and increased their arguments for a return of Khūrī to the presidency, which was deemed unacceptable by US mediators.

153 Only a week after they were originally due to take place – see Karāmi and Karāmi, *Wāqi' Al-Thawra Al-Lubnānīya*, 298.

154 Minutes of the Parliamentary Session on 31 July 1958. Retrieved from: http://www.legallaw.ul.edu.lb/PeriodSessionLandingPage.aspx?SessionID=2250.

155 Gendzier, *Notes from the Minefield*, 346.

156 According to Robert Murphy, American special envoy to Lebanon, the government only controlled about 30 per cent of the territory at one point – see Murphy, *Diplomat among Warriors*, 401.

157 K. S., 'The Lebanese Crisis in Perspective', 380.

158 Gendzier, *Notes from the Minefield*, 346.

Another actor that also played a significant role in mediation and conflict resolution was the American special envoy to Lebanon Robert Murphy, who had arrived in Beirut two days after the Marines landed. Many have argued that he was at the heart of the resolution of the crisis, though others have highlighted the more central role of McClintock. See Juan Romero, 'Discourse and Mediation in the Lebanese Crisis of 1958', *Middle Eastern Studies* 48, no. 4 (2012): 583.

159 Fouad Boutros, *Mémoires* [Memoires], ed. Jana Tamer (Beirut: Les Éditions L'Orient Le Jour/Les Messageries du Levant, 2010), 64.

160 Qubain, *Crisis in Lebanon*, 28.

161 Seven days after the landings, for example, the Communist Party of Lebanon called on its supporters to 'fight the greedy invaders with every arm in [their] possession. [To] Kill them wherever [they] find them with bullets of [their] guns and machine-guns. [To] Aim [their] bombs at them. attack them with everything that [came] to [their] hands'. See Agwani, *The Lebanese Crisis, 1958*, 298.

162 Malcolm H. Kerr, 'Review: Lebanese Views on the 1958 Crisis', *Middle East Journal* 15, no. 2 (1961): 216.

Chapter 5

DELAYING THE INEVITABLE?

The crisis of 1958 was seen, both historically and contemporarily, as the culmination of the flaws of the Lebanese system. Specifically, political institutions that were meant to reinforce a power-sharing system were evidently no longer reflecting the true demographic proportions of the country. Even though no census had been conducted since 1932,[1] the reality of the Christian/Muslim ratio had become obvious to everyone: the Christians no longer enjoyed a numerical majority that entitled them to a greater number of political posts. This reality, coupled with the 'no victor, no vanquished' formula adopted by those left standing after 1958, signified that substantial reforms were bound to occur during the next few years in Lebanon. Additionally, the personal convictions of Fu'ād Shehāb – the general-turned-president – and his distaste for sectarian politics propelled him to attempt a fundamental change in the Lebanese political structure.

During the 1950s, Sham'ūn had tried to increase the institutional legitimacy of the state while also pushing for a particular idea of the state in an effort to also develop its societal legitimacy. Institutionally, Sham'ūn's efforts proved futile, in no small part because of his decision to adopt a minimalist position where the state's role was mostly restricted to administrating between traditional and sectarian dynamics. The result was a continuation of corruption through communal patron–client relationships in addition to institutional inefficiency. Similarly, the rise in economic growth only served to exacerbate existing inequalities that fell along confessional and regional lines. In terms of foreign policy, a field so vital to Lebanese national identity, Sham'ūn was perceived, by the Muslim population, to have betrayed both the neutrality which was so vital to confessional equilibrium and the Lebanese position within the Arab world, one embodied by the expression of Lebanon's 'Arab face'. Instead, Sham'ūn developed a close relationship with the United States and, in light of 'Abd al-Nāṣer's rise, further alienated the Muslims from a common idea of the state, thus losing any potential for societal legitimacy in the process.

In essence, Shehāb endeavoured to undo all the steps taken by Sham'ūn. The policies taken by the state during the 1950s were perceived to be the main factor that led to the crisis of 1958, and Shehāb viewed a modernization[2] of the state as a necessity, since he believed that the Lebanese 'had not yet succeeded in building a nation'. Thus, Shehāb believed that he must strive to build a 'healthy' state which can allow the Lebanese who are drawn to it to be 'elevated to the rank of nation'.[3] His policies during his tenure, which expanded the Lebanese state to an unprecedented degree, came to be known collectively as 'Chehabism', and while there is no clear definition for this term, it came to represent a number of political principles.[4] Firstly, that national unity can only be achieved through a strong, centralized state that is free of sectarian tension and requirements; secondly, that socio-economic development should remain a state initiative if inequality is to be avoided; thirdly, that an affirmation of Lebanon's Arabness is necessary both for its internal stability and for its existence in the Middle East; and fourthly, that in order to effect the aforementioned reforms, the role of the Lebanese army must be strengthened.[5] Chehabism would remain in effect even after Shehāb's term had ended. Consequently, this chapter will focus on Lebanese state-building during Shehāb's years so as to continue observing the role that political legitimacy played during the development of the Lebanese state, especially during the years preceding the start of the civil war in the 1970s.

Reconciliation and reform

When Shehab first took over from Sham'ūn in September 1958, he attempted to install a representative but progressive cabinet. Thus, on 24 September, he named a cabinet of eight members, four Muslims and four Christians, who, while reflective of the different facets of the Christian community, had not been supporters of the Sham'ūn regime.[6] Part of Shehab's reasoning for this was that the Sham'ūnists and the Katā'ib had become too extreme, and were no longer able to control their followers and henchmen, though he had left some hope for the 'much more moderate' Jumayyil – leader of the Katā'ib.[7] Feeling unrepresented, the Christian 'loyalists' launched a counter-revolution, an offensive of 'killings and kidnappings' which lasted about three weeks until the four-man government[8] was formed in October.[9] That government would gain a unanimous vote of confidence from parliament.[10]

Though they had all participated in the crisis one way or another, the members of the new government were ready to support – at least for the time being – Shehāb in a project of reconciliation that was deemed necessary. Additionally, Shehāb's reform project had brought with it a promise of more accurate representation within public institutions for the Muslim population, a key demand by the Muslim-dominant opposition. For the Christian members of the cabinet, this was their opportunity to maintain some checks on the extent of the upcoming reforms, in order to preserve what they felt should be the character and organization of the state.[11] It was clear Shehāb noticed that the state had not achieved the legitimacy it needed to function effectively and maintain stability. He argued that the 1958 conflict was but a reflection of the deeper crisis of national unity. On 21 November 1959, Shehāb argued that 'building a state cannot occur unless the people put their enthusiasm, their heart, their will, and their toughness in the endeavour'.[12] A year later, he also asserted that 'building a society does not occur unless national unity is built, which is itself dependent on building a society'.[13] Having witnessed the culmination of societal and institutional illegitimacy in 1958, Shehāb continued to stress the need for state- and nation-building in Lebanon throughout his term.

Institutional changes

On 6 December 1958, the Shehāb regime created a new institution: the Central Body for Administrative Reform (CBAR). The CBAR's main mission was to 'assess all organs of state administration with the aim of increasing standards within and turning those organs into valid tools that perform the missions entrusted to them in a manner that coincides, to the greatest extent possible, to the needs of the country'.[14] The CBAR, which was crucially made up of a majority of professionals from outside the state, was then charged to recommend any changes for the government to effect. Six days later, a law was officially put in effect, which gave Rashīd Karāmī's government the 'right to enact legislative decrees for a period of six months'.[15]

Bureaucratic changes

The following months would see the Lebanese public administration undergo the biggest changes since the independence of the country. A total of 162 legislative decrees were issued by June 1959, 'dealing with every basic aspect of government organization and policy'.[16] These decrees were mainly of two kinds; many dealt with the organization (or reorganization) of existing institutions, since part of the CBAR's mission was to identify unnecessary overlap and excessive personnel. These included the state's public administration,[17] the diplomatic corps,[18] the internal security forces[19] and the State Consultative Council.[20] A second group of legislative decrees focused on establishing new institutions or rules. The most significant of these is what became known as the Personnel Law:[21] an extensive and detailed text which aimed to clearly define the responsibilities, privileges, benefits and limits of government employees. Crucially, Article 96 of the decree stipulated that confessional balance must be respected as per the constitution, indicating that the removal of confessionalism from the Lebanese political system was still far from an immediate requirement.[22] Other important institutions created at the time were the Council for Money and Credit,[23] the Central Inspection Service[24] and the Public Service Council.[25] The last two were of particular importance as they were assigned to the office of the prime minister, allowing the latter to have enough autonomous power within the state to challenge the main executive power: that of the president. Additional autonomous bodies, such as the Authority for Investment in the Port of Tripoli and the Lebanese Fruit Office, were also created to monitor, regulate and encourage socio-economic development in the areas outside Beirut.

Despite the extensive legislation produced within the early years of Shehāb's term, and while almost all of them addressed the modernization of the state in theory, it is almost impossible to judge the performance of all these drastic changes on their own, as they were intended for deeper, long-term change not only in the organization of state bureaucracy but also in the transformation of values associated with government employment within Lebanon. In 1961, Ralph Crow and Adnan Iskandar argued that it would be 'a generation before this [transitional] stage [in administration] would be complete and before a new and more consistent pattern of behaviour could be stabilized'.[26] Additionally, the limited time which the CBAR had to study these organizations and recommend the right measures taken also hampered the potential for meaningful change within public administration. Shehāb himself, a self-declared upholder of the National Pact,[27] was also wary about affecting so deep a transformation that it could threaten the traditional dynamics of Lebanese political life, or aggravate a certain community. Thus, many of the reforms made in the first two years of his term, though revolutionary in a sense, still maintained the supremacy of sectarianism and the dominance of patron–client relationships. In fact, in some cases, the ministers themselves – all four of who had traditionally operated within sectarian circles – stood in Shehāb's way when it came to the removal or replacement of certain top-level officials.[28] Similarly, members of parliament were already feeling threatened by the exceptional power they had given to the government.[29]

Nevertheless, the administrative reforms of 1959 were seen, overall, as a hugely necessary step in the modernization of the Lebanese state. Their significance was highlighted by one Shīʿa member of parliament later that year, ʿAlī Bazzī, who proclaimed that, as a whole, the legislative decrees formed the second-most important event in Lebanese state-building, after the acquisition of independence in 1943.[30] According to Samuel Huntington, 'political modernization involves the rationalization of authority, the differentiation of structures, and the expansion of political participation'.[31] Whether or not they would prove successful, the reforms during Shehāb's early term signify, at the very least, an attempt to ensure the rationalization of authority through heavier centralization, institutionalization and inspection of public institution and services. Similarly, the CBAS's work focused on the true differentiation of structures by attempting to remove the ad hoc nature of power within Lebanese state institutions, usually based on social standing and prestige, and by also addressing the issue of functional overlap due to lack of planning and communication as well as corruption. Shehāb's attempt to modernize the state through the first two aspects mentioned by Huntington is apparent, but it would remain to be seen whether or not the Lebanese political context could absorb such changes to its institutional life. As for the increase in political participation, Shehāb left that goal for his socio-economic development plan. Nevertheless, these bureaucratic changes were meant to help the state acquire institutional legitimacy, very much in line with Weber's 'rational authority'.[32]

Development plan

On 22 November 1959, Shehāb declared in his 'message to the nation' that Lebanon had entered a 'new life', one which meant the 'disappearance of the spirit of discord and hatred', and in which a new 'public life' has protected the country 'from corruption and sedition'.[33] A few weeks earlier, Raymond Eddeh had quit his post over differences with Jumayyil and Shehāb.[34] The president, in his bid to achieve national unity, added five members to form a government that – with the exception of Jumayyil's inclusion – resembled the one he put together when he first came to office.[35] It was also decided that parliament would be dissolved and re-elected a year before the end of its term, as Shehāb saw it necessary for deputies to reflect new political opinions that were not as extreme as those at play in 1957.

Accordingly, a new electoral law was drafted which enlarged parliament from sixty-six to ninety-nine members, while only adding one constituency (making the total twenty-seven) so as to still reflect local wishes as much as possible.[36] This move proved successful, as the new parliament reflected much of the support that Shehāb had received. The elections also allowed for the return of many that Sham'ūn had excluded from the chamber like Kamāl Junblāṭ and Ṣā'ib Salām, while also containing many new faces,[37] though members of what would become Shehāb's main opposition – Sham'ūn himself and Eddeh – were elected as well.[38] The increased number of seats also naturally meant that a bigger number of the 1958 opposition were now represented in parliament.

On 20 July, two days after the new parliament convened for the first time and elected a new speaker, Shehāb tendered his resignation. In an address to the Lebanese public, he declared that he had only accepted the presidency because he saw it necessary to step in during Lebanon's 'darkest days'.[39] He also stated that he had, from the off, set himself a timetable in which he wanted to effect the change that he did. After 'all conditions necessary for the return of the normal exercise of authority have been met', he thus considered his mission complete and decided to resign with his 'conscience at ease'.[40] Immediately, a strong reaction came about as a result of Shehāb's resignation, both from members of the public and from political leaders. Junblāṭ immediately prepared a petition for the president to revoke his decision, emphasizing in it the risk of another crisis, and implying that his mission was not as complete as he would've liked. That petition would end up bearing the signatures of more than 90 per cent of members of parliament.[41] Later that day, Shehāb accepted that his task wasn't complete and rescinded his resignation, which prompted celebrations throughout the country.

Following his return, Shehāb decided not to settle for bureaucratic reforms: after appeasing much of the Lebanese population (i.e. the under-represented Muslims and the frustrated, progressive Christians) with these changes, he set out to initiate his own plans for socio-economic development and the modernization of Lebanon as a whole, and he had acquired the popular mandate he needed.[42] He started by surrounding himself with a combination of technical professionals and military men that he could count on not to get caught up in sectarian politics.[43]

In 1960, Shehāb commissioned the 'Institut de Recherche et de Formation en vue du développement' (IRFED), founded by a close advisor of his, Louis-Joseph Lebret,[44] to undergo a two-year study of the 'needs and possibilities of development in Lebanon'.[45] The IRFED reports would end up confirming what Shehāb – and most Muslim Lebanese – suspected: that despite the economic boom of the 1950s, regional (and thus, sectarian) inequality throughout Lebanon had been growing to an unsustainable degree.[46] The evidence provided by IRFED also reinforced Shehāb's own view of Lebanese politics: that, while traditional rivalries and one-sided policies like Sham'ūn's play their part in instability, it was actually socio-economic demands and the feeling of unfairness that was at the heart of the Muslim insurrection of 1958.[47] Accordingly, the IRFED report argued that the 'difficulties encountered through creating a sense of citizenship and the establishment of national cohesion cannot be overcome but incrementally, and on the condition that the different sections of society largely feel enriched from national economic solidarity'.[48] The study found that the solution was not to increase 'global revenue' but to revamp the entire economic structure and the way resources are distributed.[49] Thus, the IRFED developed a plan that aimed to increase state effectiveness while better spreading 'prosperity' among the Lebanese society.[50]

Starting in 1960, Shehāb began to implement the reforms tasked by the CBAR, though he 'knew better' than to trust the historically ineffective Lebanese government to do so. He named Ṣā'ib Salām as prime minister in an effort to appease the Beiruti leader after two years of the Tripolitan Karāmī at the helm, and decided to have a totally representative government of eighteen members, the largest in Lebanese history at that point.[51] He also kept both Junblāṭ and Jumayyil (the latter through his cousin Maurice who was appointed minister) involved in governmental activities because they could provide him with communal support (especially among the Maronites) and because, notwithstanding their political stances, they both led parties that claimed to fight for socio-economic reform.[52] Shehāb also insisted on the creation of a new Ministry for Administrative Reform in Salām's government, in which he inserted the Jesuit priest André Le Genissel to take charge of social legislation and, specifically, the preparation of a policy draft for a social security programme.[53]

Shehab knew that his reforms needed more time than his presidential term would allow but, without sacrificing the sanctity of the constitution (i.e. through another amendment), he planned on doing as much as he could during his time and to set up a foundation for his successor.[54] With the support of an extensive government, and most of parliament, the president had a clear lane to implement as much of the IRFED recommendations as he could. From 1960 to 1964, he would personally issue over two hundred decrees, with parliament promulgating an additional 490 ordinary laws.[55] Shehāb himself defended the high number of decrees by arguing that any necessary proposals he would send to parliament were 'guaranteed a burial'.[56] He also firmly believed in the IRFED report's recommendations which argued for a more extensive state, with a much wider scope than the one already present in a Lebanon 'that wanted to guarantee a maximum of liberalism'.[57] The IRFED report further recommended a degree of ministerial cooperation, hence Shehab's insistence on inserting individuals that he deemed as qualified within the different ministries. Of the new institutions which the IRFED advised the creation of, the Litani River Development Plan was one which Shehāb immediately attended; its objective was to provide water for the south and the Biqāʿ, so as to finally take advantage of the longest Lebanese river.[58] Additionally, Shehāb set up the Green plan, a semi-autonomous organization that aimed to encourage irrigation and the expansion of cultivated areas.[59] Throughout the early 1960s, the state also ensured that funds remained available in a Credit Bank for Tourism, Agriculture and Industry.[60]

Not unlike his bureaucratic changes, Shehāb's socio-economic plan was very much in line with the suggestions of modernization theory. The attempt to eradicate regional economic isolation and integrate all the underdeveloped areas into a cohesive, regulated, national economy is seen as one of the key stages of social modernization.[61] Additionally, increasing state capacity while eradicating corruption and satisfying changing social needs is seen as a stabilizing combination that also helps the state achieve institutional legitimacy. And, most importantly, the increase in the scope of the state as well as the socio-economic integration of the peripheral areas through the increase in education, communication and media aimed to increase the rate of social participation in the political system.[62]

While it is difficult to obtain exact, year-by-year statistics for the period of Shehāb's term and beyond, some studies and certain research, in addition to official statistics taken periodically, allow for a broad picture of the results of the regime's policies. These results are divided between socio-economic and political, and grouped in Tables 5.1 and 5.2.

Summary

Tables 5.1 and 5.2 allow for a number of conclusions that can help assess Shehāb's term as president, and specifically his policies of modernization and development. Firstly, on the socio-economic level one can clearly notice that the economy under Shehāb continued to grow, recovering after the crisis of 1958 to unprecedented levels and continuing to expand throughout the rest of the 1960s. Still, while Shehāb's policies focused on allaying issues of inequality and the development of the peripheral areas (as evidenced by the quality of life index), the 1960s did not see a fundamental change in the structure of the economy, with the tertiary market still dominating much of the percentage of the GNP throughout the decade. During that time, the share of both the agriculture and industry sector continued to diminish, but their equivalent share in the labour force remained stable. A survey of Muslim and Christian agricultural villagers in the Biqāʿ in the early 1960s showed that there was very little trust in the government's ability to improve their circumstances or their ability to make a better living from working in agriculture.[63] The figures suggest that this had not changed much by the end of the decade.

Similarly, Shehāb's policies do not seem to have caused a major change of trend in international trade as the export/import ratio had also only barely increased by 1968. At a developmental level, Shehāb's focus on improving the standard of living in the areas surrounding Beirut and the Mountain seemed to have borne fruit, as the 1960s saw an improvement in the quality of life in those outer regions,

Table 5.1 Socio-economic Indicators

	1956	1957	1958	1960	1961	1964	1966–9	1968	1970	1971
GNP in LL[a]	2,851 m	2,880 m	2,537 m	3,246 m	3,478 m	4,334 m	5,111 m	5,328 m	5,787 m	6,337 m
Income per Capita in $[b]				362		449				
Percentage of National Income by Household %[c]				*Lower 50*: 18 *Next 40*: 38 *Upper 10*: 44						*Lower 50*: 17 *Next 40*: 35 *Upper 10*: 48
Ordinary Budget as Percentage of GNP[d]			13.7		14.5	23.2				
Percentage of GNP by Economic Sector (Agriculture, Banking/ Insurance, Commerce/Trade, Government Others)[e]					*Agriculture*: 18.5 *Industry Energy Consumption*: 16 *Others*: 65.5		*Agriculture*: 12 *Banking/ Insurance*: 4 *Commerce/ Trade*: 33 *Government*: 8 *Industry*: 13 *Others*: 30			

Table 5.1 Socio-economic Indicators (continued)

	1956	1957	1960	1964	1966–9	1968	1970	1971
Percentage of Labour Force by Economic Sector[f]		*Agriculture*: 48.9 *Industry*: 12 *Construction*: 7.3 *Transport*: 5.3 *Commerce*: 18.8 *Finances*: 0.44 *Government*: 3.36 *Others*: 10.7			*Agriculture*: 50 *Industry*: 11 *Banking/ Insurance*: 0.4 *Commerce/ Trade*: 11 *Government*: 23			
Expenditures of State-Affiliated Autonomous Authorities in LL[g]		±69,900,000		±225,140,000				
Quality of Life Index by Region[h]			*Central*: 2.24 *North*: 2.13 *South*: 1.53 *Biqāʿ*: 1.47 *Rural areas*: 1.69				*C*: 2.59 *N*: 2.52 *S*: 2.20 *B'*: 2.00 *R*: 2.23	
Export/Import Ratio[i]	0.24					0.28		
Number of Primary and Secondary Students in Private/Government Schools[j]			*Private*: ±170,000 (61%) *Government*: ±105,000 (38%)	*Private*: ±245,000 (58%) *Government*: ±173,000 (41%)				*Private*: ±464,000 (63%) *Government*: ±268,000 (36%)

(continued)

Table 5.1 Socio-economic Indicators (continued)

	1959	1960	1961	1971	1972
Percentage of Students per Population by Region[k]	Beirut: 18.8 Mountain: 17.4 North: 16.4 Biqā‘: 13.5 South: 13.2			Beirut: 38.3 Mountain: 34.4 North: 20.0 Biqā‘: 17.6 South: 17.2	
Number of University Students[l]		±4,000	±17,000		

[a] This GNP is set against the market prices of 1972–4. See Gaspard, *A Political Economy of Lebanon, 1948–2002: The Limits of Laissez-Faire*, 262–3.
[b] See Hudson, 'Democracy and Social Mobilization in Lebanese Politics', 254.
[c] See Gaspard, *A Political Economy of Lebanon, 1948–2002: The Limits of Laissez-Faire*, 75.
[d] See Hudson, *The Precarious Republic: Political Modernization in Lebanon*, 308.
[e] For 1961: see Labaki, 'L'Économie Politique Du Liban Indépendant, 1943–1975 [The Political Economy of Independent Lebanon, 1943–1975]', 180. For 1966–9: see Salem, *Modernization without Revolution: Lebanon's Experience*, 42.
[f] For 1957: see Institut de Recherche et de Formation en Vue du Developpement Harmonisé, *Besoins et Possibilités de Développement Du Libon; Étude Préliminaire. Mission IRFED-Liban*, 1960–1. Tome 1, 87.
For 1966–9: see Salem, *Modernization without Revolution: Lebanon's Experience*, 42.
[g] See Hudson, *The Precarious Republic: Political Modernization in Lebanon*, 311.
[h] See 1961: see Labaki, 'L'Économie Politique Du Liban Independant, 1943–1975 [The Political Economy of Independent Lebanon, 1943–1975]', 174–6. Labaki recognizes that his index is synthetic but does not elaborate on its creation.
Overall, Labaki argues that Muslim-dominant regions have grown more than Christian-dominated ones, e.g. South = 70% Muslim; North = 40% Muslim; Bioā' = 60% Muslim; Central = 70% Christian.
[i] See Owen, 'The Economic History of Lebanon, 1943–1974: Its Salient Features', 34.
[j] Includes pre-primary, primary, intermediate and secondary education. See Bashshur, 'The Role of Education: A Mirror of a Fractured National Image', 50
[k] See Kliot, 'The Collapse of the Lebanese State', 59.
[l] See el-Khazen, *The Breakdown of the State in Lebanon, 1967–1978*, 71.

Table 5.2 Political Indicators

	1953	1957	1960	1964	1965	1963	1969
Total Number of Civil Servants[a]			±16,000		19,161		24,227
Number and Percentage of Party Members in Parliament[b]	*44 Members:* Total: 8–10 Percentage: 24	*66 Members:* Total: 12 Percentage: 18	*99 Members:* Total: 33–37 Percentage: 35	*99 Members:* Total: 27 Percentage: 27		*99 Members:* Total: 38 Percentage: 38	
Occupation of Members of Parliament[c]	*44 Members:* Landlords: 40.9% Lawyers: 34.1% Businessmen: 6.8 Professionals: 18.2%	*66 Members:* Landlords: 33.3% Lawyers: 36.3% Businessmen: 11.1% Professionals: 19.0%	*99 Members:* Landlords: 23.0% Lawyers: 29.0% Businessmen: 14.0% Professionals: 34.0%	*99 Members:* Landlords: 23.2% Lawyers: 27.3% Businessmen: 17.2% Professionals: 32.3%			
Occupation of New Members of Parliament[d]	*44 Members:* Landlords: 46.1% Lawyers: 23% Businessmen: 0 % Professionals: 30.8%	*66 Members:* Landlords: 11.5% Lawyers: 38.5% Businessmen: 15.4% Professionals: 23.1%	*99 Members:* Landlords: 13.5% Lawyers: 21.2% Businessmen: 15.4% Professionals: 50%	*99 Members:* Landlords: 17.9% Lawyers: 25% Businessmen: 25% Professionals: 32.1%			

(continued)

Table 5.2 Political Indicators (continued)

	1943	1943–58	1958	1962	1969	1958–75
Number of Troops in Lebanese Armed Forces[e]			±10,000		±12,000	
Religion of Lebanese Officers in the Armed Forces[f]		*Christians:* 65.5% (Maronites 43.8%) Muslims: 33.9% (Sunnis 14.7%)				*Christians:* 55% (Maronites 34.8%) *Muslims:* 45% (Sunnis: 15.3%) (Shīʿa: 15.3%)
Total Percentage of Christians in State Administration[g]	62			53		

[a] For 1960: see Crow, 'Confessionalism, Public Administration, and Efficiency in Lebanon', 178.
For 1965: Numbers exclude Ministry of Defence. See Salem, *Modernization without Revolution: Lebanon's Experience*, 77.
[b] For all years excluding 1968: see Suleiman, 'The Role of Political Parties in a Confessional Democracy: The Lebanese Case', 684. For 1968: See Zuwiyya, 1972, *The Parliamentary Election of Lebanon 1968*, 92.
[c] See Hudson, 'The Electoral Process and Political Development in Lebanon', 178.
[d] See Malsagne, *Fouad Chehab, 1902–1973: Une Figure Oubliée de Mistake Ubanaise [Fu'ād Shehāb, 1902–1973: A Forgotten Figure of Lebanese History]*, 244.
[e] For 1958: see Barak, *The Lebanese Army: A National Institution in a Divided Society*, 55. Barak bases this number on Sham'ūn's own memoires and US ambassador's correspondence at the time. For 1969: see Steinberg and Paxton, *The Statesman's Year-Book 1969–1970: Statistical and Historical Annual of the States of the World for the Year*, 1125. Although, Hudson seems to suggest that this figure grew to over 15,000 'during Shehāb's term' – see Hudson, *The Precarious Republic: Political Modernization in Lebanon*, 312.
[f] See Barak, *The Lebanese Army: A National Institution in a Divided Society*, 26.
[g] See Hudson, *The Precarious Republic: Political Modernization in Lebanon*, 320.

though the increase in the ratio of educated people still didn't match the equivalent rate for the Beirut and Mountain populations. And while the share of students in public – as opposed to historically communitarian, private – schools increased by the end of Shehāb's term, it would end up significantly declining by 1972, though how much of that is because of Shehāb's policies or those of his successor is still up for debate, and will be broadly addressed later in the chapter.

Similarly, the decade of the 1960s saw changes on the political level, ones that suggested a trend towards modernization as well. The main transformation in the state's activity, as assumed by modernization theory, is its expansion in size. The number of civil servants during Sham'ūn's term was already deemed to be excessive, especially for a country in which most of the personal status laws are governed by communal institutions. And yet, that number continued to grow during Shehāb's term and would ultimately increase by almost 50 per cent by the end of the decade. Similarly, with Chehabism reliant on the power and prestige of the military, members of the armed forces also increased during that time, with some sources indicating an even higher increase than that suggested by the statistics above. Moreover, as economic indicators show, the share of the labour force taken up by government workers also dramatically increased throughout the decade. Politically, one can see a clear trend of modernization within parliament that rises in 1960 but also shows a slight decline by 1964. This is evidenced both by the number of political party members and by the share of new entrants to parliament that were professionals and lawyers as opposed to traditional landlords and/or businessmen, as well as the overall make-up of parliament itself.

On this issue, however, there are two – interlinked – issues that must be taken into consideration: firstly, that the presence of political parties in the Lebanese parliament was also there prior to Shehāb's term – for example, 24 per cent of deputies in the forty-four-member parliament of 1953 were party members – and secondly, that Lebanese political parties are quite different in their nature than Western-style political parties, which are usually advocated for by modernization theorists. To that end, in his study of Lebanese political parties in 1967, Michael Suleiman begins by arguing that 'inasmuch as what pass for political parties in the country differ from "modern political parties", some deviation from, or alterations of, more conventional definitions is obviously necessary'.[64] Similarly, Hudson's 1966 study of competitiveness in the Lebanese electoral scene also sheds light on some truths about the relation between socio-economic modernization and political modernization, through the relation between development and democratic competitiveness.[65] While there is a constant increase in national and regional competitiveness during parliamentary elections since 1947, what wasn't there was a clear correlation between urban development and electoral competitiveness. In fact, Beirut ranked last in competitiveness despite it being the most urbanized and developed (therefore most socially mobilized) region in the country.[66] Similarly, the rural areas of the south showed more competitiveness than the urbanized city of Tripoli.[67] As a result, Hudson ponders on whether or not the removal of confessionalism – an inherent obstacle to modernization and a strong characteristic of rural Lebanon – would make the electoral process 'more democratic'.[68]

And finally, Shehāb's goal of reducing inequal representation both in the administrative and the military sector also showed signs of success, as the percentage of Christians declined to reflect the growing Muslim population that, with the continued absence of a census, were becoming more convinced of their overall majority. However, while the Muslim population at the time was nearly equally divided between Shīʿa and Sunnis, the former's disadvantageous positions meant that the latter, along with the overrepresented Druze, were more able to take advantage of these changes and secured 'the lion's share of administrative posts reserved' for Muslims.[69] Subsequently, the Shīʿa, whose population and social influence was growing, remained under-represented and alienated within and by the Lebanese state.[70]

Societal changes

If one is to look at the societal legitimacy of the state during Shehāb's presidential term, one cannot but accept the fact that the president enjoyed popular support as well as the approval of many of the political elite in Lebanon. The mere fact that his term did not end in a crisis that involved armed violence or a forced resignation – quite the opposite, as he was asked by many to remain as president – is a testament to the significant backing he enjoyed throughout his presidential tenure. Still, the previous chapters of this book have highlighted the fact that Lebanese state had never enjoyed a sufficient degree of societal legitimacy up to the point of Shehāb's presidency. In that context, support for the president himself did not, on its own, signify that an idea of the state, its identity and what it represented for the Lebanese communities, was widespread among the political factions in Lebanon. Indeed, one is more likely to be successful in defending the *regime's* legitimacy as opposed to the *state's*, in the case of Shehāb. The following will thus focus on the policies undertaken by the Chehabist state which, when considered along with previous regimes as well as its immediate successor, serve to alienate a section of the Lebanese society in a similar way that the Khūrian and Shamʿūnist states had done.

Early signs of discontent The events of Shehāb's resignation and return in 1960 were telling in many ways. There are some that saw it as a political manoeuvre which allowed him to consolidate power and thus embark on the reforms he had in mind with a sort of leeway that he might not have enjoyed otherwise. Ghassān Tuweynī, the editor of the Nahār newspaper, called it the 'greatest manoeuvre planned by a military mind, or executed by a politician', since it showed him as indispensable to the country's well-being.[71] Overall, such arguments mainly circulated within the Christian community, by those who distrusted Shehāb's ability to protect the Christian identity (or idea) of the state.[72] After all, the new parliament included a much higher degree of Arab nationalists, which itself – along with some of the usual accusations of interference that accompany Lebanese elections – made the

Christians feel 'uneasy about the outcome'.[73] Most, however, saw Shehāb's decision to be completely in line with his previously demonstrated principles, mainly his dislike of the Lebanese political game. Others even drew parallels with De Gaulle's role within the French state after the Second World War, one that also ended with the French president tendering his resignation.[74]

In any case, it is usually held, historically, that Shehāb's presidential mandate (in the sense of an application of his own policies) did not truly begin until after 20 July 1960. This date is thus also crucial in understanding the political legitimacy of the Lebanese state during his next four years at the helm. There was no doubt that Shehāb, and the possibility of change which he embodied, enjoyed relatively widespread popularity. Particularly, it was the first time that a Maronite president had received that much support from the Muslim population that had felt disenfranchised for so long. Shehāb himself was very aware of the feeling of frustration among the Muslim population, and the need to 'bring them back in', both institutionally by giving them more representation and societally by pushing for a more Arab character of the state.[75] In other words, the state had, for the first time, the *potential* for achieving societal legitimacy through the support of both major communities. But the early signs of Christian discontent need to remain unignored. During the day of his resignation and return, the French ambassador at the time – Robert de Boisséson – noted that celebrations of Shehāb's return were louder in Muslim-dominated areas like Basta than those in Christian-dominated ones like Ashrafieh.[76] As Kamal Salibi noted, 'By and large, the establishment of the Shihāb régime was seen by the Christians as a reverse.'[77] Specifically, the more radical elements of the Christian community saw in his ascendance to the presidency a sign of defeat in the 1958 conflict.

After all, the formation and development of the Lebanese state meant that it was much harder for Lebanese Christians to feel alienated from it: firstly, the community and the Maronite Church itself had been the primary elements in creating the state. Secondly, there was no doubt that most Christians had become aware that, while they did not enjoy a demographical majority within Lebanese society, they were still overrepresented in parliament and continued to hold most top-level jobs in the administration. The Maronites in particular still felt empowered by maintaining their hands on the positions of president and chief commander of the armed forces. This was considered a natural entitlement for the Christians, and they continued to regard themselves as the primary defenders of the Lebanese entity. This was certainly reflected in the Katā'ib's decision to cooperate with Shehāb's regime so as to maintain a 'watchful eye' on the character of the state and to preserve its Christian identity.[78] Finally, there was also a stronger attachment to the Lebanese state on the part of the Christians simply because there was a feeling of no alternative choices. Notwithstanding Syrian nationalists (many of whom were from Christian backgrounds), most Lebanese Christians did not identify with any other political entity, nor did they have the geographical option of turning to any immediate neighbours – a feeling that many Sunnis held for so long with the overwhelming proximity of Syria and Egypt. These circumstances are crucial in explaining how the alienation of many Christians occurred during the reign of Shehāb and his successor. That feeling, a first for the Christians within Lebanon, developed at a much slower pace than previously seen with the Muslims and, by early 1970s, proved to be just as threatening – if not more so – to the stability of the Lebanese state. The following will show how, slowly but surely, the idea of the state espoused by Chehabism gradually pushed many Christians away from the Lebanese state.

Political policies and reactions

Thus, while he succeeded in gaining the support of many traditionalists and reformists, there was no doubt that Shehāb was an alienating figure from the moment he became president. For Sham'ūn loyalists, many of whom became members of his newly founded National Liberal Party (NLP), Shehāb represented the opposite of what the former president was fighting for: close relationships with the West (particularly the United States), economic liberalism and the maintenance of the Christian idea of the state. Similarly, Eddeh's National Bloc (NB), which had not directly participated in the 1958 crisis, was also unsatisfied with Shehāb's election. While not as anti-Arabist as his father was, Raymond Eddeh was still apprehensive about having a military general as president, and remained worried about Shehāb's accommodating policies towards the surrounding Arab states, specifically Nāṣer. While it is hard to gauge whether or not the NLP and the NB represented the thinking of most Christians (the Katā'ib, after all, were also popular and cooperated with the regime), Kamal Salibi, like others, argued at the time that the two parties together 'truly represented the Christian ethos'.[79]

As for the SSNP,[80] the founders – and many members – of which were Greek Orthodox, they had chosen to fight alongside Sham'ūn in 1958 against Nāṣer's version of socialism as well as Syrian Ba'thism. For them, Shehāb also represented Lebanon's capitulation to Nāṣer and pan-Arabist ideals which flew in the face of their secular form of Syrian nationalism. What further alienated them from Chehabism was that, at a time when governments were formed by eighteen ministers and administrative jobs were created to ensure full representation, they never had any political representation as a party and were few and far between within the administrative apparatus of the state.[81] Even the Katā'ib, considered the most organized of the Christian organizations – both politically and as a paramilitary group – was dismissed by many Christians and, through their decision to associate with Shehāb's regime and its reforms, 'did not enjoy much Christian popularity after 1958'.[82]

The fears of those Christians, and the SSNP, were only confirmed when Shehāb decided to meet Nāṣer in March of 1959. Foreign policy, an indicator of Lebanese political identity since the creation of the National Pact, would again prove to be the president's most alienating area of policy. Shehāb organized the meeting with the Arab leader on the Syrian–Lebanese borders. The resulting 'communiqué' – seen as a victory by Shehāb – included a promise by Nāṣer to respect Lebanese independence and not interfere in its affairs. In return, Shehāb promised solidarity with the Arab cause without having to openly support Nāṣer's international disputes.[83] It has also been argued that the agreement included, both implicitly and explicitly, an acknowledgement by Shehāb of Nāṣer's supremacy in the region, a commitment by both sides not to participate in alliances – neither covert nor overt – that could hinder the other's internal stability and a promise by Nāṣer to remove Syrian restrictions put in place since 1958 on Lebanese goods as well as his word that the UAR would defend Lebanon from external infiltration.[84] For Shehāb, Lebanese sovereignty was at the core of his Chehabism, and he had personally seen how external penetration could intensify the existing tensions among the Lebanese communities. Thus, obtaining these assurances from Nāṣer was key, and the latter had, by 1959, better understood the fragility of Lebanese stability, and was content with having a president he approved of at the helm.[85] Similarly, Shehāb knew he needed a free hand if he was to effectively develop the state and apply significant reforms in accordance with his vision.[86]

There was also no doubt that Nāṣer saw this accord with Shehāb as a win of his own. As the end of the 1950s was approaching, the former had been growing to be an even more divisive figure within the Arab world, and had begun to face heavy internal opposition from within Syria, where the emergent Ba'th party were growing tired of his policies towards the eastern portion of the UAR. Similarly, the revolution of 1958 in Iraq had not panned out exactly how he would've liked, after the prime minister – leader of the revolution 'Abd al-Karīm Qāssem – became reluctant to tie Iraq to the UAR, politically, and preferred a much more Iraqi-focused brand of nationalism, which put him at odds with the pro-Nāṣer Iraqi branch of the Ba'thist Party.[87] On top of that, there was also the looming presence of his historical rival: the Arab monarchies of Jordan and Saudi Arabia. Thus, having a stable and relatively subdued political situation in Lebanon became necessary for Nāṣer, as any alternative could aggravate the already-sceptic Christians who might then push for the return of a Sham'ūn-like figure to the presidency. Whether or not the Lebanese state was capable of warding off external infiltration, however, was another story. In September 1960, for example, the UAR consulate in Beirut was bombed by suspected 'agents of Jordan', which naturally prompted accusations by the UAR that Lebanese authorities were either assisting or ignoring covert Syrian exiles operating within Lebanese territory to bring down Nāṣer's regime.[88] For Shehāb, his strategic appeasing of Nāṣer was simply explained as follows: 'I see it as my duty to respect the aspirations of half the Lebanese population [the Muslims] that respect and adore, even deify, a nationalist hero like 'Abd al-Nāṣer.'[89]

The coup of 1961

In late September 1961, a coup d'état was successfully conducted in Syria by a group of disgruntled army officers and an anti-Nāṣer government was installed which resulted in the break-up of the UAR.[90] A few weeks later, Salām's government was made to resign in large part because of its inability to decide on the recognition of the new Syrian government and a clear Lebanese position.[91] Karāmī was thus brought back as prime minister and would continue to serve as such until the end of Shehāb's term.[92] Spurred on by this change in current, the SSNP was approached by a group of officers within the Lebanese army who had become disgruntled with what they perceived as Shehāb's treasonous obedience to Nasserism.[93] Subsequently, on New Year's eve 1961, the SSNP and its sympathizers within the armed forces attempted and failed to execute a coup d'état the goal of which 'was to establish a civilian caretaker government to oversee the implementation of fundamental reforms', which included the removal of confessionalism, to follow a policy of 'genuine' neutrality, to establish more radical socio-economic reforms and to work with surrounding countries on the eventual creation of Levantine nation-state.[94]

While the fact that the regime had got wind of the coup beforehand helped easily dismantle the operation, it seemed that neither Shehāb nor the Deuxième Bureau were aware of the involvement of army officers in the coup. This disturbed Shehāb deeply, as he had built his political gravitas upon the success of the army as a unified institution and, as mentioned above, he had seen in it the hope of national unity through values like honour and loyalty. Indeed, Manaḥ al-Ṣulḥ, who served in the Ministry of Information during Shehāb's term, argued that a new stage of Shehāb's term began with the failed coup, which was also the 'occasion of a successful coup': that of Shehāb on himself.[95] In fact, Shehāb's political policies after the coup of 1961 were markedly different from his earlier ones: while he was willing to tolerate some of the more traditional leaders of the opposition so long as their local activities did not get in the way of his more global reforms, the SSNP coup was seen as an insult to his tolerance, his pride and his trust.[96] After all, since Shehāb was not a traditional leader within the Lebanese political scene, and since he lacked his own social base, he had always turned to his officers and the army – for which he was seen as the godfather – as a support system and a mark of success that he could point to whenever doubts about him emerged. Even before 1961, there were many who accused Shehāb of using the armed forces to accomplish his means. Specifically, the 1960 elections had brought with it many suspicions that the 'Deuxième Bureau', the intelligence branch of the Lebanese army, intervened to ensure Shehāb's opponents did not win many seats.[97] Nevertheless, the elections were still regarded as relatively peaceful and free on the whole.[98] The same would not be said of the elections of 1964.

The rise of the Deuxième Bureau

Following the events of December 1961, there was a clear change in Shehāb's limits to using the army as a political tool. After the coup, he authorized an extensive and unforgiving purge of, firstly, the army, and then the country itself. For the rest of his term, he gave the Deuxième Bureau a 'free hand to deal with the SSNP and other "subversive" elements in Lebanon', though the clandestine nature of this purge meant that a culture of secrecy and suspicion quickly spread throughout the country.[99] According to a member of the NB at the time, 'all non-Chehabist citizens were suspected accomplices of the "parti populaire syrien" [the traditional name of the SSNP]', and there were some claims of Christian support for the coup had it succeeded.[100] As they carried out these actions, the officers of the Deuxième

Bureau became more involved in politics than the army had ever been up to that point. Their activities ranged from surveillance and intimidation to arrests and questioning, even going so far as to establish ties with gangs in Beirut, the Biqā' and 'Akkār to hinder the power of traditional populist leaders like Ṣā'ib Salām, who by the mid-1960s had grown to resent the president.[101] In a matter of years, Shehāb had successfully developed a very powerful intelligence network which, in his eyes, was the best deterrent for attempts at power like the coup of 1961. As a result, the army came to be seen as Shehāb's own political party, and many who carried this perception came to look at him as no different than the other traditional leaders who rely on a degree of political and, when necessary, violent power. The rise of the Bureau also concerned many parliamentarians, chief among whom was Raymond Eddeh, who increasingly felt like the legislative power was being weakened.[102]

Organization of the Bureau During that time, the head of the Bureau, Antūn Sa'd, declared a new policy of 'absolute security'.[103] This meant a shift from the Bureau's earlier activities of retroactive policing to a more hands-on approach of intelligence that aimed to prevent any insurrections or radical opposition from taking place.[104] In 1962, the Central Cell was created within the Bureau, with Sa'd as its head and Gaby Laḥūd – a captain in the army – acting as his second in command. The Cell was then divided into five departments that each centred around: internal security, external security, military affairs, information and the refugee situation. Each department enjoyed an autonomy in its undertakings and an independent budget, while the overall budget for military intelligence was raised to LL1.7 m.[105] Laḥūd served as the liaison between all five departments which put him in a special position of power and heavy influence.[106] Shehāb, who had retained the unofficial role of leader of the army, had his say on every high-ranking appointment within the Bureau and every decision that had the potential to impact the country's stability.[107]

In accordance with its new policy, and its increased capabilities, the Bureau began infiltrating most aspects of Lebanese socio-political life. It planted agents in various organizations including parties, exclusive clubs and associations – especially those that had displayed a distaste for the regime and Chehabism in general. It was clear that such activities were a result of the shock of the SSNP's attempted coup. At the same time, the Bureau never hesitated to conduct similar activities against allied groups and organizations, so as to ensure no disturbance to or deviation from the status quo was able to thrive.[108] The Bureau also reinforced its existing relationships with influential members of Lebanese society, for the sake of gathering as much data as possible, on the condition that this was always done covertly to avoid any questions.[109]

By the final year of Shehāb's term, the Bureau's presence had been felt throughout the Lebanese political arena. Raymond Eddeh, an opposer of the regime since 1960, had continuously called out the alarming level of political involvement on the part of the army intelligence, though the regime's influence on the press was able to ensure his criticism did not resonate across the country.[110] He, along with other legislators, brought up the issue in parliament time and again but were mostly ignored and muted through the Bureau's influence on the press.[111] In the meantime Chehabist politicians, who still enjoyed the support of many sections of Lebanese society, maintained that the president was unaware of the Bureau's excessive behaviour, that he did not condone it and that he was not responsible for it in any way.[112] In addition, when directly accused, the Bureau could, and would, always argue that it was working to reduce the tension post-1958 and to demilitarize many of the armed groups that formed in the late 1950s, and that its excessive measures formed an adequate response in order to protect honest civilians. Shehāb himself also provided similar arguments when pressed on the issue, and he also argued that with all the foreign intelligence agencies working to influence the Lebanese political climate, 'it was only right' that the state had one of its own that could attempt to ensure stability.[113]

The 1964 elections Still, it wasn't until the elections of 1964 that the Bureau's presence was truly felt among the general population. With the presidential elections expected later in the year, Shehāb's supporters and the Bureau were inclined to ensure a favourable outcome that would fill the parliament with enough Chehabists to get Shehāb re-elected.[114] The latter, for his part, had given indication as early as the fall of 1963 that he was not intending to remain as president once his term ended.[115] Nevertheless, both the Bureau and the Chehabists were hoping for a change of heart on Shehāb's part when faced with pressure put on him by a parliament overwhelmingly supporting his re-election. Additionally, most surrounding states (especially Egypt) and the bigger powers were more than satisfied with Shehāb's external policies and the stability that had ensued therefrom, and thus were also pushing for his re-election.[116] Subsequently, the Bureau put all their efforts in ensuring Chehabists dominated parliament so the regime can remain in control of the legislative side of the state. In the build-up to the elections, the Bureau concentrated on identifying those candidates that could present a threat to Shehāb and proceeded to dismantle their 'election keys'.[117] It directly attacked their influence and prestige among their supporters by blocking their abilities to dish out favours and jobs, excluding them from certain public services, and freezing their assets and businesses. It was also able to bring in some candidates towards Chehabism by ways of intimidation, bribery and threats.[118]

As a result of the Bureau's efforts, the two biggest opponents to Shehāb (both politically and with regard to the position of president), Sham'ūn and Eddeh, lost their seats by very close margins. Out of parliament and legally weak, the two continued to feverishly oppose the direction in which Shehāb was taking the Lebanese state and the now-obvious influence of the Bureau, while their supporters, shocked by this loss, grew more upset than ever. The Christian opposition front grew further when the Maronite Patriarch M'ūshī, who had opposed Sham'ūn during the 1958 crisis and as a result had his popularity in Christian circles diminished, also felt alienated by Shehāb after the latter relied on more secular professionals for advice.[119] That feeling of alienation was not limited to the Christian camp, either. Ṣā'ib Salām had also grown disillusioned with the regime, mostly because the Bureau had backed rival gangs in Beirut in exchange for information and compliance, which had significantly diminished his local influence.[120] By 1964, Salām had become such an opponent to Shehāb's re-election that he allied with Sham'ūn despite their intense and violent rivalry during 1958. He even further worsened his relationship with once-ally Nāṣer, sending a letter to UAR ambassador 'Abd al-Ḥamīd Ghālib accusing him of interfering in Lebanese affairs.[121] While the Sham'ūn-Eddeh-M'ūshī-Salām bloc was nowhere near strong enough in parliament to stop Shehāb's re-election, it has been argued that his decision to not pursue a second term was in part taken in light of such opposition, especially from the three big Christian leaders.[122]

With none of the other traditional Maronites standing for president, Pierre Jumayyil took it upon himself to run for the position, though the vehemently Christian character of the Katā'ib, their paramilitary history and Jumayyil's personal relations with the rest of the Chehabists meant that he did not have a realistic chance at winning. Instead, Shehāb practically handpicked his successor: Charles Ḥelū, a previous member of the Constitutional Bloc who like many others migrated over to Chehabism with the disappearance of their party in the 1950s, and had served as minister of education.[123] Ḥelū satisfied all the criteria for Shehāb and was also a satisfactory successor for all external parties, chief among them Nāṣer, and, most importantly, by the Bureau itself, though it was rumoured that they preferred Ḥelū's weak political standing – he had no personal following of his own – since it allowed them to continue intervening in political affairs as they saw fit. That rumour would haunt Ḥelū for much of his presidential tenure, and would make him, eventually, desperate to escape Shehāb's shadow.

Of the three presidents whose regimes ruled over independent Lebanon, there was no doubt that Shehāb was the least controversial or polarizing. One could argue with relative ease that he got further than his predecessors in engendering the idea of the state in almost all sections of the Lebanese community. He certainly made sure not to alienate the Muslim community like Sham'ūn had done in the 1950s; in fact his tenure can be better compared to that of Khūrī who, as another Maronite leader, was more than willing to accommodate the Muslim–Arab vision into the idea of the state. Shehāb's reluctance to be as active, internationally, as his predecessors, and his insistence on the need for socio-economic development across the country, along with the Maronites' special position within the state, put him in the perfect position to allay some fears from the big communities.

As he strove to focus on internal policies, however, Shehāb's idea of the Lebanese state necessarily implied a more involved administration that could regulate where previous regimes hesitated to do so. This flew in the face of the mainly Christian conception of the 'merchant republic' in which entrepreneurs can play all the cards they have – and pull any strings they need to – in order to move up the social ladder without any impedance on the part of the state, and at the expense of those who do not have enough capital or pull to do the same (and who were predominantly Muslim). The state's increased use of the Deuxième Bureau to ensure a stable path for Chehabism only served to confirm these fears by politicians like Eddeh, who accused Shehāb of running a police state in the style of many other Arab leaders. After the failed coup of 1961 of yet another alienated organization, the SSNP, the regime felt it necessary to increase its intelligence network and the reach of its influential arm across the country. This newer character of the state, one even more involved and aware in its citizens' business, further isolated Eddeh and his allies, while Sham'ūn and Salām – and their supporters – were also made to feel alienated through the Bureau's covert activities. The final nail in the coffin of the Christian front against Shehāb was the opposition of the Maronite Patriarch M'ūshī, who had been excluded from his traditional advisory role to the Maronite president.

In light of such policies and reactions, it actually becomes more plausible to compare Shehāb to both Sham'ūn and Khūrī in that, while they all espoused to stick to a neutral internal and foreign policy, all three of them found it an unsustainable method to engender a common idea of the state, both in terms of character and identity. And while Shehāb arguably had the best run at such an endeavour, the fact that a Christian front – which would be joined by Jumayyil a few years later – was formed in opposition of the state for the first time in modern Lebanon's history was telling of the alienation that had occurred under the new president, just as it had under his predecessors. In other words, Shehāb, like his predecessors, cannot be judged to have succeeded in gaining societal legitimacy for the Lebanese state, despite the hope that many had placed in him. His successor, Ḥelū, would have to deal with the consequences.

Notes

1 There is enough evidence that lack of an updated census was itself a deliberate policy on the part of key Maronite officials that feared revealing the true discrepancies in the confessional numbers.

See Rania Maktabi, 'State Formation and Citizenship in Lebanon: The Politics of Membership and Exclusion in a Sectarian State', in *Citizenship and the State and the Middle East: Approaches and Applications*, ed. Nils A. Butenschøn, Uri Davis, and Manuel S Hassassian (Syracuse, NY: Syracuse University Press, 2000), 146–78.

2 One definition of modernization in Lebanon, with which Shehāb's policies seem to agree, is presented by Elie Salem. He defined modernization as a 'process by which a country adapts, transforms or replaces its traditional institutions and patterns of life under the influence of the new science and technology that arose during the Renaissance in western Europe and has since spread throughout the world'. See Salem, *Modernization without Revolution*, 2.

3 Fu'ād Butros, *Al-Mudhakkarāt* [Memoires] (Beirut: Dār al-Nahār, 2009), 53.

4 The term was first coined by journalist Georges Naccache during a conference of the Cénacle Libanais in 1960. He described a 'new style of politics', as opposed to an ideology or philosophy – see Marwān Ḥarb, *Al-Shihābiya: Ḥudūd Tajribat Al-Taḥdīth Al-Siyāsī Fī Lubnān* [Chehabism: Limits of the Experience of Political Modernisation in Lebanon] (Jdeydet al-Matn: Dār Sā'ir al-Mashriq, 2012), 53.

Also see Naccache, Georges. November, 1960. 'Un Nouveau Style: Le Chehabisme', *Cénacle Libanais*. Retrieved from: https://www.fouadchehab.org/wp-content/uploads/doc/bk/naccache-fr.pdf.

5 There was, and has been, a debate over the role of the Lebanese army during Shehāb's term, as will be seen in this chapter. Some writers do not believe that the army formed a central tenet of Chehabism.

Marwan Ḥarb, for example, does not mention it in his discussion on Shehāb's politics, though he acknowledges that the latter viewed the army as a 'school for national unity'. See Marwan Harb, *Le Chehabisme Ou Les Limites d'une Experience de Modernisation Politique Au Liban* [Chehabism: Limits of the Experience of Political Modernisation in Lebanon] (Author, 2008), 71.

Others like Nasser Kalawoun, however, have argued that it is at the heart of the Chehabism doctrine – see Nasser M. Kalawoun, *The Struggle for Lebanon: A Modern History of Lebanese-Egyptian Relations* (London: I.B. Tauris, 2000), 76.

Regardless of Shehāb's personal intention to involve the army in politics, there can be no doubt of the vital role the army played as an institution in the application of Chehabism. This was even mentioned by Naccache himself: 'This political paradox – the salvaging of democracy by the [Lebanese] military power – is certainly the central point of the Shehābian experience' – see Kalawoun, 22.

6 Malsagne, *Fouad Chéhab, 1902–1973*, 210.

7 Gendzier, *Notes from the Minefield*, 351.

8 This government, seen as the ultimate reflection of the 'no victor, no vanquished' formula upon which reconciliation was to be based, included: Rashid Karāmī appointed as prime minister and in charge of finance, economy, the press and national defence; Jumayyil appointed minister of public works, communications, education, public health and agriculture; Ḥussein al-'Uwayni appointed foreign minister and in charge of justice and government planning; and Raymond Eddeh appointed minister of the interior and in charge of labour affairs, social affairs, as well as in charge of affairs relating to the postal, telegraph and telephone services.

See minutes of Parliamentary session on 17 October 1958.

Retrieved from: http://www.legallaw.ul.edu.lb/PeriodSessionLandingPage.aspx?SessionID=2219.

9 Tabitha Petran, *The Struggle over Lebanon* (New York: Monthly Review Press, 1987), 53.

10 Though sixteen of the twenty-six members of parliament were absent. See minutes of Parliamentary session on 17 October 1958.

11 The Katā'ib in particular changed its political mission and started seeing itself as a defender of the state, and to maintain some pushback on the 'enemy within', that is, the Muslim population – see Petran, 54.

12 Tūfī' Anīs Kfūrī, *Al-Shehābiyya Wa Siyāsat Al-Mawqaf* [Chehabism and the Policy of Decision] (Beirut: Author, 1980), 162.

13 Kfūrī, 143.

14 See Decree issued on 6 December 1958. Retrieved from: http://www.legallaw.ul.edu.lb/Law.aspx?lawId=197599.

15 See Law promulgated on 12 December 1958. Retrieved from: http://www.legallaw.ul.edu.lb/Law.aspx?lawId=198307.

That law had been voted for in parliament a few weeks before. See parliamentary session on 12 November 1958. Retrieved from: http://www.legallaw.ul.edu.lb/PeriodSessionLandingPage.aspx?SessionID=22.

16 Crow and Iskandar, 'Administrative Reform in Lebanon 1958–1959', 300.

17 See Legislative Decree issued on 16 June 1959. Retrieved from: http://www.legallaw.ul.edu.lb/Law.aspx?lawId=179570.

18 See Legislative Decree issued on 15 June 1959. Retrieved from: http://www.legallaw.ul.edu.lb/Law.aspx?lawId=178645.
19 See Legislative Decree issued on 22 June 1959. Retrieved from: http://www.legallaw.ul.edu.lb/Law.aspx?lawId=182239.
20 See Legislative Decree issued on 12 June 1959. Retrieved from: http://www.legallaw.ul.edu.lb/Law.aspx?lawId=244498.
21 See Legislative Decree issued on 12 June 1959. Retrieved from: http://www.legallaw.ul.edu.lb/Law.aspx?lawId=179571.
22 Salem, *Modernization without Revolution*, 95.
23 See Legislative Decree issued on 12 June 1959. Retrieved from: http://www.legallaw.ul.edu.lb/Law.aspx?lawId=193762.
24 See Legislative Decree issued on 12 June 1959. Retrieved from: http://www.legallaw.ul.edu.lb/Law.aspx?lawId=244295.
25 See Legislative Decree issued on 12 June 1959. Retrieved from: http://www.legallaw.ul.edu.lb/Law.aspx?lawId=257678.
26 Crow and Iskandar, 'Administrative Reform in Lebanon 1958–1959', 306.
27 On 23 September 1958, when he was officially sworn in as president, Shehāb proclaimed the following: 'In the hour in which I swear to protect the Constitution, I promise – and ask for your promise – to remain loyal to the unwritten constitution: our National Pact. For it is the Pact that has united us in our belief in Lebanon.'
See Statement of Constitutional Oath on 23 September 1958. Fouad Chehab Foundation. Retrieved on 11 July 2019 from: http://www.fouadchehab.org/wp-content/uploads/doc/bk/koutab1.pdf.
28 Bāssem Al-Jisr, *Fu'ād Shehāb, Dhālika Al-Majhūl* [Fu'ād Shehāb, the Unknown] (Beirut: Sharikat al-Maṭbū'āt lil-Tawzī' wal-Nasher, 1988), 54.
29 In late July 1959, for example, a debate occurred over a legislative decree issued by the government a month before concerning the resignation of government employees. A parliamentary committee judged the government to have overstepped its boundaries, and a vote of confidence ensued. This time around, the government gained the vote of confidence by only twenty-eight votes, with sixteen voting against and five abstaining.
See minutes of Parliamentary session on 30 July 1959. Retrieved from: www.legallaw.ul.edu.lb/PeriodSessionLandingPage.aspx?SessionID=2264.
30 See minutes of Parliamentary session on 30 July 1959.
31 Samuel P. Huntington, *Political Order in Changing Societies* (New Haven, CT: Yale University Press, 2006), 93.
32 See Weber, *Economy and Society*.
33 See *Messages à la Nation Libanaise* [Messages to the Lebanese Nation]. Fouad Chehab Foundation. Retrieved on 10 July 2019 from: http://www.fouadchehab.org/wp-content/uploads/doc/bk/discours1.pdf.
34 Sālīḥ' Ja'yūl Juway'id and Fātīma 'Abd al-Jalīl Yāsir, 'Rīmūn Iddeh Wa Dawrahū Al-Siyāsī Fī Lubnān [Raymond Eddeh and His Political Role in Lebanon]', *Majallat Jāmi'at Dhī Qār* 12, no. 3 (2017): 346.
35 Hudson, *The Precarious Republic*, 300.
36 In fact, ten of the twenty-six electoral districts were single-sect districts – see Michael C. Hudson, 'The Electoral Process and Political Development in Lebanon', *Middle East Journal* 20, no. 2 (1966): 184.
Also see Malsagne, *Fouad Chéhab, 1902–1973*, 233.
37 According to Stéphane Malsagne, fifty-one out of the ninety-nine members elected were first-time deputies – see Malsagne, 224. Thirty-three of those newcomers had

never even presented themselves as candidate before – see Nicola A. Ziadeh, 'The Lebanese Elections, 1960', *Middle East Journal* 14, no. 4 (1960): 377.

38 Bāssem Al-Jisr, *Fu'ād Shehāb* [Fu'ād Shehāb] (Beirut: Fouad Chehab Foundation, 1998), 41–2.

39 See *Message à la Nation* on 20 July 1960. Fouad Chehab Foundation. Retrieved on 8 July from: http://www.fouadchehab.org/wp-content/uploads/doc/doc/off/resign60-fr.pdf.

40 See *Message à la Nation*.

41 Malsagne, *Fouad Chéhab, 1902–1973*, 233.

42 Two months after the last governmental legislative decrees, he issued a decree of his own in which he expanded the presidential office (which had been reorganized a few months before) in a manner which would allow him to surround himself with 'apolitical' professionals and military personnel that he could trust. See Al-Jisr, *Fu'ād Shehāb, Dhālika Al-Majhūl*, 52.

The expansion of the Office allowed him to affect substantive change in different areas of Lebanese socio-economic life. See Decree issued on 27 August 1959. Retrieved from: http://www.legallaw.ul.edu.lb/Law.aspx?lawId=196203

43 In fact, as one story goes, Shehāb once brought up the names of two people – Eliās Sarkīs and Shafīq Muḥarram – he was considering appointing to his administration during a governmental meeting. He asked whether the ministers had heard of the two. When they replied that they hadn't, he concluded: 'Now I have two reasons to appoint them, then.' See Al-Jisr, 52.

44 Louis-Joseph Lebret had been an officer in the French navy during the First World War, and after joining the Dominican Order at the end of the war, had focused his efforts on the reshaping of the modern economy into a 'human economy'. From then on, he travelled many parts of the developing world 'seeking solutions to the dramatic crisis of under-development'. See Vincent Cosmao, 'Louis-Joseph Lebret, O.P. 1897–1966: From Social Action to the Struggle for Development', *New Blackfriars* 51, no. 597 (1970): 64.

45 That would become the title of the extensive report submitted by the IRFED.

46 Malsagne, *Fouad Chéhab, 1902–1973*, 303.

47 The report also argued that, strictly speaking, Lebanon is not 'under-developed' overall. It was only in the areas of the north, the north-east and the south (all of which contain a Muslim majority) that one can speak of under-development. 'If Lebanon fails to attend to these inequalities and to address the discrepancies in standard of living, it will face significant social problems like the events of 1958.'

See Institut de Recherche et de Formation en Vue du Développement Harmonisé, *Besoins et Possibilités de Développement Du Liban; Étude Préliminaire. Mission IRFED-Liban, 1960–1961. Tome I*, 26.

48 Institut de Recherche et de Formation en Vue du Développement Harmonisé, 17.

49 Institut de Recherche et de Formation en Vue du Développement Harmonisé, 18.

50 Institut de Recherche et de Formation en Vue du Développement Harmonisé, 21.

51 Mājid Khalīl Mājid, *Tārīkh Al-Ḥūkūmāt Al-Lubnāniya 1926–1966: Al-Ta'līf, Al-Thiqa, Al-Istiqāla* [The History of Lebanese Governments 1926–1966: Formation, Confidence, Resignation] (Beirut: Author, 1997), 141.

52 Al-Jisr, *Fu'ād Shehāb, Dhālika Al-Majhūl*, 62.

53 Malsagne, *Fouad Chéhab, 1902–1973*, 257.

54 Nadā Ḥassan Fayād, *Al-Dawla Al-Madaniya: Tarjibat Fu'ād Shehāb Fī Lubnān* [The Civil State: Fu'ād Shehāb's Experiment in Lebanon] (Beirut: Muntada al-Ma'ārif, 2011), 160.

55 Malsagne, *Fouad Chéhab, 1902–1973*, 277.

56 Malsagne, 278.

57 See Institut de Recherche et de Formation en Vue du Développement Harmonisé, *Besoins et Possibilités de Développement Du Liban; Étude Préliminaire. Mission IRFED-Liban, 1960–1961. Tome II* [Requirements and Possibilities of Development in Lebanon; A Preliminary Study. IRFED-Liban Mission, 1960–1961. Volume II], ed. Louis-Joseph Lebret (Beirut: Wizārat al-Taṣmīm al-ʿĀm, 1963), 206.

58 Petran, *The Struggle over Lebanon*, 56.

The importance of making use of the Litānī river was not only one of providing service but also of appeasing the growingly frustrated Shīʿa population of the south who felt like they were second-class citizens.

In 1960, Shīʿa deputy Jaʿfar Sharaf al-Dīn accused the government of letting Tyre 'fall[s] short of what a civilized place should be', and elaborated on all the services that the region around city is 'deprived from'. See minutes of Parliamentary session on 10 August 1960. http://www.legallaw.ul.edu.lb/PeriodSessionLandingPage.aspx?SessionID=2316.

59 Petran, 56.

60 See Law promulgated on 10 February 1960 concerning the availability of $5 m to the Credit Bank for the benefit of industrialists. Retrieved from: http://www.legallaw.ul.edu.lb/Law.aspx?lawId=165649.

Also see Decree issued on 15 March 1963 concerning the organization and general principles of hotel and tourism loans. Retrieved from: www.legallaw.ul.edu.lb/Law.aspx?lawId=176687.

Also see minutes of Parliamentary session on 31 July 1961 in which a further LL10 m was approved for the Credit Bank. Retrieved from: www.legallaw.ul.edu.lb/PeriodSessionLandingPage.aspx?SessionID=2343.

61 See, for example, Gino Germani, 'Stages of Modernization', *International Journal* 24, no. 3 (1969): 463–85; J. Tyson Chatagnier and Emanuele Castelli, 'The Arc of Modernization: Economic Structure, Materialism, and the Onset of Civil Conflict', *Political Science Research and Methods* 7, no. 2 (2019): 233–52.

62 See table 8 for a 'Summary of Social-Mobilization Trends', in Hudson, 1985, *The Precarious Republic*, 78.

63 The survey asked the villagers (160 of whom were Christians and 246 Muslim): 'How satisfied are you with the way government affairs are handled?' Over 90 per cent of both Christians and Muslim replied with either 'Not very well satisfied' or 'not at all satisfied'. Similarly, when quizzed on the value of outside help, about half of each community responded answered negatively, while the majority of those that were positive towards it 'volunteered the opinion foreign aid, to have any chance of being effective, must by-pass the Lebanese government'.

See George C. Fetter, 'A Comparative Study of Attitudes of Christian and of Moslem Lebanese Villagers', *Journal for the Scientific Study of Religion* 4, no. 1 (1964): 48–59.

64 He goes on to argue that 'Lebanese parties are not, in the main, electoral organizations but ideological groupings, primarily interested in gaining converts to their various causes.' As a result, Suleiman decide to use broader definitions for a political party that focus on the representation of a cause and the competition for power. For example, he suggests E. E. Schattschneider's definition: 'a political party is first of all an organized attempt to get [political] power'. See Michael Suleiman, *Political Parties in Lebanon: The Challenge of a Fragmented Political Culture* (Ithaca, NY: Cornell University Press, 1967), xvi–xvii.

65 Hudson, 'The Electoral Process and Political Development in Lebanon', 174.
66 See Hudson, 183.
67 Hudson, 183.
68 Hudson, 184.
69 See previous chapters.
70 Kamal Salibi, 'Lebanon under Fuad Chehab 1958–1964', *Middle Eastern Studies* 2, no. 3 (1966): 219.
71 See al-Nahār newspaper on 22 July 1960.
72 Though there were some Lebanese Muslims who, even though offered support for Shehāb, also saw his resignation as a premeditated move to push through further changes – see Malsagne, *Fouad Chéhab, 1902–1973*, 235.
73 See FO 371/158939.
74 Malsagne, 233.
75 Owen, 'The Political Economy of Grand Liban, 1920–1970', 29.
76 Malsagne, *Fouad Chéhab, 1902–1973*, 234.
77 Kamal Salibi, *Crossroads to Civil War: Lebanon, 1958–1976* (Delmar, NY: Caravan Books, 1976), 3.
78 In fact, it was after 1959 that the Katā'ib really embarked on the militarization of their party members, expanding their paramilitary, propaganda and intelligence activities on an unprecedented scale. See Petran, *The Struggle over Lebanon*, 54.
79 Salibi, *Crossroads to Civil War*, 4.
80 Syrian Social Nationalist Party (see previous chapters).
81 Part of the alienation of the SSNP was due to their refusal to be involved in Shehāb's government and administration as well.

See Adel Beshara, *The Politics of Frustration: The Failed Coup of 1961* (New York: Routledge, 2005).

For a perspective of the SSNP, see 'Abdallah S'ādeh, *Awrāq Qawmiya: Mudhakarāt Al-Ductūr 'Abdallah S'ādeh* [Nationalist Papers: The Memoirs of Dr. 'Abdallah S'ādeh] (Beirut: Author, 1987).
82 Even as six of their seven candidates were successful in the 1960 elections, many of their electoral victories were attributed to their strategic alliances with the other communities (e.g. the Armenian Tashnaq party in Beirut) in addition to support from the regime itself, which went as far as intimidating opponents' voters in some cases. See Salibi, *Crossroads to Civil War*, 4–6.
83 Kalawoun, *The Struggle for Lebanon*, 77.
84 Kalawoun, 78.
85 Butros, *Al-Mudhakkarāt*, 109.
86 See Tūfī' Anīs Kfūrī, *Al-Shehābiyya, Madrasat Ḥidātha Ru'yawiya* [Chehabism, a School of Visionary Modernity] (Beirut: Raidy Printing Group, 2012), 390–400.
87 Muḥammad Souheil Taqqūsh, *Tārīkh Al-'Irāq (Al-Ḥadīth Wal-Mu'āsir)* [History of Iraq (Modern and Contemporary)] (Beirut: Dār al-Nafā'is, 2015), 272.

For a brief history of the coup and Iraq, see Stacy Holden, *A Documentary History of Modern Iraq* (Gainesville: University Press of Florida, 2012).
88 Kalawoun, *The Struggle for Lebanon*, 81.
89 Ḥarb, *Al-Shihābiya*, 81.
90 Kamāl Dīb, *Tārīkh Sūriya Al-Mu'āsir: Min Al-Intidāb Al-Faransī Ila Ṣayf 2011* [The Modern History of Syria: From the French Mandate to the Summer of 2011] (Beirut: Dār al-Nahār, 2011), 207–8.

91 Additionally, Salām had cut down his cabinet to only eight members, which angered many who had now established positions of power through his former eighteen-man government. See Hudson, 'The Electoral Process and Political Development in Lebanon', 302.
92 Karāmi's cabinet would become the longest-serving one in Lebanese history up until that point – see Kalawoun, *The Struggle for Lebanon*, 103.
93 Nicholas Nassīf, *Al-Maktab Al-Thānī: Ḥākim Fī Al-Ẓol* [The Deuxième Bureau: Ruler in the Shadows] (al-Zal'a, Lebanon: Mukhtārāt, 2005), 85.
94 Beshara, *The Politics of Frustration*, 123.
95 The first stage, Manaḥ claimed, began during Khūrī's term as he was establishing his prestige within the army. The second started with his election to the presidency and lasted until the coup of 1961.
See Ghassān Sharbel, *Lubnān – Dafāter Al-Ru'asā'* [Lebanon – Presidents' Records] (Beirut: Riad El-Rayyes Books, 2014), 165.
96 Barak, *The Lebanese Army*, 66.
97 Pierre Eddeh, brother to Raymond, and who lost his seat in East Beirut to a Katā'ib candidate, accused the Deuxième Bureau of intimidating his supporters and keeping them away from polling stations. See Salibi, *Crossroads to Civil War*, 5.
Similarly, the SSNP accused the army of intervening when they lost their only seat in parliament during the elections of 1960. See Beshara, *The Politics of Frustration*, 63.
98 See FO 371/158939.
99 Barak, *The Lebanese Army*, 67.
100 Rodrigue El Houeiss, *Raymond Eddé Ou Une Certaine Idée Du Liban – Souvenirs Politiques* [Raymond Eddé or a Certain Idea of Lebanon – Political Memories] (Paris: L'Harmattan, 2017), 50–1.
101 See Petran, *The Struggle over Lebanon*, 58–9; Barak, *The Lebanese Army*, 67–8.
102 Sem'ān, Sem'ān 'Īd *Rīmūn Iddeh: Damīron Lan Yamūt* [Raymond Eddeh: A Conscience That Never Dies] (Beirut: Dār al-Jīl, 2000), 260.
103 Nassīf, *Al-Maktab Al-Thānī*, 127.
104 Nassīf, 132.
105 Nassīf, 132.
106 He would go on to become Sa'd's successor as head of the Army Intelligence.
107 Nassīf, 139.
108 Nassīf, 141.
109 Nassīf, 141.
110 Salibi, *Crossroads to Civil War*, 6.
111 In August 1962, for example, Sleymān al-Ali (a former supporter of Sham'ūn) talked of prisoners held without charge and tortured by the Deuxième Bureau. He claimed that, when he enquired about the issue to the prosecutors, he was told that it was none of his business and that the Bureau was handling the prisoners' case.
See minutes of Parliamentary session on 14 August 1962: http://www.legallaw.ul.edu.lb/PeriodSessionLandingPage.aspx?SessionID=2415.
In June 1963, Eddeh accused the government of plotting with the army to diminish the role of parliament in order to strengthen the executive. He specifically mentions how, ever since an extra LL12 m was given to the Ministry of Information, the press had not published any dissenting views, especially when they were proclaimed by members of parliament. There were also accusations that officers in the Deuxième Bureau openly interfere in parliamentary elections, as well as local ones like in Jbeil.

See minutes of Parliamentary session on 28 June 1963: http://www.legallaw.ul.edu.lb/PeriodSessionLandingPage.aspx?SessionID=2451.

112 Nassīf, *Al-Maktab Al-Thānī*, 139.

113 Nassīf, 140.

114 A two-thirds majority is needed for a constitutional amendment that would allow Shehāb to be re-elected. See Article 77 of the *Lebanese Constitution as promulgated on May 23, 1926*. Retrieved from World Intellectual Property Organization on 23 May 2019: https://www.wipo.int/edocs/lexdocs/laws/en/lb/lb018en.pdf.

115 Al-Jisr, *Fu'ād Shehāb*, 63–4.

116 Al-Jisr, 64.

117 The term used by many Lebanese to indicate the campaigning that occurs prior to parliamentary elections which includes endorsement by influential figures, promises of favours and services by the campaigner, and the spending of personal money for publicity.

118 Nassīf, *Al-Maktab Al-Thānī*, 145.

119 There is enough evidence to point to the fact that, up to that point, the Maronite Patriarchs had opposed all three Lebanese presidents, perhaps due to them representing a more secular threat to the Church's influence in Maronite circles. See Hudson, *The Precarious Republic*, 129.

120 Éric Verdeil, *Beyrouth et Ses Urbanistes: Une Ville En Plans (1946–1975)* [Beirut and Its Urbanists: Planning a City] (Beirut: Presses de l'IFPO, 2010), 91.

121 Johnson, 'Factional Politics in Lebanon', 62.

122 Salibi, *Crossroads to Civil War*, 21.

123 Charles Ḥelū, *Mudhakarātī 1964–1965* [Memoires 1964–1965] (Beirut: Author, 1984), 45.

The fact that Shehāb personally picked Ḥelū as his successor was also confirmed by Gābī Laḥūd of the Deuxième Bureau – see Ghassān Sharbel, *Dhākirat Al-Istikhbārāt* [Memories from the Intelligence Service] (Beirut: Riad El-Rayyes Books, 2007), 208.

For a brief history of Ḥelū's political history, see Charles Ḥelū, *Ḥayāt Fī Zikrayāt* [Life in Memories] (Beirut: Dār al-Nahār, 1995).

Chapter 6

DESCENT INTO CIVIL WAR

While the later years of Shehāb's presidency certainly served to aggravate many in the Christian population, the situation was still somewhat far from leading up to a civil war. After all, while many Christian leaders had been excluded from power (Raymond Eddeh managed to recapture his seat during a by-election in 1965), the Katā'ib were still co-opted into governmental and legislative positions while the Muslims, though not exactly overjoyed, were mostly satisfied with the improvement of their official representation during Shehāb's years. Thus, the following will highlight some of the events which helped further alienate the Christian community from the Lebanese state and also intensified the tension between the two main communities in the country, with the particular addition of an external actor: the Palestinian liberation movement.

Charles Ḥelū's tenure as president was seen very much as the continuation of Chehabism. But the reality proved to be somewhat different. The fact was that Ḥelū was stuck between a rock and hard place from the moment he became president. With rumours spreading that he was simply put in place by the Bureau to allow them to continue pulling the strings behind closed doors, his election was possibly the most unspectacular one up to that point in Lebanese history. With no political, confessional or military base, Ḥelū was 'essentially alone'.[1] Subsequently, the events of his tenure will prove to be the final link in the chain that has connected political illegitimacy from the formation of the Lebanese state to its collapse during the 1970s.

Early reforms

Nevertheless, being a firm believer in Chehabism, he set out to carry on his predecessor's mission of internal reform and nation-wide development. In 1965, Ḥelū's government, again headed by Karāmī, was granted exceptional legislative powers once more so as to continue to carry on a purge on the state administration. According to Ḥelū, who refused to term the subsequent decrees as a 'purge', the objective of the reforms was to 'try to impose new and stricter standards on the administrative relations between the state and the citizen, and to eliminate any shade of leniency with regards to the execution of the law and public rules'.[2] The main method for reform was the creation of the Unified Body, an ad hoc unit made up of members of Civil Service Council and the Central Inspection Service to study the bureaucracy and recommend dismissals. The Unified Body was given the incomparable power of having the final say on specific posts and its decisions were declared not subject to revision.[3] In order to save their reputation, civil servants were advised to tender their resignations and given a grace period before being asked to leave. Ultimately, over two hundred individuals were dismissed, and the purge went 'as far as the system could tolerate'.[4] The purge itself was met by support from most labour and trade organizations as well as the press, though it was naturally opposed by many traditional leaders who feared losing their men from the state bureaucracy or, even worse, a connection with which they could promise special services and favours.

Nevertheless, the issue of sectarianism remained an obstacle to the efficiency of state administration. The culture of the 'wāsta' remained as strong as ever, even within the state itself.[5] After the reforms, Karāmī's government, which had been formed with the exclusion of any parliamentarians (apart from himself), resigned, after which it was back to the old formula of MPs being involved in parliament which, within the Lebanese system, immediately allowed for an opportunity on their part to take advantage of such situations and place their own men within state bureaucracy. In addition, it wasn't just political unwillingness that functioned as an obstacle, but the lack of public outrage at corruption: there simply was, as one journalist put it, a 'conspiracy of shoulder-shrugging'.[6]

Moreover, the culture of corruption remained rampant *within* the state during that time. A survey conducted in 1971 showed that 60 per cent of civil servants recommended the use of an 'influential mediator' for anyone 'seeking to transact official government business', while 65 per cent of Lebanese citizens surveyed claimed that they already sought such mediators.[7] Further still, parliamentarians surveyed in 1972 conceded that their election was still as dependent as it ever was on the guaranteeing of personal services and favours for their constituents.[8] This would seem normal in most democratic elections where representatives are accountable to their constituents except for, firstly, the personal nature of these favours and, secondly, the fact that the Lebanese Constitution demands that 'a member of the Chamber shall represent the whole nation' and is thus theoretically accountable to the Lebanese society as a whole as opposed to his own district.[9] Another series of questionnaires conducted earlier in the late 1960s showed similar results. Crucially, two specific questions showed that there was 'no strong confidence in the integrity, objectivity and effectiveness of these institutions [the CSC and the CIS] to eliminate corruption'.[10]

The PLO and the 1967 war

By the time Ḥelū officially became president, he had already had a taste of regional politics and the impact they could have on societal state-building in Lebanon. In 1964, after being elected as president, but before having been sworn in, he was sent by Shehāb to attend an Arab League summit in Alexandria in September 1954. During an earlier January summit that year, as a response to Israel's River Jordan Project, the United Arab Command (UAC) was created to prepare a military plan to defend and protect Arab counterpart project for Jordan river.[11] The UAC, as an initiative championed by Nāṣer, was based in Cairo and headed by an Egyptian general. Though Lebanon had 'kept a low profile', it 'had no choice but to agree' with the resulting decision to create the UAC, although the government was under much Christian pressure to refrain from any collective action.[12] In between the January and the September summit, an Arab Palestinian Congress was held in Jerusalem which established the Palestine Liberation Organization (PLO) and the Palestine National Charter, both of which called for the liberation of Palestine in accordance with the territorial boundaries set during the British mandate period, that is, before the creation of the state of Israel.[13] Since many believed that either Shehāb or the Bureau, or both, had brought Ḥelū to the presidency, the latter began to immediately feel the pressures of the Lebanese presidency and pushed to displace himself from the shadow of his predecessor. Thus, during the September summit, he presented many reservations to the autonomy that had been given to the UAC and to its Egyptian commander. Among other things, Ḥelū insisted that the Lebanese government maintain ultimate authority over the UAC and that it be consulted on any action taken on Lebanese soil. Despite objections by the other Arab states, and accusations of Lebanese opportunism and isolationism, Nāṣer acquiesced to Ḥelū's demands.[14]

During the 1967 Arab–Israeli war, Lebanon, due to its historically hesitant position on the Israeli conflict, did not actively contribute to combat activities, instead remaining content to allow the restricted use of its territory for Syrian and Jordanian troops, as well as Palestinian guerrillas while officially remaining as passive as a state can be in times of war.[15] Though the war was over in less than a week, it was the aftermath that proved to set the course for the breakdown of the Lebanese state. Tensions had already been flaring up within Lebanon over the issue of Israel and the question of Lebanon, and the Christians' commitment to the Palestinian cause. For the Christians, the agenda remained the same as it had been since 1948: to morally support the Palestinian struggle without endangering, in any way, the sovereignty or special character of the country. For Muslims, however, the Palestinian struggle, especially when endorsed by Nāṣer, was as much their own as it was the Palestinians'. As leftist groups and parties, declaring solidarity with the Palestinians, grew in the late 1980s, so too did the number of Muslim youth, Lebanese or otherwise, willing to join these movements that were quick to take on a paramilitary form.[16] These developments further aggravated the Christians: for example, in March 1967, M'ūshī delivered a 'warrior-priest' speech when he accused the Cairo-sponsored Beirut Arab University of producing 'commandos' and called on the state to clean up these 'subversive elements' instead of being idle.[17] By the end of the month, three Maronite leaders supposedly met with Helū to discuss these issues, claiming the support of half the Druze and 'all' the Shī'a population, though 'it was the grievances of their own community that bothered them'.[18]

The Cairo Agreement

By 1969, the question of the Palestinian guerrillas operating in Lebanon had become the most divisive issue in Lebanon since Shamʿūn's endorsement of the Eisenhower Doctrine. A year earlier, Jmayyil had joined Shamʿūn and Eddeh to form the Tripartite Alliance, a political group that together held most if not all Christian popular support. They had achieved an overwhelming victory in the 1968 parliamentary elections and were even assumed to be gaining support by Ḥelū himself, who was doing all he can to try and uphold the tenets of Chehabism while not creating enemies within his own confession.[19] In December of 1968, the Israeli Defence Forces raided the Lebanese airport outside Beirut and destroyed over twelve planes that had been parked on the runway (and were empty) as a result of an earlier operation by Lebanese-based Palestinian guerrillas on an Israeli airliner. As this attack threw the issue of the Palestinian struggle to the forefront of Lebanese politics, the first months of 1969 were characterized by clashes between the Lebanese Army and armed Palestinian fighters. The Bureau had maintained a heavy degree of control over the Palestinian refugee camps up until 1967, when the Palestinians began to turn many of those camps into military bases.[20] As the clashes between the two forces intensified, the country became more divided between Christians who supported the army and claimed to defend the sovereignty of Lebanon, and the Muslim who accused the 'Christian army' of treachery to the Arab cause and conspiracy to silence the Palestinian struggle. Heavy clashes ensued in late April of 1969, which resulted in further protests and the declaration of a state of emergency in many of Lebanon's big cities.[21] By May, Yāsser 'Arafāt, who had become the head of the PLO, went so far as to declare that 'no rules apply to the *Fida'iyīn*,[22] neither in Lebanon nor outside it'.[23] 'Arafāt, knowing he could count on the support of most Lebanese Muslims and almost all leftist groups, had become more provocative. Meanwhile, the Christians were only too happy to lend their support to military clashes against what they considered to be an intentional encroachment on Lebanese sovereignty. What followed was a political crisis as Rashīd Karāmī refused to form a government while the issue remained unsolved, and the country remained without a government for months.

On 31 May, Ḥelū delivered a letter to the country in which he argued that the issue wasn't the lack of support from Lebanon to the Palestinian struggle but the recurring attempt to impose a fait accompli on the Lebanese state and territory.[24] The crisis would only be resolved by the creation of the Cairo Agreement, an understanding brokered by Nāṣer between the PLO, represented by 'Arafāt, and the Lebanese state, represented by head of the army Emile Bustānī. The Agreement allowed, among other things, the facilitation of passage to the Palestinian 'commandos', the independence and autonomy for the 'Armed Struggle Command to control the activities of all those belonging to its member organisations' and the responsibility of the latter 'for ensuring that they do not interfere in Lebanese affairs'.[25] While the crisis had been resolved by the time Emile Bustānī arrived back to Lebanon, the damage had already been done. The Lebanese state, deprived of any societal legitimacy, had begun its dissent into disintegration as the Cairo Agreement would prove to be the last straw for many Christian parties like the Katā'ib and the NLP, both of which would not take long to start setting up military bases of their own in order to combat the Palestinian–Muslim alliances that continued to form. A year later, the Christian Tripartite Alliance ensured Sleymān Franjieh would be elected as president, and in the summer of 1971, a Christian columnist for al-Nahār wrote,

> The claim has been until now that the state is the servant of the citizens but in reality, the citizens are the servants of the state. Four regimes since independence have failed to reverse this situation and it has been getting worse to the extent that the 'citizens' class felt for the first time, with the election of President Franjieh, that it had placed its own representative at the head of the other 'class'.[26]

Yet despite such optimism over the supposed representativeness of Franjieh's term, his presidential tenure would lead into the Lebanese civil war only a few years later.

So how did Chehabism, as a philosophy of political reform under Shehāb and Ḥelū, perform as a tool for political legitimacy and state survival? Institutionally, the policies undertaken in the 1960s definitely improved many of the public institutions' performances in delivering services, though the extent to which this performance increased tends to be overstated in some situations. After all, clientelism and overall corruption – mainly based on confessional or familiar ties – persisted throughout the decade.[27] Rather, it is the creation, and the rise, of new institutions that focused on socio-economic development that helped increase the scope (as opposed to the strength) of state capacity and authority. Examples of these include the regional developmental funds, the Litānī River project and the Personnel Law. The strength of these institutions, nevertheless, still depended on them being shielded from confessional interests, a characteristic of Lebanese legislative and executive life. Thus, for Chehabism to ensure its own realization, it had to circumvent many of the existing 'democratic', power-sharing institutions: the rise in power of the Deuxième Bureau would be the epitome of this circumvention. Societally, Shehāb managed to keep foreign infiltration (relatively) at bay through a combination of a foreign policy that appeased the hegemon of the region, Nāṣer, maintained ties with traditionally friendly countries like France through his own personal connections and enforced a tighter grip on traditional areas of infiltration (i.e. confessional elites) through the use of the extensive intelligence network. His 'neutrality', however, was perceived by many in the Christian community (and the SSNP) as a resignation of Lebanese independence, and an acceptance of Nasserism as the form of Arabism which Lebanon adhered to. This, combined with what was now perceived as an anti-democratic state,[28] led to a gradual and incremental alienation of most of the Christian community.

With these policies, Chehabism managed to amend the Pact's formula of negative legitimacy through the introduction of more 'dictatorial' elements. It would certainly be an exaggeration to label Shehāb or Ḥelū as dictators, but the distaste for Lebanese politics and the extensive use of more covert and forceful components to their policies assuredly pushed the state more in the direction of authoritarianism than ever before. Forms of totalitarian, absolutist or dictatorial states around the Middle East had certainly proven to be effective methods to ensure state survival, as the examples of Saudi Arabia, Egypt, Syria and Jordan showed. Yet the National Pact was not compatible with those types of regimes, and while Chehabism only slightly nudged the state in that direction, it had done enough to disturb the delicate balance needed for the state to survive despite its illegitimacy. The fact that the alienation of the Lebanese Christians is an inherently longer process than that of the Muslim communities only served to delay the consequences of Chehabism's effect on the state's legitimacy. Those effects would be felt a few years later, during the term of Sleymān Frangieh.

The early 1970s: Groundwork for civil war

Under the 'era' of Chehabism, the state had, paradoxically, undergone many changes, and yet did not itself transform in any essential way. The modernization undergone in the 1960s allowed for better socio-political mobilization which introduced new players in the political arena: the army (and in particular the Deuxième Bureau), the workers' unions and syndicates,[29] the city-dwellers that developed their own demands (such as the Beiruti university students) and, most importantly, the usually marginalized Shī'a community. The insertion of new actors onto the political scene had not, however, managed to provide a path away from the confessional politics that dominated the Lebanese state, despite mounting a significant challenge to the old elites. The National Pact was still unmodified after all, and was still the basis of the state, which meant that political power still resided within each community, and citizens continued to be defined by their confession.

Sleymān Frangieh's win in the presidential election of 1970 not only signified a counter-offensive on behalf of the major Christian parties against the alienation they had suffered under Chehabism but was also meant to herald a return of the old elites to power. The state could, in theory, return to the old formula of illegitimacy as agreed upon by those in communal leaders. After all, feelings of alienation were common during presidential terms in Lebanon, such as the Muslims experienced under Sham'ūn, and the system had time and again found a way to rebalance itself to the illegitimacy it desperately needed to survive. The following section, however, will highlight the different changes that occurred both inside and outside Lebanon during the years of Frangieh's term, which made the legitimacy (or illegitimacy) crisis of the 1970s different from that of previous ones. The nature of these developments will shed light on how the state could not return to the old formula and would therefore crumble by the end of Frangieh's term.

Internal changes

It is clear that Frangieh's election occurred at a very sensitive time in Lebanese history. His presidency came amid a period of relatively radical change in Lebanese politics, particularly characterized by three phenomena.

First among these was the establishment of a reformist, 'neutral' (and usually professional) class that saw in Chehabism the salvation of Lebanon. The idea of a modern, efficient and expansive Lebanese state had always existed in certain circles but it was only in the 1960s that such ideas were finally tested through Chehabism, and having been somewhat underwhelmed with Ḥelū's performance as president, Chehabists were distraught by the fact that their candidate Eliās Sarkīs lost the presidential election by just one vote.[30] Nevertheless, they could still boast a good number of MPs for the first two years of Frangieh's term: the *Nahj* bloc had twenty-seven seats out of ninety-nine, only second to the twenty-eight seats of the Tripartite Alliance (which was a much weaker, fragile, grouping of three different leaders).[31]

The second phenomenon was the change in the political nature of the Shīʿa as a more independent and self-conscious community. The history of Lebanon had not been short of important Shīʿa politicians and clergymen, especially after the entrenchment of the National Pact and the guaranteed position of speaker of parliament. And while those elites certainly made their voices heard more loudly as time went on, the community as a whole had been characterized by feudalistic families, and pragmatic alliances that served the interests of the few among them. But it was under the cleric Mūsa al-Ṣadr that a more modern form of political activism emerged within the community, especially as Shīʿa families relocated to more central areas of the country. The rapid urbanization of the Shīʿa of the South during the 1960s and 1970s occurred, for the most part, due to a combination of the depression of the southern agricultural sector,[32] and a hasty migration process which was sparked by the Palestinian–Israeli conflict which took place in and around southern villages.[33] The result was a loss of influence for the older families like al-Asʿad and al-Khalīl not least because, as the poorer Shīʿa mixed with Beiruti families that were able to receive services from their confessional elites in the city, the newcomers were let down by the inability of the traditional Shīʿa families to do the same for them.[34]

It is in this environment that Mūsa al-Ṣadr, chairman of the newly formed Supreme Shiʿite Islamic Council (SSIC),[35] thrived. He arrived in Lebanon (his ancestral home, though he was born in Iran) as the new mufti of Tyre, and he initially refused to associate himself with any political agenda: 'There are those who … have linked my initiatives to political movements – local, Arab, and foreign – without shame, without any evidence', he insisted.[36] Nevertheless, it would not take long for Al-Ṣadr to label himself as 'Imam of the community'. Through this title, he modernized the notion of the religious cleric and inserted into it elements of socio-economic – and inevitably political – activism. As such work pushed him further and further into the intricacies of the Lebanese political 'game', he began to take on a much more advocative role, and mended broken linkages between the Shīʿa of the south and those of the Biqāʿ to issue more concrete demands for the whole confession through speeches, petitions and calls for strikes. His charisma carried him to the upper echelons of the Lebanese elites relatively quickly, and prior to the war, he had become on good terms with many Christian clergyman and political leaders, especially those that would seek to ally themselves with

Shīʿa constituencies to weaken Sunni positions. As a stark contrast to his early apolitical rhetoric, his later declarations became very similar to other Lebanese politicians. He would, for example, establish an idea for the state and push for the creation of ʻan Arabic, democratic, non-confessional Lebanon with a fair regime that guarantees rewarding opportunities for everyone'.[37]

With regard to the Palestinians, al-Ṣadr had developed a mixed relationship with the PLO and the guerrilla warfare they were undertaking. While he was always an advocate for the Palestinian cause, and remained eager to show himself as an 'Arab' as opposed to the foreigner 'Persian' image with which his critics would label him, he was also very aware of the Shīʿa community's frustration with the Palestinians' carelessness towards the well-being of southern villages. He was once quoted as saying that the Shīʿa sympathized with the Palestinians, but that their 'sympathy no longer extends to actions which expose our people to additional misery and deprivation'.[38] The Palestinian operations, after all, were resulting in Israeli counterattacks that demolished southern Shīʿa villages. And yet al-Ṣadr could not escape presenting himself as a promoter for the Palestinian cause, urging them to 'bear arms and to train'.[39] His savvy balancing of the Palestinian issue in relation to Shīʿa political demands became a famous characteristic of his. In a similar act of tightrope walking later in the 1970s, he tried to maintain his pacifist image by going on a hunger strike as a protest to the violence that erupted in April of 1975, only to confess five days later that his movement (Amal) had been forming a militia of its own to deter Israeli assaults on Lebanon, particularly in the South.[40]

The third political phenomenon that Lebanon saw in the late 1960s was the rise in the ideological nature of political activism and dialogue. The fact that political affiliations were being labelled as 'left' and 'right' was, on its own, unprecedented on a national scale in Lebanon. Indeed, much of the way in which normally confessional conflicts were ideologized was a result of the void left by the decline of Nasserism and the need to reshape Arab nationalism. In the late 1960s, as Leftist parties were given room to grow and expand, the Lebanese Communist Party (LCP), having been banned for so long, began affiliating itself with Arabist issues and developed particularly close ties with the Palestinian National Liberation Movement (otherwise known as Fatah) after the 1967 war.[41] Within the LCP itself, a new faction had risen up, made up of individuals that had grown tired of Soviet non-interference and the USSR's support of the Egyptian and Syrian governments that were not always themselves supportive of the Palestinian cause. This faction would, not long after, take over leadership in the party.[42] The LCP would end up forming the 'Popular Guard' to support the Palestinian guerrillas fighting in Jordan during the late 1960s, while the regional communist parties in Syria, Iraq, Jordan and Lebanon would collectively form their own fidāʾī force known as al-Ansār.[43] Around the same time, Muḥsin Ibrahim formed the Organisation of Communist Action in Lebanon by merging the Organization of Lebanese Socialists and the 'Socialist Lebanon' group. The political literature emerging from such groups linked confessionalism and the power-sharing system to bourgeois politics and stressed the link with the Palestinian revolution as a means of fighting bourgeois imperialism.[44] In the meantime, Arab nationalist parties also continued with their growing momentum. Specifically, with the decline of Nasserism and the stability of the Baʿthist regime in Syria, branches of Baʿthism in Lebanon were able to expand in the early 1970s, with leading member Abd al-Majīd Rifāʿī becoming an MP in 1972, while leftist Nasserist Najāḥ Wakīm also won a seat in the same elections.[45] Even the SSNP, after having the leaders of the 1961 coup released in the late 1960s, drastically changed their political and ideological structures. After a conference held in December 1969, the party took the decision to support Arabist movements (and particularly Baʿthism) and also put much focus on the Palestinian revolution as an expression of such aspirations.[46] Such a collection of different ideologies and principles all came to be known as the 'Muslim-left' by the mid-1970s, despite their ideological differences.

While these groups would form a somewhat steadfast front in defence of the Palestinian guerrilla movement, and later on against the 'Christian-right', they were unsuccessful in evolving from a pragmatic, para-militaristic alliance to a united ideological faction. One example of the differences that continued to exist between them is illustrated in a speech given by Mūsa al-Ṣadr in May of 1976, in which he condemned 'those that call for complete secularism' (which would normally include communists, socialists and Baʿthists) and he claimed that they are no different 'from atheists and Israelis'.[47] Adeed Dawisha also argued this point on how

> the divisions in Lebanon began gradually to assume a left v. right, rather than a straightforward Moslem v. Christian, character. Nevertheless ... it is important not to over-exaggerate the ideological nature of the conflict, for it is certainly true that the vast majority of those labelled 'Rightists' were Christians, in the same way that the forces of the Left showed a massive preponderance of Moslems over Christians.[48]

In fact, student and worker strikes and demonstrations on class issues, usually involving the Palestinian struggle, became part of the culture, according to Fawwāz Ṭrābulsī, to the extent that many did not know what they were demonstrating for a lot of the time.[49] In fact, in a survey conducted by Halim Barakat in 1970, he concluded that 'sectarianism is the most highly significant determining factor of attitudes towards the Palestinian Resistance Movement'.[50] The mishmash of confessionalism and class struggle became itself a recurring phenomenon, as the following speech by Mūsa al-Ṣadr shows:

> It is intolerable for the Front [i.e. the Christian-majority Lebanese Front] to be so arrogant in its dealings with the Muslims, to treat them as though they are traitors. The ruling right bears responsibility because it ignored the Shia and the south since the dawn of independence. They are deprived. They have become the proletariat of Lebanon. Let no one fool himself. Every oppression leads to an explosion.[51]

Nevertheless, with all these changes occurring in a relatively short time, the state's normal, stable, illegitimacy was bound to be affected. Firstly, it meant one more voice needed to be heard in the power-sharing game. In other words, the equation changed from Christian and Muslim (with the latter being spearheaded by the Sunni community) to Christian, Sunni and Shīʿa. It is thus not surprising that Frangieh's first few years were characterized by something akin to the post-war 'troika' of president, prime minister and speaker of parliament all needing to coordinate, politically.[52] The state being normally 'accepted' as illegitimate, it could only continue to be so in such an equation if it elevated the Shīʿa to the same level as the Christians and the Sunnis, in terms of ensuring their representativeness within state institutions. In a relatively calm climate, this would already have been a daunting test on a state so riddled with deadlock and too rigid to conduct such change in a short time. It would find this change near-impossible during the tense situation which plagued the 1970s. The second issue which challenged the norm of illegitimacy associated with the Lebanese state was the Palestinian revolutionary movement, which left the state with too much to do in too little time. It had to choose a clear policy with regard to the Palestinian struggle which meant, once again, deciding on a particular identity where ambiguity had helped it survive for so long.

In light of such pressure, Frangieh's first two years in term were surprisingly characterized by relative stability. While it would turn out to be the calm before the storm, the stability was down to the president's mix of 'Khūrīan' and Chehabist decisions. On the one hand, he started by appointing a traditional Sunni leader (his ally Ṣā'ib Salām) as prime minister and, with the Speaker Kāmil al-Asʿad on their side, fulfilled all his obligations under the National Pact. Yet, to also satisfy demands for further reform which was expected by so many, he and Salām appointed a young and technocratic government: the 'Youth Cabinet'.[53] He faced two issues with this combination, however. With regard to his Khūrīan tactics, Frangieh's relationship with Salām was nowhere near as strong as Khūrī's was with Riād al-Ṣulḥ. Similarly, al-Ṣulḥ himself had much more widespread support (and much less competition for it) within the Sunni community. Finally, the nature of Lebanese politics had changed and political expectations by both the Sunni community and the Shīʿa community had dramatically increased in that time. It was thus unsurprising that tension between the prime minister and the president grew fairly quickly, and that the speaker himself got involved between the two as well. As for any aspirations of him carrying on the Chehabist tradition, his own personal background and those of his allies (e.g. Salām and/or the Maronite elites) as traditional regional elites meant that he had no chance of carrying the same authenticity as a military man like Shehāb, or a relative unknown like Ḥelū.

Regional changes

Another major factor which played an important part in weakening the state's position to maintain normal illegitimacy was the continuously changing regional environment. While Shehāb and Ḥelū still had to deal with external penetration into Lebanese politics, their policy was a relatively simple one: keep Nāṣer happy, and in his capacity as Arab leader he would ensure stability in Lebanon, in particular by keeping the Syrian regime relatively 'tame'.[54] With Nāṣer gone, though, the competition for leadership in the Arab world grew, and the rise of Mu'ammar al-Qadhāfi in Libya, the succession of Anwar al-Sadāt in Egypt and, most importantly, the ascent of Ḥāfiz al-Assad in Syria meant that Lebanon was vulnerable on all fronts, and there wasn't any single broker with which to conduct deals. Instead, the country had to learn to stave off infiltration from all sides.

Syria posed a particularly large problem, being Lebanon's only Arab neighbour and having finally established some sort of governmental stability. It was finally strong enough to undertake an effective neighbourhood policy and pursue its interests in Lebanon, not unlike what it had done during the days of the French mandate. According to Itamar Rabinovich, by 1973–4, Syria had replaced Cairo as 'the external center [*sic*] of allegiance and guidance for Lebanese Muslims and acquired virtual veto power over major decisions concerning Lebanon's domestic and foreign policies'.[55] Indeed, with much of the division in the Arab World in the 1970s revolving around whether or not to pursue non-military action towards the Israeli problem, al-Assad's regime realized that it could only pursue such solutions if it not only cooperated closely with Palestinian guerrillas but also maintained tight control over their movements. It would do so through the use of state sponsorship of Palestinian commando factions such as al-Sā'iqa, which had been set up by the Syrian state, and the Palestinian Liberation Army.[56] Seeing the need to retain political backing from a stronger regime such as al-Assad's, Palestinian resistance organizations agreed to retain much of their military operations in the more fragile states of Jordan, initially, and Lebanon during the 1970s.

In essence, al-Assad was able to develop a multifaceted network through which he could significantly influence Lebanese politics. Through his Ba'thist contacts, he had a hand in shaping Arab nationalist policies and tendencies within the Sunni elite; through his agreements with many organizations within the PLO and his political leverage over the Palestinian movement in general, he could influence the intensity of Palestinian activity within Lebanon; through his close confessional relationship with the Shī'a community, particularly after 1973,[57] he could coordinate with leaders such as Mūsa al-Ṣadr; and finally, thanks to his tight grip on the Syrian state, he could influence the Lebanese government more directly through political and economic actions, such as the closing of the border. It is also worth mentioning that Sleymān Frangieh and al-Assad knew each other personally, as the former had given al-Assad shelter during the coup that occurred in Syria in March of 1962.[58] With such potential influence, combined with aspirations to extend Syrian control of its overly liberal – and thus unpredictable – neighbour, it would only be natural that Syria would be the first to step in after the initial instances of civil war in 1975–6, seeing an opportunity to finally shape Lebanese politics in accordance with Syrian policy. And through maintaining Lebanon as a buffer zone, Syria could guarantee the stability of its own borders while also ensuring a balance of power between itself and Israel.[59]

Al-Assad himself had also learned how to perfectly situate himself with regard to the two global superpowers. He maintained the Ba'thist relationship with the USSR which supplied him with weapons, equipment and technicians/advisors.[60]

And yet, the Syrian government 'zealously guarded their independence from Moscow', much to the frustration of the Soviets.[61] One example is US Secretary of State Henry Kissinger's role in negotiating a disengagement agreement between al-Assad and Israel with regard to the Golan Heights. Kissinger was able to acquire al-Assad's agreement to disengage with Israel (in May 1974) only a month after Syria's president had returned from a trip to Moscow which resulted in a new arms deal.[62] So while al-Assad maintained his established relationship with the USSR, he also managed to become an occasional ally to the United States and an essential part of American policy in the Middle East. For the Americans, his regime offered a source of stability, an ability to control Palestinian guerrillas and, after 1974, Syria effectively stopped being a direct threat to Israel. As a result, al-Assad was given somewhat of a free rein in Lebanon. In fact, when Syrian forces crossed the borders to intervene in the Lebanese conflict in 1976, more objection was found from the Soviet side than the American side.[63] These circumstances meant that Lebanese politics were more directly affected by Syrian policy than by more global interests. As Élizabeth Picard put it, 'The Lebanese crisis and the Syrian policy in Lebanon are only indirectly and circumstantially influenced by the configuration of the Cold War to which they subscribe.'[64]

In many cases, regional powers were very direct in expressing their interests vis-à-vis the Lebanese internal tension. For example, in February 1973, when former head of the armed forces Emile Bustānī was implicated in a bribery case, his immediate recourse was to flee to Syria and its foreign minister, 'Abd al-Ḥalīm Khaddām, who would become the new Ghālib,[65] proclaimed him as a 'guest' and sheltered him from a 'plot' by the Lebanese military.[66] Another example occurred in May of the same year 1973, when only a few weeks after the Israeli raid in Beirut, Libya's Mu'ammar al-Qadhāfi expressed his wish that the Palestinian forces take over the airport in Beirut. Such declarations shed light on the internal Lebanese situation. For instance, a speech by al-Assad in 1976 clarified many nuances about the left–right struggle in Lebanon, and the intentions of those involved. In his speech, al-Assad described a meeting he had had with Junblāṭ as follows:

> [Jumblatt] said: 'Let us discipline [the Maronites]. We must have decisive military action. They have been governing us for 140 years and we want to get rid of them.' At this point, I realized that all the masks had fallen. Therefore, the matter is not as we used to describe it. It is not as we were told. The matter is not between the Right and Left or between progressives and reactionaries. It is not between Muslim and Christian. The matter is one of vengeance. It is a matter of revenge which goes back 140 years.[67]

In the midst of this state of these regional changes, Lebanon somehow managed to sidestep getting involved (directly) in the Arab–Israeli war of 1973, and while the Arab coalition would end up on the losing side once again, many outlooks were changed afterwards. On the one hand, al-Assad started pursuing an independent policy of political settlement and bargaining with Israel through the United States. On the other hand, the Palestinian forces, seeing that states like Syria and Egypt were considering making peace with Israel, developed fears that an Arab–Israeli settlement would be drafted at their expense.[68] This resulted not only in divisions within the Palestinian camp but also in a general acceleration of militarization in Lebanon.[69]

With such developments, and the increase of influence from regional forces mingled with existing prejudices in Lebanon, whether painted with an ideological or a confessional brush, the state was not able to handle this vast amount of pressure. Institutionally, the old balance of power had truly pushed its limits of keeping foreign interests at bay, and was no longer sustainable. Societally, polarization had peaked over the Palestinian issue. Once it became clear that the state would not be able to support the Palestinian cause in a manner in which it was acceptable to the broad Muslim-left, nor could it maintain the independence and specialness which was so treasured by the Christian-right, the state faced a level of illegitimacy which it had not encountered previously. To put it in its most simple terms, the developments of the early 1970s ensured that it stopped being convenient for any of the major communities to tolerate the state anymore, the National Pact as an instrument of survival had run its course and the state had lost all hope for legitimacy, even the 'negative legitimacy' which had kept it afloat for so long. Ironically, the illegitimacy of the state would finally be admitted by a Maronite leader, the head of the Katā'ib no less, the self-professed gatekeepers of the raison d'ètre of the state, in 1975. Only a few hours after the infamous Ain al-Remmāneh incident, Pierre Jmayyil spoke the following words on Radio Lebanon: 'There is not one government, but many in Lebanon. The authority of the state does not cover the whole state.'[70]

A decade of Chehabism

Overall, Chehabism was characterized – especially early on – by a modernizing policy: increased state scope and strength; socio-economic development that matches the rate of social mobilization; an increase in the total number of ideological, modern, political parties and their incorporation into state institutions; and higher degree of professionalism and technocracy within state legislature and executive power. And yet, despite these developing changes to the state, those policies could not change the fundamental make-up of the state itself. Sectarianism, not only as an institutional characteristic but also as a socio-economic phenomenon, remained as strong as ever. Administrative corruption and favouritism, while taken away from the hands of traditional leaders, remained the preferred method for both politicians and their constituencies.

Moreover, a cross-community feeling of underrepresentation endures, and Lebanon continued to be 'penetrated' by external powers, specifically its immediate neighbours like Nāṣer who, while not as directly as he had previously done, remained a major influencer in internal politics.[71] Subsequently, the obstacles that had hindered institutional legitimacy remained there, as they had been since the creation of the state in 1920. While these failures of institutional state-building can be attributed to the fact that Shehāb did not have enough time or willpower to undergo more radical changes in the state structure, the signs were still there to show that Chehabism as a school of thought was not an adequate tool of state-building that could achieve legitimacy for the Lebanese state on an institutional level. In fact, as Michael Hudson, a modernization theorist, put it at the time, 'Lebanon's historic problems are not disappearing: parochialism if anything is aggravated by social change.'[72]

On the societal level, the events of Ḥelū's term only served to exacerbate the complete lack of identification from most members of both Christian and Muslim communities with the state. Its policy of 'positive neutrality', hailed by Chehabism as the only solution for a sustainable foreign policy that could avoid damaging societal legitimacy, had proven completely untenable in the tension-ridden environment of the Middle East in the late 1960s. The shocking loss of the 1967 war in such a short time, combined with the increased impatience of the Palestinians to rely on bigger Arab powers to 'win back their country for them' meant that the state had to choose a side, just as it was forced to do so in 1958. And while Ḥelū tried to use legality and concepts such as sovereignty and independence in order to control the movements and actions of the Palestinian guerrillas, his own actions could only ever be perceived negatively when taken in the context of the history of the Lebanese state. As a result, though the Christians had fallen back into a unified front once they perceived a threat to their only hope of a state, the Muslims had, just as much, grown tired of waiting for the Lebanese state to adapt to their own ideas and values.[73]

With such a volatile environment in place, Sleymān Frangieh's term had very little hope of restoring the 'negative legitimacy' formula that the Pact had taken advantage of for so long to ensure the survival of the state. Within only a few years, 'the country's domestic situation had deteriorated to such an extent that it was practically unrecognisable from the tranquil Lebanon of the Shihab [*sic*] period'.[74] The introduction of new elements to Lebanese political life like the rising demands of the Shīʿa, new ideological labels and the rise of a stable and powerful Syria only served to diminish the chance of the state regaining its tolerated illegitimacy. These circumstances combined with the continuously increasing activities of the Palestinian movement in Lebanon to complete a threat to state survival. Over fifty years of political illegitimacy had finally caught up with the Lebanese state, and the abnormally positive relation between illegitimacy and stability in Lebanon was lost by mid-1970, as the state collapsed and the country plunged into a fifteen-year civil war.

Notes

1 Sharbel, *Lubnān – Dafāter Al-Ruʾasāʾ*, 66.
2 Ḥelū, *Ḥayāt Fī Zikrayāt*, 211.
3 Salem, *Modernization without Revolution*, 101.
4 Salem, 101.

5 'Wāsta' is the Lebanese colloquial term for any form of connection, be it familial, regional or political, in which clientelism is used to dish out and/or obtain specific favours or job positions.

Writing in 1968, Samir Khalaf argued that, in Lebanon, 'the *wasta* [*sic*] mentality has virtually become institutionalized' – see Samir Khalaf, 'Primordial Ties and Politics in Lebanon', *Middle Eastern Studies* 4, no. 3 (1968): 262, https://doi.org/10.1080/00263206808700103.

6 'A new Levant?' (1966, 2 April). *Economist*, 28+.

7 David R. Smock and Audrey C. Smock, *The Politics of Pluralism: A Comparative Study of Lebanon and Ghana* (Oxford: Elsevier, 1975), 117.

8 Smock and Smock, 117.

9 See Article 27 of the *Lebanese Constitution as promulgated on May 23, 1926*. Retrieved from World Intellectual Property Organization on 23 May 2019: https://www.wipo.int/edocs/lexdocs/laws/en/lb/lb018en.pdf.

10 Kisirwani, 'Attitudes and Behavior of Lebanese Bureaucrats', 178.

11 Kalawoun, *The Struggle for Lebanon*, 111.

12 Kalawoun, 111.

13 Hassouna, *The League of Arab States and Regional Disputes*, 267–8.

14 Kalawoun, *The Struggle for Lebanon*, 114.

15 See Michael B. Oren, *Six Days of War: June 1967 and the Making of the Modern Middle East* (New York: Oxford University Press, 2002).

16 Farid el-Khazen, *The Breakdown of the State in Lebanon, 1967–1978* (London: I.B. Tauris, 2000), 73.

17 Are they being pushed, or are they pulling? (1967, 15 April). *Economist*, 241+.

18 Are they being pushed, or are they pulling? (1967, 15 April). *Economist*.

19 Sharbel, *Lubnān – Dafāter Al-Ru'asā'*, 73.

20 Nassīf, *Al-Maktab Al-Thānī: Ḥākim Fī Al-Ẓol*, 270.

21 See *al-Anwār* newspaper on 23–25 April 1969.

22 The plural form of *Fidā'ī*, the term used to denote a Palestinian fighter whose goal was to liberate Palestine.

23 See *al-Anwār* newspaper on 11 May 1969.

24 Ḥelū would articulate the official stance of most Christian parties and groups: 'It is natural … that we hold on to the logical conclusions of Lebanese sovereignty and safety.' See el-Khazen, *The Breakdown of the State in Lebanon, 1967–1978*, 150.

25 See Unofficial Text of the Cairo Agreement between the Lebanese Authorities and Palestinian Commando Organisations in Khadduri (ed.) International Documents on Palestine. 1972.

26 Kisirwani, 'Attitudes and Behavior of Lebanese Bureaucrats', 5.

27 As Michael Hudson argued, 'sectarian feelings [under Shehāb] were reduced to their former level, just beneath the surface of ordinary political life' (116). See Hudson, *The Precarious Republic*, 116.

28 This perception and framing of Chehabism as anti-democratic was specifically adopted by Raymond Eddeh, who became increasingly worried about the armed forces' involvement in politics, and saw in it a similar process that had occurred in the neighbouring Arab states.

'I used to always say to him,' Eddeh said about Shehāb, 'that the military should only be involved in military concerns, but his [Shehāb's] behaviour showed the opposite and indicated that he supported the army unconditionally.' See Sem'ān, *Rīmūn Iddeh*, 327.

29 Shehab's socialism gained him popularity among the urban world and those aspiring to overcome under-development (mostly Muslim).

Especially when Communist party was banned since 1947 and PSP was caught up in its feudal traditions. He instead received support from the syndicates/unions which represented around 90 per cent of the syndicate movement. In 1962, the General Confederation of Lebanese Workers (CGTL) was created – it represents seventy syndicates, that is, 60 per cent of 'syndicalized' workers (22,000 out of 37,000). The CGTL openly supported Shehab through its al-Awassef journal. Similarly, the Worker Liberation Front ('Front de Libération ouvrière') which includes the Régie syndicate, rail syndicate, port de Beyrouth syndicate, etc. also proclaimed that 'its policy is that of the regime'. See Malsagne, *Fouad Chéhab, 1902–1973*, 310–11.

30 Even worse for Chehabists, Sarkīs had actually won the most votes (forty-five) in the first round of voting (Frangieh only won thirty-eight). It was in the run-off between the two that many, including the ten MPs who voted for Pierre Jmayyil, moved their votes for Frangieh. See *al-Anwar* newspaper on 18 August 1970.

31 Meir Zamir, 'The Lebanese Presidential Elections of 1970 and Their Impact on the Civil War of 1975–1976', *Middle Eastern Studies* 16, no. 1 (1980): 50.

32 Shanahan, *The Shi'a of Lebanon*, 33.

33 See Shaery-Eisenlohr, *Shi'ite Lebanon*, 31.

According to the governor of southern Lebanon, the number of southerners who had left for the Lebanese interior, particularly the Beirut area, reached 22,853 persons by the summer of 1970. See Fuad Jabber, 'The Palestinian Resistance and Inter-Arab Politics', in *The Politics of Palestinian Nationalism*, ed. William B. Quandt, Fuad Jabber and Ann Mosely Lesch (Berkeley: University of California Press, 1973), 190.

34 Nir, *Lebanese Shi'ite Leadership, 1920–1970s*, 99.

35 The SSIC was formed by al-Ṣadr in May 1969, and gave the community an unprecedented confessional independence from the general Islamic Council 'which had been conducted under Sunni hegemony for years'. See Nir, 103.

36 The main reason for this failure was the lack of clientelist infrastructure through which older elites could help the poorer families that had occupied the southern suburbs of Beirut, the city being already divided up between Maronite and Sunni elites.

See Fouad Ajami, *The Vanished Imam: Musa Al Sadr and the Shia of Lebanon* (Ithaca, NY: Cornell University Press, 1986), 85.

37 Ṣādiq Al-Nābulsi, *Mūsa Al-Ṣadr: Masār Al-Taḥadiyāt Wal-Taḥawulāt* [Mūsa Al-Ṣadr: The Path of Challenges and Transitions] (Beirut: Markaz al-Ḥaḍāra li Tanmiyat al-Fikr al-Islāmī, 2013), 214.

38 Quoted in Ajami, *The Vanished Imam*, 162. Also see *al-Nahar* newspaper on 27 May 1970 and 2 June 1970.

39 Ajami, 125.

40 Ajami, 169.

al-Ṣadr had already proclaimed during a parade in Tyre in May of 1974 that the 'era of conversation [was] over, and there [was] no going back'. His speech was met with a 'breath-taking abundance' of celebratory gunfire. See *al-Nahar* newspaper on 6 May 1974.

41 el-Khazen, *The Breakdown of the State in Lebanon, 1967–1978*, 73.

42 Dina Kehat, 'Dilemmas of Arab Communism: The Case of the Syrian Communist Party, 1969–73', in *The USSR and the Muslim World: Issues in Domestic and Foreign Policy*, ed. Yaacov Ro'i (New York: Routledge, 1984), 285.

43 Kehat, 277.
44 el-Khazen, *The Breakdown of the State in Lebanon, 1967–1978*, 74.
45 el-Khazen, 74.
46 el-Khazen, 74.
47 See *Al-Nahar* newspaper on 24 May 1976.
48 Adeed I. Dawisha, *Syria and the Lebanese Crisis* (London: Macmillan Press, 1980), 27.
49 Fawāz Ṭrābulsī, *Ṣūrat Al-Fata Bil-Aḥmar: Ayām Fil-Silm Wal-Ḥarb* [The Picture of the Boy in Red: Days in Peace and in War] (Beirut: Riad El-Rayyes Books, 1997), 108.
50 Halim Barakat, 'Social Factors Influencing Attitudes of University Students in Lebanon towards the Palestinian Resistance Movement', *Journal of Palestine Studies* 1, no. 1 (1971): 94.
51 Ajami, *The Vanished Imam*, 178.
52 In fact, Frangieh, Ṣā'ib Salām and Kāmil As'ad had all been part of an ad hoc 'Central Bloc' prior to Frangieh's election. See Dan Naor, 'The Quest for a Balance of Power in Lebanon during Suleiman Frangieh's Presidency, 1970–76', *Middle Eastern Studies* 49, no. 6 (2013): 991.
53 Naor, 991.
54 In an interview in 2007, Sāmi Sharaf, advisor to Nāṣer at the time, confirmed the agreement of such a policy during the meeting between Nāṣer and Shehāb in 1959. In fact, Sharaf claims that Nāṣer was so satisfied with Shehāb that he assured the latter that 'the UAR is at his disposal in all that he desires and decides on'. See *al-Akhbar* newspaper on 1 November 2007.
55 Itamar Rabinovich, *The War for Lebanon: 1970–1983* (Ithaca, NY: Cornell University Press, 1984), 37.
56 Naomi Joy Weinberger, *Syrian Intervention in Lebanon: The 1975–76 Civil War* (New York: Oxford University Press, 1986), 131.

Assad's relationship with Yāsser 'Arafāt and Fatah, however, was much more problematic. See 'Alā Butros, *Al-Stratījīya Al-Sūriya Fī Lubnān Bayn Al-Assad Al-Ab Wal-Assad Al-Ibn: 1970–2009* [The Syrian Strategy in Lebanon between Assad the Father and Assad the Son: 1970–2009] (Beirut: al-Furāt, 2011), 58.
57 In 1973, the Shī'a religious authorities officially recognized the Alawite sect (to which Assad and many of the key position-holders in the Syrian state belonged to) as a part of the wider Shī'a community. See Weinberger, *Syrian Intervention in Lebanon*, 112.
58 Alain Ménargues, *Asrār Ḥarb Lubnān* [Secrets of the War of Lebanon] (Beirut: Librairie Internationale, 2004), 23.
59 Butros, *Al-Stratījīya Al-Sūriya Fī Lubnān Bayn Al-Assad Al-Ab Wal-Assad Al-Ibn*, 70.
60 In fact, after securing power, Assad 'made it one of his immediate goals … to reassure the USSR of Syria's future course', and its adherence to developing 'relations with the socialist camp, particularly with the friendly USSR'. See Efraim Karsh, *Soviet Policy towards Syria since 1970* (New York: Palgrave Macmillan, 1991), 68.
61 Galia Golan, 'The Cold War and the Soviet Attitude towards the Arab–Israeli Conflict', in *The Cold War in the Middle East: Regional Conflict and the Superpowers 1967–73*, ed. Nigel J. Ashton (New York: Routledge, 2007), 65.
62 See Salim Yaqub, 'Scuttle Diplomacy: Henry Kissinger and the Middle East Peace Process, 1973 1976', in *Imperfect Strangers: Americans, Arabs, and U.S.–Middle East Relations in the 1970s* (Ithaca, NY: Cornell University Press, 2016), 145–82.

Although Assad had initially rejected any deal, the end-product was a much clearer agreement, including the following commitment by Assad: 'There will be no firing across the lines by anyone. There [will be] no possibility for organized armed bands to cross into Israel. No fedayeen (terrorist) can be stationed in the front areas.' See Yinon Shlomo, 'The Israeli–Syrian Disengagement Negotiations of 1973–74', *Middle Eastern Studies* 51, no. 4 (2015): 646.

For the reported arms deal, see *al-Anwar* newspaper on 14 April 1974.

63 The Soviets were worried about the unilateral nature of the intervention, especially its effect on the Palestinian revolutionary movement. See Élizabeth Picard, *Liban-Syrie, Intimes Étrangers: Un Siècle d'Interactions Sociopolitiques* [Lebanon-Syria, Intimate Strangers: A Century of Sociopolitical Interactions] (Paris: Actes Sud, 2016), 181.

64 Picard, 180.

65 Egyptian Ambassador to Lebanon during Nāṣer's regime – see previous sections.

66 See *Al-Nahar* newspaper on 13 February 1973.

67 Sam Younger, 'The Syrian Stake in Lebanon', *World Today* 32, no. 11 (1976): 401–2.

68 See Weinberger, *Syrian Intervention in Lebanon*, 134.

69 Weinberger, 134.

70 Edgar O'Ballance, *Civil War in Lebanon, 1975–92* (New York: Palgrave Macmillan, 1998), 2.

71 In fact, Egypt's ambassador Ghālib was at one point 'known to the Lebanese by the colonial title of the High Commissioner'. See James Craig, *A History of the Middle East Centre for Arab Studies* (London: Macmillan, 1998), 115.

Also see Salibi, *Crossroads to Civil War*, 18.

72 Hudson, *The Precarious Republic*, 330.

73 In fact, a survey conducted in Lebanese universities in the early 1970s showed that, in response to the statement 'What is needed in the Lebanese political system is revolution, not reform', 50 per cent of Sunnis, 68 per cent of Shī'a and 57 per cent of Druze either agreed or strongly agreed, as opposed to only 24 per cent of Maronites who answered the same. See Halim Barakat, *Lebanon in Strife: Student Preludes to the Civil War* (Austin: University of Texas Press, 1977), 63.

74 Dawisha, *Syria and the Lebanese Crisis*, 22.

CONCLUSION

By 1976, talks of the Lebanese state being 'on the verge of disintegration', another civil war that had reached 'its fourth phase' and of '15 "official" militias with a total strength of a 150,000 men and 300,00 firearms' became common.[1] The Lebanese state had begun to break down, as the broad Muslim-left and the Palestinian liberation forces were pitted against a mainly Christian front in a country-wide divide reminiscent of 1958. A decade later, the state's collapse was all but confirmed: 'In the 1980s, Lebanon cannot be considered to be a sovereign independent state, and its government controls neither most of the territory of the state nor its people.'[2]

There have been many causes – direct and indirect – reasoned to have launched the Lebanese civil war, which lasted for fifteen years, but this book has maintained that one cannot look at any incident in isolation. Nor is it appropriate to situate the conflict in its immediate temporal context. The nature of the war and the actions and decisions of all sides, internal and external, demand that it be looked at as another link in a long chain that had been forming throughout the history of the Lebanese state. Just as the creation of the state of Greater Lebanon is itself a somewhat arbitrary point for the start of this research, justified only by the theoretical framework (i.e. legitimacy) in which this book has operated, so too is the decision to satisfactorily end the research during the last years of Shehāb's term and the start of Charles Ḥelū's. There is no doubt that the 1967 war, three years into the latter's tenure, and the increased presence and activities of Palestinian guerrillas throughout the late 1960s served to aggravate tensions between the Muslim and the Christian communities. Similarly, the continued disenfranchisement of the Shīʿa population, which was only increasing in numbers, became crucial to the developments of the war in the late 1970s and 1980s. On top of that, regional and international interests in the country and the Middle East played a crucial role in the undergoing of the fifteen-year-old conflict. Still, this research has argued that the political circumstances of the state – in particular its inability to maintain political and institutional stability, which includes the occurrence of the civil war – stem from the experience of Lebanese state-building. In particular, that state-building experience has failed in allowing the state to obtain the political legitimacy – institutional and societal – that could prevent or correct those circumstances. In essence, the structure of the Lebanese case in this book has followed, and thus proven the existence of, the causal chain which lies at the heart of Lebanese political instability.

The causal chain of Lebanese illegitimacy

It was firstly shown how the political environment in the Lebanese territories prior to the creation of the state was in no way conducive to a legitimate political authority that could rule over all of what would become the state of Greater Lebanon. In particular, the different communities within those territories had started to receive, and implement, eighteenth- and nineteenth-century European ideas of nationalism while also developing their own within the context of the Ottoman Empire. Those feelings of political aspiration and forms of self-determination were clearly and undoubtedly contradictory, on a material level in terms of what constituted the Lebanese 'nation' and with regard to the format and structure of a possible Lebanese state. Three factors then came into play to ensure the illegitimacy of the new state: the fact that those political communities coincided with ethno-religious dividing lines, the fact that the new state was based on a form of confessionalism which englobed (both literally and symbolically) all of these contradictory opinions and the fact that the French mandate which oversaw the state openly backed one particular state-building project (that of the Maronites). The combination of these three conditions provides a sufficient explanation for why the resulting Lebanese state is an illegitimate one, however one defines the concept of political legitimacy.

Chapter 2 focused on the period of the French mandate over the state of Greater Lebanon. The illegitimacy of the latter, exacerbated by the constant interference on behalf of the mandatory power, created a series of conditions that made it virtually impossible for the Lebanese state to develop adequately, both in terms of institutional function and in terms of acceptability on the part of its citizens. Not only did the state authority (i.e. a combination of domestic and French institutions) have to constantly deal with pushback on the part of the alienated Muslim communities, making much of its expected functions impossible to fully execute, but it also suffered from internal divisions on the part of the powerful Maronite community wherein a disagreement arose over the identity of the state itself, to which the French had to continuously adjust and on which they had to constantly arbitrate. Elements of traditional feudal-like relations and personal power politics also hindered the state's performance, while the regional schemes of both the French and the English, which were shaped by their own considerations, also served to hinder Christian–Muslim relations at the time. Thus, the period of the Lebanese state under the mandate proved to be the first where the new state found itself in a vicious circle in illegitimacy. In other words, political illegitimacy, itself a result of the conditions prior to the creation of the state, created further conditions that caused the state of Greater Lebanon to remain, institutionally and societally, illegitimate.

However, the end of the mandate period brought with it the creation of the National Pact, a formula of supposed social and political cohabitation concocted between two leaders, one Maronite and the other Sunni. The National Pact was the direct result of the state's illegitimacy, specifically its societal illegitimacy. It was painted as the only way in which the divided communities can live peacefully under one state: it rejected both extreme Christian and Muslim identities, it put the utmost emphasis on national consensus with regard to political decisions and it established the principle of proportional representation within the state. The period succeeding the French mandate is the focus of Chapter 3. It shows how the Pact failed in answering the most fundamental questions about Lebanese state-building: a way for the state to gain strength and effectiveness, and a reason for the population to identify with the idea of the state. Institutionally, the Pact quickly rose to become the highest norm, both legally and politically, to the extent that its preservation came at the expense of effective governance. Instead, so as to keep to the 'confessional code' while avoiding interference in political affairs could cause sectarian tension (which, it was found, encompassed almost all affairs). Societally, the Pact was too ambiguous to be able to successfully establish a Lebanese identity and an idea of the state which most, if not all, communities could accept. Its weaknesses were quickly uncovered especially when dealing with issues of foreign policy, where the Lebanese state had to recurrently choose the extent to which it was willing to embrace the Arab unity which most of its neighbours aspired for. That choice regularly pit the extremes of Christian isolationism and their historical attachment to the West against the Muslim counterpart which called for more political proximity to the Arab environment. In both cases, the National Pact – which became the raison d'être for the post-mandate Lebanese state – plunged the state deeper into the trap of illegitimacy which it had found itself in.

Despite the illegitimacy which the new Lebanese Republic inherited from the National Pact, however, the first independent Lebanese presidency showed the manifestation an abnormal phenomenon. Khūrī, who had been the co-creator of the Pact, understood exactly how the latter could, despite its illegitimacy, ensure the survival of the state itself. The Pact guaranteed positions of power for both the Christians and the Muslims, and remained sufficiently vague about Lebanon's relation with its Arab surroundings that both Christians and Muslims could find a way to identify with the state. In addition, the communities themselves being guaranteed a voice within the state, they could – it was hoped – democratically steer the state towards an identity that could unite the country. At best, the consensus needed for this power-sharing system could be achieved, in which case the state will have achieved some form of legitimacy. At worst, the consensus could not be achieved and the state would simply remain irrelevant to the internal workings of the communities. While the possibility of consensus would rarely (if ever) be realized, the latter option of an out-of-the-way state was easily achievable with Khūrī at the helm. This formula of illegitimacy, while unable to bring about an acceptance of the state's right to rule, managed to ensure toleration of the state's existence on the part of the different communities, and the Lebanese state under these conditions could be said to have achieved a tolerated illegitimacy, or a 'negative legitimacy'. This can be defined as a situation in which groups do not agree on the primary principles and values under which they want to be governed, but

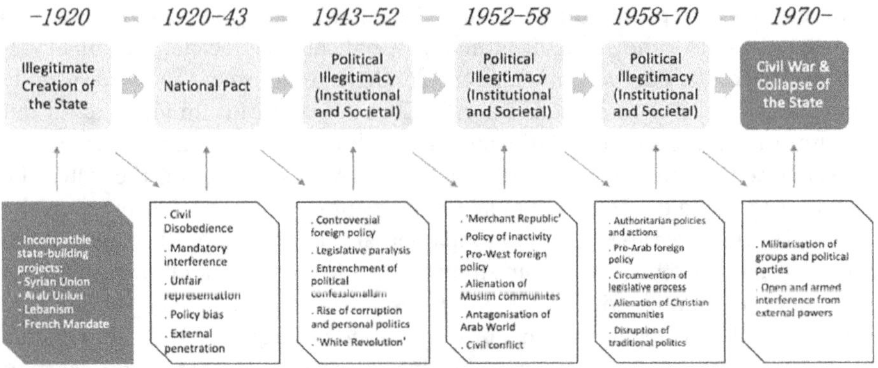

Figure C.1 Schema of the causal link established in the previous chapters.

instead undertake a tit-for-tat agreement with the state as one would expect to see with external forms of governance such as a UN mission. In other words, the state is for all intents and purposes illegitimate, yet this does not result in its failure or in rampant political instability. Instead, groups agree to partake in the power-sharing system precisely because the state serves as a guarantor for overall illegitimacy. The state remains illegitimate in the eyes of all its groups, thus providing each of them with a degree of satisfaction (and ensuring partial compliance) while public institutions themselves remain inhibited due to the power-sharing system.

Chapter 4 begins with Bishāra al-Khūrī's forced resignation in 1952, itself a result of the inability of his term to solve the fundamental Lebanese issues, and his tendency to take advantage of a state which gave the president overwhelming power while setting up a legislative deadlock ready to be abused. The causal chain established so far has linked the illegitimacy state up to that point to the National Pact of 1943, itself the result of the mandatory state, which itself was linked to the creation of the state in accordance with French and Maronite interests. Out of all Lebanese presidents in the twentieth century, perhaps no one understood the inherent weakness of the state more than Kamīl Shamʿūn, its second president post-1943. It did not take him long to brush off most calls for fundamental reform and instead set the state down the path of inactivity and non-interference, with the vision of turning Lebanon into a 'merchant republic', one characterized by economic liberalism and free enterprise. The first years of his term passed with relative stability, though it eventually became clear that non-interference created socio-political gaps that could only be filled by those with a socio-economic advantage, which had historically been the Christians. As inequality increased, or was at the very least *perceived* to have increased by those on the losing end, regional circumstances also reminded Shamʿūn that indifference or complete neutrality was not a sustainable option for the foreign policy of the Lebanese state. The National Pact continued to be the source of political illegitimacy. Nevertheless, when Shamʿūn moved away from the spirit of the Pact by accepting the Eisenhower Doctrine in the face of Nāṣer-led Arab opposition which the Muslim population identified with, he was faced with an uprising led by the Muslim communities.

Subsequently, the Pact also showed itself to be the only thing on which the majority of Lebanese communities could agree on. A pattern thus started to emerge: stability in the Lebanese political scene can only exist when the Pact, source of illegitimacy, was being adhered to. In other words, stability could only be achieved when the state was considered illegitimate *by everyone*. The sustainability of such a formula, however, would prove to be much more difficult: with illegitimacy remaining at the heart of the state and creating an atmosphere of distrust, and constant attempts at unachievable compromise, it did not take much to tip the delicate balance and cause crisis after crisis.

Fu'ād Shehāb's tenure as president came after the 1958 civil conflict and most were optimistic of his ability to reconcile the country, again under the National Pact which was seen to have been breached by Sham'ūn. Shehāb also clearly saw the shortcomings of the Pact with regard to state effectiveness and efficiency. As a result, he undertook a more authoritarian (relative to Lebanon) route which allowed him to circumvent the sluggish legislative and administrative processes. This method, on its own, faced some backlash by those who felt that Lebanese democracy (however faulty) was being ignored or overrun, yet Shehāb remained convinced that his much-needed reforms would justify the means. As he relied more and more on political and executive autonomy, however, Shehāb made what were seen as consecutive concessions to regional powers, in particular to Nāṣer. Despite appeasing a majority of the centrist politicians, and in particular the majority of the previously disenfranchised Muslim powers, Shehāb progressively learned that a Lebanese state strong enough to intervene in communal and traditional relations, and one that adhered to Arab-friendly politics, would alienate most Christians in the country, just as the opposite had done to the Muslim population the decade before. By the end of the 1960s, and after the second 'Chehabist' term, the Christians leaders had, for the first time since the creation of the state, united in what they perceived to be a threat to their communal existence. Another section of the Lebanese population became alienated from the state, as the Muslims had been earlier in the country's history. After the Christian community pushed back in the 1970s, however, the years of Sleymān Frangieh's term saw the exacerbation of those feelings of alienation on all sides, including the more politically conscious Shī'a. No longer espousing a negative legitimacy, the state finally crumbled under the decades of illegitimacy which it had been struggling with from its inception.

The National Pact, by now a clear cause *and* consequence of political illegitimacy, had, time and again, spurred the state to undertake extreme (in the eyes of the different communities) measures in order to overcome the weaknesses of this 'national agreement'. As a direct result, the formula which had become the cornerstone of the country's survival was also at the heart of all its periods of instability. The National Pact had created an environment in which all parties knew that the state was illegitimate, and it was simply a question of how long each community would be able to tolerate this status quo. The history of the Lebanese state showed that it would simply take a relatively small series of circumstances to nudge one of the Lebanese communities into a space of alienation. And in all of those cases, the state would – sooner or later – bear the consequences.

These empirical observations have shown a clear causal relation between the process of the creation of the Lebanese state and its continued illegitimacy throughout its development in the twentieth century. Figure C.1 can thus outline the causal chain established in this book.

Additionally, this book has shown how the existing theories on legitimacy – and specifically legitimacy in state-building – prove inadequate in explaining the shortcomings of the state in Lebanon. In essence, the theories fail to sufficiently take into account the multifaceted nature of legitimacy which, in the Lebanese case, needs to exist both on the institutional and the societal level. The reason for this particular requirement with regard to the Lebanese state is relatively simple and direct: the existence of the National Pact as the fundamental building bloc to political governance. Undoubtedly, there is no set majority formula that determines when the state's right to rule is no longer accepted (even in the most democratic of countries). But one contextual element of societal legitimacy is the objective set out by the state itself, either through its initial formation or, in the case of many former colonial entities, through its independence process. In Lebanon's case, accepting that no national identity had previously existed within the Lebanese territories, the Pact established two crucial conditions for the state to exist: on the one hand, it stressed the official representativeness of all communities through an entrenchment of the confessional system into a consociational state. In this power-sharing system, the state was expected to meet the demands of both the individual rights of its citizens and the group rights of its communities. On the other hand, it required both overarching sides (the Christians and the Muslims, composed of mainly the Maronites and the Sunnis) to forego their attachment to the West and the Arab world, respectively. This attachment, present for centuries beforehand, had grown to form part of the identity of these two groups. Thus, the Pact demanded that the state not only reflect a neutral idea which neither group reflected but, through practical necessity, form a new idea in which the state was neutral towards these two international, and internal, currents. Thus, the Pact demanded that the state possess both institutional and societal legitimacy.

Because of those demands, different approaches to state-building – institutional or societal – become inadequate in explaining the contradictory developments of the Lebanese state throughout the twentieth century. In particular, the prescriptions of each approach fall flat when they encounter the same obstacles that contradict their own principles. In this sense, the institutional approach, which focuses on the perfection of the organizational and operational aspects of the state, struggles to explain why the existing traditions and communal institutions clash with the establishment of impersonal, modernized state bureaucracies. Similarly, those institutionalists who advocate for doing away with the power-sharing system have to deal with the fact that, with an insistence on democratic institutions, they cannot override the wishes of the Lebanese communities that wish to preserve such a system without risking the descent into an autocratic state, as the experience of Fu'ād Shehāb's later years showed. On the other hand, the societal approach, while easily analysing the reason behind societal illegitimacy within the state, struggles to analyse why and how the existing Lebanese state can remain as representative as possible without fundamentally crumbling. In other words, the state cannot remain viable and at the same time representative of contradictory ideas and identities which the different communities espouse. Therefore, the natural conclusion for any societal approach to Lebanese state-building is for the state to either embark on a nation-building programme, which it has historically failed to do due to a combination of corruption and internal resistance because of the power-sharing nature of its institutions, or to disappear entirely.

Jeffrey Herbst has argued that, in the case of some African countries, the latter alternative should be considered a possibility.[3] For such an alternative to become realistic, however, the international community would need to let go of its attachment to the current state system, its definition for 'failed states' and its worry of a slippery slope that could lead to the creation of microstates. There is evidence to show that, politically and academically, the concepts of the state and state-building are dominated by Euro-centric – or Western-centric – assumptions and presuppositions. Western states are seen as 'successful' examples of state-building and, in that respect, are in possession of the legitimacy they need to continuously change shape and adapt to their societies' needs without risking wide scales of instability that could threaten the existence of these states. These states, however, are products of their own histories, and centuries of political developments leading into state-building in the West mean that those models might not be as applicable to other countries as one would like to think. Indeed, the events of the last decade and the unprecedented scale of immigration to European and North American countries have shown that those states themselves can clash with other cultures, especially those that carry with them elements of group thinking and communal loyalties. It is partly for such circumstantial reasons, and for the fear of falling into the same assumptions, that this particular research has focused solely on the Lebanese case and has not claimed any generalizable characteristic of the explanation it provides for Lebanese state-building. In the case of the latter, it could be time, just as Herbst argued, to start looking at alternatives that could satisfy the legitimacy criteria which seem to be central to the functioning and viability of governance.

Such conceptual alternatives could be particularly useful in the Lebanese case since the end of the civil war and the establishment of the Tā'if agreement in 1990, which was meant to make the state even more representative by distributing powers more evenly to the Sunni and Shīʿa communities within the state, have hardly succeeded in providing institutional or societal legitimacy to the Lebanese state. One need only look at the occupations of Israel and Syria from the present until 2000 and 2005, respectively; the development of Ḥizballah's internal state-building which has rivalled that of the state; the nature of the June war of 2006; the series of assassinations that plagued the country at the time; and the recurrent political crises between 2008 and 2019 as examples of the inability of the state to deal with the institutional pressures which are put on it. Subsequently, if there is one aspect of this research that could be generally applicable to comparative cases, it is that institutional and societal legitimacy are key for any successful, viable and governing apparatus.

Stability, on the other hand, is not as positively (or proportionately) linked to legitimacy as the existing theories assume that it is. In fact, institutionally, the Lebanese case has shown that the country has experienced its most stable periods when the country was left to its devices – that is, without external infiltration – and the weakness of state institutions was simply circumvented by internal subnational actions. This was the case for the initial years of the first two presidents' terms, and most of Shehāb's presidential tenure is characterized by the regimes' ability to ward off external penetration and to resist the temptation to embark on a wholesome political plan to shape the state. Institutionally, both al-Khūrī and Sham'ūn maintained a minimal state, one which could be easily bypassed and the ineffectiveness of which could be ignored, or at the very least tolerated, to a certain degree. Meanwhile, Shehāb strengthened many new institutions and reformed some of the old, but did not go so far as to change the fundamental character of the state. Instead, he chose to bypass much of the old, corrupt institutions wherein a culture of favouritism had become too widespread and as a result the bureaucracy itself could not be relied upon. In either case, institutional illegitimacy did not stand in the way of relative stability, though whether or not that would be sustainable in the long term is up for debate, since the feeling that the Lebanese state was too minimal, weak and ineffective was just as widespread in 1975 as it had been in 1958 and in the early 1940s. Even Shehāb himself, when refusing to run for president once more in 1970, declared – as part of his reasons – that the political structures in Lebanon 'do not seem to be to consist an adaptive instrument to the needs of Lebanese recovery'.[4] This flew in the face of Shehāb's rhetoric during his term in which he affirmed his belief in the Lebanese political structure and argued that the system itself was innocent, yet was simply being taken advantage of.[5]

On the other hand, societally, stability in Lebanon has been congruent with illegitimacy on the national scale: when *all* the communities have perceived the state as illegitimate, but have been content with it being out of the way of their own internal manoeuvres, the country experienced periods of stability. This has been the case during the early years of Khūrī's term, Sham'ūn's term, Shehāb's term and even some of the periods of political crises in the 2010s. This 'illegitimate legitimacy' is not a new idea for the Lebanese case, as Binder wrote in 1966:

> When we ask on what bases legitimacy is accorded to the Lebanese regime, we are struck by the fact that the major support of the present regime stems from the willingness of a majority of Lebanese to put up with a regime which is not legitimate in order to prevent it from assuming a legitimacy which is disapproved. In a sense, we might say that the Lebanese regime enjoys a 'neutral legitimacy', that it is established upon principles which arc neither strongly approved nor strongly disapproved.[6]

The evidence at the time showed that Binder's neutral legitimacy had actually been internalized within many of Lebanon's communities, as they mostly resort to instigating instability when they feel that the state is moving away from this illegitimacy, such as during the predominantly Muslim insurrection of 1958 or the increased Christian antagonism towards the state in the late 1960s. Still, Binder's concept fails to account for the institutional weakness of the state which has also resulted in periods of instability, as it had done in 1951–2 and the various governmental crises throughout the twentieth century. Similarly, Michael Suleiman and Michael Hudson have argued that 'Lebanon's political system rests upon a tradition of *non-legitimacy* and dispersed, balanced, power'.[7] Their concept of 'non-legitimacy' suffers from the same drawbacks as Binder's idea, and the heavy political and administrative centralization of the state means that their second claim is not as reflective of reality as the evidence shows. It is with the benefit of retrospect, theoretical advancement and time that this book has re-assessed such brief statement from Binder and Suleiman, and has attempted to further their notions to develop the hypothesis of negative legitimacy.

Effectively, the attribution of negative legitimacy to the state, as has been argued by this book, allows for a much more nuanced understanding of the relationship between state and society in pre-war Lebanon, something which has been desperately needed in developing countries where traditional conceptions have simply failed to explain political dynamics. While undoubtedly shaped by its colonial past and the regional tensions it has found itself in, the essence of the Lebanese state's current predicament can be explained through this legitimacy-based, holistic perspective on the development of Lebanese state-building since 1920. Once established, however, this approach opens up more fundamental questions with regard to the future prospects of the Lebanese state. First and foremost, a similar study needs to be conducted regarding post-war Lebanon and the 'Taif Republic', though the fact that the system itself has barely changed would imply that negative legitimacy is still very much present to this day in Lebanon.

The second point that needs to be addressed is the desirability of this negative legitimacy: though it might ensure periods of stability, is it worth the risk of living in an illegitimate state where public institutions are rarely relied on? After all, those who work to preserve the status quo have relied time and again on warning their supporters of the chaos that would ensure by questioning the viability of the state as it is. What would the alternative look like for the Lebanese? That, in this author's opinion, will always remain for them to decide. The final, wider question that this analysis poses is on the nature of the state itself: if it is ultimately defined by its legitimacy above all else, what does this tell us about alternative political systems that vary from the traditional notion of the state, but retain the legitimacy so desperately needed for a functioning system (the key being the term 'functioning' and its definition)? Technology and innovation have been shattering the administrative barriers of the state for the last few decades (with Europe being the strongest example), and the traditional idea of the state in relation to competing ideas of a transnational and regional nature is being challenged daily. Is it somewhat ironic then that in Lebanon, groups define themselves based on their existence in and around the modern state, a foreign apparatus that is supposed to have been imported to the region? These are questions that legitimacy-based approaches could help answer.

As for any study applying a legitimacy-based analysis to Lebanon after 1990, it would undoubtedly have to adjust for certain changes in the Lebanese political landscape. While there is no immediate reason to suppose that such a study would produce a drastically different assessment of the state's institutional legitimacy, one has to acknowledge that, for the most part, both the Sunni and the Shīʿa communities have displayed an acceptance of the adjusted political formula that was hitherto non-existent within these groups, at least not in a widespread manner. Naturally, the new troika which allows for a fairer share of political representation played a major part in this, as did the fact that the Lebanese Constitution now begins by defining Lebanon as unequivocally 'Arab'. As such, in terms of societal legitimacy, the situation has changed in quite a significant manner.

Nevertheless, to look at this period as a definitive, as opposed to an ongoing, transition is a risky, if not perilous, proposition. Generally speaking, the right–left divide which was used in Lebanon during the Cold War to increase tensions has been slowly but surely replaced by the rise of Iran on the one hand and the increasing influence of the Gulf states, led by Saudi Arabia and backed by the United States, on the other. Crucially, however, both of these axes, while increasingly polarizing in Lebanon's case, have not displayed enough direct expansionist potential to compete with, for example, Nāṣer's form of Arabism in the 1950s. In fact, extreme (in the ideological sense) versions of Arabism have virtually disappeared from the political scene in the Middle East. This can also be argued to have helped engender the idea of the state on the societal level in Lebanon, with virtually no separatist or irredentist movements cropping up within the Sunni or Shīʿa community as there had been done in the past.

Another regional element to consider is the rise of Daʿesh (or the Islamic State) during the mid-2010s and, more importantly, what that represented in terms of challenging existing state borders. While Daʿesh's power has greatly diminished, the effects of its attempted 'revolution' on the internal borders of the region are still felt today, as the Kurdish community's newfound autonomy in the Levant can attest to. And while the Daʿesh threat did not manifest itself as strongly in Lebanon, Hezbollah's infamous campaign against the Islamist group in Syria was often justified as a pre-emptive measure and showed the malleability of borders around Lebanon. The prerequisites and implications of the disregard for Syrian–Lebanese borders and sovereignty is another interesting event worth appraising if one is to thoroughly assess institutional and societal legitimacy of Lebanon in the 2010s.

Naturally, the rise of Hezbollah itself as an unmatched rival to the state's security institutions, and subsequently some of its public services, is perhaps the standout change in post-war Lebanon. It represents an unprecedented phenomenon in Lebanese politics and one could argue it indicates an astute understanding by Shīʿa leadership of negative legitimacy and how to take advantage of the unique ineptitude of Lebanese public institutions. But in a sense, through its self-declared mandate to liberate Israeli-occupied Lebanese territories and a periodic reference to its Lebanese origins, Hezbollah has arguably helped convince many in the Shīʿa community to continue to accept the Lebanese state. Conversely, the antagonistic stance taken by Hezbollah towards the Sunni-supported axis in the region can also be argued to have pushed the Lebanese Sunni community to stand up for the state in a way that they have never felt the need to do before. If one were to accept such a statement, however, then the crucial question becomes about how conditional such acceptance from both sides is, and how far it has gone to actually help increase societal legitimacy within Lebanon, as opposed to entrench the negative legitimacy in which the different communities feel threatened by any pressure that forces one idea of the state over another. In other words, at what point (if at any) does reactionary tolerance for the state become unconditional acceptance? These are central considerations for an inquiry into legitimacy in post-war Lebanon, and this author hopes that this book and the analysis therein could provide some guidance for such a study. Moreover, it is my hope that legitimacy-based studies can provide a road map for political solutions to the people in Lebanon. Their benefit, as well as that of all citizens living under illegitimate rule, should, in my humble opinion, remain the focal point of academic endeavours like these.

Notes

1 See Naveed Ahmed, 'The Lebanese Crisis: The Role of the PLO', *Pakistan Horizon* 29, no. 1 (1976): 32; Middle East Research & Information Project, 'Lebanon's Civil War: The Fourth Phase', *MERIP Reports*, 1976; Eric Rouleau, 'Crisis in Lebanon', *Journal of Palestine Studies* 5 (1976): 234.
2 N. Kliot, 'The Collapse of the Lebanese State', *Middle Eastern Studies* 23, no. 1 (1987): 54.
3 See Herbst, 'Responding to State Failure in Africa'.
4 Antoine Nasri Messarra, *Le Modèle Politique Libanais et Sa Survie: Essai Sur La Classification et l'Aménagement d'un Système Consociatif* [The Lebanese Political Model and Its Survival: An Essay on the Classification and the Layout of a Consociational System] (Beirut: Librairie Orientale, 1983), 144.
5 Messarra, 145.
6 Leonard Binder, 'Political Change in Lebanon', in *Politics in Lebanon*, ed. Leonard Binder (New York: Wiley, 1966), 309.
7 Suleiman, *Political Parties in Lebanon*, 289.

BIBLIOGRAPHY

Archival sources

British National Archives, Foreign Office

FO 371 General Correspondence (Syria and Lebanon)
FO 406 Confidential Print, Eastern Affairs
FO 484 Confidential Print, Lebanon

U.S. National Archives

Lebanon, Palestine, Syria, Trans-Jordan: Records of the U.S. Department of State, 1836–1944
Confidential U.S. State Department central files: Lebanon, 1945–9
Confidential U.S. State Department central files: Syria 1945–9

French National Archives

Archives Nationales d'Outre-mer (ANOM, Aix-en-Provence), cote 50065
Archives Nationales d'Outre-mer (ANOM, Aix-en-Provence), cote 50507

United Nations Archives

Official Records of the General Assembly – UNSCOP: A/364/Add.2 PV.38
Statistical Office of the United Nations Department of Economic and Social Affairs

Oberlin College Archives

Archives of the Lebanese Maronite Patriarchate
Documents relating to former Lebanese President Fu'ād Shehāb – Fouad Chehab Foundation
King-Crane Commission Digital Collection

Newspapers and journals

a-'Irfān
al-'Ahd al-Jadīd
al-'Amal
al-Akhbar
al-Anwar
al-Mihmāz
al-Qabas
Beirut
L'Orient
Le Jour
Le Monde
Lisān al-Ḥāl

Works cited

'Awād, Walīd. *Aṣḥab Al-Fakhāma: Rou'asā' Lubnān* [Masters of Luxury: Presidents of Lebanon]. Beirut: al-Ahliyya lil-Nashr wal-Tawzī', 1977.
Abisaab, Rula. 'Shiite Beginnings and Scholastic Tradition in Jabal Amil in Lebanon'. *Muslim World* 89 (1999): 1–21.
Abou, Sélim. *Le Bilinguisme Arabe-Français Au Liban: Essai d'Anthropologie Culturelle* [Arab-French Bilingualism in Lebanon: An Essay on Cultural Anthropolgy]. Paris: Presses universitaires de France, 1962.
Abu-Husayn, Abdul Rahim. *The View from Istanbul: Lebanon and the Druze Emirate in the Ottoman Chancery Documents, 1546–1711*. London: I.B. Tauris, 2004.
Agwani, M. S. *The Lebanese Crisis, 1958: A Documentary Study*. London: Asia Publishing House, 1965.
Agwani, M. S. 'The Lebanese Crisis of 1958 in Retrospect'. *International Studies* 4, no. 4 (1962): 248–329.
Ahmed, Naveed. 'The Lebanese Crisis: The Role of the PLO'. *Pakistan Horizon* 29, no. 1 (1976): 31–46.
Ajami, Fouad. *The Vanished Imam: Musa Al Sadr and the Shia of Lebanon*. Ithaca, NY: Cornell University Press, 1986.
Akl, Georges, Abdo Ouadat and Edouard Hunein, eds. *The Black Book of the Lebanese Elections of May 25, 1947 (An Account Translated from the Arabic Original)*. New York: Phoenicia Press, 1947.
Akzin, Benjamin. *State and Nation*. London: Hutchinson University Library, 1964.
Al-'Aẓem, Khāled. *Mudhakarāt Khāled Al-'Aẓem, Al-Jeld Al-Thānī* [Khāled Al-'Azem's Memoirs, Volume Two]. Beirut: al-Dār al-Mutta7ida lil-Nasher, 1973.
Al-Ḥāj, Bader. *Al-Judhūr Al-Tārīkhiya Lil-Mashrū' Al-Ṣahyūnī Fī Lubnān* [Origins of the Zionist Project in Lebanon]. Beirut: Dār Muṣbāḥ al-Feker, 1982.
Al-Ḥallāq, Ḥassān. *Al-Tayārāt Al-Siyāsiya Fī Lubnān 1943–1952* [Political Currents in Lebanon 1943–1952]. Beirut: Ma'had al-'Inmā' al-'Arabi, 1982.

Al-Ḥallāq, Ḥassān. *Mu'tamar Al-Sāḥil Wal-Aqḍiya Al-Arb'a, 1936* [The Conference of the Coast and the Four Districts, 1936]. Beirut: Dār al-Nahār, 1983.
Al-Ḥallāq, Ḥassān. *Tārīkh Lubnān Al-Mou'āṣir 1913–1952* [Modern History of Lebanon 1913–1952]. Beirut: Dār al-Nahḍa al-'Arabiyya, 2010.
Al-Ḥoṣ, 'Abed al-Raḥman Maḥmūd. *Lubnān Fī 'Ahd Al-Ra'īs Kamīl Sham'ūn* [Lebanon under President Kamīl Sham'ūn]. Beirut: Maṭba'at al-Hilāl, 1953.
Al-Jabūrī, Jāsem Muḥammad. 'Mawqaf Lubnān Fī Jāmi'at Al-Duwal Al-'Arabiyya Min Al-Qadiya Al-Filastiniya [Lebanon's Position within the League of Arab States on the Palestinian Cause]'. *Majallat Abḥāth Kulliyat Al-Tarbiya Al-Asāsiya* 6, no. 2 (2007): 76–106.
Al-Jisr, Bāssem. *Fu'ād Shehāb, Dhālika Al-Majhūl* [Fu'ād Shehāb, the Unknown]. Beirut: Sharikat al-Maṭbū'āt lil-Tawzī' wal-Nasher, 1988.
Al-Jisr, Bāssem. *Fu'ād Shehāb* [Fu'ād Shehāb]. Beirut: Fouad Chehab Foundation, 1998.
Al-Khālidi, Muḥammad F. *Al-Mu'āmara Al-Kubra 'ala Bilād Al-Shām: Dirāsat Taḥlil Lil-Nosef Al-Aqal Min Al-Qurn Al-'Ashrin* [The Great Conspiracy against the Levant: An Analysis of the First Half of the Twentieth Century]. Beirut: Dār al-Rāwī lil-Nasher wal-Tawzi', 2000.
Al-Matni, 'Azīz. *Kamāl Junblāṭ: 'As'ila Wa Ḥaqā'iq* [Kamāl Junblāṭ: Questions and Truths]. al-Mokhtāra, al-Shūf: Dār al-Taqadumiya, 2010.
Al-Muwāfi, 'Abd al-Ḥamīd Muhammad. *Maṣr Fī Jāmi'at Al-Duwal Al-'Arabiyya: Dirāsa Fī Dawr Al-Dawla Al-Akbar Fī Al-Tanẓīmāt Al-'Iqlīmiyya 1945–1970* [Egypt within the League of Arab States: A Study in the Role of the Greatest State in Regional Organisations 1945–1970]. Cairo: al-Hay'a al-Maṣriya al-'Āma lil-Kitāb, 1983.
Al-Nābulsi, Ṣādiq. *Mūsa Al-Ṣadr: Masār Al-Taḥadiyāt Wal-Taḥawulāt* [Mūsa Al-Ṣadr: The Path of Challenges and Transitions]. Beirut: Markaz al-Ḥaḍāra li Tanmiyat al-Fikr al-Islāmī, 2013.
Al-Rā'ī, Bāsem. *Mīthāq 1943: Tajadhur Al-Hawiya Al-Waṭaniya Al-Lubnāniya* [1943 Pact: Genesis of Lebanese National Identity]. Zouk Mosbeh: al-Markaz al-Mārūnī lil-Tawthīq wal-Abḥāth, 2009.
Al-Rayyes, Fāyez. *Al-Qura Al-Junūbiyya Al-Sabe'*. Beirut: Mou'assasat al-Wafā', 1985.
Al-Shidyaq, Tannus. *Kitab Akhbār Al-A'yan Fi Jabal Lubnan* [Book on Dignitaries in Mount Lebanon]. Beirut: Publications de l'Université Libanaise, 1970.
Al-Ṣulḥ, Sāmī. *Lubnān: Al-'Abeth Al-Siyāsī Wal-Maṣīr Al-Majhūl* [Lebanon: Political Futility and the Unknown Destiny]. Beirut: Dār al-Nahār, 2000.
Al-Ṣulḥ, Sāmī. *Mudhakarāt Sāmī Bek Al-Ṣulḥ, Ṣafaḥāt Majīda Fī Tārīkh Lubnān* [Memoirs of Sāmī Bek Al-Ṣulḥ, Glorious Pages of Lebanese History]. Beirut: Maktabat al-Fikr al-'Arabi wa Maṭba'atihā, 1960.
Al-Ṣulḥ, Sāmī, and Salīm Wakīm. *'Aḥtakim Ila Al-Tārīkh* [An Appeal to History]. Beirut: Dār al-Nahār, 1970.
Al-Tāhiri, Ḥamdi. *Siyāsat Al-Ḥokm Fī Lubnān: Tārīkh Lubnān Min Al-Intidāb Ḥatta Al-Ḥarb Al-Ahliya, 1920–1976* [Regime Policy in Lebanon: Lebanes History from the Mandate to the Civil War, 1920–1975]. Paris: Manshūrāt Asmar, 2006.
Al-Yasū'y, Salāḥ Abu Jawdeh. *Hawiyat Lubnān Al-Waṭaniya: Nash'atuhā Wa 'Ishkāliyātihā Al-Ṭā'ifiya* [Lebanese National Identity: Origin and Confessional Issues]. Beirut: Dār al-Mashriq, 2008.
Āmil, Mahdī. *Fī Qadāyā Al-Tarbiya Wal-Siyāsa Al-Ta3līmiya* [On the Issues of Education and Pedagogic Policies]. Beirut: Dār al-Fārābī, 1991.
Āmil, Mahdī. *Madkhal Ila Naqḍ Al-Fikr Al-Tā'ifī: Al-Qadiya Al-Falastīniya Fī Īdiyōlojiyat Al-Būrjwāziya Al-Lubnāniya* [An Introduction to a Critique of Sectarianism: The

Palestinian Cause in the Ideology of the Lebanese Bourgeoisie]. Beirut: Dār al-Fārābī, 1989.
Arab Information Center. *Basic Documents of the League of Arab States*. New York: Arab Information Center, 1955.
Arif, Mona. 'Constructing the National Past: History-Writing and Nation-Building in Nasser's Egypt'. *Shorofat 1*, 11 December 2017.
Armstrong, John A. *Nations before Nationalism*. Chapel Hill: University of North Carolina Press, 1982.
Armstrong, Lincoln. 'A Socio-Economic Opinion Poll in Beirut, Lebanon'. *Public Opinion Quarterly* 23, no. 1 (1959): 18–27.
Atiyah, Najla Wadih. *The Attitude of the Lebanese Sunnis towards the State of Lebanon*. Unpublished Masters thesis. University of London, 1973.
Attié, Caroline. *Struggle in the Levant: Lebanon in the 1950s*. London: I.B. Tauris, 2004.
Barak, Oren. *The Lebanese Army: A National Institution in a Divided Society*. Albany: State University of New York Press, 2009.
Barakat, Halim. *Lebanon in Strife: Student Preludes to the Civil War*. Austin: University of Texas Press, 1977.
Barakat, Halim. 'Social Factors Influencing Attitudes of University Students in Lebanon towards the Palestinian Resistance Movement'. *Journal of Palestine Studies* 1, no. 1 (1971): 87–112.
Baroudi, Sami E. 'Divergent Perspectives among Lebanon's Maronites during the 1958 Crisis'. *Critique: Critical Middle Eastern Studies* 15, no. 1 (2006): 5–28.
Bashshur, Munir. 'Higher Education and Political Development in Syria and Lebanon'. *Comparative Education Review* 10, no. 3 (1966): 451–61.
Bashshur, Munir. 'The Role of Education: A Mirror of a Fractured National Image'. In *Toward a Viable Lebanon*, edited by Halim Isber Barakat, 42–98. London: Croom Helm, 1988.
Bayḍūn, Aḥmad. *Riād Al-Ṣulḥ: Fī Zamānihi* [Riād Al-Sulḥ: In His Time]. Beirut: Dār al-Nahār, 2011.
Bayhum, Muḥammad J. *'Urubat Lubnān, Tatawuraha Fi Al-Qadīm Wal-Hadīth* [Lebanese Arabness, Its Past and Modern Development]. Beirut: Dār al-Riḥānī, 1969.
Bayhum, Muḥammad J. *Al-'Urūba Wal-Shu'ūbiyāt Al-Ḥadītha* [Arabism and the Modern Shu'ūbiyāt]. Beirut: Maṭābi' Dār al-Kishāf, 1957.
Bayhum, Muḥammad J. *Lubnān Bayna Mashriq Wa Maghreb: 1920–1969* [Lebanon, in between East and West: 1920–1969]. Beirut: Author, 1969.
Bayhum, Muḥammad J. *Qawāfil Al-`Urūba Wa Mawākibouhā Khilāl Al-`Uṣūr: Al-Juz' Al-Thānī* [The Procession of Arabism and Its Convoys throughout the Ages: Part Two]. Beirut: al-Kashāf Press, 1948.
Beetham, David. 'Max Weber et La Légitimité Politique [Max Weber and Political Legitimacy]'. *Revue Européenne Des Sciences Sociales* 33, no. 101 (1995): 11–22.
Benjamin, Jacques. 'La Minorité En Etat Bicommunautaire: Quatre Études de Cas [Minorities in Bicommunal States: Four Case Studies]'. *Canadian Journal of Political Science/Revue Canadienne de Science Politique* 4, no. 4 (1971): 477–96.
Beshara, Adel. *The Politics of Frustration: The Failed Coup of 1961*. New York: Routledge, 2005.
Binder, Leonard. 'Political Change in Lebanon'. In *Politics in Lebanon*, edited by Leonard Binder, 283–328. New York: Wiley, 1966.
Birdal, Murat. *The Political Economy of Ottoman Public Debt: Insolvency and European Financial Control in the Late Nineteenth Century*. London: I.B. Tauris, 2010.

Boutros, Fouad. *Mémoires* [Memoires]. Edited by Jana Tamer. Beirut: Les Éditions L'Orient Le Jour/Les Messageries du Levant, 2010.

Bracha, Guy. '"The Germans Are Coming!": The Jewish Community of Beirut Facing the Question of Jewish Immigration from Germany'. *Leo Baeck Institute Year Book* 61 (2016): 41–54.

Britt, George. 'Lebanon's Popular Revolution'. *Middle East Journal* 7, no. 1 (1953): 1–17.

Buheiry, Marwan R. *Beirut's Role in the Political Economy of the French Mandate, 1919–39. Papers on Lebanon.* Oxford: Centre for Lebanese Studies, 1986.

Butros, 'Alā. *Al-Stratījīya Al-Sūriya Fī Lubnān Bayn Al-Assad Al-Ab Wal-Assad Al-Ibn: 1970–2009* [The Syrian Strategy in Lebanon between Assad the Father and Assad the Son: 1970–2009]. Beirut: al-Furāt, 2011.

Butros, Fu'ād. *Al-Mudhakkarāt* [Memoires]. Beirut: Dār al-Nahār, 2009.

Buzan, Barry. *People, States and Fear: An Agenda for International Security Studies in the Post-Cold War Era.* Boulder, CO: Lynne Rienner, 1991.

Caix, De. 'L'Organisation Donnée à La Syrie et Au Liban: De 1920 à 1923 et La Crise Actuelle [The Set Organisation for Syria and the Lebanon: From 1920 to 1923 and the Current Crisis]'. In *Une Tutelle Coloniale: Le Mandat Français En Syrie et Au Liban* [Colonial Guardianship: The French Mandate in Syria and the Lebanon], edited by Gérard D. Khoury, 394–456. Paris: Belin, 2006.

Caix, Robert de. 'Lettre à M. Le President Du Conseil, Ministre Des Affaires Étrangères'. In *Une Tutelle Coloniale: Le Mandat Français En Syrie et Au Liban* [Colonial Guardianship: The French Mandate in Syria and the Lebanon], edited by Gérard D. Khoury, 375–89. Paris: Belin, 2006.

Caix, Robert de. 'Lettre Au Général Gouraud [Letter to General Gouraud]'. In *Une Tutelle Coloniale: Le Mandat Français En Syrie et Au Liban* [Colonial Guardianship: The French Mandate in Syria and the Lebanon], edited by Gérard D. Khoury, 372–4. Paris: Belin, 2006.

Catroux, Georges. *Deux Missions En Moyen-Orient: 1919–1922* [Two Missions in the Middle East: 1919–1922]. Paris: Plon, 1958.

Chaigne-Oudin, Anne-Lucie. *La France et Les Rivalités Occidentales Au Levant 1918–1939* [France and the Oriental Rivalries in the Levant 1918–1939]. Paris: L'Harmattan, 2006.

Chaitani, Youssef. *Post-Colonial Syria and Lebanon: The Decline of Arab Nationalism and the Triumph of the State.* London: I.B. Tauris, 2007.

Chalabi, Tamara. *The Shi`is of Jabal `Amil and the New Lebanon: Community and the Nation-State, 1918–1943.* New York: Palgrave Macmillan, 2006.

Chamoun, Camille. *Crise Au Moyen Orient* [Crisis in the Middle East]. Paris: Gallimard, 1963.

Chatagnier, J. Tyson, and Emanuele Castelli. 'The Arc of Modernization: Economic Structure, Materialism, and the Onset of Civil Conflict'. *Political Science Research and Methods* 7, no. 2 (2019): 233–52.

Chatterjee, Partha. *The Nation and Its Fragments: Colonial and Postcolonial Histories.* Princeton, NJ: Princeton University Press, 1993.

Chevallier, Dominique. 'Comment l'Etat a-t-Il- Été Compris Au Liban? [How Was the State Understood in the Lebanon?]'. In *Lebanon: A History of Conflict and Consensus*, edited by Nadim Shehadi and Dana Haffar Mills, 210–23. London: I.B. Tauris, 1988.

Chiha, Michel. *Visage et Présence Du Liban* [The Face and Presence of Lebanon]. Beirut: Editions du Trident, 1984.

Cobban, Helena. *Lubnān: 400 Sana Min Al-Tā'ifiya* [Lebanon: 400 Years of Confessionalism]. Edited by Samīr 'Atalla. London: Highlight Publications, 1985.

Cobban, Helena. *The Making of Modern Lebanon*. London: Hutchinson Education, 1985.

Cohen, Ronald. 'Legitimacy, Illegitimacy, and State Formation'. In *State Formation and Political Legitimacy*, edited by Ronald Cohen and Judith D. Toland, 69–94. Oxford: Transaction Books, 1988.

Connor, Walker. 'Nation-Building or Nation-Destroying?' *World Politics* 24, no. 3 (1972): 319–55.

Cosmao, Vincent. 'Louis-Joseph Lebret, O.P. 1897–1966: From Social Action to the Struggle for Development'. *New Blackfriars* 51, no. 597 (1970): 62–8.

Crabbs, Jack Jr. 'Politics, History, and Culture in Nasser's Egypt'. *International Journal of Middle East Studies* 6, no. 4 (1975): 386–420.

Craig, James. *A History of the Middle East Centre for Arab Studies*. London: Macmillan, 1998.

Crow, Ralph E. 'Religious Sectarianism in the Lebanese Political System'. *Journal of Politics* 24, no. 3 (1962): 489–520.

Crow, Ralph E. 'The Civil Service of Independent Syria, 1945–58'. Unpublished doctoral thesis. University of Michigan, 1964.

Crow, Ralph E., and Adnan Iskandar. 'Administrative Reform in Lebanon 1958–1959'. *International Review of Administrative Sciences* 27, no. 3 (1961): 207–93.

Curtis, Gerald L. 'The United Nations Observation Group in Lebanon'. *International Organization* 18, no. 4 (1964): 738–65.

Daher, Massoud. 'The Lebanese Leadership at the Beginning of the Ottoman Period: A Case Study of the Ma`n Family'. In *Syria and Bilad Al-Sham under Ottoman Rule*, edited by Peter Sluglett and Stefan A4 - Malczycki Weber Matt, 323–46. Leiden: Brill, 2010.

Dawisha, Adeed I. *Arab Nationalism in the Twentieth Century: From Triumph to Despair*. Princeton, NJ: Princeton University Press, 2003.

Dawisha, Adeed I. *Syria and the Lebanese Crisis*. London: Macmillan Press, 1980.

Daye, John. 'Syrianist Orientations in the Thought of Mikha`il Nu`ayma'. In *The Origins of Statehood: Histories, Pioneers and Identity*, edited by Adel Beshara, 190–209. London: Routledge, 2011.

Dīb, Kamāl. *Tārīkh Sūriya Al-Mu'āsir: Min Al-Intidāb Al-Faransī Ila Ṣayf 2011* [The Modern History of Syria: From the French Mandate to the Summer of 2011]. Beirut: Dār al-Nahār, 2011.

Dorn, Walter A. *Air Power in UN Operations: Wings for Peace*. Farnham: Ashgate, 2014.

Eisenberg, Laura Zittrain. *The Communal Pact of National Identities: The Making and Politics of the 1943 National Pact. Papers on Lebanon*. Oxford: Centre for Lebanese Studies, 1991.

Eisenberg, Laura Zittrain. 'Desperate Diplomacy: The Zionist-Maronite Treaty of 1946'. *Studies in Zionism* 13, no. 2 (1992): 146–63.

Eisenberg, Laura Zittrain. *Lebanon in Early Zionist Imagination, 1900–1948*. Detroit: Wayne State University Press, 1994.

el-Khazen, Farid. *The Breakdown of the State in Lebanon, 1967–1978*. London: I.B. Tauris, 2000.

el-Solh, Raghid. *Lebanon and Arabism: National Identity and State Formation*. London: I.B. Tauris, 2004.

Entelis, John P. 'Party Transformation in Lebanon: Al-Kata'ib as a Case Study'. *Middle Eastern Studies* 9, no. 3 (1973): 325–40.

Eveland, Wilbur. *Ropes of Sand: America's Failure in the Middle East*. New York: W. W. Norton, 1980.

Fanṣa, Nadhīr. *Ayām Ḥusni Al-Za'īm* [The Days of Ḥusni Al-Za'īm]. Beirut: Dār al-'Āfāq al-Jadīda, 1982.

Farah, Caesar E. *The Politics of Interventionism in Ottoman Lebanon, 1830–1861*. London: I.B. Tauris, 2000.

Farrūkh, 'Omar. *Difā'an 'an Al-'Elem, Difā'an 'an Al-Waṭan* [In Defence of Knowledge, in Defence of the Country]. Beirut: Beirut Arab University, 1977.

Fawaz, Eli. 'What Makes Lebanon a Distinctive Country?' In *Lebanon: Liberation, Conflict and Crisis*, edited by Barry Rubin, 25–35. New York: Palgrave Macmillan, 2009.

Fayād, Nadā Ḥassan. *Al-Dawla Al-Madaniya: Tarjibat Fu'ād Shehāb Fī Lubnān* [The Civil State: Fu'ād Shehāb's Experiment in Lebanon]. Beirut: Muntada al-Ma'ārif, 2011.

Fayyad, Halim Faris. 'The Effects of Sectarianism on the Lebanese Administration'. American University of Beirut, 1956. https://scholarworks.aub.edu.lb/bitstream/handle/10938/5000/t-161.pdf.

Fetter, George C. 'A Comparative Study of Attitudes of Christian and of Moslem Lebanese Villagers'. *Journal for the Scientific Study of Religion* 4, no. 1 (1964): 48–59.

Firro, Kais. 'Ethnicizing the Shi`is in Mandatory Lebanon'. *Middle Eastern Studies* 42, no. 5 (2006): 741–59.

Firro, Kais. *Inventing Lebanon: Nationalism and the State under the Mandate*. London: I.B. Tauris, 2002.

Firro, Kais. 'Lebanese Nationalism versus Arabism: From Bulus Nujaym to Michel Chiha'. *Middle Eastern Studies* 40, no. 5 (2004): 1–27.

Fish, W. B. 'The Lebanon'. *Geographical Review* 34, no. 2 (1944): 235–58.

Frankel, Ephraim A. 'The Maronite Patriarch: An Historical View of a Religious Za'im in the 1958 Lebanese Crisis'. *Muslim World* 66, no. 4 (1976): 246–58.

Frayha, Nemer. 'Education and Social Cohesion in Lebanon'. *Prospects* 33, no. 1 (2003): 77–88.

Friedman, Isaiah. 'The McMahon-Hussein Correspondence and the Question of Palestine'. *Journal of Contemporary History* 5, no. 2 (1970): 83–122.

Fromkin, David. *A Peace to End All Peace: The Fall of the Ottoman Empire and the Creation of the Modern Middle East*. New York: Henry Holt, 1989.

Ftūnī, 'Ali 'Abed. *Tarīkh Lubnān Al-Ṭā'ifī* [Lebanese Confessional History]. Beirut: Dār al-Fārābī, 2013.

Fukuyama, Francis. 'The Imperative of State-Building'. *Journal of Democracy* 15, no. 2 (2004): 17–31.

Galal, Amin A. *The Modernization of Poverty: A Study in the Political Economy of Growth in Nine Arab Countries, 1945–1970*. Leiden: Brill, 1974.

Gaspard, T. *A Political Economy of Lebanon, 1948–2002: The Limits of Laissez-Faire*. Leiden: Brill, 2004.

Gellner, Ernest. *Nations and Nationalism*. Oxford: Blackwell, 1983.

Gendzier, Irene L. *Notes from the Minefield: United States Intervention in Lebanon and the Middle East*. New York: Columbia University Press, 2006.

Germani, Gino. 'Stages of Modernization'. *International Journal* 24, no. 3 (1969): 463–85.

Giddens, Anthony. *The Nation-State and Violence: Volume Two of a Contemporary Critique of Historical Materialism*. Berkeley: University of California Press, 1985.

Gilliot, Cl., R. C. Repp, K. A. Nizami, M. B. Hooker, Chang-Kuan Lin and J. O. Hunwick. '`Ulama'. In *Encyclopaedia of Islam, Second Edition*, edited by P. Bearman, Th. Bianquis, C. E. Bosworth, E. van Donzel and W. P. Heinrichs, 2nd edn, X:801b. Leiden: Brill, 2012. http://referenceworks.brillonline.com/entries/encyclopaedia-of-islam-2/ulama-COM_1278.

Golan, Galia. 'The Cold War and the Soviet Attitude towards the Arab–Israeli Conflict'. In *The Cold War in the Middle East: Regional Conflict and the Superpowers 1967–73*, edited by Nigel J. Ashton, 59–73. New York: Routledge, 2007.
Griffith, Sidney Harrison. *The Church in the Shadow of the Mosque: Christians and Muslims in the World of Islam*. Princeton, NJ: Princeton University Press, 2008.
Hakim, Carol. *The Origins of the Lebanese National Idea, 1840–1920*. Berkeley: University of California Press, 2013.
Hakim, Georges. 'The Economic Basis of Lebanese Polity'. In *Politics in Lebanon*, edited by Leonard Binder, 57–69. New York: Wiley, 1966.
Hamzeh, Nizar A. 'Clientalism, Lebanon: Roots and Trends'. *Middle Eastern Studies* 37, no. 3 (2001): 167–78.
Ḥanna, George. *Al-'Aqda Al-Lubnāniyya* [The Lebanese Tangle]. Beirut: Dār al-'Elm lil-Malāyīn, 1957.
Ḥanna, George. *Min Al-Iḥtilāl … Ilā Al-Istiqlāl* [From Occupation … to Independence]. Beirut: Matbaʻat Dār al-Funūn, 1946.
Hanrieder, Wolfram. *West German Foreign Policy, 1949–1963: International Pressure and Domestic Response*. Stanford, CA: Stanford University Press, 1967.
Ḥarb, Marwān. *Al-Shihābiya: Ḥudūd Tajribat Al-Taḥdīth Al-Siyāsī Fī Lubnān* [Chehabism: Limits of the Experience of Political Modernisation in Lebanon]. Jdeydet al-Matn: Dār Sā'ir al-Mashriq, 2012.
Harb, Marwān. *Le Chehabisme Ou Les Limites d'une Experience de Modernisation Politique Au Liban* [Chehabism: Limits of the Experience of Political Modernisation in Lebanon]. Unpublished Masters thesis. Beirut: Université Saint-Joseph, 2007.
Harik, Iliya F. *Politics and Change in a Traditional Society: Lebanon, 1711–1845*. Princeton, NJ: Princeton University Press, 1968.
Harris, William. *Lebanon: A History, 600–2011*. New York: Oxford University Press, 2012.
Hassouna, Hussein A. *The League of Arab States and Regional Disputes*. Dobbs Ferry, NY: Oceana, 1975.
Haykal, Muḥammad Ḥussein. *Sanawāt Al-Ghilyān, Al-Jiz' Al-Awal* [The Boiling Years, Part One]. Cairo: Markaz al-'Ahrām lil-Tarjama, 1998.
Hazran, Yusri. 'Between Authenticity and Alienation: The Druzes and Lebanon's History'. *Bulletin of the School of Oriental and African Studies* 72, no. 3 (2009): 459–87.
Hazran, Yusri. 'Lebanon's Revolutionary Era: Kamal Junblat, The Druze Community and the Lebanon State, 1949 to 1977*'. *Muslim World* 100, no. 1 (2010): 157–76.
Hazran, Yusri. *The Druze Community and the Lebanese State: Between Confrontation and Reconciliation*. New York: Routledge, 2014.
Ḥelū, Charles. *Ḥayāt Fī Zikrayāt* [Life in Memories]. Beirut: Dār al-Nahār, 1995.
Ḥelū, Charles. *Mudhakarātī 1964–1965* [Memoires 1964–1965]. Beirut: Author, 1984.
Herbst, Jeffrey Ira. 'Responding to State Failure in Africa'. *International Security* 21, no. 3 (1997): 120–44.
Hershlag, Zvi Yehuda. *Introduction to the Modern Economic History of the Middle East*. Leiden: Brill, 1980.
Hess, Clyde G., and Herbert L. Bodman. 'Confessionalism and Feudality in Lebanese Politics'. *Middle East Journal* 8, no. 1 (1954): 10–26.
Heydemann, Steven. *Authoritarianism in Syria: Institutions and Social Conflict, 1946–1970*. Ithaca, NY: Cornell University Press, 1999.
Himadeh, *Economic Organisation of Syria*, Beirut: American Press, 1936.
Hitti, Philip K. *Syria: A Short History*. New York: Macmillan, 1961.

Hitti, Philip K. *The Origins of the Druze People and Religion: With Extracts from Their Sacred Writings*. New York: Columbia University Press, 1928.

Hokayem, Antoine, Da'd Bou Malhab Atallah and J. Charaf. *Documents Diplomatiques Français Relatifs à l'Histoire Du Liban et de La Syrie à l'Époque Du Mandat, 1914–1946* [French Diplomatic Documents Concerning the History of Lebanon and Syria at the Time of the Mandate, 1914–1946]. Paris: L'Harmattan, 2003.

Holden, Stacy. *A Documentary History of Modern Iraq*. Gainesville: University Press of Florida, 2012.

Holsti, K. J. *Taming the Sovereigns: Institutional Change in International Politics*. Cambridge: Cambridge University Press, 2004.

Hottinger, Arnold. 'Zu'amā' and Parties in the Lebanese Crisis of 1958'. *Middle East Journal* 15, no. 2 (1961): 127–40.

Houeiss, Rodrigue El. *Raymond Eddé Ou Une Certaine Idée Du Liban – Souvenirs Politiques* [Raymond Eddé or a Certain Idea of Lebanon – Political Memories]. Paris: L'Harmattan, 2017.

Hourani, Albert. 'From Jabal `Āmil to Persia'. *Bulletin of the School of Oriental and African Studies* 49, no. 1 (1986): 133–40.

Hourani, Albert. 'Lebanon: The Development of a Political Society'. In *Politics in Lebanon*, edited by Leonard Binder, 13–30. New York: Wiley, 1966.

Hudson, Michael C. 'The Electoral Process and Political Development in Lebanon'. *Middle East Journal* 20, no. 2 (1966): 173–86.

Hudson, Michael C. *The Precarious Republic: Political Modernization in Lebanon*. Boulder, CO: Westview Press, 1985.

Hughes, Matthew. 'Collusion across the Litani? Lebanon and the 1948 War'. In *The War for Palestine: Rewriting the History of 1948*, edited by Eugene L. Rogan and Avi Shlaim, 204–27. Cambridge: Cambridge University Press, 2007.

Hughes, Matthew. 'Lebanon's Armed Forces and the Arab-Israeli War, 1948–49'. *Journal of Palestine Studies* 34, no. 2 (2005): 24–41.

Huntington, Samuel P. *Political Order in Changing Societies*. New Haven, CT: Yale University Press, 2006.

Hurewitz, J. C. 'Lebanese Democracy in Its International Setting'. In *Politics in Lebanon*, edited by Leonard Binder, 213–38. New York: Wiley, 1966.

Hurwitz, Leon. 'Contemporary Approaches to Political Stability'. *Comparative Politics* 5, no. 3 (1973): 449–63.

Institut de Recherche et de Formation en Vue du Développement Harmonisé. *Besoins et Possibilités de Développement Du Liban; Étude Préliminaire. Mission IRFED-Liban, 1960–1961. Tome I* [Requirements and Possibilities of Development in Lebanon; A Preliminary Study. IRFED-Liban Mission, 1960–1961. Volume I]. Edited by Louis-Joseph Lebret. Beirut: Wizārat al-Taṣmīm al-ʿĀm, 1963.

Institut de Recherche et de Formation en Vue du Développement Harmonisé. *Besoins et Possibilités de Développement Du Liban; Étude Préliminaire. Mission IRFED-Liban, 1960–1961. Tome II* [Requirements and Possibilities of Development in Lebanon; A Preliminary Study. IRFED-Liban Mission, 1960–1961. Volume II]. Edited by Louis-Joseph Lebret. Beirut: Wizārat al-Taṣmīm al-ʿĀm, 1963.

Ismail, Mounir. *Le Régime de La Mutasarrifiya Du Mont Liban 1861–1915* [The Regime in the Mutsarrifiya of Mount Lebanon 1861–1915]. Beirut: Edition des Oeuvres Politiques et Historiques, 2002.

Ja'ja', Ghāzī. *Al-Batriark Mār Anṭūn Butrus 'Arīḍa, 1863–1955* [The Patriarch Mār Antūn Butrus 'Arīḍa, 1863–1955]. Beirut: Dār Bshāriā lil-Nasher, 2006.

Ja'yūl Juway'id, Sāliḥ', and Fātīma 'Abd al-Jalīl Yāsir. 'Rīmūn Iddeh Wa Dawrahū Al-Siyāsī Fī Lubnān [Raymond Eddeh and His Political Role in Lebanon]'. *Majallat Jāmi'at Dhī Qār* 12, no. 3 (2017): 337–69.

Jabber, Fuad. 'The Palestinian Resistance and Inter-Arab Politics'. In *The Politics of Palestinian Nationalism*, edited by William B. Quandt, Fuad Jabber and Ann Mosely Lesch, 155–216. Berkeley, University of California Press, 1973.

James, Paul. *Nation Formation: Towards a Theory of Abstract Community*. London: Sage, 1996.

Jasay, Anthony de. *The State*. Indianapolis, IN: Liberty Fund, 1998.

Jaulin, Thibaut. 'Démographie et Politique Au Liban Sous Le Mandat. Les Émigrés, Les Ratios Confessionnels et La Fabrique Du Pacte National [Demographics and Politics in Lebanon under the Mandate. Emigrants, Confessional Ratios, and the Fabric of the National Pact]'. *Histoire et Mesure* 24, no. 1 (2009): 189–210.

Johnson, Michael. *Class & Client in Beirut: The Sunni Muslim Community and the Lebanese State, 1840–1985*. London: Ithaca Press, 1986.

Johnson, Michael. 'Factional Politics in Lebanon: The Case of the "Islamic Society of Benevolent Intentions"'. *Middle Eastern Studies* 14, no. 1 (1978): 56–75.

Junblāṭ, Kamāl. *Rub' Qarn Min Al-Niḍāl* [A Quarter-Century of Struggle]. al-Mukhtāra: Dār al-Taqadumiya, 1987.

Kalawoun, Nasser M. *The Struggle for Lebanon: A Modern History of Lebanese-Egyptian Relations*. London: I.B. Tauris, 2000.

Karam, Georges Adib. *L'Opinion Publique Libanais et La Question Du Liban (1918–1920)* [Lebanese Public Opinion and the Question of Lebanon (1918–1920)]. Beirut: Publications de l'Université Libanaise, 1981.

Karāmi, Nādia, and Nawāf Karāmi. *Wāqi' Al-Thawra Al-Lubnānīya* [The Reality of the Lebanese Revolution]. Beirut: Maṭba'at Karam, 1959.

Karsh, Efraim. *Soviet Policy towards Syria since 1970*. New York: Palgrave Macmillan, 1991.

Kaufman, Asher. 'Phoenicianism: The Formation of an Identity in Lebanon in 1920'. *Middle Eastern Studies* 37, no. 1 (2001): 173–94.

Kaufman, Asher. *Reviving Phoenicia: In Search for Identity in Lebanon*. London: I.B. Tauris, 2004.

Kaufman, Asher. ' "Tell Us Our History": Charles Corm, Mount Lebanon and Lebanese Nationalism'. *Middle Eastern Studies* 40, no. 3 (2004): 1–28.

Kawtharānī, Wajīh. *Al-Ittijāhāt Al-Ijtmā'iyya Al-Siyāsiyya Fī Jabal Lubnān Wa Mashriq Al-'Arabi* [Socio-Political Objectives in Mount Lebanon and the Arab Levant 1860–1920]. Beirut: Ma'had al-Inmā' al-'Arabi, 1978.

Kehat, Dina. 'Dilemmas of Arab Communism: The Case of the Syrian Communist Party, 1969–73'. In *The USSR and the Muslim World: Issues in Domestic and Foreign Policy*, edited by Yaacov Ro'i, 272–89. New York: Routledge, 1984.

Keohane. 'Political Authority after Intervention: Gradations of Sovereignty'. In *Humanitarian Intervention: Ethical, Legal, and Political Dilemmas*, 275–98. Cambridge: Cambridge University Press, 2003.

Kerr, Malcolm H. 'Review: Lebanese Views on the 1958 Crisis'. *Middle East Journal* 15, no. 2 (1961): 211–17.

Kerr, Michael. *Imposing Power-Sharing: Conflict and Coexistence in Northern Ireland and Lebanon*. Dublin: Irish Academic Press, 2006.

Kfūrī, Tūfī' Anīs. *Al-Shehābiyya, Madrasat Ḥidātha Ru'yawiya* [Chehabism, a School of Visionary Modernity]. Beirut: Raidy Printing Group, 2012.

Kfūrī, Tūfī' Anīs. *Al-Shehābiyya Wa Siyāsat Al-Mawqaf* [Chehabism and the Policy of Decision]. Beirut: Author, 1980.

Khalaf, Samir. *Civil and Uncivil Violence in Lebanon: A History of the Internationalization of Communal Conflict*. New York: Columbia University Press, 2002.

Khalaf, Samir. 'Primordial Ties and Politics in Lebanon'. *Middle Eastern Studies* 4, no. 3 (1968): 243–69. https://doi.org/10.1080/00263206808700103.

Khalīfeh, 'Issām Kamāl. *Abḥāth Fī Tārīkh Lubnān Al-Mu'āṣer* [Studies in Lebanese Contemporary History]. Beirut: Dār al-Jalīl, 1985.

Khoury, Gérard D., ed. *Une Tutelle Coloniale: Le Mandat Français En Syrie et Au Liban* [Colonial Guardianship: The French Mandate in Syria and the Lebanon]. Paris: Belin, 2006.

Khoury, Philip Shukry. *Syria and the French Mandate: The Politics of Arab Nationalism, 1920–1945*. Princeton, NJ: Princeton University Press, 1987.

Khūrī, Bishāra. *Ḥaqā'iq Lubnāniyya, Al-Jiz' Al-Awal* [Lebanese Truths, Part One]. Beirut: 'Awrāq Lubnāniyya, 1961.

Khūrī, Bishāra. *Ḥaqā'iq Lubnāniyya, Al-Jiz' Al-Thāleth* [Lebanese Truths, Part Three]. Beirut: 'Awrāq Lubnāniyya, 1961.

Khūrī, Bishāra. *Ḥaqā'iq Lubnāniyya, Al-Jiz' Al-Thānī* [Lebanese Truths, Part Two]. Beirut: 'Awrāq Lubnāniyya, 1961.

Kisirwani, Marun Yusef. 'Attitudes and Behavior of Lebanese Bureaucrats: A Study in Administrative Corruption'. Unpublished doctoral thesis. Indiana University, 1971.

Kiwan, Fadia. 'La Perception Maronite Du Grand-Liban [Maronite Perception of Greater Lebanon]'. In *Lebanon: A History of Conflict and Consensus*, edited by Nadim Shehadi and Dana Haffar Mills. London: I.B. Tauris, 1998.

Kliot, N. 'The Collapse of the Lebanese State'. *Middle Eastern Studies* 23, no. 1 (1987): 54–74.

Kurki, Milja. *Causation in International Relations: Reclaiming Causal Analysis*. Cambridge: Cambridge University Press, 2008.

Lapierre, Jean. *Le Mandat Français En Syrie: Origines, Doctrine, Exécution* [The French Mandate in Syria: Origins, Doctrine, Execution]. Paris: Librairie du Recueil Sirey, 1936.

Leenders, Reinoud. *Spoils of Truce: Corruption and State-Building in Postwar Lebanon*. Ithaca, NY: Cornell University Press, 2012.

Lijphart, Arend. 'Consociational Democracy'. *World Politics* 21, no. 2 (1969): 207–25.

Lijphart, Arend. *Thinking about Democracy: Power Sharing and Majority Rule in Theory and Practice*. New York: Routledge, 2008.

Little, Douglas. 'His Finest Hour? Eisenhower, Lebanon, and the 1958 Middle East Crisis'. *Diplomatic History* 20, no. 1 (1996): 27–54.

Little, Robert D., and Wilhelmina Burch. *Air Operations in the Lebanon Crisis of 1958*. Washington, DC: USAF Historical Division Liaison Office, 1962.

Louet, Ernest. *Expédition de Syrie: Beyrouth – Le Liban – Jérusalem, 1860–1861. Notes et Souvenirs* [Expedition of Syria: Beirut – Lebanon – Jerusalem, 1860–1861: Notes and Souvenirs]. Paris: Amyot, 1862.

Lowrance, Sherry. 'Nationalism without Nation: State-Building in Early Twentieth-Century Palestine'. *Middle East Critique* 21, no. 1 (2012): 81–99.

Ma, Shu-Yun. 'Nationalism: State-Building or State-Destroying?' *Social Science Journal* 29, no. 3 (1992): 293–305.

Maḥmūdī, Aḥmad Khalīl. *Lubnān Fī Jāmi'at Al-Duwal Al-'Arabiyya, 1945–1958* [Lebanon in the League of Arab States, 1945–1958]. Beirut: al-Markaz al-'Arabi lil-Abḥāth wal-Tawthīq, 1994.
Mājid, Mājid Khalīl. *Tārīkh Al-Ḥūkūmāt Al-Lubnāniya 1926–1966: Al-Ta'līf, Al-Thiqa, Al-Istiqāla* [The History of Lebanese Governments 1926–1966: Formation, Confidence, Resignation]. Beirut: Author, 1997.
Makki, Muḥammad Kāẓim. *Munṭalaq Al-Ḥayat Al-Thaqāfiya Fi Jabal 'Āmel* [The Beginnings of Cultural Life in Jabal 'Āmel]. Beirut: Dār al-Zahra, 1991.
Maktabi, Rania. 'State Formation and Citizenship in Lebanon: The Politics of Membership and Exclusion in a Sectarian State'. In *Citizenship and the State and the Middle East: Approaches and Applications*, edited by Nils A. Butenschøn, Uri Davis and Manuel S. Hassassian, 146–78. Syracuse, NY: Syracuse University Press, 2000.
Maktabi, Rania. 'The Lebanese Census of 1932 Revisited. Who Are the Lebanese?' *British Journal of Middle Eastern Studies* 26, no. 2 (1999): 219–41.
Malsagne, Stéphane. *Fouad Chéhab, 1902–1973: Une Figure Oubliée de l'histoire Libanaise* [Fu'ād Shehāb, 1902–1973: A Forgotten Figure of Lebanese History]. Paris: Karthala, 2011.
Malsagne, Stéphane. 'L'Armée Libanaise de 1945 à 1975: Du Socle National à l'Effritement [The Lebanese Army from 1945 to 1975: From National Bedrock to Disintegration]'. *Vingtième Siècle. Revue d'histoire* 124 (2014): 15–31.
Malsagne, Stéphane. *Sous l'oeil de La Diplomatie Française: Le Liban de 1946 à 1990* [In the Presence of French Diplomacy: Lebanon from 1946 to 1990]. Paris: Geuthner, 2017.
Masters, Bruce Alan. *Christians and Jews in the Ottoman Arab World: The Roots of Sectarianism*. Cambridge: Cambridge University Press, 2001.
McLaurin, R. D. 'Lebanon and Its Army: Past, Present, and Future'. In *The Emergence of a New Lebanon: Fantasy or Reality?*, edited by Edward E. Azar, 79–114. New York: Praeger, 1984.
Meier, Daniel. 'Borders, Boundaries and Identity Building in Lebanon: An Introduction'. *Mediterranean Politics* 18, no. 3 (2013): 352–7.
Ménargues, Alain. *Asrār Ḥarb Lubnān* [Secrets of the War of Lebanon]. Beirut: Librairie Internationale, 2004.
Messarra, Antoine Nasri. *Le Modèle Politique Libanais et Sa Survie: Essai Sur La Classification et l'Aménagement d'un Système Consociatif* [The Lebanese Political Model and Its Survival: An Essay on the Classification and the Layout of a Consociational System]. Beirut: Librairie Orientale, 1983.
Meyer, A. J. 'Entrepreneurship and Economic Development in the Middle East'. *Public Opinion Quarterly* 22, no. 3 (1958): 391–96.
Middle East Research & Information Project. 'Lebanon's Civil War: The Fourth Phase'. *MERIP Reports*, 1976.
Migdal, Joel S. *State in Society: Studying How States and Societies Transform and Constitute One Another*. Cambridge: Cambridge University Press, 2001.
Miller, David Hunter. *My Diary at Conference of Paris – Volume IV – Documents 216–304*. New York: Appeal Printing Company, 1919.
Mitchell, Timothy. 'The Limits of the State: Beyond Statist Approaches and Their Critics'. *American Political Science Review* 85, no. 1 (1991): 77–96. https://doi.org/10.1017/s0003055400271451.
Mizrahi, David Hunter. 'La France et Sa Politique de Mandat En Syrie et Au Liban (1920–1939) [France and Its Mandate Policy in Syria and the Lebanon (1920–1939)]'. In *France, Syrie et Liban 1918–1946: Les Ambiguïtés et Les Dynamiques de La Relation*

Mandataire [France, Syria and Lebanon 1918–1946: Ambiguity and the Dynamics of the Mandatory Relationship], edited by Nadine Méouchy, 35–71. Damascus: Presses de l'IFPO, 2002. http://books.openedition.org/ifpo/3162.
Morris, Benny. 'Israel and the Lebanese Phalange: The Birth of a Relationship, 1948–1951'. *Studies in Zionism* 5, no. 1 (1984): 125–44.
Mühlbacher, Tamirace Fakhoury. *Democracy and Power-Sharing in Stormy Weather: The Case of Lebanon*. Wiesbaden: VS Verlag für Sozialwissenschaften, 2009.
Murphy, Robert. *Diplomat among Warriors*. Garden City, NY: Doubleday, 1964.
N.a. *Lubnān Fī 'Ahd Al-Istiqlāl* [Lebanon during the Era of Independence]. Beirut: Dār al-Aḥad, 1947.
Naef, Silvia. 'La Presse En Tant Que Moteur Du Renouveau Culturel et Littéraire: La Revue Chiite Libanaise Al-'Irfân [The Press as a Motor for Cultural and Literal Renewal: The Lebanese Shiite Journal Al-'Irfân]'. *Asiatische Studien: Zeitschrift Der Schweizerischen Gesellschaft Für Asienkunde – Études Asiatiques: Revue de La Société Suisse d'études Asiatiques* [Asian Studies: Journal of the Suiss Society for Asian Studies] 50 (1996): 385–98.
Naor, Dan. 'The Quest for a Balance of Power in Lebanon during Suleiman Frangieh's Presidency, 1970–76'. *Middle Eastern Studies* 49, no. 6 (2013): 990–1008.
Nassīf, Nicholas. *Al-Maktab Al-Thānī: Ḥākim Fī Al-Ẓol* [The Deuxième Bureau: Ruler in the Shadows]. al-Zal'a: Mukhtārāt, 2005.
Nicolle, David. *The Great Islamic Conquests AD 632–750*. Essex: Osprey, 2009.
Nir, Omri. *Lebanese Shi'ite Leadership, 1920–1970s: Personalities, Alliances, and Feuds*. Cham: Palgrave Macmillan, 2017.
Nir, Omri. 'The Shi'ites during the 1958 Lebanese Crisis'. *Middle Eastern Studies* 40, no. 6 (2004): 109–29.
O'Ballance, Edgar. *Civil War in Lebanon, 1975–92*. New York: Palgrave Macmillan, 1998.
O'Zoux, Raymond. *Les États Du Levant Sous Mandat Français* [The States of the Levant under the French Mandate]. Paris: Larose, 1931.
Obeid, Anis. *Druze and Their Faith in Tawhid*. Syracuse, NY: Syracuse University Press, 2006.
Oren, Michael B. *Six Days of War: June 1967 and the Making of the Modern Middle East*. New York: Oxford University Press, 2002.
Ottaway, Marina. 'Nation Building and State Disintegration'. In *State Building and Democratization in Africa: Faith, Hope, and Realities*, 83–98. Westport, CT: Praeger, 1999.
Owen, Roger. 'The Economic History of Lebanon, 1943–1974: Its Salient Features'. In *Toward a Viable Lebanon*, edited by Halim Isber Barakat, 27–42. London: Croom Helm, 1988.
Owen, Roger. 'The Political Economy of Grand Liban, 1920–1970'. In *Essays on the Crisis in Lebanon*, edited by Roger Owen, 23–32. London: Ithaca Press, 1976.
Pacha, Auguste Adib. *Le Liban Après La Guerre* [Lebanon after the War]. Cairo: Imprimerie Paul Barbey, 1919.
Paine, S. C. M. *Nation Building, State Building, and Economic Development: Case Studies and Comparisons*. New York: M.E. Sharpe, 2010.
Parsons, Talcott. *Societies: Evolutionary and Comparative Perspectives*. Englewood Cliffs, NJ: Prentice Hall, 1966.
Persen, William. 'Lebanese Economic Development since 1950'. *Middle East Journal* 12, no. 3 (1958): 277–94.

Petran, Tabitha. *The Struggle over Lebanon*. New York: Monthly Review Press, 1987.
Picard, Élizabeth. *Liban-Syrie, Intimes Étrangers: Un Siècle d'Interactions Sociopolitiques* [Lebanon-Syria, Intimate Strangers: A Century of Sociopolitical Interactions]. Paris: Actes Sud, 2016.
Pipes, Daniel. *Greater Syria: The History of an Ambition*. Oxford: Oxford University Press, 1990.
Podeh, Elie. 'The Struggle over Arab Hegemony after the Suez Crisis'. *Middle Eastern Studies* 29, no. 1 (1993): 91–110.
Podeh, Elie. 'The Symbolism of the Arab Flag in Modern Arab States: Between Commonality and Uniqueness'. *Nations and Nationalism* 17, no. 2 (2011): 419–42.
Qubain, Fahim I. *Crisis in Lebanon*. Washington, DC: Middle East Institute, 1961.
Quinn, Josephine Crawley. *In Search of the Pheonicians*. Princeton, NJ: Princeton University Press, 2018.
Ra'd, Layla. *Tārīkh Lubnān Al-Siyāsī Wal-Iqtiṣādī, 1958–1975* [Lebanese Political and Economic History, 1958–1975]. Tripoli: Maktabat al-Sā'iḥ, 2005.
Rabinovich, Itamar. *The War for Lebanon: 1970–1983*. Ithaca, NY: Cornell University Press, 1984.
Rafeq, Abdel Karim. 'Social Groups, Identity and Loyalty, and Historical Writing in Ottoman and Post- Ottoman Syria'. In *Les Arabes et l'Histoire Créatrice* [Arabs and Formative History], edited by Dominique Chevallier, 79–93. Paris: Presses de l'Université du Paris-Sorbonne, 1995.
Ramadān, 'Omar K. 'Al-'Inqisām Al-Waṭani Al-Lubnāni Fī `Ahd Al-Intidāb 1920–1943 [National Division in Lebanon during the Mandate 1920–1943]'. *Majallat Dirāsāt Tārīkhiyya* 16 (2014): 209–72.
Rochemonteix, Camille de. *Le Liban et l'Expédition Française En Syrie, 1860–1861. Documents Inédits Du Général A. Ducrot* [Lebanon and the French Expedition in Syria, 1860–1861. Unedited Documents of General A. Ducrot]. Paris: Picard, 1921.
Rogan, Eugene L., and Avi Shlaim, eds. *The War for Palestine: Rewriting the History of 1948*. Cambridge: Cambridge University Press, 2007.
Romero, Juan. 'Discourse and Mediation in the Lebanese Crisis of 1958'. *Middle Eastern Studies* 48, no. 4 (2012): 567–87.
Rondot, Pierre. 'Lebanese Institutions and Arab Nationalism'. *Journal of Contemporary History* 3, no. 3 (1968): 37–51.
Rouleau, Eric. 'Crisis in Lebanon'. *Journal of Palestine Studies* 5 (1976): 233–43.
Russell, Malcolm B. *The First Modern Arab State: Syria under Faysal, 1918–1920*. Minneapolis, MN: Bibliotheca Islamica, 1985.
S., K. 'The Lebanese Crisis in Perspective'. *World Today* 14, no. 9 (1958): 369–80.
S'ādeh, 'Abdallah. *Awrāq Qawmiya: Mudhakarāt Al-Ductūr 'Abdallah S'ādeh* [Nationalist Papers: The Memoirs of Dr. 'Abdallah S'ādeh]. Beirut: Author, 1987.
Sa'īd, Amīn. *Al-Thawra Al-'Arabiyya Al-Koubra* [The Great Arab Revolt]. Cairo: `Īsa al-Bābi al-Ḥalabi and Co. Press, 1934.
Saab, Hassan. 'The Rationalist School in Lebanese Politics'. In *Politics in Lebanon*, edited by Leonard Binder, 271–82. New York: Wiley, 1966.
Sachedina, Abdulaziz A. 'Activist Shi`ism in Iran, Iraq and Lebanon'. In *Fundamentalisms Observed*, edited by Martin E. Marty and R. Scott Appleby, 403–56. Chicago: University of Chicago Press, 1991.
Salameh, Franck. *Language, Memory, and Identity in the Middle East: The Case for Lebanon*. New York: Lexington, 2010.

Salem, Elie Adib. *Modernization without Revolution: Lebanon's Experience.* Bloomington: Indiana University Press, 1973.

Salibi, Kamal. *A House of Many Mansions: The History of Lebanon Reconsidered.* London: I.B. Tauris, 1988.

Salibi, Kamal. *Crossroads to Civil War: Lebanon, 1958–1976.* Delmar, NY: Caravan Books, 1976.

Salibi, Kamal. 'Lebanon Under Fuad Chehab 1958–1964'. *Middle Eastern Studies* 2, no. 3 (1966): 211–26.

Salibi, Kamal. 'The Maronites of Lebanon under Frankish and Mamluk Rule (1099–1516)'. *Arabica* 4, no. 3 (1957): 288–303.

Salibi, Kamal. *The Modern History of Lebanon.* New York: Praeger, 1965.

Sālim, Yūsif. *50 Sana Min Al-Nās* [50 Years of People]. Beirut: Dār al-Nahār, 1998.

Salloukh, Bassel F., Rabie Barakat, Jinan S. Al-Habbal, Lara W. Khattab and Shoghig Mikaelian. *The Politics of Sectarianism in Postwar Lebanon.* London: Pluto Press, 2015.

Samné, Georges. 'Questions Orientales [Oriental Questions]'. *Correspondance D'Orient*, April 1928.

Sarufīm, Antūn. *Wazīfat Al-Intikhābāt Al-Niyābiya Fī Lubnān* [The Role of Parliamentary Elections in Lebanon]. Beirut: Dār al-Fārābī, 2015.

Sayigh, Rosemary. 'The Bilingualism Controversy in Lebanon'. *World Today* 21, no. 3 (1965): 120–30.

Schulze, Kristen E. *Israel's Covert Diplomacy in Lebanon.* Basingstoke: Palgrave Macmillan, 1998.

Selzer, Michael. 'Nation Building and State Building: The Israeli Example'. *Phylon* 32, no. 1 (1971): 4–22.

Sem'ān, Sem'ān 'Īd. *Rīmūn Iddeh: Damīron Lan Yamūt* [Raymond Eddeh: A Conscience That Never Dies]. Beirut: Dār al-Jīl, 2000.

Sha'ib, Ali A M. *Maṭāleb Jabal 'Āmel: Al-Waḥda, Al-Mousāwāt Fī Jabal Lubnān* [Demands of Jabal 'Āmel: Unity, Equality in Mount Lebanon]. Beirut: Al Mu'assasa al-Jāmi'iyya Lil-Dirāsāt wal-Nashir, 1987.

Shaery-Eisenlohr, Roschanack. *Shi'ite Lebanon: Transnational Religion and the Making of National Identities.* New York: Columbia University Press, 2008.

Shanahan, Rodger. *The Shi'a of Lebanon: Clans, Parties and Clerics.* London: I.B. Tauris, 2005.

Sharbel, Ghassān. *Dhākirat Al-Istikhbārāt* [Memories from the Intelligence Service]. Beirut: Riad El-Rayyes Books, 2007.

Sharbel, Ghassān. *Lubnān – Dafāter Al-Ru'asā'* [Lebanon – Presidents' Records]. Beirut: Riad El-Rayyes Books, 2014.

Shehadi, Nadim. *The Idea of Lebanon: Economy and State in the Cénacle Libanais 1946–54.* Oxford: Centre for Lebanese Studies, 1987. https://www.lebanesestudies.com/wp-content/uploads/2012/03/4defaf75.-Economy-and-State-in-the-Cenacle-Libanais-Nadim-Shehadi-1987.pdf.

Shlaim, Avi. 'Israeli Interference in Internal Arab Politics: The Case of Lebanon'. In *The Politics of Arab Integration*, edited by Giacomo Luciani and Ghassan Salamé, 232–55. New York: Croom Helm, 1988.

Shlomo, Yinon. 'The Israeli–Syrian Disengagement Negotiations of 1973–74'. *Middle Eastern Studies* 51, no. 4 (2015): 636–48.

Simon, James A. 'The Creation of Greater Lebanon, 1918–1920: The Roles and Expectations of the Administrative Council of Mount Lebanon'. University of Utah, 1995.

Smith, Anthony D. *Nationalism and Modernism: A Critical Survey of Recent Theories of Nations and Nationalism*. London: Routledge, 1998.
Smith, Anthony D. 'Nations Before Nationalism? Myth and Symbolism in John Armstrong's Perspective'. *Nations and Nationalism* 21, no. 1 (2015): 165–70.
Smock, David R., and Audrey C. Smock. *The Politics of Pluralism: A Comparative Study of Lebanon and Ghana*. Oxford: Elsevier, 1975.
Sorby, Karol R. 'Lebanon: The Crisis of 1958'. *Asian and African Studies* 9, no. 1 (2000): 76–109.
Soueid, Yassine. *Corps Expéditionnaire de Syrie: Rapports et Correspondance 1860–1861* [Syria Expeditionary Corps: Rapports and Correspondance 1860–1861]. Beirut: Naufal, 1998.
Stewart, Desmond. *Turmoil in Beirut: A Personal Account*. London: Wingate, 1958.
Stone, Christopher. 'The Ba'albakk Festival and the Rahbanis: Folklore, Ancient History, Musical Theater, And Nationalism in Lebanon'. *Arab Studies Journal* 11, no. 2 (2003): 10–39.
Suleiman, Michael. *Political Parties in Lebanon: The Challenge of a Fragmented Political Culture*. Ithaca, NY: Cornell University Press, 1967.
Syrien, Comité Central. 'La Syrie Devant La Conférence. Mémoire à Monsieur Georges Clémenceau et à MM. Les Délégués Des Puissances Alliées et Associées à Cette Conference [Syria Facing the Conference. Memorandum Addressed to M. Georges Clémenceau and to the Delegates of the Allie]'. Bibliothèque Nationale de France, January 1919. https://gallica.bnf.fr/ark:/12148/bpt6k9399754.
Tah, Ghassān Fawzī. *Hawiyat Lubnān ('ind Al-Kiyāniyīn – Al-Qawmiyīn – Al-Islāmiyīn)* [Lebanese Identity (in Lebanism – in Nationalism – in Islamism)]. Beirut: al-Markaz al-Islāmī lil-Dirāsāt al-Fikrīyah, 2009.
Tamari, Steven. 'Arab National Consciousness in Seventeenth and Eighteenth Century Syria'. In *Syria and Bilad Al-Sham under Ottoman Rule*, edited by Peter Sluglett and Stefan Weber, 309–22. Leiden: Brill, 2010.
Tanenbaum, Jan Karl. 'France and the Arab Middle East, 1914–1920'. *Transactions of the American Philosophical Society* 68, no. 7 (1978): 1–50.
Taqī al-Dīn, Suleimān. *Al-Taṭawur Al-Tārīkhī Lil-Mushkila Al-Lubnāniya*. Beirut: Dār Ibn Khaldūn, 1977.
Taqqūsh, Muḥammad Souheil. *Tārīkh Al-'Irāq (Al-Ḥadīth Wal-Mou'āsir)* [History of Iraq (Modern and Contemporary)]. Beirut: Dār al-Nafā'is, 2015.
Tarabein, Ahmad. *Al-Waḥda Al-'Arabiyya Fī Tārīkh Al-Mashriq Al-Mou'āsir 1800–1958* [Arab Unity in the Contemporary History of the Near East 1800–1958]. Damascus: University of Damascus, 1970.
Tilly, Charles. 'Cities and States in Europe'. *Theory and Society* 18, no. 5 (1989): 563–84.
Tilly, Charles. *Coercion, Capital, and European States, AD 990–1992*. Cambridge: Blackwell, 1990.
Tilly, Charles. *The Formation of National States in Western Europe*. Princeton, NJ: Princeton University Press, 1975.
Tilly, Charles. 'War Making and State Making as Organized Crime'. In *Bringing the State Back In*, edited by Peter B. Evans, D. Rueschemeyer and T. Skocpol, 169–91. Cambridge: Cambridge University Press, 1985.
Ṭrābulsī, Fawāz. *A History of Modern Lebanon*. London: Pluto Press, 2007.
Ṭrābulsī, Fawāz. *Ṣilāt Bilā Waṣl: Mishāl Shīḥa Wal-'Īdiyōlōjiya Al-Lubnāniya* [Connections without Association: Michel Chiha and the Lebanese Ideology]. Beirut: Riad El-Rayyes Books, 1999.

Ṭrābulsī, Fawāz. *Ṣūrat Al-Fata Bil-Aḥmar: Ayām Fil-Silm Wal-Ḥarb* [The Picture of the Boy in Red: Days in Peace and in War]. Beirut: Riad El-Rayyes Books, 1997.
Tueynī, Gebrān. *Fī Waḍe' Al-Nahār – Maqālāt Moukhtāra* [In the Nahār's Situation – Selected Articles]. Beirut: Dār al-Nahār, 1939.
Verdeil, Éric. *Beyrouth et Ses Urbanistes: Une Ville En Plans (1946–1975)* [Beirut and Its Urbanists: Planning a City]. Beirut: Presses de l'IFPO, 2010.
Weber, Max. *Economy and Society: An Outline of Interprative Sociology.* Berkeley: University of California Press, 1978.
Weber, Max, David Owen, Tracy B. Strong. *The Vocation Lectures*. Indianapolis: Hackett, 2004.
Weinberger, Naomi Joy. *Syrian Intervention in Lebanon: The 1975–76 Civil War.* New York: Oxford University Press, 1986.
Weiss, Max. *In the Shadow of Sectarianism: Law, Shi'ism, and the Making of Modern Lebanon*. Cambridge, MA: Harvard University Press, 2010.
Weiss, Max. 'The Historiography of Sectarianism in Lebanon'. *History Compass* 7, no. 1 (2009): 141–54.
Yaqub, Salim. 'Scuttle Diplomacy: Henry Kissinger and the Middle East Peace Process, 1973 1976'. In *Imperfect Strangers: Americans, Arabs, and U.S.–Middle East Relations in the 1970s*, 145–82. Ithaca, NY: Cornell University Press, 2016.
Yin, Robert K. *Case Study Research: Design and Methods*. London: Sage, 2009.
Younger, Sam. 'The Syrian Stake in Lebanon'. *World Today* 32, no. 11 (1976): 399–406.
Youssef, Ḥamlāwi Jalāl. 'Musṭafa Al-Naḥas Basha Wa Dawrahu Fī Al-Ḥaraka Al-Waṭaniyya Al-Maṣriyya 1879–1952 [Mustafa Al-Naḥas Basha and His Role in the Egyptian National Movement 1879–1952]'. University of Biskra, 2017.
Z'aytir, Akram. *Yawmīyāt Akram Z'aytir: Al-Ḥaraka Al-Waṭanīya Al-Filastīnīya, 1935–1939* [Diaries of Akram Z'aytir: The Palesitinian National Movemement, 1935–1939]. Beirut: Mu'assasat al-Dirāsāt al-Filastīnīya, 1980.
Zamir, Meir. 'Emile Eddé and the Territorial Integrity of Lebanon'. *Middle Eastern Studies* 14, no. 2 (1978): 232–5.
Zamir, Meir. 'Faisal and the Lebanese Question, 1918–20'. *Middle Eastern Studies* 27, no. 3 (1991): 404–26.
Zamir, Meir. *Lebanon's Quest: The Road to Statehood 1926–1939*. London: I.B. Tauris, 1997.
Zamir, Meir. *The Formation of Modern Lebanon*. Leiden: Dover, 1985.
Zamir, Meir. 'The Lebanese Presidential Elections of 1970 and Their Impact on the Civil War of 1975–1976'. *Middle Eastern Studies* 16, no. 1 (1980): 49–70.
Zernatto, G., and Alfonso G. Mistretta. 'Nation: The History of a Word'. *Review of Politics* 6, no. 3 (1944): 351–66.
Ziadeh, Nicola A. 'The Lebanese Elections, 1960'. *Middle East Journal* 14, no. 4 (1960): 367–81.
Zisser, Eyal. *Lebanon: The Challenge of Independence*. London: I.B. Tauris, 2000.
Zisser, Eyal. 'The Downfall of the Khuri Administration: A Dubious Revolution'. *Middle Eastern Studies* 30, no. 3 (1994): 486–511.
Zisser, Eyal. 'The Maronites, Lebanon and the State of Israel: Early Contacts'. *Middle Eastern Studies* 31, no. 4 (1995): 889–918.
Zogheib, Penelope. 'Lebanese Christian Nationalism: A Theoretical Analyses of a National Movement'. Unpublished Masters thesis. Northeastern University, 2013.

INDEX

'Abd al-Nāṣer's, Jamāl 99, 115, 124, 128, 129–32, 134, 153, 168–9, 173, 185–7, 192–3, 195, 204–5
Abi al-Lama', Khalīl 61
Aboultaif , Eduardo Wassim 10
'Akkār 133, 171
'Akl, Saīd 123
Akzin, Benjamin 4
Ali, Muhammad (of Egypt) 20
Allenby, (General) Edmund Henry 31
'Āmel (Jabal) 24, 52, 54, 58, 60, 62
'Āmeli/ites 52, 53, 58, 59, 60
Arabism/ist 9, 15, 22, 24, 45, 63, 83–7, 92, 101–2, 123, 125, 134, 168, 187, 190–1, 210
'Arafāt, Yāsser 186
Aristotle 35
Armstrong, John A. 4
Arslān
  'Ādil 77, 99
  Nihād 97
al-As'ad
  Aḥmad 95, 133
  family 95, 189
  Kāmil 52, 122, 192
al-Assad, Ḥāfiz 193, 194

B'albak 53–5, 95
Ba'th (*see also* Ba'thism/ist) 168–9, 191, 193
Baghdad Pact 129
Bashir al-Shihabi/Bashir II (Emir) 20, 26
Bayhum
  'Abdallah Bey 59
  Muḥammad Jamīl 10, 123
Beirut
  communities 46, 49, 51, 53, 62, 67, 117, 118, 119, 158, 188–9
  political figures 31, 89, 90, 130, 158, 169,
  political views 35, 49, 51, 52, 53, 58, 62, 94
  territory 49, 51, 53, 66, 94, 132, 155, 159, 165, 186, 194
Binder, Leonard 209
Biqā' 19, 23, 34, 159, 161–2, 171
Bracha, Guy 89
Britain (*see also* the UK, British) 31–3, 35–6, 49–50, 52–3, 64–6, 85, 90, 93, 118, 128–30
Bustānī, Emile 186, 194

Cairo Agreement 186, 187
Catroux, (Colonel) Georges 46, 64
Central Body for Administrative Reform (CBAR) 155, 156, 158
Chatterjee, Partha 3
Chehabism/ist 13, 154, 165–6, 168–9, 170–3, 183, 186–9, 192, 195–6
Church (Maronite) 21, 28, 89–90, 97, 133, 167
Clemenceau, Georges 29
Cobban, Helena 11
Cold War 118, 127–30, 139, 194, 210
Comité Central Syrien (CCS) 28, 29, 30
Communism/ist 118, 128, 133–5, 136, 190–1
Conference of the Coast 61, 63
Conseil des Comités Libano-Syriens d'Egypte (CCLS) 28, 30
consociationalism 10, 11
Constitutional Bloc 60–4, 82, 84–5, 173
Corm, Charles 47, 123
de Beaufort [General], Charles-Marie-Napoléon d'Hautpoul 21, 22, 25, 26, 28
de Caix, Robert 46, 48, 50–2, 57, 59

Da'esh (*see also* Islamic State) 210
al-Da'uq, 'Omar 31
Dawisha, Adeed 191
De Jouvenel, Henri 54
Deuxième Bureau

rise under Shehāb 170, 171, 172, 173
under Ḥelū 185, 186, 187, 188
Druze(s) 1, 18–23, 26, 28, 35, 47, 50–1, 53, 58, 67–9, 96–7, 121, 125, 166, 185

Eddeh
Emile 47, 58–64, 82–6, 89–80, 93–5
Pierre 121
Raymond 137, 157, 168, 171–4, 183, 186
Egypt (*see also* Egyptian) 20, 28, 30, 64–5, 83–4, 87, 99, 124, 127–32, 167, 172, 185, 188, 190, 193–4
Eisenhower Doctrine 130–1, 133, 135–6, 139, 186, 204
Emirate (Lebanese) 19–20, 22–3, 26

Fakhoury Mühlbacher, Tamirace 10–11
Far'ūn, Henri 86–7, 95, 97, 117–18, 133, 136–7
Faysal I Al-Hashemi (Emir) 31–2, 46, 56
France (*see also* French) 20–3, 25–7, 28–35, 45–54, 56–8, 60–2, 64–7, 81, 84–6, 89, 91, 93, 98, 115, 119–20, 123–5, 129–30, 167, 187, 193, 202–4
Frangieh
Ḥamīd 91, 95
Sleymān 187–9, 192, 193, 196, 205
Farrūj, 'Omar 125
Fukuyama, Francis 120

Gellner, Ernest 4
Ghālib, 'Abd al-Ḥamīd 173, 194
Giddens, Anthony 3–4
Gouraud, (General) Henri 46, 48–9
Greater Lebanon 1, 13, 17–18, 23–5, 33–5, 45–53, 58, 67, 123, 201–2
Greater Syria/n 28, 29, 46, 54, 87, 93, 98–9, 101
Greek Catholic 1, 28, 50, 68
Greek Orthodox 1, 28, 46, 50–3, 57, 59, 65, 67–8, 95, 123, 168

al-Hajj, Kamāl Yūsif 125
Hakim, Carol 9
al-Hallaq, Hassan 9
Hasbaya 34, 55
Ḥelū, Charles 173–4, 183–7, 189, 192, 196, 201
Hezbollah 210–11
Hitti, Philip 23
Hourani, Albert 9–10
Houstoun-Boswall, William 93–4
Hudson, Michael 12, 165, 196, 209
Huntington, Samuel 156
Hurewitz, J. C. 10
Hurwitz, Leon 6
Hussein bin Ali Al-Hashimi (Sharīf) 25, 31, 32

identity 2, 4–5, 7–9, 13, 17–19, 23–4, 30, 48–9, 56–60, 66, 81, 83–4, 86–8, 92, 94, 115, 121, 123, 125–6, 131, 137–8, 153, 166–8, 174, 192, 202–3, 206
Institut de Recherche et de Formation en vue du développement (IRFED) 157, 158
Israel
Arab-Israeli conflict 1, 82, 88, 89, 91, 92, 99, 102, 185, 189, 193, 195
state 89, 90, 98, 99, 185, 186, 190, 193, 194, 207

al-Jazā'iri, Sa'id 31
Jew(s) (*see also* Jewish) 24, 89–91, 126
Jewish Agency 89–90
al-Jisr, Muḥammad 59
Jordan (*see also* Jordanian) 51, 87, 99, 124, 127, 129, 169, 185, 188, 190, 193
Jumayyil
Maurice 158
Pierre 86, 95, 122, 137, 154, 157–8, 173–4, 186, 195
Junblāṭ, Kamāl 93–4, 96–7, 100, 121–2, 125, 137, 157–8, 194
Junblati(s) 125

Karam, Joseph 87
Karam, Yousef 28
Karāmī
'Abd al-Ḥamīd 82, 85–7, 94–7
Rashid 129–30, 137, 155, 158, 183–4, 169, 186
Katā'ib (*see also* Phalangists) 59, 65, 86, 90, 95–8, 122, 131, 133, 154, 167–8, 173
Kedourie, Elie 10
Kerr, Michael 11
Khaddām, 'Abd al-Ḥalīm 194

Khāled (Grand Mufti), Muḥammad Toufiq 62
al-Khalīl
family 189
Kāzim 133
Khūrī, Bishāra 60–1, 63–6, 81–6, 88, 91–6, 99–102, 115–17, 127, 129, 131–2, 136, 166, 173–4, 192, 203–4, 208
Khūrian 166
King-Crane Commission (*see also* KCC) 33–5

Laḥūd, Gaby 171
Lammens, Henri 23
language
Arabic 24, 32, 66, 124
French 125
Lebanese 58
League of Arab States (*see also* Arab League) 82–6, 91–2, 98, 128, 130–1, 135
League of National Action 59
League of Nations 57
Lebanese Armed Forces (*see also* Lebanese army) 91, 134, 136, 154, 164, 170, 186
Lebanese Communist Party (LCP) 190
Lebanism/ist 19, 22, 24, 34–5, 45–7, 49, 52, 57, 61, 66, 82–3, 85–7, 90, 95, 123, 134
Lebret (Père), Louis-Joseph 157
legitimacy 2, 5–13, 17–8, 22, 26, 30, 33, 35, 45–9, 51–2, 54, 56–8, 65–7, 81–4, 88–90, 92–5, 97, 99–100, 102, 116, 119–20, 126–8, 134, 136–7, 139, 153–6, 159, 166–7, 174, 183, 187–8, 191–2, 195–6, 201–11
Lijphart, Arend 11
Lipset, Seymour Martin 35
Litani (river) 53, 158

Mālik, Charles 130
Malsagne, Stephan 9
Mandate (British) 35, 52–3, 185
Mandate (French) 22–3, 33, 35, 45–7, 50–4, 56–8, 60–1, 64, 66, 81–4, 90, 95, 98, 115, 123, 125, 193, 202–3
Mardam, Jamīl 98
Maronite Patriarch 21, 28, 60
'Arīḍa 60, 61, 85, 86, 89, 90, 94,
Ḥubaysh 21
Mas'ad 22
M'ūshī 133, 172, 174
Maronite(s) 1, 18–23, 25–6, 28–30, 35, 46–7, 49–50, 52, 57, 60, 63–5, 67–9, 85, 87, 89–90, 94–8, 100–1, 117, 125–7, 133, 158, 164, 167, 172–4, 185, 192, 194–5, 202–4, 206
al-Matnī, Nasīb 133
Max Weber 5–7, 22, 120, 156,
Mediterraneanism/ist 85, 86, 123
Mistretta, Alfonso G. 3
Mitchell, Timothy 4
Mt. Lebanon (*see also* the Mountain) 19–23, 25–6, 28, 30, 34–5, 46–7, 52–4, 61, 82–3, 93–4, 98, 123, 159, 162, 165
Mubārak, Igantius 89, 90, 94, 97, 99
Muslim Conference 62
Mutasarrifiyya (*see also* Mutassarrif) 21, 28

Nādi al-Ahli 59
Najjada/i 59, 65, 133
Nakhleh, Amīn 97
Nami, Ahmed Damad 54
Nasserism/ist 118, 128–9, 133, 170, 187, 190–1
nation and state 3–5
nation-building 2–3, 5, 8–9, 18, 24, 26, 36, 45, 47–8, 54, 57–9, 64–7, 81, 102, 115, 120, 122, 124–6, 139, 155, 207,
National Bloc
Lebanese 60, 82, 93, 94, 97, 122, 168
Syrian 59, 61, 62
National Liberal Party (NLP) 168, 187
National Pact 13, 64–7, 81–9, 91–102, 115–6, 119–28, 129–31, 134, 136–9, 156, 168, 187–9, 192, 195–6, 202–6
nationalism 9, 18–23, 35, 54, 63, 65, 82, 84, 97–8, 124, 128, 133, 168–9, 190, 202
during First World War 18
Maronites, Druze 19–22
Mt Lebanon 19–22
Shī'a 23–4
Sunni 24–5

'Oseyrān, 'Ādil 95, 99, 133
Ottoman 17–20, 22–5, 28, 31, 35, 45, 47, 49, 52, 121, 202

Palestine 1, 35, 52, 90, 91, 95, 98, 185
Palestinian
  cause 91, 92, 94, 95, 97, 183, 185, 186, 189, 190, 192–3, 195, 201
  militias 183, 186, 187, 189, 190, 191, 193, 194, 196, 201
  Palestinian Liberation Organisation (PLO) 184, 185, 186, 190, 193
  people 91, 97, 99, 117, 127, 185
Paris Peace Conference 32
Parliament (Lebanese) 56, 61, 63–5, 81–4, 87, 90, 92–7, 100–1, 116, 121–2, 128–9, 132, 154, 156–8, 163–7, 171–3, 184, 186, 189, 192
Parsons, Talcott 5, 7
Pasha, Auguste Adib 25, 26, 28, 32
Pāsha, Jamal 31
Phoenicianism/ist 47, 123
Picard, Élizabeth 194
Pluralism/ist 10, 48, 126, 134
power-sharing 8, 10–11, 17, 47, 57, 81, 87, 100–1, 120, 123, 125–6, 138, 153, 187, 190, 192, 203–4, 206–7
Puaux, Gabriel 64

al-Qadhāfi, Mu'ammar 193–4
Qubain, Fahim 138

Rashaya 34, 53, 55
Representative Council 49–50, 53–6
Rifā'ī, Abd al-Majīd 191
Roché, Louis 120

Sa'd, Antūn 171
S'ādeh, Antūn 94, 97
al-Ṣadr, Mūsa 189, 190, 191, 193,
Salām, Ṣā'ib 122, 130–1, 157–8, 169, 171–4, 192
Salame, Ghassan 10
Salameh, Franck 9
Salibi, Kamal 9–10, 167, 168
Sarkīs, Eliās 189
Saudi Arabia 84, 129, 130, 169, 188, 210
Sawda, Yusuf 25, 28, 85
Sham'ūn, Kamīl 13, 93–6, 100, 115–22, 127–39, 153–4, 157–8, 166, 168–9, 172–4, 186, 188, 204–5, 208
Sham'ūnist 118, 154, 166
Shehāb, Fu'ād 91, 101, 131, 134–9, 153–9, 165–74, 183–7, 192, 195, 201, 205, 208
Shī'a(s) (*see also* Shiite) 18, 22–5, 28, 50, 52–3, 58–9, 63, 67–8, 82, 86, 89, 94–5, 133, 156, 166, 185, 188–90, 192–3, 196, 201, 205, 207, 210
  Metawali(s) 23, 86
Shīḥa, Michel 25, 123, 124, 125, 140
Sidon 54, 58, 135
Smith, Anthony D. 4
SSNP/Parti Populaire Syrien 59, 65, 97–100, 133, 168, 170–1, 174, 187, 191
state-building 2–3, 5–10, 12, 17–9, 24–6, 28–31, 35, 45, 47–8, 50, 54, 56–8, 63–5, 81, 87–8, 92, 100, 102, 115–20, 121, 123, 127, 136–9, 154, 156, 184, 195, 201–2, 206–9
Suleiman, Michael 165, 209
al-Ṣulḥ
  Kāzim 63
  Riāḍ 60, 61, 63, 81, 82, 83, 84, 85, 86, 93, 94, 95, 96, 97, 99, 100
  Sāmī 92, 100, 122, 130
  Taqī al-Dīn 133
Sunni(s) 1, 18, 22–5, 28, 49–53, 58–60, 62–3, 65, 67–8, 82–4, 86, 89, 92, 94–6, 100–1, 117–19, 129, 164, 166–7, 190, 192–3, 198, 203, 206–7, 210–11
Supreme Shi'ite Islamic Council (SSIC) 189
Syria–Mount Lebanon League of Liberation (SMLL) 28, 30
Syrian nationalism/Syrianism 31, 45–6, 49, 52, 53, 54, 59, 60, 61, 82, 86, 94, 98, 123, 167, 168

Tābet, Ayūb 65
al-Tahiri, Hamdi 9
Taqiyya 20, 23
Trabulsi, Fawwaz 9
Trād, Petro 65
Tripartite aggression 129
Tripartite Alliance 186–7, 189
Tripoli
  political events 34, 46, 53, 54, 58, 61, 63, 132, 135

territory 47, 52, 54, 59, 118, 155, 165
Tripolitan(s) 53, 85, 97, 158
Turkey (*see also* Turkish) 32, 51, 128–9
Tuweynī, Ghassan 122, 133–4, 139, 166
Tyre 29, 34, 55, 59, 189

United Arab Command/UAC 185
United Arab Republic/UAR
1950s 132, 133, 135, 136
under Shehāb 169, 173
United National Front 132, 133, 134, 137
United Nations
General Assembly 91
Observer Group in Lebanon 135–6
Secretary General 136
Security Council 135–6
Special Committee on Palestine 90
United States (*see also* America, American) 30, 32–3, 128, 130, 132, 134, 136–7, 139, 153, 168, 194, 207, 210
University
American University of Beirut 128
Beirut Arab University 185
students 162, 188
USSR (*see also* Soviet Union) 132, 134, 135, 190, 193, 194
al-ʿUweynī, Ḥussein 100

Wakīm, Najāḥ 191
World War I 18, 22, 23, 25, 28, 30, 31
World War II 128, 167

Yāfi, ʿAbdallah 96, 122, 128, 130
Yin, Robert 2

Zaʿīm, Ḥusni 98, 100
Zamir, Meir 10
Zernatto, Guido 3
Zionism/ist 89–92
Zisser, Eyal 10–11

www.ingramcontent.com/pod-product-compliance
Lightning Source LLC
Chambersburg PA
CBHW062142300426
44115CB00012BA/2013
* 9 7 8 0 7 5 5 6 4 4 1 8 6 *